KINDRED ARTS:
BIOGRAPHIC WRITING AND
PSYCHODYNAMIC THERAPY,
COMPLEXITIES AND COMPLICATIONS

KINDRED ARTS:

Biographic Writing and Psychodynamic Therapy, Complexities and Complications

by Esther Urdang, PhD

International Psychoanalytic Books (IPBooks)
New York • http://www.IPBooks.net

Published by IPBooks, Queens, NY
www.IPBooks.net

ISBN: 978-1-956864-73-1

(Previously published in 2014 as: *Parallels between Writing Biographies and Clinical Practice: Impact. Influence. Value.*
Publisher: NASW Press; ISBN: 978-0871014504.)

To my dear grandchildren

Haley Brown, Jacqueline (Q) Urdang, Zoe Brown, and Sam Goodman Urdang

With love from Grandma

Contents

About the Author

Esther Urdang, PhD (Simmons), MSS (Adelphi), LICSW, has practiced for many years in mental health and family agencies, hospitals, and private practice. At Boston College Graduate School of Social Work for 27 years, she taught clinical courses as Adjunct Associate Professor and was Assistant Director of Field Education. Subsequently, Dr. Urdang was a Research Advisor at Smith College School for Social Work. Her published papers include *In Defense of Process Recording, The Discipline of Faculty Advising, The Video Lab: Mirroring Reflections of Self and the Other, Becoming a Field Instructor: A Key Experience in Professional Development,* and *Awareness of Self—a Critical Tool.* She has received the Simmons Alumni Special Recognition Award for her writing, twice for papers and once for the first edition of her textbook: *Human Behavior in the Social Environment: Interweaving the Inner and Outer Worlds.* She has written its third edition for Routledge Press.

.

Acknowledgments

Warmest thanks are extended to my husband, Elliott B. Urdang, MD, MA (in Russian), for his support and encouragement. He generously contributed his linguistic talent for editorial assistance and was constantly available to help me cope with technical issues and computer breakdowns.

The unending moral and intellectual support of Gwen Urdang Brown, Erik Urdang, Jerry Brown, Marguerite Dorian, Pam and Peter Kosseff, and Joan and Wendell Thompson is deeply appreciated.

I wish to express my deep gratitude and love to my late parents, my mother, Rose Klepper, and my father, Mendel Klepper, MD.

I wish to thank the biographers and autobiographers and the theorists whose work has dealt with the issues at the heart of this book.

I also wish to dedicate this work to the memory of my dear colleagues, Carolyn Thomas, professor emeritus; Matthew L. Pisapia, former director of field education; and Professor Robert Castagnola of Boston College Graduate School of Social Work and his wife, Charlotte, for their encouragement and spirit of caring and healing.

Acknowledgments for Permission to Quote

Thanks to Professor Harry Ricketts for kind permission to quote excerpts from *Rudyard Kipling: A Life* by Harry Ricketts, © Harry Ricketts, 1999, as well as for assistance in determining copyright of other materials.

Thanks to Professor Dr. Maria I. Diedrich for kind permission to quote excerpts from *Love Across Color Lines: Frederick Douglass and Otillie Assing* by Maria I. Diedrich, © Maria I. Diedrich, 1999.

Thanks to Professor Paula R. Backscheider for kind permission to quote excerpts from *Reflections on Biography* by Paula R. Backscheider, © Paula R. Backscheider, 1999.

Thanks to Jack Thomas (JBW), literary executor of the Estate of Charles E. Carrington, for excerpts from *The Life of Rudyard Kipling,* by Charles E. Carrington, © Charles E. Carrington, 1955.

Thanks to Geoff Browne, Webmaster, Uplyme, England, for his kind assistance. *The Nature of Narrative,* Scholes, Phelan, & Kellogg (2006). © 1968 by Oxford University Press, Inc. By permission of Oxford University Press, USA.

Handbook of Psychobiography, edited by William Todd Schultz (2005). © 2004 by Oxford University Press, Inc. By permission of Oxford University Press, USA.

Thanks to Rebecca Fraser for excerpts from *The Brontës: Charlotte Brontë and Her Family* by Rebecca Fraser, Ballantine Books. ©

Rebecca Fraser, 1988. With thanks to Ed Victor Ltd (with the kind assistance of Sarah Williams).

Thanks to Professor William S. McFeely for excerpts from *Frederick Douglass* by William S. McFeely. Copyright © 1991 by William S. McFeely. Used by permission of W.W. Norton & Company, Inc. (with the kind assistance of Elizabeth Clementson).

Thanks to Cushing Memorial Library and Archives, Texas A & M University, for the use of items of Alice "Trix" MacDonald Fleming (with the kind assistance of Larry Mitchell).

The Doctor, The Detective & *Arthur Conan Doyle: A biography of Arthur Conan Doyle,* by Martin Booth, first published by Hodder & Stoughton, 1997, © The Estate of Martin Booth, with thanks to Aitken Alexander Associates (with the kind assistance of Imogen Pelham).

The kind permission of the New York Review of Books to excerpt *The Powers of Doctor Johnson,* by Andrew O'Hagan (with the kind assistance of Patrick Hederman).

Daddyji, Oxford University Press—By Ved Mehta, Copyright © Ved Mehta, 1979, with thanks to David Godwin Associates (with the kind assistance of Caitlin Ingham).

Sound-shadows of the New World, Oxford University Press—By Ved Mehta, Copyright © Ved Mehta, 1987, with thanks to David Godwin Associates (with the kind assistance of Caitlin Ingham).

Excerpts from Kipling Papers, quoted by Harry Ricketts in *Rudyard Kipling: A Life,* reproduced with the kind permission of the National Trust (with the assistance of Nikita Hooper, National Trust Images) and the Library Special Collections, University of Sussex (with the assistance of Rose Lock, Senior Archive Assistant).

Thanks to Daniel Stashower for kind permission to quote excerpts from *Teller of Tales: The Life of Arthur Conan Doyle* by Daniel Stashower, © Daniel Stashower, 1999.

Thanks to Prof. Richard Holmes for kind permission to quote excerpts from *Footsteps: adventures of a romantic biographer* by Richard Holmes, © Richard Holmes, 1985, with thanks to David Godwin Associates (with the kind assistance of Caitlin Ingham).

What became of Arthur Conan Doyle's father? The last years of Charles Altamont Doyle, by Allen Beveridge MD, with thanks to the Journal of the Royal College of Physicians of Edinburgh, © 2006 Royal College of Physicians of Edinburgh (with the kind assistance of Susan I. Laurence).

Thanks to the Kipling Manuscript Collection, Rice Library, Marlboro College, Marlboro, Vermont, for permission to use an excerpt from the Collection quoted in *Rudyard Kipling: A Life,* by Harry Ricketts (with the kind assistance of Emily Alling, Library Director).

Thanks to Peggy Perdue, librarian for the Arthur Conan Doyle Collection at the Toronto Public Library (Toronto Reference Library) for helpful research.

Thanks to Mr. John Walker, Honorary Librarian, The Kipling Society, London, for vital assistance with copyright search.

Introduction

I am a clinical social worker and social work educator. I am also hopelessly addicted to biographical writings. Charlotte Brontë was my first in-depth biographical subject, and photographs that I took during a visit to her home, the Parsonage at Haworth, appeared in my office at Boston College. Excerpts from her writings and biographies enlivened my classes. She soon found herself in good company, as other biographical subjects joined her.

Discussions of biographies and autobiographies then appeared in the first and second editions of my textbook, *Human Behavior in the Social Environment: Interweaving the Inner and Outer Worlds* (Urdang, 2002, 2008); I was impressed with how biographical writings captured so much of human experience. There was the voice of Maya Angelou (1997), poignantly recalling growing up with her grandmother in the South and the support and solidarity she experienced in her black community. Mark Vonnegut (1975) shared his insights into his bizarre world of schizophrenia.

Over time, I came to appreciate how much biographies and autobiographies can tell us about the ways in which people evolve through life; we see individuals overcoming (or succumbing to) adversity and learn how early childhood experiences and relationships affected (or did not affect) them. These readings also shed light on historical, social, and cultural events affecting lives and illuminate the continual interweaving of a person's inner and outer worlds.

Then I came to realize that biographers struggle with questions that also concern clinical social workers and mental health practitioners: how the subjectivity of the author affects all aspects of the biographical enterprise (as subjectivity affects all aspects of clinical work); how biographers (and clinicians) feel about their subjects (and their clients); and how these feelings can change over time. This can have an impact on the biographer's representation of the subject to readers and on the clinician's ongoing relationship to the patient. In both fields, there are decisions to be made about which data to select and who are the significant people in the subject's (or client's) life.

My conviction grew that biographical and autobiographical writings in and of themselves, as well as reflective analysis of them, can contribute to clinical education and enrich the general reader. The nonclinical reader of biographies also has an interest in learning how people experience life, what motivates them, what kinds of relationships they have, and what dark secrets may lurk in their backgrounds. How did Rudyard Kipling survive being placed in a rigid and punitive private foster home in England from age six until 12 without seeing his parents, who remained in India? How do we explain the changes in Arthur Conan Doyle, a physician, an intellect, and the creator of Sherlock Holmes, who stunned his friends and much of the public by turning to spiritualism in late adulthood, claiming to have conversations with dead souls, an admiration for mediums, and a belief in fairies?

These thoughts have motivated me to write this volume about reading, studying, and enjoying biographies. The goals of this book are threefold: The first is to emphasize the relevance of the life course perspective, examining how people develop and evolve (or regress) over their life span. This perspective uses the biopsychosocial framework, which interweaves inner and outer worlds.

The second goal is to explore methodological issues embedded in constructing biographies, such as collecting evidence, evaluating "witness" accounts (including correspondence), and handling gaps in information and uncertainties, "the things that go missing" (Lee, 2005, p. 5). This exploration can further the development of those critical analytical abilities that can enrich all readers: These skills are necessary for the work of both biographers and clinicians as they delve into the biopsychosocial worlds of their subjects and clients. Does the author share uncertainties with us, as did Glendinning (1999), in her biography of Jonathan Swift, when she acknowledged to the reader her dilemmas about "knowing," including problems of conflicting evidence, lack of data, and the fact that "it is all so long ago" (p. 2)?

Finally, the relationship of the biographer to the subject (or the autobiographer's self-presentation to the reader) is a major point of interest. What was the autobiographer's motivation in writing about his or her life or a biographer's motivation in choosing a particular person as a subject? Did the biographer have personal contact with the subject, and if so, what was its nature? Did the relationship change over time? How the writing of the book affected the writer is an intriguing question to which we cannot always find the answer but which is sometimes revealed. The ways in which these complex processes in the relationship of the biographer or autobiographer with their subject parallel similar processes in the clinician-client relationship are discussed throughout. These discussions should have particular relevance for clinicians.

Doris Kearns and Lyndon Johnson developed a complex emotional relationship during their ongoing contact, as she lived at his ranch while writing his biography. Her discussion of the many examples of Johnson's "transference" and [her] countertransference … suggest [ed] that this is likely to be a primary difficulty in nearly any opportunity to do "psycho biography up close" (Elms & Song, 2005, p. 307). The well-known transference and countertransference complexities (inner feelings and conflicts unconsciously expressed in relation to one another by patient and therapist) are present in therapy in a similar fashion. Biographers can also have emotional reactions to subjects they do not know. I noted this phenomenon in my past writings:

> Biographers also have emotional involvement with their subjects even if they have never met, and even if the subjects have been long dead. Maria Diedrich (1999), for example, wrote the biography of Ottilie Assing (who died 66 years before Diedrich was born), focusing on Assing's relationship to Frederick Douglass. Diedrich observed that her own family "were served Assing-Douglass fare for breakfast, lunch, and dinner, and for years" (p. viii). (Urdang, 2008, pp. 148–149)

Just as biographers attempt to convey to their readers "how the world looks from inside another person's experience" (Conway, 1998, p. 6), so do clinicians seek understanding of their clients' experiential worlds.

Both biographers and clinicians are also affected by their theoretical orientations, which can affect their search for evidence as well as their interpretation of this evidence. Multiple books have been written about the same person, often with different presentations and perspectives. The proliferation of biographies about Abraham

Lincoln, for example, has not ebbed with time; stories of his life continue to be written. What is there about Lincoln that casts this spell over us?

As we look to biographers to answer this, we find no definitive explanation but rather a multiplicity of explanations offered by Lincoln's many biographers: "the bearded man in the stovepipe hat seems much like a hologram, a medium for our fears and fantasies" (Shenk, 2005, p. 39). Lincoln is not unique among biographical subjects in being a "hologram" onto whom writers can project their own fantasies, perspectives, and agendas. Multiple studies have also been done of others as well. Those of Sigmund Freud, for example, have at times been "sympathetic," while others have created "an enormous number of intellectually and politically charged alternative accounts of Freud and his work" (Runyan, 2005a, p. 21). Biographies of the controversial Charles Darwin follow a similar pattern (Runyan, 2005a).

Biographers can be misled by the ways subjects choose to present (or misrepresent) themselves. For example, Lord Byron "liked to fictionalize himself in his poetry and even his letters" (Barton, 2002, p. 8). Similarly, patients may also impede their therapists from knowing them, using such strategies as "masking, pretending, and denying so that the [patient's] self-estrangement in the end cannot be fully overcome" (F. Wyatt, 1986, p. 207).

Both biographers and clinicians face ethical dilemmas in terms of protecting privacy and confidentiality. Some people do not want biographies written of them. Thomas Hardy solved this problem by writing his own biography, under the "authorship" of his wife (Tomalin, 2006). Charles Dickens was not alone in burning many of his personal papers and letters to keep them from biographers. Some families withhold important materials (as did Conan Doyle's family for many years) and may demand editorial and sometimes censorship rights over what is written. Kipling's daughter fired a number of his biographers and then demanded oversight of Charles Carrington's work when she selected him as Kipling's biographer. Clinicians can also be constrained by clients and families who are resistant to intervention or share only "partial" truths.

It has been argued that autobiographies are more "reliable" than biographies because they provide an authentic, firsthand portrayal of the subject's life and experiences. But do all writers wish to share what they know about themselves and their lives? Some take great pains to conceal the truth. Saint Augustine "set the problem for all subsequent autobiographies: How can the self know itself?" (Spengemann, 1980, p. 32). Conan Doyle's (1924) autobiography omitted details of his life he may have considered shameful (such as his father's alcoholism and mental illness), while placing emphasis on his own achievements and bravery. Jean Piaget's autobiographies focused on the development of his psychological theories, omitting details of his personal life (Urdang, 2008; Voneche, 2001).

The Autobiography of Alice B. Toklas was published in 1933, but as Malcolm (2003) pointed out, this was actually written by her partner Gertrude Stein. Then in 1954, Toklas wrote *The Alice B. Toklas Cook Book,* which was "more than a cookbook and memoir; it could almost be called a work of literary modernism" (Malcolm, 2003, p. 59). Malcolm discussed this conundrum: "Was Stein imitating Toklas when she wrote in Toklas's voice in the 'Autobiography,' or did she invent the voice, and did Toklas then imitate Stein's invention when she wrote the 'Cook Book'"? It is impossible to say" (p. 59).

So, you may ask, is there value in reading any biographical materials if both biographies and autobiographies are not definitive and are colored by the subjectivities and biases of both the subjects and their writers? Yes, I will argue in this book, there is great value in reading biographical materials. First, we need to accept the premise that people wish both to reveal and to conceal aspects of their inner and outer worlds and that multiple contradictions and paradoxes abound within all of us. We need to relinquish the search for complete knowledge of the subject: "biography has to omit and to choose. In the process some things go missing" (Lee, 2005, p. 36). But if we can accept these limitations, a wealth of knowledge, insight, and pleasure becomes available to us. At the same time, such complexities and contradictions may shed light on deeper truths.

Perhaps, though, the most compelling reason to read biographies is to connect with other people, to learn how others experience life: "we *want* to know how the world looks from inside another person's experience, and when that craving is met by a convincing narrative, we find it deeply satisfying" (Conway, 1998, p. 6). Lee (2005) observed that the "endlessly absorbing" motivation is that "we keep catching sight of a real body, a physical life … [James] Joyce with a black felt hat, thick glasses and a cigar, sitting in Sylvia Beach's bookshop in Paris" (pp. 2–3).

Holroyd (2002) highlighted biography's existential purpose, providing the reader with not only a sense of connection to others but a sense of continuity of the past, present, and future:

> By recreating the past we are calling on the same magic as our forefathers did with stories of their ancestors round the fires under the night skies. The need to do this, to keep death in its place, lies deep in human nature, and the art of biography arises from that need. This is its justification. (Holroyd, 2002, pp. 30–31)

This book is intended for students, teachers, and practitioners in social work and the human service and medical professions, such as psychology, psychiatry, medicine, and nursing, as biographical study can contribute to increased clinical knowledge and insight. These studies afford a unique opportunity to examine individual lives over the life span and to apply (and question) clinical theories. It is also written for the general audience of biography readers who wish to increase their understanding of the complexities of life and the intricacies involved in recording the life of oneself or of another and to find a framework for analyzing these works. The general reader may also benefit from the discussions of mental health theory and practice included in this book. Certainly, mental health problems, including eating disorders, bipolar disorders, incest, suicide, and gambling addictions, pervade media coverage today, in both real-life and fictional forms. The discussions of clinical terms and concepts, such as denial, unresolved grief, abandonment, therapy, and transference, are probably familiar to many; if not, in this book these terms can be easily comprehended. In fact, seeing these terms come alive in biographical discussions may further illuminate these concepts for all readers.

Biographical study serves to counter current trends in the mental health fields, which often exclusively favor the application of evidence-based, quantitative measures and cognitive-behavioral and technological approaches to clinical work and which largely de-emphasize exploring the past, developing empathy, and understanding experiential worlds.

The goals of this book are compatible with recent attempts to introduce narrative theory to clinicians and to "humanize" medical education as well: A number of medical schools now include courses in humanities, with some emphasizing studies of "narratives," in an effort "to restore a sense of meaning and healing to counter the dehumanizing effects of technological explosion" (Thernstrom, 2004, p. 44).

Writers such as Robert White (Runyan, 2005a) have stressed how the study of individual lives can contribute to increased psychological knowledge of both normal development and psychopathology. Challener (1997), exploring the development of resilience in childhood, found similarities in his autobiographical studies to outcomes from general research.

Studies of lives provide insight into many aspects of the human condition, such as attachment and its vicissitudes, loss, family breakdown, the impact of economic factors and poverty, the effects of physical illness, struggles with anxiety, depression and mental illness, war, cultural values, and cultural conflict. We observe ways people adapt and cope and how love, imagination, creativity, and finding meaning in activities such as politics and religious movements can have healing functions.

Rationale for the selection of the life stories

The process of choosing these particular subjects was somewhat idiosyncratic and did not follow any given methodology. I was moved by these subjects in different ways, and as I got to know them, I wanted to know them better. I felt that the stories of their lives would contribute insights into varieties of human experience that were interwoven with diverse social, historical, and cultural milieus. However, the book's underlying orientation and analysis can be applied to studying many other biographical and autobiographical subjects not included.

I followed five of the six subjects over the course of their lives, all but one of whom lived into late adulthood (that is, 65 or older). Charlotte Brontë died prematurely at 39. Ved Mehta, still living, is my only autobiographical subject. He discusses his childhood and his life through his middle adulthood.

With the exception of Ottilie Assing and Ved Mehta, multiple biographies have been written about these subjects, offering readers a range of perspectives about their lives. A multiplicity of perspectives is also provided through the many letters these subjects wrote and received. In addition, they were often the subjects of newspaper or magazine articles or were discussed in biographies of others. Three of the biographical subjects also wrote autobiographies (Douglass, 1845, 1855, 1882; Doyle, 1924; Kipling, 1937), which are sources referred to in their life stories.

Although I did not use this as a selection criterion, all six of my subjects had enormous willpower and determination and exercised forceful self-agency. They all had much to overcome, and they overcame a lot. Each subject was, as Backscheider (1999) described, a "special individual, the person who makes something of life" (pp. 100–101). In addition to strength and resilience, each person also had conflicts, struggles, and vulnerabilities that are part of their portraits.

Overview

I have arranged this book according to four major themes: the biographer's involvement with the subject and the autobiographer's self-exploration and the clinical parallels; the biopsychosocial framework; narrative theory; and gathering, evaluating, and interpreting evidence. To tackle these themes, I have written chapters that focus on theory and chapters that put those theories into practice by exploring the life of a prominent literary/historical figure, and I have alternated these chapters so that the life stories clearly illustrate the theoretical concepts in the chapters preceding them. For example, chapter 5 introduces the biopsychosocial framework, and chapter 6 illustrates this framework in the presentation of the life course of Arthur Conan Doyle. The life course is a theme illustrated in all the biographies, giving the reader an opportunity to follow the ups and downs of individual's lives and to compare lives.

Clinical concepts, such as loss, illustrated by Douglass's grandmother's coerced abandonment of him under slavery, are interwoven throughout the book. Some theoretical concepts, such as self-objects and disenfranchised grief, are introduced and discussed. It is anticipated that readers unfamiliar with these concepts will gain familiarity with them and their relevance to biographical and clinical material.

Case illustrations have been taken from various sources, including published and unpublished case material. For published material, sources are given; for unpublished case material, the identities of clinicians and clients are not disclosed, and anonymity and confidentiality are maintained.

A brief outline of each chapter is presented below to give the reader an overall sense of the organization of the book and the pairings of the chapters.

Chapter 1 explores the history of biographies and autobiographies, as they have appeared in different forms at different times, shaped by sociocultural and historical forces.

Chapter 2 focuses on some of the ways authors have become emotionally involved in the biographic enterprise. Immersion in a subject's life, usually over a lengthy period of time, affects biographers in different ways; this may evolve and change over time, with parallels to the therapeutic relationship. This chapter also discusses motivations for writing autobiographies and the impact of the process of self-exploration on the autobiographer.

Chapter 3 presents the life course of Charlotte Brontë, with a particular focus on her relationship to her biographer and contemporary, Elizabeth Gaskell. Gaskell's motivations for portraying a "tragic" and "pious" image of Charlotte are discussed. The concept of self-objects is exemplified by Charlotte, whose many early losses led to her neediness for approval, closeness, and security from others.

Also paired with chapter 2 is chapter 4, on Ved Mehta, a contemporary writer born in India, who became totally blind as a result of meningitis when he was almost four years old. How blindness affected his life is a major theme in his autobiographies, which he wrote after his psychoanalysis enabled him to write with new insight. His further explorations of his past through autobiographical writing and his articulation of his struggles with blindness offer rich clinical insights.

Chapter 5 introduces the biopsychosocial framework as the conceptual model used here in the examination of the biographical process. This synthesizing model, which interweaves both inner and outer worlds, is also the foundation of social work practice. The life course perspective, also discussed in this chapter, presents a dynamic and fluid model of life, emphasizing change, transitions, turning points, and the concept of human agency. The biopsychosocial framework applied here emphasizes psychodynamic theory.

The life course of Sir Arthur Conan Doyle is presented in chapter 6, following the biopsychosocial model. Conan Doyle's life course exemplifies a radical change, as he became an extreme avowed spiritualist. This raises the question of whether this unexpected dramatic shift represented a "discontinuity" in his identity and life course.

Chapter 7 discusses narrative theory, which focuses on story-telling, looking at how the narrator's subjectivity influences the narration. The concept of narrative discourse is also stressed—that is, the interactions and reactions of narrators and their audiences. This theory is relevant for the study of biography and has been extensively applied clinically as well.

Chapter 8 gives an account of the life of Frederick Douglass, the renowned abolitionist and former slave, and his long-standing relationship with Ottilie Assing, a German journalist. They were involved intellectually, politically, and romantically. Douglass's narratives (his three autobiographies) and the use of his narratives in his skillful orations were influential in the abolitionist movement. Douglass's and Assing's self-presentations were central to their concerns.

Chapter 9 focuses on the process of gathering, reading, evaluating, and interpreting biographical materials, including such variables as perspective and objectivity; these are also relevant for clinicians. Ethical dilemmas such as invasion of privacy and vulnerability are also discussed.

Chapter 10 examines the life of Rudyard Kipling, dealing with the evaluation of evidence as discussed in the last chapter. Kipling's life course and work present controversy around the validity of his portrayal of his childhood foster home experience. The validity and meaning of data are also a fundamental issue in clinical situations.

As a biography addict, I am certain that biographies are a source of reading pleasure in and of themselves. But I also feel that they can be read with a discerning mind along the various dimensions I will discuss in this book. Clinical processes can also be "read" for what lies behind the scenes, along similar lines. Perhaps you will both enjoy and read with a critical eye what is presented here, as well.

SECTION I

STUDYING BIOGRAPHY AND AUTOBIOGRAPHY

CHAPTER 1

History and Development of Biographical Writings and Psychobiography

Early History

Stories of the lives of others or oneself have appeared in many forms over the ages, from cave drawings, through oral traditions, to the modern biography and memoir. When writing was invented, documents "incised in clay, chiseled on stone, painted on papyrus, inked on paper," allowed important historical and biographical data to be gathered and retained (Hamilton, 2007, p. 12). *The Epic of Gilgamesh, King of Ur,* dating back to 2,000 BCE, is the oldest written literary story of a life (Hamilton, 2007), the narrative of the king of Sumeria and his good friend Enkidu.

It is not known whether this epic poem is a historic account with some literary liberties taken or if it is a myth. This controversy highlights "the eternal questions that hang over biographical portraiture to this very day" (Hamilton, 2007, p. 15):

> Where does fact end and interpretation begin? Is biography essentially the chronicle of an individual's life journey (and thus a branch of history, employing similar processes of research and scholarship), or is it an art of

human portraiture that must, for social and psychological constructive reasons, capture the essence and distinctiveness of a real individual to be useful both in its time and for posterity? (Hamilton, 2007, p. 15)

Greek and Roman men were taught how to deliver a "eulogy or encomium praising dead figures" and how to write about people important in their own lives (Hamilton, 2007, p. 20). The so-called "professional biographer" of those times was "the compiler, who put together collections of essays about statesmen, soldiers, or philosophers" (p. 20). Tensions developed between those advocating the encomium ("expected to drip with didactic praise") and those supporting the life chronicle ("which opened up the coffins of the dead to more searching curiosity"; p. 23).

The Greek historian, biographer, and essayist Plutarch, who lived from 46 to 120 AD, emphasized the individuality of the subject; his best-known work is *Parallel Lives,* a series of biographies of famous Greeks and Romans. Plutarch has been described "as near a patron saint as biographers have" (Pachter, 1985, p. 12); he asserted that biographers should create portraits of their subjects: " 'I must be allowed to give my more particular *attention to the marks and indications of the souls of men'* " (quoted in Pachter, 1985, p. 12, emphasis added). Plutarch's philosophy has revived, and today many biographers aim to present an authentic portrait of their subjects, emphasizing their individuality and humanity.

Conway (1998) has observed a consistency in biographical form in Western cultures over time, as "archetypal life scripts for men and women" (p. 7). Men's biographical narratives follow the theme of the "odyssey," which is "a journey through many trials and tests, which the hero must surmount alone through courage, endurance, cunning, and moral strength"; ultimately he returns home triumphantly (p. 7). Emphasis is placed on the hero's will and self-agency. *The Epic of Gilgamesh, King of Ur,* predating Homer's *Odyssey,* described one such journey. Women's autobiographies were different in style from the male odyssey books and, even in later periods generally downplayed the role of the authors' self-agency in their own lives (Conway, 1998). For example, in the late nineteenth and early twentieth centuries, women's autobiographies conveyed the impression that their behavior was determined by external circumstances, rather than asserting they had an active role in their destinies. Social reformer Jane Addams, discussed at the end of this chapter, exemplified this trend (Conway, 1998). Although she made major social changes in her Chicago community, as director of Hull House, and achieved international acclaim, she underplayed her involvement and her contributions.

Religious writers incorporated the concept of the journey; their "odysseys" were their own inner struggles, which they successfully mastered along their path toward conversion. Saint Augustine's *Confessions* illustrates this model. Stories of journeys also exist in non-Western cultures (Carbaugh, 2001). The Blackfeet, for example, a Native American tribe living in northern Montana, highlight their interest in returning home in their narratives:

> Traveling and longing for home is . . . a deeply ingrained plot in many people's oral and written literatures. In fact, in some Blackfeet tales, if we didn't know better, we might suspect, as an early compiler of traditional lodge tales wrote, some "might have been taken bodily from the Odyssey." (Carbaugh, 2001, p.118)

The history of biography is circuitous, with progress as well as lapses and backsliding. As the Roman Empire declined, so did "the first golden age of biography" (Hamilton, 2007, p. 34).

The Middle Ages

During the Dark Ages, the spread of Christianity flourished, with an emphasis on religious writings, a reversion to commemorative biographies, and the development of *hagiography,* the stories of saints.

The subject of major biographical interest during this time was Jesus of Nazareth; stories of his life proliferated. Church leaders condemned and destroyed versions of Christ's life of which they disapproved, such as chronicles written by Gnostic writers (Hamilton, 2007). As a consequence, the four Gospels became the accepted versions of Christ's life and teachings.

During the fifth century AD, the landmark *Confessions,* written by Saint Augustine, were addressed to God, but other Christians were also the intended audience (Hamilton, 2007). The concept of *confession* used by Augustine was adopted by later autobiographers and novelists who "link autobiographical truth to confession of the self's past sins" (Barbour, 1992, p. 10). Although Augustine emphasized the religious life and his conversion experience, the *Confessions* contain so much more.

Saint Augustine insightfully described his psychological struggles, his conflicts between passion and conscience, and his spiritual and moral evolution. Augustine's emphasis on self-awareness is "thought to mark *the beginning of autobiographical reflection* as we have come to know it" (Freeman & Brockmeier, 2001, p. 80, emphasis added). Augustine was perceptive about the development of memory and the processes by which people's past experiences, present experiences, and thoughts of the future are "woven together." Such reflection on one's past life can alter when looked at from one's current perspective. This concept is highlighted in discussions of narrative theory: "the past of a life becomes ordered in the light of the present, an ordering which I have called *retrospective teleology*" (Brockmeier, 2001, p. 276). Saint Augustine, memory, and retrospective teleology and its relevance to clinical practice are discussed further in chapter 7.

Women's Early Autobiographies

Women generally had little or no role in public life throughout both antiquity and the Middle Ages and were notably excluded from politics and theology. In the Middle Ages, however, they had more prominent roles and exercised more "self-direction" within the monasteries and abbeys for women, although their freedom was circumscribed within monastic life (Conway, 1998, p. 11).

Religious life also saw the beginnings of women's autobiography, in which writers discussed their religious feelings and their "meditation about the nature of God and the recording of direct experience of divine illumination" (Conway, 1998, p. 12). Such writers included the German Abbess Hildegard of Bingen, in the 12th century; the English Dame Julian of Norwich, author of the *Book of Shewings to the Anchoress Julian of Norwich* in 1393; and the Spanish mystic Saint Teresa of Avila, whose *Life of St. Teresa by Herself* was written in 1562–1565 (Conway, 1998).

Reflecting on her religious experience, Saint Teresa of Avila, as Conway (1998) observed, uses the image of a garden being fed by streams of water to convey her sense of the operation of grace in her consciousness. Her guide to her readers on the techniques of prayer and meditation is practical and vividly written. Her entire history is a story of a relationship with God, although her powers of expression make every monk, nun, confessor and family member live in the reader's mind. She is direct and plainspoken about the insignificance of the will in coming to know God. (p. 12)

Conway (1998) stresses that Saint Teresa's lack of emphasis on her felt "will" is typical of women's writings Hamilton (2007) notes the paradox that the church, while suppressing secular biographies, including those of the classical era, opened up the possibilities of autobiography. Although initially of a religious nature, the autobiographical emphasis on self-reflectiveness, the exploration of one's inner life, and the evolution of individual morality would remain key features as religious forces receded and were rivaled by secular interests.

The Renaissance

During the Renaissance, with its greater intellectual freedom, artistic expression, creativity, and gifted in-depth portrait painting, such as that of Rembrandt, biography also progressed. Plutarch's works were rescued from oblivion and circulated. Cellini, a gifted goldsmith, wrote his (very secular) autobiography. In England, Holinshed's extensive history of Great Britain "fueled as many as twelve of

William Shakespeare's historical-biographical plays. Biography was approaching its second golden age" (Hamilton, 2007, p. 64).

Shakespeare had a strong influence on biographical writings, especially because of his psychological understanding of the complexities of his characters; his depictions of their inner struggles, interpersonal relationships, and conflicts over political power; and the complex interplay of these dynamics (Hamilton, 2007). Shakespeare tended to choose characters from the historic past; portraits of more contemporaneous subjects had to be handled with circumspection. Ever present was the danger of disapproval by the monarch or prominent establishment figures; this dilemma of so-called "subversive biography—especially about living people"—has persisted over time (Hamilton, p. 67). Although beheadings are not in style today, lawsuits do proliferate.

Hamilton (2007) referred to Sir Walter Raleigh as biography's "first martyr" (p. 74). Raleigh, after a successful multifaceted career as a soldier, explorer, and writer, was tried in 1663 as a spy for Spain. Condemned to execution, a great public protest followed, and his sentence was commuted to incarceration in the Tower of London. During the 10 years of his imprisonment, he wrote *The History of the World*, published in 1614 as an anonymous work. His history ended at 168 BC because he feared offending contemporary officials.

When the book became very popular, King James I had it withdrawn for various objections, "but specially for being too sawcie in censuring princes" (Hamilton, 2007, p. 71). Although circumspect in some ways, Raleigh nevertheless made negative remarks about sitting monarchs, noting that comparisons could be drawn between early rulers and modern ones. Raleigh was again tried, ostensibly not for the book but for what Hamilton implies were trumped-up political reasons; Raleigh was convicted by a "kangaroo court" and executed the next day, October 29, 1618 (Hamilton, 2007, p. 71).

Raleigh observed that writing historical biographies served two purposes: to use contemporary understanding to gain insight into the figures of the past and to learn how past behaviors can throw light on present misbehaviors. He was concerned with "the political—involving moral and political censure" (Hamilton, 2007, p. 76).

Raleigh made other insightful observations about the writing of biographies: "There can be many opinions and perspectives on an individual's life. The biographer must look beneath the surface appearances of the subject's life to find the inner man or woman.

> In studying people, one finds great diversity in their thoughts and feelings and that every person has a fancy and cognition differing: there being nothing wherein Nature so much triumpheth, as in its dissimiltude. From whence it commeth, that there is found so great diuersity of opinions; so strong a contrariety of inclinations; so many naturall and vnnatural; wise, foolish; manly, and childish affections, and passions in Mortall Men. (Raleigh, quoted in Hamilton, 2007, p. 78).

Samuel Pepys, born in 1633, 15 years after Raleigh's death, incorporated in his diaries the ongoing political turmoil of the times, including the execution of Charles I, the reign of Cromwell, and the restoration of Charles II to the English throne (Tomalin, 2002). Men powerful, wealthy, and successful one day could suddenly find themselves in prison as power changed hands. Pepys himself was briefly imprisoned in the Tower of London, charged with treason.

Although writers needed to exercise caution, the reading public's strong interest was accommodated by a continual supply of life stories. Life depictions also became popular in painting, sculpture, and the theater (Hamilton, 2007). Many life stories were commemorative; others tended to follow Plutarch's dictum to paint life "portraits." Izaak Walton's *Lives* (of Donne, Wotton, Hooker, and Herbert) was considered one of the most notable of this genre for his time (Hamilton, 2007) and was among those biographies "that broke the mould" (Backscheider, 1999, p. 127).

There was keen interest in learning about new discoveries and explorations of the world and the conquest of the wilderness. Narratives by Christopher Columbus, John Smith, and Captain James Cook relating segments of their lives were among those exciting interest in the reading public. These stories were a new "version of the classical odyssey" (Conway, 1998, p. 9).

The Renaissance was an expansive period; great strides were made in intellectual and artistic expression, science, and exploration. There was greater freedom to move away from religious to secular themes. The numbers of those capable of and interested in reading increased. However, freedom to express criticism of current governments and rulers was restricted; violators faced death or imprisonment.

The Age of Johnson

In the 18th century, the middle class was growing, as was its appetite for learning and for books. At the same time, many writers felt constrained by the risks of writing anything other than idealized accounts of lives. There were strict libel laws with serious consequences for those writers who tarnished the reputations of people still living (Hamilton, 2007). These laws did not cover individuals who were no longer living, which enabled biographers such as Samuel Johnson to deprecate aspects of the lives of deceased subjects.

This period has often been referred to as the "Age of Johnson" (Jarrett, 1999, p. 40), in deference to Dr. Samuel Johnson, who was then one of the most prominent men in London society. He was best known for his *Dictionary,* among other literary accomplishments. Johnson found himself frustrated by the proliferation of books extolling people, amounting to hagiographies "or the Lives of the Saints" (Hamilton, 2007, p. 89). One should not write only about people's virtues, he claimed: "'If nothing but the bright side of characters should be shewn,' he pointed out, 'we should sit down in despondency, and think it utterly impossible to imitate them in *any thing.'* . . . for the purpose of biography was, he recognized, to allow the audience to empathize with, or project onto, the life portrayed" (Hamilton, 2007, p. 89).

When Johnson wrote the *Lives of the Poets,* published in 1779, "biography came of age" (Holroyd, 2002, p. 22). Although immensely successful, this book also received strong public disapproval because of Johnson's discussion of his subjects' flaws and their "domestick privacies." For example, Johnson excoriated Milton's political views as those of a "surly and acrimonious republican" (Dunn, 1908, p. 136). When Johnson was 53 and already famous, he met James Boswell, who was then 22. Although quite dissimilar in many ways, they developed a strong friendship, and Boswell became his biographer. Boswell and Johnson, and their collaboration, are discussed further in chapter 7.

Rousseau and Autobiographies

When Boswell was writing during the Enlightenment, a strong interest developed among the middle class throughout Europe in writing personal accounts of life experiences, through media including diaries, journals, and letters (Hamilton, 2007). Self-contemplation was considered an important step toward personal development. The greater freedom of the political climate was also conducive to writing autobiographies. This is when Rousseau (in 1770) wrote his ground breaking *Confessions*. It was published in 1781, three years after he died (Hamilton, 2007).

Different from the religious orientation of Augustine's *Confessions,* Rousseau's book was a secular tract with a political agenda that influenced future autobiographical writing. Rousseau discussed his childhood experiences as important influences throughout his adult life. This created a precedent for later autobiographers to "record the shaping influences of [their] childhood" (Conway, 1998, p. 19). Brooks (1984) asserts that Rousseau's work "stands as the emblematic emergence of the biography of the individual personality, announcing the typical focus and concern of modern narrative" (p. 268). He "stands at the inception of the case history, the use of narrative to grasp patterns of behavior through time and to trace their etiology" (p. 269).

Rousseau elevated the significance of the emotional life; he felt that man should be "governed by his senses and feelings," rather than being controlled by "externally imposed laws of conduct" (Conway, 1998, p. 8). Although he observed that people needed others "to serve as a foil bringing out [their] true colors and character" (Olney, 1998, p. 413), Rousseau saw himself as an exception to this rule. It was his intention "to *offer himself as an other* so that readers may have a 'piece de comparaison' by means of which they might know themselves" (Olnet, 1998, p. 413, emphasis added).

Paradoxically, although Rousseau set himself up as the epitome of truthfulness, exhorting his readers to follow his model, he did not have the ability to see himself from the perspective of others. Hamilton (2007), Barbour (1992), and Olney (1998) see him as a master of self-deception who was seldom aware of the consequences of his own behavior. When Rousseau actually confessed to doing something wrong, "he presents himself as an innocent victim of a corrupting environment" (Barbour, 1992, p. 15).

In one such example, Rousseau rationalized his placement of all five of his children in an orphanage (notorious then for poor conditions and a high mortality rate):

> I will be content with a general statement that in handing my children over for the State to educate, for lack of means to bring them up by myself, by destining them to become workers and peasants instead of adventurers and fortune-hunters, I thought I was acting as a citizen and a father, and looked upon myself as a member of Plato's Republic. (Rousseau, quoted in Olney, 1998, p.144)

In another reference to this Foundlings' Home, Rousseau adds:

> I should do the same thing again with even fewer misgivings if the choice were still before me, and I am sure that no father is more affectionate than I would have been towards them once habit had time to reinforce my natural inclination. (quoted in Olney, 1998, p. 192)

Rousseau did not seem aware of the inherent contradictions in his behavior: While railing against the negative influences of corrupt society, preferring the development of the "natural man," he nevertheless turned his children over to the care of the state, placing them in an environment hardly conducive to a natural flowering of the personality.

Olney (1998) can recall "no other autobiographer or life-writer or self-writer... as thoroughly and as continuously self-deceived as Rousseau" (p. 147). He adds that present-day "confessions" have roots in Rousseau's precedent-setting *Confessions:*

> ...my impression is that in our time... literary confession owes almost nothing to Augustine and almost everything to Rousseau. *True Confessions—which* are neither true nor confessions—set the tone for our time and they come more or less directly out of Rousseau. (Olney, 1998, p. 147)

Rousseau's *Confessions* had a political agenda. He "rejects" the French "corrupt aristocratic society" and supports the "new democratic man," which he asserts himself to be (Conway, 1998, p. 8). He emphasizes "sincere self-examination as the key to his vision of humanity freed from the corruptions of modern civilization" (Clemit, 2005, p. 168).

Rousseau wrote in the politically turbulent years preceding the French Revolution (and seven years before the American Revolution). In France, *Confessions* made a powerful impression on the population at large and became a model for others to write their "frank, self-justifying memoirs of their conversion to the principles of liberty and equality" (Clemit, 2005, p. 161). *Confessions* also had a profound influence on the "English radical intelligentsia of the

1790's" (Clemit, 2005, p. 161). William Godwin, an English writer and social critic influenced by Rousseau, considered self-reflection and autobiographical writings to be essential to his own political development (Clemit, 2005).

Committed to the principles of freedom, Godwin was convinced that biographical writing was the key to social reform. "He dismissed the history of mass movements in favor of 'individual history,' or *biography,* which contributed to general progress of mind by encouraging attention to the *internal causes of human behaviour"* [italics added] (Clemit, 2005, p. 163). Godwin subsequently focused on his own development and wrote autobiographical pieces.

> Just as Rousseau used autobiography to demonstrate how he became a philosopher, Godwin constructed his personal history so as to elucidate the foundations of his adult identity as social critic... he organized his past experiences into a pattern, which reflects his own understanding of human nature. (Clemit, 2005, p. 170)

Initially, Godwin insisted on total openness in discussing his past: "'to tell the truth & the whole truth, as far as I could discern it'" (quoted in Clemit, 2005, p. 173). Godwin later modified this stance, in large measure because of the negative public reaction to his publication of his wife's posthumous *Memoirs* in 1798, a book of "unprecedented biographical frankness" (Clemit, 2005, 174). Godwin's wife was Mary Wollstonecraft, who, years before her marriage,, had established a reputation as a liberated, radical feminist. She was "that rarest of things in eighteenth century England, a woman freelance reviewer and writer, living entirely by her own pen" (Holmes, 1985, p. 90).

In espousing the need for circumspection in revealing personal truth, Godwin emphasized the importance of understanding who the audience might be that would be receiving this "truth." Although narrative theory had not been conceptualized at this point in history, Godwin's following statement foresees the theory's *dialogic* principle. "Truth, practically speaking… arises from the relative character & disposition of two persons or things, the speaker & the hearer, the words uttered, & the temper of him by whom the words are received" (Godwin, quoted in Clemit, 2005, p. 174).

The Proliferation of Autobiographical Writings

Autobiographies became increasingly popular after the American and French Revolutions; readers were eager to hear details about these revolutionary events from the leaders, participants, and witnesses. Individual rights were receiving recognition, and interest in learning about the development and functioning of the mind was growing. Autobiographies appeared in four formats: "memoir, apologia, essay, and confessional" (Hamilton, 2007, pp. 100–101). The memoir may focus on the writer's memories, feelings, and emotions or conversely may be an extended "memorandum" on the writer's public achievements. The apologia is a work of autobiographical self-justification, and the confessional is a self-critical autobiographical work, at least formally, on the surface. The autobiographical essay is a brief examination of subject matter important in the writer's life, expressing the writer's slant on the issues in question. Eager to read autobiographies of others, people of all ages also kept diaries of their own.

Life narratives became popular. Often they were written by unknown people who recorded unusual and dramatic events in their lives, such as narratives by women who had been taken hostage by Indians: Mary Rowlandson's (1635–1678) memoir is an early example. Accounts of escapes from slavery also became popular. The discussion of narratives is expanded in chapter 5.

Benjamin Franklin

Benjamin Franklin, writing during the same period as Rousseau, focused on the pragmatics of his success rather than chronicling his past traumas or drawing on introspection, as Rousseau had done. His autobiography was basically "a memoir, a record of public achievements and... character formation" (Barbour, 1992, p. 117). Franklin was truly a "man for all seasons," whose contributions included scientific discoveries (for example, the theory of electricity) and inventions (such as the Franklin stove and the lightning rod), political leadership (in the formation of the U.S. government and serving as an ambassador to France), and philanthropy. His autobiography did not display "any complexity... or hidden aspects of Franklin's character. The autobiography displays little consciousness of a constantly developing sense of individuality, and no interest in how the autobiographical act itself necessitates further reformulations of identity" (Barbour, 1992, p. 117).

Although Franklin emphasized the development of self-agency and individualism, Barbour (1992) observes that it would be incorrect to say that Franklin did not have a "social conscience" (as some of his detractors contend); in fact, Franklin had "a genuine appreciation of the interconnectedness of individuals in society and a concern for community" (Barbour, 1992, p. 85). "His many inventions... were at once contributions to the practice of philanthropy and that of science. He refused to take a patent for his stove [because] … " 'we should be glad of an Opportunity to serve others.' " (Barbour, 1992, p. 100).

Although dedicated to intellectual and scientific pursuits, Franklin nevertheless had reservations about relying totally on rationality and acknowledged the complexities of human nature. "So convenient a thing is it to be a *reasonable Creature,* since it enables one to find or make a Reason for everything one has a mind to do" (quoted in Barbour, 1992, p. 28). Although Franklin was not alluding to Rousseau in this context, it is a fitting description of Rousseau's rationalizations.

The Victorian Age

The quality of biographical writings declined during the Victorian Age; writing regressed to a pre- Johnsonian phase. The whitewashed, external, and proper lives of people were presented, and encomiums flourished. This decline accompanied the emphasis on social class, concern focused on social advancement, and a focus on creating a proper image in society; any biographical materials detracting from a person's social standing were not tolerated. Hamilton (2007) observes that Thomas De Quincey's autobiography about his drug addiction, *Confessions of an English Opium Eater,* published in 1821, would probably not have been published after his death in 1859 because of these changing social mores.

The expansion of the British Empire, with its emphasis on imperialism, colonization, and missionary activity, enhanced feelings of patriotism and the exercise of "public virtue," as did the development of "Victorian evangelism, fear of poverty, and moralizing" (Hamilton,

2007, pp. 109–110). Rudyard Kipling (discussed in chapter 10) exemplified this viewpoint, extolling the virtues of imperialism, supporting the Boer War, and shouldering the "white man's burden."

The Victorian age also saw the development of the "profession of 'biographer'" (Hamilton, 2007, p. 120). Biographers, usually men, were generally commissioned to write the lives of prominent subjects, themselves nearly always men; rarely were women subjects of biographies, although Queen Victoria was an exception. A notable double exception to this custom was the commission of the female novelist, Elizabeth Gaskell, by Charlotte Brontë's father, to write Charlotte's biography (discussed in chapters 2 and 3).

Hamilton (2007) observed that although these biographers were writing encomiums, they did nevertheless make a lasting contribution, as their books were usually carefully researched and well documented, leaving detailed records of the lives of fascinating and important individuals, including explorers, politicians, and scientists, which future biographers could use.

During this period, John Forster was a successful biographer of English and Irish writers, such as Jonathan Swift (at that point already long deceased). When Forster wrote the life of Dickens, whom he had known personally, he included details about Dickens's difficult marriage and his emotional fragility. The result was that his book met with angry rejection. Hamilton (2007) emphasizes that public anger was directed not at Dickens's indiscretions but at Forster, for his indiscretion in revealing these details to the public.

Hamilton (2007) credits the rise and popularity of Victorian fiction during this time in large measure to the demise of good biographical writing. Audiences hungering for life stories turned to the new extraordinary novels depicting fictional lives, which also incorporated personal flaws, "immoral" behaviors, and social problems, such as Dickens's *David Copperfield,* Charlotte Brontë's *Jane Eyre,* Hawthorne's *The Scarlet Letter,* and Tolstoy's *Anna Karenina.*

Lytton Strachey

As the Victorian period came to an end, another landmark biographer appeared, as significant in his day as Samuel Johnson and James Boswell had been in theirs. *Eminent Victorians* by Lytton Strachey, published in 1918, was radically different from the prevailing sanitized encomiums (Miller, 2001). Strachey wrote about four eminent public personalities of the 19th century—Cardinal Manning, Florence Nightingale, Thomas Arnold, and General Gordon—with the purpose of "dethroning" them and exposing their alleged inadequacies and deceptions: "Its abrasive, even satiric, tone was designed to undermine the idols of a bankrupt age and reveal their feet of clay" (Miller, 2001, p. 145).

Strachey was also concerned with the style and format of biographical writing; his "biographical essays are masterpieces of wit and polish" (Miller, 2001, p. 145).

Strachey wrote in a time of profound political and social change: The Victorian age, which had witnessed tremendous growth of the British Empire and the development of a self-righteous imperialism, was over (Backscheider, 1999). World War I, with its rhetoric of patriotism, ended in tragic disaster for England and all of Europe; America, too, suffered many losses on the battlefield. The meaningless slaughter of young men was catastrophic, the battle strategies unrealistic and hopeless, the devastation unbelievable.

Disillusionment permeated the biographical sphere—this was not the time for hero worship or for memorializing leaders responsible for this debacle. Hamilton, citing Richard Altick, noted that in both the United States and England, "'book-length debunking of reputations became a literary fad,'" which found a large market of readers (2007, p. 152). The reputations of many subjects other than political and military leaders were also debunked. For example, in 1929, Langbridge wrote *Charlotte Brontë: A Psychological Study,* a negative portrayal whose goal was to stop "'the foolish fashion of canonising Charlotte'" (Miller, 2001, p. 145).

Freud, Psychoanalytic Theory, and Psychobiography

Sigmund Freud and the development of psychoanalysis were major influences during this period, affecting writers, biographers, the medical community, and the general public. Freud felt that it was his fate to "'agitate the sleep of mankind'" (Gay, 1988, p. xvii); this agitation was intense in his day and persists to the present. Although he remains a controversial figure, Freud has contributed lasting insights relating to unconscious drives and motives, fantasies, dreams, subjectivity, and psychological conflict and brought the discussion of sexual attitudes and behaviors "out of the closet."

Freud also had a specific influence on biographical writings per se, as he proposed a method for conducting such studies and wrote what he felt was a model biographical essay on Leonardo da Vinci. *Leonardo da Vinci and a Memory of His Childhood* was published in 1910 (Runyan, 1982) and is often cited as marking the beginnings of psychobiography. Freud's study on Leonardo has been generally disparaged. Although credited with elucidating very useful concepts for constructing a psycho biography, Freud nevertheless did not himself follow them in his study (Elms, 2005a). For example, he did not avoid basing "arguments upon a single clue" or "pathographizing the psycho biographical subject" (pp. 40, 42). Freud's discussion focused on an early childhood dream reported by Leonardo and stressed the development of Leonardo's inferred putative homosexuality. Freud's essay has been "attacked not only for dragging the great Leonardo in the mud . . . but also for serious factual errors and lapses in logic" (Elms, 2005a, p. 210).

In examining the development of psychobiography, it is important to clarify the distinction between the *discipline* of psychobiography and the more general usage of this term to describe the reliance on psychological theory (often psychoanalytic theory) as a basis for constructing biographies. Psychobiography, as a specific discipline, generally has a more limited goal than producing a full-scale biography: "It often targets one facet of a life at a time, a more or less discrete episode or event or action" (Schultz, 2005c, p. 9). Psychobiographers generally start out with a question or a mystery that needs to be explored, and their assessment of a person's life revolves around answering it. Schultz (2005a), for example, was intrigued with the life and art of Diane Arbus, particularly the questions of what drew her to photograph the lives of eccentrics and people she termed "freaks" (p. 112).

There are many adherents (both biographers and readers) of psychologically oriented biographies; however, there is also opposition to this practice from proponents of particular social issues, such as oppression. "The term 'Freudian biography' is now an even more derogatory term than 'psychobiography' " (Elms, 1994, p. 4). In their own defense, some authors have chosen "more innocuous labels for their work: *Life History, Narratology, Psychological Biography*" (p. 4).

Authors have not infrequently misapplied psychoanalytic theory to their writings. Some psychoanalytic biographies use specific early events or relationships to explain everything about the person; this" 'key to personality' (whether they found it in, say, the dominant father, the dead mother, or the rivalrous brother) meant that subtlety and complexity were often sacrificed for the sake of fitting the evidence into a consistent, preordained pattern" (Miller, 2001, p. 144). Elms (1994) has observed that the practice of defining the behaviors and relationships of adults primarily on the basis of their childhood experiences is so common that Erik Erikson has "given the process a gently sarcastic label: 'originology' " (p. 4). Rosamond Langbridge's *Charlotte Brontë: A Psychological Study* (1929) was "indirectly influenced by a bastardized watered-down version of psychoanalytic thinking—psychosomatic illness and sexual repression feature in her account" (Miller, 2001, pp. 144–145).

Biographies based primarily on psychological theories often fail to present a comprehensive picture of the subject's life. Many have reduced the subject's life to psychological development, omitting social, cultural, and historical contexts; they may emphasize psychopathology and leave out important life transitions and adult development. Runyan (1982) discussed three types of "reductionist" flaws:

> One...is that psychological factors are overemphasized at the expense of external social and historical factors.... A second...is that psychobiography focuses excessively on psychopathological processes and gives insufficient attention to normality and creativity.... A third...is to explain adult character and behavior exclusively in terms of early childhood experience while neglecting later formative processes and influences. (pp. 208–209)

Psychoanalysis, which ushered in a new era in understanding the personality, has itself evolved in new directions, with the development of ego psychology, object relations theory, and self-psychology; psychodynamic theory, incorporating these later concepts, is espoused by many clinicians and writers today. Ego psychology focuses on ego functioning and adaptation to the external world; object relations theory emphasizes attachment, loss, the internalization of important relationships, and the development of identity; and self-psychology centers on the development of a cohesive self and self-objects. (These concepts are discussed in detail in chapter 5.) The psychodynamic orientation is a much broader and comprehensive approach to understanding people. While incorporating Freudian concepts of an inner mental life, it includes additional concepts, such as attachment, the development of identity, and patterns of social relationships.

Backscheider (1999) has observed that writers as well their audiences use a "national language of psychology" (p. 114); many psychoanalytic concepts, such as the ego and the Oedipus complex, are explicitly or implicitly embedded in biographical writings. In current psychodynamic theory, the ego is recognized as a set of functions important in helping the person adapt to the external world. Previously, the ego was seen as focusing exclusively on mediating the conflicts between the drives and the superego (conscience). The Oedipus complex, based on the ancient myth of Oedipus, who unknowingly married his mother and killed his father, postulates that during the Oedipal phase, children have strong attachments to the parent of the opposite sex and experience jealousy and rivalrous anger toward the parent of the same sex. Although these conflicts are generally worked through (at about five to six years of age), difficulties in resolving these feelings may occur and may underlie neuroses, character disorders, and relationship disturbances.

Backscheider (1999), quoting Storrs, a British psychiatrist and author, emphasized that the internal life of subjects is often explored by biographers, and many psychodynamic concepts" 'have become so incorporated into intellectual discourse that biographers automatically employ them without always realizing whence they came' " (Storrs, quoted in Backscheider, 1999, p. 114). The inner life of individuals is interwoven into the fabric of this book.

The 20th and 21st Centuries

The dynamic 20th century burst with profound and rapid changes in every sphere of life: political, biological, social, psychological, technological, legal, and philosophical. Major advances took place in human rights for women and minorities. Technological advances in communication were phenomenal, including the rapid development of radio, film, TV, and the Internet. Great intellectual ferment occurred in all fields, with cross-fertilization of ideas among disciplines. Medical advances prolonged the life span. The sexual revolution altered sexual behavior and brought a new openness and public discussion of sexuality. What was now seen as "proper" to include in life studies was greatly expanded to include intimate details of lives.

Biographies and autobiographies were affected by all these changes in many ways. The 1960s through the 1990s saw "the most astonishing display of biographical outpouring ever witnessed. It was a veritable second Renaissance—a passionate, irrepressible fascination with individuality and individuals that could not be stopped" (Hamilton, 2007, p. 205).

Major strides were made in expanding subjects to be discussed, and biographers experimented with new techniques (Holroyd, 2002), such as those of the novelist or short story writer. This created new issues of contention: When these techniques are used, some wondered whether it was "legitimate for a biographer to borrow from the techniques of the fiction writer," for example, by creating or re-creating dialogue between the subject and others. Another consideration is the extent to which biographers, by sharing their thoughts about biographical decision making, ought to "make themselves audible" to the reader rather than remaining invisible in the background (Backscheider, 1999, pp. xix–xx).

Factors significantly influencing the writing of biographies and autobiographies today are presented below; there is ongoing interaction among all of them.

Mass Communication

Radio was a dramatic advance in the evolution of mass communication: Audiences could now hear for themselves from people from all walks of life around the globe; the immediacy of an event was transmitted to wide audiences. World War II was the first time broadcast journalists brought news directly from the battlefield to the public.

Movies captured public interest, increasing in popularity when soundtracks were added in 1928. Initially, films focused on fictional stories; documentaries were later added, following a liberalization of privacy and libel laws (Hamilton, 2007). This legal evolution galvanized biographers and autobiographers as well as filmmakers, radio and television broadcasters, researchers, and journalists to pursue the representation of individual lives in greater depth. Now they could "fulfill Samuel Johnson's vision of biography as an account that included both virtue *and* vice" (Hamilton, 2007, p. 204). Biographies in all forms became very popular. An interest in past lives was supplemented by an interest in current lives and events; biography was "increasingly becoming a record of the *present* in America" (Hamilton, 2007, p. 223).

Today television has a Biography channel and features special programs on other channels dedicated to the stories of lives. Hollywood produces many well-attended biopics. The burgeoning interest of people in sharing accounts of their lives and reading accounts of others is also seen in the proliferation of Internet messaging, including Weblogs (i.e., blogs) and online diaries.

The public's interest in the lives of celebrities continues. Broadcasting details of their life crises is routine. For example, in the summer of 2009, when Michael Jackson died, a "media frenzy" scrutinized the causes of Jackson's death, his finances, family conflict, and the ongoing custody disputes over his children.

Support for Human Rights and Diversity

The various revolutions in human rights have led to widespread interest in the stories of women, blacks, lesbians, gay men, and bisexual individuals, post-colonials, and other marginalized minorities (Hamilton, 2007).

Feminism and women's rights has had a major impact on biographical writings, both in terms of subject matter and style. Women now regularly write biographies and are the subjects of biographies. Greater interest has also been given to the stories of women involved in the lives of famous men. One such book (Flanders, 2001) discusses the four Macdonald sisters, living in Victorian England. They attained fame in terms of their own talents and attributes, as well as because of the men they married (the artist Burne-Jones and the Royal Academician Edward Poynter) or mothered (Rudyard Kipling and Prime Minister Stanley Baldwin).

Women's studies developed as a new field of scholarship, and there has been a remarkable production of research related to women's history. Other newly developed and growing academic fields include African American studies and gay and lesbian studies, which include extensive biographical and autobiographical works.

Feminist Biographies and Autobiographies

During the Progressive Era, many American women were educated and entered fields such as education, social work, and nursing. Jane Addams, a social worker and director of the Hull Settlement House in Chicago, gained international fame as a social reformer. Although an activist, she did not write in an "active" voice and did not express her own will (or "agency"). Conway (1998) observed that this tended to be typical of women reformers of that period:

> Through her extensive use of conditional tenses and the passive voice, Addams is able to conceal her own role in making the events of her life happen and to conform herself to the romantic image of the female, seeming to be all emotion and spontaneity, and to be shaped by circumstances beyond her control. Once we grasp her skill in doing this we have learned an important point about later-nineteenth- and early-twentieth-century women's

autobiography. We can be sure that whenever women autobiographers are hiding behind the passive voice and the conditional tense, they are depicting events in which they acted forthrightly upon a preconceived, rational plan. (Conway, 1998, pp. 49–50).

As feminism evolved in the latter part of the 20th century, it made contributions to biography in terms of style, placing emphasis on details of "private, domestic, or intimate sphere[s]" of the lives of both men and women (Backscheider, 1999).

Feminist biographers gave prominence to emotionality and to relationships, studying the involved social networks that women form and observing the different ways the subject interacts with others— this is "now a demand placed on all biographers" (Backscheider, 1999, p. 156). However, there have also been male biographers, including Richard Holmes and Michael Holroyd, who have given attention to these issues. Holroyd's *Lytton Strachey,* for example, details Strachey's involvement with the intricate network of relationships and romances of the Bloomsbury group.

Finally, Backscheider (1999) credits feminists with focusing on the relationship of the biographer and the subject, though credit also needs to be shared with Boswell (Hamilton, 2007), Michael Holroyd (2002), Richard Holmes (1985), and George Moraitis (2003), among others.

Feminist biographers can have special problems, including overinvolvement and bias fostered by being intensely engaged with their subjects (Backscheider, 1999). Overidentification with a subject can be fueled by social factors, such as identification with a social movement or shared feelings of social oppression:

> Sometimes, however, such engagement can be perilous,
> and books should carry warning labels for readers. Among
> the problems women biographers have admitted are iden-
> tifying too closely, taking too much for granted, refusing
> to deal with things that are too personally charged... and
> refusing to include things that, in our opinions, reinforce
> debilitating stereotypes of women. (Backscheider, 1999,
> p. 160)

In writing of Mary Wollstonecraft's relationship with her lover Imlay, Richard Holmes (1985) has noted that Imlay has been "bad mouthed" in most biographical accounts; but Holmes views Imlay in a more positive light and wants to convey how much Imlay had meant to Mary. Holmes implies that Imlay's "bad press" is due to writers' overinvolvement with and protectiveness of Wollstonecraft. "Poor Gilbert Imlay! Subsequent biographers of Mary, mostly feminist writers, have torn him limb from limb.... They have condemned him for shallowness, bad faith, bad manners. But it never seemed like that to me" (Holmes, 1985, p. 110).

The 20th and 21st centuries saw an explosion of technological, psychological, political, and artistic advances. Advances have been made in the sphere of human rights, and women and minorities have an important presence. There is greatly increased interest in biographies, autobiographies, and memoirs.

Personal Memoirs and Confessions

Some biographies and autobiographies focus on special events or adventures. The early fascination with stories of adventure, exploration, and escape that began during the Enlightenment continues to the present. People want to read firsthand accounts of war experience, space exploration, survival of boat and plane crashes, experiences of coping with a spouse's extramarital affairs, and so forth. If an "interesting" person is convicted of an "interesting" crime and imprisoned, this story also has special public appeal.

One popular venue is the "success" story—how the protagonist overcame difficult social and economic circumstances to become important and successful. Biographers have told of their religious conversions and of overcoming (or coping with) their physical illness. These narratives have been described as *quest stories* (Frank, 1995, p. 115). The first such quest narrative has been attributed to the 17th-century poet John Donne, "who recast his illness... into a spiritual journey" (Frank, 1995, p. 116).

Some writers present psychological or mental health problems as another form of a quest narrative. Mark Vonnegut (1975) has described his bout with schizophrenia; Kay Redfield Jamison (1996), a clinical psychologist, has shared her struggle with her own bipolar illness; and William Styron (1990) portrayed the onset and course of his depression and brush with suicide. Clifford Beers's (1908/1925) account of his years of struggle with manic-depressive disorder became a rallying point for his development of the mental health movement.

Some autobiographies are written as confessions, which may include apologies. The fictional autobiographies of Kierkegaard, Dostoevsky, and Camus were "first-person confessions, public articulations of a guilty conscience" (Barbour, 1992, p. 21). For some writers, "introspection and self-accusation" is the highest good and can eclipse "kindness, justice, or loyalty to any conviction or person" (Barbour, 1992, p. 21). This trend in confessional autobiography has had an impact on other writers, "demanding more intimate, more challenging, more *revealing* exposure of the individual self and selves" (Hamilton, 2007, p. 194).

Some confessional autobiographies are not always truthful; fraudulent autobiographies are not uncommon (Yagoda, 2009). A scandal erupted in 2006 surrounding the memoir *A Million Little Pieces,* by James Frey, which was found to contain many untruths. His book and the subsequent fraud were publicized on Oprah Winfrey's TV show (Grossman, 2006; Wyatt, 2006). Deception and fraud in autobiographies are discussed further in later chapters.

Family Lives Revealed

Writers sometimes recount their difficulties in overcoming and coping with painful family relationships. Nuland's (2003) autobiography focused on his father and their relationship: "I am writing this book to help me come to terms with my father. I am writing this book to finally make peace with him, and perhaps with myself" (Introduction [unpaged]).

A major breakthrough in revealing highly sensitive material about homosexuality was made when Nigel Nicolson's *Portrait of a Marriage* was published in 1973, depicting the marriage of his famous bisexual parents (both biographers), Harold Nicolson and Virginia Sackville-West. Although maintaining a close relationship with each other, they each had relationships with same-sex lovers.

Edmund Gosse, the English writer and critic, published a book anonymously in 1907, an expose of his father: *Father and Son: A Study of Two Temperaments.* Gosse's father was a well-known naturalist and geologist, with a strong religious faith; but what Gosse described was his father's tyranny and abuse. This book contributed to the trend toward exposé, which flowered later in the century, with accounts of parental psychological, physical, and sexual abuse (Hamilton, 2007). Sometimes the parents were celebrities such as Joan Crawford, whose daughter wrote *Mommie Dearest,* describing her traumatic experiences growing up with her alcoholic mother (Hamilton, 2007).

Copyright Laws and Privacy

Although biographers gained freedom to write about living people through the passage of libel laws in the 1960s, biographical writing became complicated again in the 1990s through the passage of stringent copyright laws. Now living celebrities and their heirs can withhold materials, sometimes to protect privacy and/or to profit from royalties. Unpublished personal letters or memos, critical resources for biographers, can also be withheld; it is generally easier for biographers to get permission to use a subject's published writings than it is to receive permission to have access to the subject's private written material, such as letters or diaries.

Copyrights now extend to the lifetime of the author plus 70 years; this precedent was established by the European Union in 1995 and accepted by the United States Supreme Court in 1998 (Hamilton, 2007). It has often led to involved legal negotiations between biographers and the estates of prospective subjects.

Biographical work on James Joyce, for example, was impeded by Joyce's family. Joyce's daughter Lucia had had a long period of psychiatric institutionalization, which the family made strenuous efforts to conceal.

Controversies Regarding Style and Genre

The boundaries between fiction and nonfiction are not always clearly demarcated: Some novelists have included biographical and historical materials (about real people and events) in their fictionalized novels. Biographers, in turn, often borrow fictional techniques from novelists, including "flashbacks, close-ups, varying points of view, and narrative tropes" (Hamilton, 2007, p. 272). Biographers try to bring their subjects to life for the reader: What do they look like? How do they talk? How do they think? Some biographers will describe the sound of the subject's voice (Backscheider, 1999). Sometimes dialogue is invented in the attempt to convey the presence of the subject, with the author using his or her intuitive sense to render what the subject probably would have said. Some writers borrow excerpts from letters the subject has written and translate the written words into spoken dialogue. In addition, some biographers, convinced that they know their subjects' thoughts and feelings, invent monologues that they feel typify the subject. In a similar manner, clinicians, especially when presenting a case to others, may also modify or embellish the client's thoughts or speech without being aware of distortions they may be introducing. This complex issue is discussed further in chapters 7 and 9.

Truman Capote wrote *In Cold Blood,* a true story based on the murder of a family in their farmhouse in Kansas during the 1950s. Capote conceptualized this book as a "'nonfiction novel,'" but Hamilton (2007) suggests that "he might more accurately have termed it 'fiction-style biography'" (p. 215). *In Cold Blood* also highlighted the involvement of the writer with the subject: Capote became emotionally involved with one of the killers he extensively interviewed. This relationship became the subject of the well-received movie *Capote.*

In *Dutch: A Memoir of Ronald Reagan,* the author, Edmund Morris (Reagan's official biographer), cast himself as a fictionalized character in the book: "...he watches himself, as a *participating* character in Reagan's life story, observing the events as they happen" (Hamilton, 2007, p. 250). This book was highly criticized; many felt that Morris had gone too far in applying this postmodern approach to a serious biography. And so the debates go on.

How to portray the life of the subject has been debated throughout the ages.

For many years, biographies portrayed only the positive aspects of a person's life, often presenting adulation of a life rather than a more balanced portrait. Over time, however, biographers such as Johnson, Boswell, and Strachey began depicting their subjects with both strengths and vulnerabilities. Although many biographers adhere to this approach today, encomiums are still written.

Psychodynamic and transactional thinking have brought to light the role of the involvement of the practitioner's self in the client-clinician relationship. Likewise, there is presently greater awareness of the role of the biographer's own personal involvement in creating the portrait of a subject, whether implicit or explicit has been said that all biographies are autobiographies. Though undoubtedly an exaggeration, there is nevertheless an involvement of the biographer in every aspect of this work, including deciding on a subject, what evidence to gather, and how to portray the person. Biographers' involvement with their subjects and the impact of the autobiographer's self-exploration on the writer are discussed in the next chapter.

CHAPTER 2

The Role of Relationships: The Biographer's Involvement with the Subject and the Autobiographer's Self-Exploration

"Living with the Subject," a chapter in Paula R. Backscheider's (1999) book, assumes that an emotional connection exists between biographers and their subjects. Although not meant in a literal sense, sometimes living with the subject is actually the case—for example, when people write about family members, friends, colleagues, or lovers. However, the biographer always develops a relationship with the subject (which is often changing and evolving), even if the biographer and subject never collaborated in the biographical enterprise or even knew one another. The relationship develops as biographers emotionally participate in the reconstructing of their subjects' lives. Richard Holmes (1985) talked of his imagined dialogues with all of his subjects, most of whom had died before he was born.

This chapter explores the impact of writing a biography on biographers, on their writing, and sometimes on their own or their subjects' lives. Occasionally we get a glimpse into the biographer's subjective world.

The encounter between Steve Jobs and his biographer, Walter Isaacson, is intriguing in this light. Jobs requested that Isaacson write his biography. They collaborated for two years. Isaacson visited him shortly before Jobs's death:

We talked about his childhood, and he gave me some pictures of his father and family to use in my biography. As a writer I was used to being detached, but I was hit by a wave of sadness as I tried to say goodbye. In order to mask my emotion, I asked the one question that was still puzzling me: Why had he been so eager, during close to 50 interviews and conversations . . . to open up so much for a book when he was usually so private? *"I wanted my kids to know me," he said. "I wasn't always there for them, and I wanted them to know why and to understand what I did."* [italics added] (W. Isaacson, 2011, p. 35)

Perhaps Jobs gained a sense of peace from knowing that his children would feel more connected to him. Perhaps he gained support, acceptance, and insight when sharing his life story. Do biographical subjects achieve therapeutic gains by engaging in the narrative process with their biographers? These speculations are worth exploring.

Harry Stack Sullivan (DeLaCour, 1996) introduced the concept of the therapist as a "participant observer" in the therapy; the biographer also becomes a "participant observer" in the life of the subject, whether actually or vicariously. The participant observer concept was a major contribution of modern anthropology; anthropologists became aware that they become inevitably involved in the lives of the people they are observing. This in turn affects the interactions between them and consequently has an impact on the behaviors of those under observation. Conversely, the anthropologists' own subjectivity is also affected.

And so biographers become participant observers as they work with their subjects, as do therapists as they engage with their patients, even when insight therapy is not the goal. Although this has not typically been their focus, cognitive therapists recently have given more attention to the therapeutic relationship, including to their own "feelings, attitudes and cognitions toward their clients" (Northcut, 1999, p. 43).

In this chapter, I will first discuss the relationship between subjects and biographers when they are known to each other and then biographers' reactions to subjects personally unknown to them. Finally, I will look at autobiographies, examining various objectives and motivations in writing them.

Subjects Who Are Personally Involved with Biographies

Is it an advantage to have the "living breathing" subject as a collaborator in the biography? Or can negative repercussions ensue? Schultz (2005c) discussed complications in working with living subjects, similar to those that emerge in work with psychotherapy clients:

> ... living psychobiographical subjects are not always preferable to dead ones. Their willingness to answer questions or respond to ideas pro or con does not lead ineluctably to enhanced validity.... Most people do not know themselves very well. Their motives may be as obscure to them as they are to us—even obscurer. They may be defensive. They may want to be thought of in ways that conflict with who they really are. They may even lie. Dead or alive, people are complicated. (p. 56)

The biographical process (and the therapeutic process), even when good rapport exists, does not proceed without impediment. Motivation can increase, or resistance can develop. Subjects (and clients) may find the intimacy of the biographic (therapeutic) relationship too threatening. Or, though benefiting from the acceptance and attention of the biographer (therapist), problems can develop if emotions or memories begin to surface that are threatening to the subject (client) or for the biographer (therapist).

Lyndon Johnson asked Doris Kearns to help him write his memoirs at his Texas ranch; while there she began her own biography of him. As Johnson's health became more fragile and he felt life ebbing away, he shared a lot with her. Kearns wrote: "He spoke of the beginnings and ends of things, of dreams and fantasies" (Elms & Song, 2005, p. 307). Sometimes she was uncomfortable listening to his outpourings:

> Kearns took notes about the intimate details of Johnson's life history as he called up his memories and free associations. She sometimes felt awkward about writing down what he was telling her so privately. But when she stopped her note-taking, Johnson would ask, *"Hey, why aren't you writing this down? Someday, someone may want to read it"* [italics added] (Elms & Song, 2005, p. 307).

Differences between the subject and the biographer may emerge regarding the interpretation of the subject's (client's) life and relationships. Alice Schroeder wrote *The Snowball,* a biography of Warren Buffet, at his request (Wayne, 2009). During this project, which lasted for five years, Schroeder had total access to his papers, and they spent many hours in interviews. However, when completed, "seeing his complicated personal life laid out in black and white left him with mixed feelings, particularly over the portrayal of his late wife, Susie" (Wayne, 2009, p. B2). Although Buffet had been open with Schroeder about his relationship with Susie, apparently the slant given to it by Schroeder made him uncomfortable. His long-time professional relationship with Schroeder, which had predated the book, deteriorated after its publication.

Collaboration between Biographer and the Subject: Samuel Johnson and James Boswell

An important landmark in the history of biography was Samuel Johnson's *Lives of the Poets,* published in 1779; with it "biography came of age" (Holroyd, 2002). Boswell wrote Johnson's biography, with his full cooperation and collaboration. At times, Bowell was actually living with the subject; their lives became intertwined.

In many respects, Johnson and Boswell were opposites, the former "immensely learned and principled," the latter "horny and irresponsible, already drinking too much." They both shared "loneliness, a tendency to depression," as well as a "tortured, guilt-ridden history with a stubborn, overbearing father"; their relationship, "with its obvious father-son overtones," was perhaps "a way to rewrite and make amends for the past."

Boswell made no secret of wanting to write Johnson's biography, and Johnson indicated that he had no objections (McGrath, 2001). Johnson was very aware that "much of what he said would be taken down by Boswell for the benefit of posterity" (Jarrett, 1999, p. 39). Boswell was not to be a biographer who worked at a distance from his subject; their lives became intertwined in many ways. Boswell's first biographical book about Johnson, *The Journal of a Tour to the Hebrides with Samuel Johnson, L.L.D.,* was published in 1785 and centered on the three-month trip they took to Scotland and the Hebrides.

Boswell and Johnson were also involved in an incredibly entangled three-way relationship involving Mrs. Hester Thrale, the wife of Henry Thrale (a successful brewery entrepreneur who was politically active in Parliament). The Thrales were captivated by Johnson and invited him to live with them, which he did for 20 years. Johnson and Mrs. Thrale developed a special relationship: "he lived in closer intimacy with her than with anyone else" (Gopnik, 2008, p. 93). Boswell managed to become a frequent guest in the Thrale home.

Both Mrs. Thrale and Boswell had a close relationship to Johnson, who was "half in love" with Mrs. Thrale but maintained a "respectful" relationship with Mr. Thrale. Boswell was jealous of Johnson's interest in Mrs. Thrale, but he was also aware "that he alone could play the role of the son that the older man never had" (Gopnik, 2008, p. 94).

Johnson and Mrs. Thrale developed an extremely close relationship; there are intimations that their relationship was sexual (Gopnik, 2008). Referring to a new biography of Mrs. Thrale *(Hester,* by Ian McIntyre), Gopnik commented that people who knew them were quite certain that it would be Mrs. Thrale, not Boswell, who would write Johnson's biography. This did not happen, although shortly after Johnson's death, she did publish a collection of anecdotes about him, which present Johnson in a different light from Boswell's representation (Gopnik, 2008).

When Mrs. Thrale became a widow in 1781, it surprised and puzzled their friends that she and Johnson did not marry. Moreover, she horrified her children and friends by marrying Signor Piozzi, a young Italian music teacher, and moving with him to Italy. Johnson lived only five months after this loss, becoming depressed and then paralyzed. He died in 1784 (Gopnik, 2008). Boswell wrote the definitive biography of Johnson, "libeling Hester throughout."

When Boswell's *Life of Samuel Johnson, L.L.D.* was printed in 1791, it became a popular sensation, "bringing praise and condemnation with equal extravagance" (Holmes, 2000, p. 369). The book was offensive to many because Boswell described Johnson's negative characteristics, bad habits, and anxieties, including his fears of death and insanity. Many of Johnson's friends were upset, as Boswell had included some of their personal conversations in the book. It was evident in the book that he had recorded what people were saying to each other at social events (obviously without their consent) (McGrath, 2001).

Many people refused to believe that this magnificent book was actually written by Boswell, who drank excessively. It was generally concluded that the book excelled because of its subject; Boswell was merely a scribe (McGrath, 2001). Opinion changed in the 20th century, when many of Boswell's papers that had been stored away in homes in Scotland and Ireland were discovered. These papers were acquired by Yale University, and the negative views of him turned around completely.

McGrath (2001) credits Boswell with being the originator of biography as it is conceived in modern times and as the "father of feature journalism," the creator of the model of the "celebrity profile" (p. 13). By being part of Johnson's story, Boswell also set a precedent for including in the narrative the efforts made by the biographer (or reporter) to meet and involve the subject in the writing project. Boswell also wrote vivid dialogue based on his own written recording of events (a precedent that challenges many biographers, past and present, who struggle to render lifelike dialogue)

(Holmes, 2000). Holmes referred to Boswell as "the godfather of English biography":

> No one before him had reconstructed another life on such a[n] epic scale ... or with such relentless, brilliant intimacy.... He spent nearly twenty years on the research ... and six years in the writing.... He wrote up thousands of pages of conversations recorded in his private Journals; collected hundreds of letters; interviewed bishops, actresses, philosophers, booksellers, blue-stockings, childhood friends and household servants.... Boswell deftly explored Johnson's lifelong melancholia, delving deep in his private *Diaries, Prayers and Annals.* He minutely observed ... [his] nervous tics and religious terrors, his Rabelaisian eating habits, his fondness for cats. (pp. 369–70)

Boswell expressed pride in the uniqueness of his work in his preface to *Life.* Boswell's statement "was the manifesto of modern biography" (Holmes, 2000, p. 370):

> "I will venture to say that [Johnson] will be seen in this work more completely than any man who has ever yet lived. And he will be seen as he really was; for I profess to write not his panegyrick, which must be all praise but his Life." (Boswell, quoted in Holmes, 2000, p. 370)

The story of the lives of Boswell and Johnson and their special relationship is especially compelling because of its contribution to the evolution of biography—perplexing technical and ethical issues are raised that remain controversial today, such as the involvement of the biographer with his subject. Familiarity with Johnson's inner and outer worlds provided Boswell with special insights. But Boswell, although committed to accurate reporting, was also emotionally involved in Johnson's life, for example, by actively resenting his rival, Mrs. Hester Thrale, which may have impaired Boswell's objectivity.

Johnson knew (and permitted) Boswell to be his biographer. Johnson, who struggled with his chronic depressive episodes, always needed people around him: "he compulsively sought out the company of men and women at all hours" to "dispel his fragmented spirits" (Lichtenberg, 1985, p. 47). Boswell became Johnson's "great mirroring responder.... Boswell the celebrity hunter, had become the pursued mirror for the great man to look into and see his best self reflected back" (Lichtenberg, 1985, pp. 48-49).

Johnson was quite aware that Boswell's recordings of his conversations and behaviors would be read by future generations (Jarrett, 1999). His wishes to impress posterity might have affected his self-presentation. Johnson seemed content and mellow in Boswell's company, and his recordings have a "benevolence absent from other records of his life" (Gopnik, 2008, p. 95). Was Johnson more mellow because of Boswell's presence as a "mirroring responder"? Or was this mellowness perhaps his chosen representation of himself with posterity in mind?

Privacy is an ethical issue: How much of a person's intimate issues, flaws, and "warts" should be exposed to the public? What should remain private and respected? Both Johnson and Boswell were criticized for reporting negative characteristics of their subjects; the attacks against Boswell were even stronger because of his inclusion of Johnson's intimate details and foibles. There is ongoing controversy about the degree of involvement biographers should have with their subjects. The historian Barbara Tuchman (1979) expressed reservations about delving too deeply into the private lives of subjects:

> Happily, in the case of the greatest English writer [Shakespeare], we know and are likely to know close to nothing about his private life. I like this vacuum, this miracle, this great floating monument of work that has no explanation at all. (p. 147)

Johnson was an important and popular figure during his lifetime; however, his writings probably would not be particularly popular today (McGrath, 2001). It was Boswell (unimportant in life) who became more important (for posterity) and who gave Johnson (fearful of death) his immortality. Boswell was cast aside by his contemporaries; his alcoholism increased, and in 1795 he died "a broken man" (McGrath, 2001, p. 13).

Boswell did not dispassionately write a biography of Johnson; their lives were intertwined, with Boswell being a "participant observer" and a "mirroring responder" to Johnson. Their relationship was marked by boundary problems: Their professional roles of biographer and subject merged with their personal lives and feelings.

Boundary issues are likewise of particular interest to practitioners, as they frequently arise in the clinical relationship: "Clinicians need to be caring, accepting and empathic in professional ways, without immersing themselves in the life of the client, becoming frightened by the client's emotions, or feeling totally responsible for 'fixing' the client's problems" (Urdang, 2010, p. 526).

In developing a unique clinical relationship, strong emotional feelings can develop in the client, the clinician, or both; this can lead to wishes to develop a "special" relationship, which can manifest itself within the treatment hour or, sometimes, outside the clinical encounter. For example, in a casework class, a male student spoke of his successful work with a boy in residential treatment. The instructor asked him: "'What will happen if the boy asks if he can move in with you?' 'Oh,' he replied, 'I have room'" (Urdang, 2010, p. 525). The student, who understood that he should not respond this way, nevertheless was experiencing protective feelings toward the boy in conflict with his professional role.

Boundary problems, often but not always sexual, are a major issue in malpractice complaints (Reamer, 2008). Many clinicians seek supervision and consultation when troubled by impulses that could transgress boundaries; conversely, some unfortunately act on their feelings without reflection.

Such boundary issues, as we shall see, were evident in the relationship of Charlotte Brontë and Elizabeth Gaskell.

Charlotte Brontë and Elizabeth Gaskell

Elizabeth Gaskell's biography, *The Life of Charlotte Brontë,* is considered "to be arguably the most famous English biography of the nineteenth century" and one of the "great works of Victorian literature" (Miller, 2001, p. 62). As its subject is a woman, it is significant historically: Prior to this, most biographies had been written by men about men. However, this book was not written to honor Charlotte Brontë's literary brilliance and artistry; to the contrary, it was written to present an idealized version of Charlotte Brontë as a pure, moral, and religious woman, a model of Victorian femininity. Her literary sisters, Emily and Anne, were also portrayed in the book.

Gaskell began writing Charlotte's biography at her father's request shortly after Charlotte's death. However, Gaskell and Charlotte had been friends, meeting for the first time after Charlotte's *Jane Eyre* was published. Gaskell had read *Jane Eyre* with interest and wanted to know more about the author, including" 'the way in which *she has suffered*. I wonder if she suffers now' " (Fraser, 1988, p. 380). Gaskell simply assumed that Charlotte had suffered before they ever met; this concept, which suffuses her discussions of Charlotte in the biography, never changed.

From their first meeting, Gaskell was eager to portray Charlotte to her own friends, to describe this new, unknown, and mysterious author, the writer of the sensational *Jane Eyre*; she was beginning to see herself as a "commentator" on Charlotte's life.

It cannot be said that Charlotte collaborated on this biography; she did, however, collaborate with Gaskell on maintaining her image of a suffering self as well as a model of Victorian piety, which suited her own representation of herself to the public. This collaboration was part of their unspoken agenda. During the course of their friendship, Gaskell became an active participant in Charlotte's life in a number of ways. Their relationship is discussed in greater detail in the next chapter.

Subjects Not Personally Involved with Their Biographer

The biographer relates to, and in a sense interrelates with, the subject, emotionally and attitudinally. This is so even where the biographical subject was never personally known to the biographer, and even when the lifetime of the subject has predated the life span of the biographer.

Baron and Pietsch (1985) explored this issue in a unique demonstration project, in which biographers met with psychoanalysts to discuss the biographies they had written. The goal was not to analyze the writers but to understand their involvement with their subjects and how their own subjectivity affected their work. The motivation for engaging in this project and their general degree of self-awareness varied with each writer.

Joseph Wall and Andrew Carnegie

Joseph Wall (1985), wrote one of the chapters in the Baron and Pietsch study. Wall had completed his biography of Andrew Carnegie 10 years before he agreed to take part; he openly admitted resistance to becoming involved. With no prior therapy experiences, he expected that this would "be a new and not very welcome experience" (Wall, 1985, p. 214).

Wall's research into Carnegie's life had been extensive: "In some ways I knew Carnegie better than he knew himself" (1985, p. 214). But remaining questions about his book troubled him, especially now that he was about to write the biography of Alfred I. Dupont. He wanted to explore why, with the vast amount of data he collected, he made decisions to include some materials and exclude others. He was uncertain about whether his "personal interaction between Carnegie and myself... should have been explicit in my biography" (p. 214)? He was, however, very aware "of the lasting effects Carnegie has had on me" (p. 214):

> ...there was a curious love-hate relationship, an identification with and at the same time an alienation from the man,

which has continued.... I still hold a proprietary interest in him—the irrational feeling that somehow Carnegie belongs to me. (Wall, 1985, pp. 214–215)

Wall (1985) spoke of the main theme he observed in Carnegie's life— his inner conflict in trying to integrate the "radical egalitarianism" of his family with his "insatiable desire for material acquisition" (p. 215). While putting enormous effort into becoming richer, Carnegie also wrote about labor rights and established "Radical" newspapers in England. In Wall's rendering, Carnegie became "a protagonist in the classical mode, torn by his own inner doubts and tensions—a *tormented hero of my designing*" (p. 216, emphasis added). Carnegie resolved his dilemma by giving money back to the public; he donated buildings and established museums and foundations.

As Wall (1985) reflected on his need to construct this theme about his subject, he realized:

> I needed this theme to reconcile myself to Carnegie, to find my own "refuge from self-questioning" about why I should choose to write upon... even empathize with... a man who was in many ways so antithetical to my own personality, ambitions and achievements. Only by offering [this] thesis... could I reconcile me, the liberal, with the me who was the biographer of Carnegie, the steel king. Quite unconsciously, I was attempting... to find a reflection of Carnegie in me and of me in Carnegie (p. 216) .

Wall (1985) also realized that Carnegie had personal psychological problems, "such as his abnormal attachment to his mother" (p. 216). Aware that this was all "rich material" for a "psychohistorian," he felt it was "not for me" and stayed away from family matters in his book (p. 217). Litchfield, Wall's psychoanalytic collaborator, raised the subject of Carnegie's young sister, Ann, dying when Carnegie was six years of age. Wall had written in his biography that it did not seem to have an effect on Carnegie, for he never brought up her name in any of his writings. Wall then observed:

> It seems to have made no impression upon me either, for I made no further mention of what must have been a traumatic experience for a young boy of six, but Litchfield saw its possible significance. Here was the effect of widespread poverty and disease brought home to a child in its most dramatic form. It could well have been the most significant event of his childhood in Scotland, an event too painful for Carnegie to wish ever to recall. (p. 219)

This reflection led to further discussion of Carnegie's "almost pathological fear of death," which Wall was aware of but did not stress in his book. Death was a word absent from Carnegie's writings; when people important to him died, he would never bring them up again. His charitable donations could also be seen as a way "to avoid total extinction" (Wall, 1985, p. 220). In ending this essay, Wall referred to Theodor Reik's *Listening with a Third Ear,* which highlights the importance for the therapist "to listen for what was not being said as well as for what is being said." Wall considered how the "additional eyes of a consultant" could be valuable to the biographer. In the same way, that is, that listening with the third ear and the extra ear of the supervisor or consultant, can be critical in the therapeutic encounter as well.

Richard Holmes

Richard Holmes (1985), the biographer of Percy Shelley and other dead writers he has restored to life, finds that to know his subjects he must first walk in their footsteps:

> [This leads to]... the creation of a fictional or imaginary relationship between the biographer and his subject... a continuous living dialogue between the two as they move over the same historical ground, the same trail of events. There is between them a ceaseless discussion, a reviewing and questioning of motives and actions and consequences, a steady, if subliminal exchange of attitudes, judgments and conclusions. It is fictional, imaginary, because of course, the subject cannot really, literally, talk back; but the biographer must come to act and think of his subject as if he can. (p. 66)

In his book *Footsteps: Adventures of a Romantic Biographer,* Holmes (1985) highlighted the cultivation of the relationship between the biographer and the subject, adding that the biographer must develop awareness of the boundaries between his own interpretations and his subject's actual thoughts. The writer must also establish the delicate boundary between empathic identification and overinvolvement. This is also a challenge for clinicians.

In his first such excursion, Holmes literally followed in the footsteps of Robert Louis Stevenson, who had hiked through French mountains outside of the town Le Monastier, accompanied by a donkey. Holmes, reading Stevenson's memoir, chose the route Stevenson had taken (but decided against the donkey) and "carried as my bible. . . .Stevenson's *Travels with a Donkey in the Cévennes"* (1985, p. 16).

Holmes's thinking about biography evolved as he followed Stevenson's path. Holmes felt that he got to know Stevenson, as well as himself, on this trip. Initially, he had no intention of writing about Stevenson; he would write poetry about his experiences of enjoying nature and hiking. However, what he jotted down were his intense emotions evoked by this experience: "black depressions" as well as "moments of intoxication and mad delight" (1985, p. 65). His emotions focused unexpectedly on "the growth of a friendship with Stevenson... the growth of an imaginary relationship with a non-existent person, or at least a dead one" (p. 66):

> ...what I experienced and recorded in the Cevennes in the summer of 1964 was a *haunting*... an act of deliberate psychological trespass, an invasion or encroachment of the present upon the past, and in some sense the past upon the present. And in this experience of haunting I first encountered—without then realizing it—what I now think of as the *essential process* of biography. [italics added] (Holmes, 1985, p. 66)

As Holmes learned more about Stevenson's life, he realized it resonated with his own life experiences and feelings. He became aware that after the "identification with the subject," "the true *biographic process* begins .... [when] the naive form of love and identification breaks down. The moment of *personal disillusion* is the moment of impersonal, objective re-creation" [italics added] (Holmes, 1985, p. 67).

67

Holmes (1985) also came to understand that Stevenson was part of a complicated social and interpersonal web—he was not an isolated "single subject." He existed "in and through his contact with other people: his books are written for his public" (p. 68). From Holmes's standpoint, the biographer cannot (and should not) invent dialogue or the subject's thoughts but needs evidence from witnesses who have conversed with the subject or read his letters.

Holmes (1985) added that the final realization he had from this journey is that life is fluid, not static; people change and their environments and circumstances change:

> ...they never existed wholly in any one place along the recorded path. You cannot freeze them, you cannot pinpoint them, at any particular turn in the road, bend in the river, view from the window. They are always in motion, carrying their past lives over into the future. (p. 69)

This journey led Holmes to "the undiscovered land of other men's and women's lives. It led me towards biography" (Holmes, 1985, p. 69).

Holmes described an initial process of deep engagement and identification with his subjects as "a Haunting," emphasizing his developing empathy and insight into his subjects. The process Holmes described has its counterpart in a clinical relationship process known as *intersubjectivity*. Today the concept of intersubjectivity expands Freud's concepts of transference and countertransference (relating primarily to internalized conflicts, especially of the past) to include consideration of the here-and-now "subjective reactions and interactions of the client and clinician" (Urdang, 1999, p. 154). Awareness of this concept can enable clinicians to become attuned "to feelings evoked in them by their clients; these feelings are then explored in a therapeutic manner" (Urdang, 2008, p. 98). As an illustration,

> Dan, who had a history of disturbed attachments, engaged in therapy, presenting with many anxieties and deep insecurities about himself. On several occasions, when the clinician made a sensitive and attuned comment to Dan, he would laugh in what felt to the clinician to be a disparaging manner. Instinctively, the clinician felt defensive, wondering if she was off the mark, and changed the subject. During one session, when Dan again laughed "at her," she realized that she was feeling put down. This time, she brought this behavior to his attention. She asked him if he realized that when she said something of a sensitive nature, he would laugh at it. He was able to discuss his discomfort with the feelings she evoked in him, which led to a meaningful interchange. The clinician speculated that perhaps his put-down of her was the way he was made to feel when he had tried to express painful feelings to others in his past. (Urdang, 2008, p. 98)

In this example, although initially feeling criticized, the clinician was able to make use of her insight in a therapeutic way with Dan.

In using video role-playing, "students sometimes enact aspects of their clients of which they have been unaware" (Urdang, 1999, p. 154). In this example, one student, Eleanor, pretends to be her client, while another student, Greg, plays the part of the clinician:

Eleanor did not know, on a conscious level, that her client was angry. But she had evidently internalized this knowledge. Playing her client allowed her to express and externalize this feeling in action, and viewing herself as her client enabled her to observe and get in touch with this feeling state in her client.

> As Eleanor-as-student watches Eleanor-as-client… she asks Greg and the instructor: "Would it be appropriate at this point to bring up any of the anger? *When doing this I didn't think of any anger, but in watching this I can see that suspicious look and a little bit of anger.* It would be a little premature, wouldn't it, to dive in so deeply?" (Urdang, 1999, p. 154)

Like Eleanor, Holmes (1985) empathetically strove to enter the experiential world of his subjects; he talked of "haunting" them, as he followed in their footsteps. But he also emphasized the need to distance oneself emotionally from the subjects, to find objectivity, and not lose one's personal boundaries. Having formulated his guidelines for being a biographer, Holmes found himself violating his own rules when he became engrossed in the life of Gerard de Nerval, a 19th-century French poet and essayist. It was in exploring Nerval's mental illness and suicide that Holmes ran into difficulty, finding that he was experiencing an "overflowing of the irrational into the normal forms of biography" (p. 249). He felt that it was not possible to understand Nerval's "madness and suicide, both from without and from within" and realized that "psychoanalysing" Nerval was not possible for him. Even Nerval's psychiatrist could not accomplish this. With Nerval, Holmes felt that he had "reached the limits of the biographical form" (p. 264):

> Instead, I found myself slipping further and further into a peculiar and perilous identification with my lunatic subject,

as if somehow I could diagnose Nerval by becoming him. As if self-identification—the first crime in biography—had become my last and only resort. (Holmes, 1985, p. 264)

Likewise, practitioners can sometimes overidentify with certain clients and in the process become overwhelmed. A patient's mental illness per se can provoke a sense of helplessness and paralyzing anxiety. For example, child welfare workers can experience secondary traumatization after hearing about severe abuse or violence, and some can experience severe emotional distress when removing children from their homes.

Autobiographies

People write books about themselves for different reasons and in different styles. It can be an account of an adventure, a trip, a political journey, and so forth. Some autobiographies are purely "historical" factual accounts of the writer's life, such as vocational experiences. Frederick Douglass's three autobiographies were written in part to emphasize the cruelty and oppression of slavery.

Some autobiographies are written to rationalize one's life and actions, as Rousseau did; some are written to express anger or to exact revenge against people who have "wronged" the writer, as Gosse did in writing his expose of his father, *Father and Son: A Study of Two Temperaments* (Hamilton, 2007).

Some writers want to convey to others how they have experienced their lives; some express that their aim is to think more deeply about their own lives, to understand themselves better, as Ved Mehta has done in his series of autobiographies. Some autobiographies are in the form of autobiographical novels, such as Sylvia Plath's *Bell Jar,* Charlotte Brontë's *Jane Eyre,* and Charles Dickens's *David Copperfield.*

The line between authenticity and deception is often blurred: It is not possible to write a flawless story of one's life without some missing pieces or distortions, whether due to memory lapses, omissions, defensiveness, or the need to protect certain people (as well as oneself). Barbour (1992) and Brockmeier and Carbaugh (2001) emphasized the importance of the integrity of the autobiographer—that is, the genuine effort to present the truth, even if there are obstacles to doing so: "Self-deception is a constant danger for the autobiographer.... Truth telling in autobiography is not only a matter of honesty in communication with others, for it concerns also honesty with oneself" (Barbour, 1992, p. 18).

Author Mary McCarthy (1957) was six years old when both her parents died suddenly in the influenza epidemic of 1918. She processes her uncertainty about the "facts" in her past life, a trait in her that Barbour (1992) applauded:

> "I submit that a form of this dialogue is intrinsic to the writing of every autobiography, although it is rarely formulated theoretically or rendered so vividly" (p. 30). McCarthy (1957) wrote that she saw her father as "a romancer, and most of my memories of him are colored, I fear, by an untruthfulness that I must have caught from him, like one of the colds that ran around the family.... Many of my most cherished ideas about my father have turned out to be false" (p. 11).

McCarthy (1957) poignantly recalled memories of a loving father, attentive and indulgent to her. Once she and her father "heard a nightingale together, on the boulevard, near the Sacred Heart convent," but then McCarthy added that "there are no nightingales in North America" (p. 11). Describing the magic of the nightingales' song, she creates an authentic experience of sharing a special relationship and a "fairy story" with her father; she also cautions the reader about the veracity of this account. "McCarthy provides a scrupulous account of how memory and imagination and historical guesswork were woven together and, guided by conscience, formed into an account of the essential truth of the past" (Barbour, 1992, p. 29).

Although the attempt at integrity is honored by many autobiographers, it is not unusual to find some others leaning more to the deception end of the spectrum. One early example of self-deception can be found in Rousseau's *Confessions.* Although Rousseau represented himself as the epitome of truthfulness, paradoxically he did not have the ability to see himself from the perspective of others. Hamilton (2007), Barbour (1992), and Olney (1998) have described him as a master of self-deception who was seldom aware of the consequences of his own behavior.

Yagoda (2009) has argued that the past 40 years "will probably be remembered as the golden age of biographical fraud. There has been about a scandal a year, and sometimes more than that" (p. 246). He has observed that one common characteristic of the fraudulent memoir is that the subjects are "victims," and most frequently the victim is "a member of an oppressed minority group" (p. 255). One such book published in 2008 was *Love and Consequences* by Margaret Seltzer, purportedly a memoir of her life "growing up half Native-American in the gangland of South Central Los Angeles," when in actuality Seltzer is a "white woman who grew up in the suburban San Fernando Valley" (Kinsley, 2008, p. 64).

At about the same time, the autobiography *Misha: A Memoire of the Holocaust* was published in France, written by Misha Defonseca, a woman who claimed she was saved from the Holocaust by being "adopted by a pack of wolves who protected her from the Nazis." This memoir was made into the French movie *Surviving with the Wolves.* When confronted with evidence of deception, Defonseca commented that the story "is not actually reality, but my reality" (Kinsley, 2008, p. 64). Her argument might hold water with some constructivists, but it does present an intriguing problem: Before the fraud has been exposed, can memoirs characterized by gross deception be distinguished by the reader from genuine memoirs that are subjective and impressionistic?

James Frey's autobiography, *A Million Little Pieces,* raised questions about the veracity of details of his self-reported drug abuse and treatment. Frey, apologizing publicly yet defending himself (also using a constructivist argument), stressed "the fundamentally subjective nature of his memoir.... "It's an individual's perception... my recollection' " and claimed that "the emotional truth is there' " (Grossman, 2006, p. 62).

David Carr, by contrast, in his recent memoir, *The Night of the Gun,* was determined to write an objective, accurate account of his own addiction and rehabilitation (Jones, 2008). Relying on his skills and experience as a columnist for the *New York Times,* he decided to "report" his story. Carr digs up his medical and police files and conducts some 60 interviews with people who knew him then and who know him now, from his parents to his rehab counselors to his grownup twin daughters. Wary of painting a distorted self-portrait, he offers up a researched composite instead. (Jones, 2008, p .640)

Carr's enormous effort to "authenticate" his life is unusual in auto-biography; one can find a large range of writing along the truth-deception continuum. Barbour (1992) has stressed that honesty in autobiography not only is important for readers, but also involves" honesty with oneself." Autobiographical writing offers authors the opportunity to reflect on their lives and potentially gain insight. Ved Mehta, discussed in chapter 4, used his autobiography as an opportunity to do this.

Autobiographical writings have been used in clinical work in a variety of ways: asking clients to enhance self-awareness by keeping diaries; using reminiscence with elderly clients; and creating life books for foster children. These are discussed further in chapter 7.

We read biographies and autobiographies for pleasure, entrusting the author with conveying an accurate portrait of the subject or himself or herself. The voice of the author tends to fade for us as we immerse ourselves in the life of the subject. But authors are always present, with subjective reactions to their subjects, and in ideas and impressions they wish to convey. With autobiographies, we tend to identify with the authors and enter their worlds. However, there is further pleasure to be gained from insights derived from looking more deeply into the motivations and attitudes of the writers.

In a similar vein, the clinician, interacting with and assessing a client, necessarily trusts his or her own objectivity. However, the subjective involvement with the client is also part of the story that needs to be considered.

CHAPTER 3

The Impact of Biographer Involvement and Bias: Charlotte Brontë and Her First Biographer, Elizabeth Gaskell

Charlotte Brontë's novels, especially *Jane Eyre,* have long fascinated readers. Even more intriguing to the public has been the story of her life and that of her two sisters, the novelists Emily and Anne. After Charlotte's early death, at 39, Elizabeth Gaskell wrote her biography, *The Life of Charlotte Brontë,* which became a classic. Gaskell emphasized Charlotte's tragic life, minimizing her literary genius. Many later biographers would follow Gaskell's example, emphasizing Charlotte's suffering and her piety.

The Life of Charlotte Brontë was immensely popular. People were fascinated by this most unusual family; their lives aroused greater interest than did the sisters' published works. New biographies were written almost every year, and their lives were imagined in plays, operas, dances, and films.

The history of Charlotte's biographies parallels the history of biography, with its changing points of view. Gaskell presented Charlotte as a model of virtuous Victorian morality. Feminists interpreted her as a symbol of feminine independence and competency, and Freudian psychobiographers highlighted her masochism and sexual conflicts. "Rather than reading her as a mature artist who had gained insight from self-analysis, or championing her as a pioneering precursor of psychoanalytical thinking, the psychobiographers tended to treat her as the victim of her own mental chaos" (Miller, 2001, p. 141). More recently, biographers and scholars have stressed Charlotte's highly developed intellectual and creative abilities.

Once Gaskell's *The Life of Charlotte Brontë* was published, visitors, referring to themselves as "pilgrims," flocked to the Brontës' home at Haworth (Miller, 2002, p. 109). The Brontë Museum was established in 1895.

This chapter examines the life of Charlotte Brontë, incorporating Gaskell's observations, her interviews with those who knew Charlotte, and her own recollections of their visits. Charlotte's correspondence is a major source of biographical materials. The modern biographies of Fraser (1988) and Miller (2001) are also frequently referred to in this chapter. In addition, Charlotte's autobiographical novels, *Jane Eyre* and *Villette,* are discussed.

It should also be noted that Charlotte's life was the main source of biographical knowledge when biographers wrote about her sisters, Anne and Emily.

Childhood

Family

Charlotte's father, Patrick Brontë, was born into a large farming family in Ireland with little money. He educated himself, taught school for six years, and tutored a minister's family. Leaving Ireland to study at Cambridge when he was 25, he received a bachelor of arts in theology and was ordained.

Patrick met his future wife, Maria Branwell, in 1812, when he was 35 and she was 30. Her family had deep roots in Cornwall and was fairly well off. "A tiny, neat woman ... she was well-read and intelligent, with a gentility and sweetness of character that, combined with her strong Methodist faith, immediately attracted Patrick" (Fraser, 1988, p. 11). They shared similar ideas and both liked to write; they were expressive people who shared their feelings with each other. Maria's letters to Patrick were full of passion and religion (Fraser, 1988, p. 15).

They were married in December of 1812 at Hartshead, where Patrick had his parish, and where their two oldest children, Maria and Elizabeth, were later born. The family then moved to Thornton, where Charlotte was born on April 21, 1816. Patrick accepted the offer of the curacy of Haworth, with an increase of salary and the rent-free use of the parsonage for his lifetime. The Brontë children now numbered six with the addition of Branwell, Emily, and Anne. Mrs. Brontë, who had given birth to Anne shortly before the move to Haworth, suffered complications from the delivery; she was not yet well when the family took their daylong trip to Haworth in a bumpy wagon.

Mrs. Brontë was ill for seven months after her arrival at Haworth. Patrick nursed her throughout her illness, then thought to be cancer but now considered to have been an "infection of the blood following a complex delivery" (Fraser, 1988, p. 27). Mrs. Brontë died in September 1821 and was buried "in the crypt of the church, thirty yards from the house" (Fraser, 1988, p. 28). Patrick Brontë "did not suffer his loss stoically, and seems to have found his children's presence a painful reminder of his wife rather than a comfort" (Fraser, 1988, p. 28). He wrote: "And when my dear wife was dead and buried and gone ... I missed her at every corner, and ... her memory was hourly revived by the innocent yet distressing prattle of my children" (quoted in Fraser, 1988, p. 28). He withdrew, eating dinner alone in his study, a habit that persisted throughout his lifetime.

The loss of their mother was traumatic for the children; the 7 months preceding this were also difficult as both parents had withdrawn from them. According to Mrs. Brontë's nurse, "'the mother was not very anxious to see much of her children, probably because the sight of them, knowing how soon they were to be left motherless, would have agitated her too much'" (quoted in Gaskell, 1870, p. 37). The nurse described the children:

> They were grave and silent beyond their years; subdued, probably, by the presence of serious illness in the house.... You would not have known there was a child in the house, they were such still, noiseless, good little creatures. Maria [the oldest child]... (Maria, but seven!)... as good as a mother to her sisters and brother. But there never were such good children. I used to think them spiritless, they were so different to any children I had ever seen....
>
> So the little things clung quietly together, for their father was busy... or with their mother, and they took their meals alone; sat reading, or whispering low, in the "children's study," or wandered out on the hill-side, hand in hand. (Gaskell, 1870, p. 41)

This description must be seen in the context of their mother's impending death; it does not capture their later imaginative play and the gaiety that pervaded their childhood. Gaskell, however, concludes: "Moreover, the little Brontës had been brought up motherless; and... knowing nothing of the gaiety and the sportiveness of childhood" (Gaskell, 1857, p. 183).

Overwhelmed by the care of his six children, Patrick Brontë asked his wife's sister, Elizabeth Branwell, to help. She came and remained a part of the household until her death, when the children were grown. An intelligent woman with strong opinions, Elizabeth Branwell enjoyed debating with Patrick and insisted on paying for her expenses at Haworth.

Although Elizabeth Branwell carried out her responsibilities to the children, she does not seem to have been a "sympathetic presence." In the children's letters home, Branwell was the only child who made "affectionate" references to her (Fraser, 1988, p. 29). We never get to hear Elizabeth Branwell's voice or understand how she experienced living at Haworth or why she remained for the rest of her life.

Two years after his wife died, Patrick tried to remarry, but the three women he courted were not interested. One wrote: it would be absurd to marry a man "'who had not some future, and six children into the bargain'" (quoted in Fraser, 1988, p. 30). As a result, Mr. Brontë stopped looking.

Gaskell painted a negative portrait of Patrick. However, although he had his idiosyncrasies, he was a devoted father and intent on developing the children's intellectual, literary, and political interests.

Stories have been told about Mr. Brontë's temper: "he was an irascible, difficult, choleric sort of man, and these traits would increase with age" (Fraser, 1988, p. 11). He told Gaskell: "Had I been numbered amongst the calm, sedate... men of the world, I should in all probability never had such children as mine have been" (Fraser, 1988, p. 11).

Around the time that Mr. Brontë received his holy orders, a Luddite uprising was arousing fears; Yorkshire men began wearing arms. Mr. Brontë "until the day of his death... wore a brace of pistols at his belt, like a pirate king" (Fraser, 1988, p. 11). He attached his pistols every morning; the children's friends always noted this, sometimes with alarm.

Mr. Brontë had an outstanding record as vicar and was "extremely active in the parish" and interested in his parishioners' lives (Fraser, 1988, p. 23). He wrote articles for newspapers and was concerned about politics, law, and injustice. He advocated having the water supply at Haworth inspected because of possible pollution. Gaskell omitted mention of any of these efforts but later revised her impression of Patrick, noting that he was a father who brought presents for his children and involved them in lively political discussions. But her basic negative opinion of him remained with her readers.

Education

Early education. Charlotte lost her mother on September 22, 1821, when she was just five years old. She had only some vague memories of her. Most of the characters in her juvenilia and heroines in her fiction were orphans (Fraser, 1988).

Maria, the oldest child, the "mother substitute" to the children, has been described as a remarkable, precocious child, who could, at the age of seven years, read a newspaper and discuss its contents. Mr. Brontë was strongly committed to his children; his earlier withdrawal was related to his grief. He taught them to read and discuss newspapers as well as current literature, including Byron and Scott: "His great gift to his children was his encouragement and enthusiasm, and pride in their progress" (Fraser, 1988, p. 32). He also emphasized that they should "believe in the validity of their opinions" (p. 33).

When Charlotte later attended school, it was noted that she "knew nothing systematically, though she surpassed even her teachers in her knowledge of poetry" (Fraser, 1988, p. 32). "She was clearly an imaginative child with a strong personality of her own" (Fraser, 1988, p. 32).

When the Clergy Daughters' School opened, Mr. Brontë took advantage of its affordable fees to seize this opportunity for the girls' education. Located about 50 miles from Haworth at Cowan Bridge, it was designed for daughters of poor Evangelical clergy; that the students were recipients of charity was frequently brought to their attention. Maria and Elizabeth were enrolled initially, followed by Charlotte and Emily. Charlotte attended between the ages of eight and 10. Maria, 12, and Elizabeth, 11, tragically died of tuberculosis contracted there; Charlotte and Emily were then removed from the school.

Charlotte, suffering through this schooling, fictionalized her experience in *Jane Eyre* (1847), renaming the school Lowood. In her novel, Mr. Brocklehurst, the cruel director, represents its actual director, the "eminent" Reverend Carus Wilson; Charlotte's sister Maria is Helen, her close friend. Although names and other identifying information were disguised, many readers, nevertheless, recognized Lowood as Cowan Bridge. Carus Wilson, a prominent and rich clergyman, was punitive, emphasizing sin, punishment, and hell. Many thought that Charlotte's portrayal of him was accurate: "Most of the phrases which Brocklehurst uses [in *Jane Eyre*] come almost verbatim from Carus Wilson's writings" (Fraser, 1988, p. 38). Peters (1986) notes that the "Cowan Bridge Controversy . . . is hardly settled today" and that evidence bears out that Charlotte depicted it truthfully, "or nearly" (p. 15).

Additional evidence supporting Charlotte's account has been gathered, including public reports of the inadequacy of the food and the school's poor health record (Fraser, 1988). In *The Life,* Gaskell carefully withheld the name and location of the school as well as the names of individuals. Nevertheless, many recognized the school and Carus Wilson, and Gaskell was sued for libel after her book's publication.

Located in a picturesque setting but run by inexperienced people, the Clergy Daughters' School was "as unhealthy as it was picturesque" (Fraser, 1988, p. 36). Situated near a river, the air was damp, the sleeping accommodations were overcrowded, and the sanitation was poor; "there was one stone privy between 60 girls and staff... . Disease could flourish" (p. 36). There often was insufficient heat, and the food was poor.

Charlotte, in the voice of Jane Eyre, described the harsh conditions at Lowood, including the poor quality of the food (Brontë, 1864, p. 60). Jane observed the inadequate portions and how the older girls coerced the younger ones into giving them their portions:

> We had scarcely sufficient to keep alive a delicate invalid. From this... resulted an abuse, which pressed... on the younger pupils: whenever the famished great girls had an opportunity, they would coax or menace the little ones out of their portion. Many a time I have shared between two claimants the precious morsel of brown bread distributed at tea-time; and after relinquishing to a third half the contents of my mug of coffee, I have swallowed the remainder with an accompaniment of secret tears, forced from me by the exigency of hunger. (Brontë, 1864, p. 60)

The inadequate clothing failed to protect the children from severe cold:

> "...we had no boots, the snow got into our shoes and melted there: our ungloved hands became numbed and covered with chilblains, as were our feet: I remember... thrusting the swelled, raw, and stiff toes into my shoes in the morning." (Brontë, 1864, p. 59)

The physical environment at the Clergy Daughters' School was unhealthy, with its poor sanitation, inadequate food, and lack of warm clothing in cold weather. Questions have also been raised about contamination of the water supply at Haworth, owing to its proximity to the graveyard at the parsonage. As noted earlier, Mr. Brontë advocated having the Haworth water supply tested. Most of the deaths of Charlotte's relatives and friends were caused by infectious diseases, primarily tuberculosis and cholera.

The impact of the beautiful and mysterious moors on the life and literature of the Brontës has been extensively discussed by biographers. Some writers have minimized the health hazards of the Brontë's environment, emphasizing the beauty and mystery of the moors. Emily has been referred to by some as "The Mystic of the Moors," the title of one of Miller's (2001) chapters.

In *Jane Eyre,* Reverend Brocklehurst's severe punitiveness permeates the atmosphere of the Lowood chapters, even in his absence when teachers carry out his orders. Visiting the school, Mr. Brocklehurst commands Jane to sit on a high stool in front of the group, while he castigates her, warning others about her evil ways.

> This girl... is a little castaway:... You must be on your guard against her; you must shun her example; if necessary, avoid her company, exclude her from your sports, and shut her out from your converse. Teachers, you must

watch her: keep your eyes on her... punish her body to save her soul: if, indeed, such salvation be possible, for (my tongue falters while I tell it) this girl, this child, the native of a Christian land... —this girl is—a liar!" (Brontë, 1864, p. 67)

Jane is later comforted by her good friend, Helen Brown, and a kindly teacher, Miss Temple. Both were sources of support. Helen Brown (who represents Maria) was an older student, sickly, and very religious, often treated unfairly by several teachers, as was Maria. When Helen asked "a slight question," she was scolded for the "triviality of the inquiry" (Brontë, 1864, p. 68). Jane reports: "I had heard her condemned... to a dinner of bread and water... because she had blotted an exercise in copying it out" (p. 68). Helen was continually badgered for her lack of neatness, as Maria had been. Maria was in a very fragile physical state. In writing *The Life,* Gaskell interviewed two of Maria's former schoolmates, who gave examples of the maltreatment and total lack of compassion Maria endured. Gaskell reports that one morning Maria was so unwell that she was unable to get up. She was ordered to dress, did so "trembling," and "went down stairs at last" (Fraser, 1988, pp. 39–40).

Maria, critically ill, was sent home in February 1825 and died on May 6. (Charlotte, remaining at school, was not present at her death.) In *Jane Eyre,* Helen, also critically ill, dies at the school but in Jane's arms. Soon after Maria's death, Elizabeth also became seriously ill and was sent home on May 31. Mr. Brontë withdrew Charlotte and Emily from the school the next day; Elizabeth died 2 weeks later. Charlotte was now the oldest child, and "she no doubt felt that upon her now fell the burden of mothering her brothers and sisters" (Fraser, 1988, p. 44).

Miss Branwell now assumed a more active role in the girls' schooling, teaching the girls "domestic virtues of sewing and light cleaning" and the "sew[ing of] samplers for the good of their souls" (Fraser, 1988, pp. 44-45). Miss Branwell was kindly but strict and not demonstrative. Mr. Brontë taught the girls standard school subjects. He "took pride in the precocious brilliance of his only son, Branwell, and carefully tutored him in the classics" (p. 45). In the afternoons, the family, including Miss Branwell, would have discussions about current events, politics, poetry, and readings from literary magazines.

An important addition to the household at that time was the new maid, 56-year-old Tabitha Aykroyd, or Tabby. Tabby knew many stories, which the children loved. She was a "motherly presence.... Their kitchen became the centre of life for the young Brontës. They sat there basking in the warmth of her loving, if sharp-tongued character... [and] delighted in her rough Yorkshire accent" (Fraser, 1988, p. 44). The girls felt a deep loyalty to her and cared for her in later life when she became ill. Although not a member of the family, Tabby was a mother substitute to the girls, more so than Aunt Branwell, who had this "assigned" role (although Branwell and Aunt Branwell were close: He was her favorite child). Forming bonds with nurturing surrogate adults (when parents are absent) can be a crucial factor in children's developing resilience. This is an issue often relevant in assessing family composition and relationships as well as other available supports.

It is not surprising that maids and housekeepers play a prominent role in many Brontë novels. A major narrator of Emily's *Wuthering Heights* is a housekeeper. In the unfriendly Reed household of *Jane Eyre,* the maid Bessie is the loving figure to a young Jane. Tabby, with all her stories, including tales of the wildness and illicit activities on the moors, was very likely an important literary influence in the sisters' subsequent writings.

The children's development of imaginative worlds and their habit of producing their own "secret plays" was critically important. This was enhanced when Mr. Brontë bought 12 wooden toy soldiers for Branwell, then nine years old. This gift immediately became "community property," as the four children, fascinated by these soldiers, created stories about them. A new world where these soldiers and their descendants lived evolved. Charlotte and Branwell chronicled the lives of these people "in a tiny, almost indecipherable hand" (Fraser, 1988, p. 49). Branwell created a new language for them, and maps drawn of this kingdom can be found at the Haworth Parsonage today.

The children later divided into two subgroups, although the foursome continued to participate "in common imaginary worlds" (Fraser, 1988, p. 53). Charlotte and Branwell, developing a special closeness, created the Glass Town stories; their collaboration continued for five years. Emily and Anne invented the world of Gondol. The worlds the children created were influenced by many literary sources. Charlotte and Branwell were "under the romantic spell of Byron"; by 12 and 13 they had read most of Byron's works (Fraser, 1986, p. 50). Charlotte and Branwell incorporated political events from newspapers into the Glass Town stories. They also created small magazines, "full of jokes and puns," for the town's inhabitants (Fraser, 1988). The "almost indecipherable" writing may have helped to keep them secret from adults.

Charlotte, at 13, composed "an impassioned account of the passing of the Catholic Emancipation Bill" (Fraser, 1988, p. 54). The artist Bewick, the author of *A General History of Quadrupeds* and *A History of British Birds*, history of British Birds was a favorite. Jane

Eyre also found his books a source of fascination. "With Bewick on my knee, I was then happy: happy at least in my way" (Brontë, 1864, p. 5). The children made drawings, another skill they cultivated, from Bewick's stories and his woodcuts. The Charlotte "to be met in the magazines and juvenilia bubbles over with excitement and jokes, and one can imagine her and Branwell's constant badinage" (Fraser, 1988, p. 56).

Elizabeth Gaskell had read a few of Charlotte's early manuscripts; "amazed by the tiny booklets filled with microscopic writing," she felt they were "examples of creative power *carried to the verge of insanity*" (Miller, 2001, p. 73, emphasis added). This is another example of Gaskell's distorted appraisal of the Brontë family, as she "remains blind" to Charlotte's creativity and playfulness. Similarly, strongly held preconceptions regarding clients, as well as excessive "pathologizing," can keep clinicians from accurately perceiving client's strengths and talents. Gaskell did acknowledge that some "jollicr fragments gave her a more positive impression of the Brontës' childhood than she had expected" (Miller, 2001, p. 73). Fraser (1988) commented that the "unhappiness and uncertainty of their early childhood predisposed Charlotte and her precocious bookish siblings to escape more than most children into the world of the imagination" (pp. 50–51). But the world of the imagination was not a solitary activity for these children, as it can be for other lonely children. Theirs was a shared enterprise.

Roe Head School. In 1830, Mr. Brontë became gravely ill with a lung infection and became worried about the family's economic future. He decided to send Charlotte to Roe Head School to prepare her to earn money as a governess (Fraser, 1988). Roe Head, a dramatic contrast from the school at Cowan Bridge, was small, with only 10 students; it was "more like a country house than a school" (Fraser,

1988, p. 62). Far from being a charity institution, it was attended by wealthy girls from local families. Miss Margaret Wooler, the director of Roe Head, was assisted by three unmarried sisters, "kindly, high minded women" (p. 62). Though not a "charity student," Charlotte's godparents paid her fees. Coming to Roe Head "in a covered cart, generally used to ferry produce... can have done nothing to alleviate the sense she would always have of being a charity child" (p. 62).

At Roe Head, she met two girls who were to become her best friends: Ellen Nussey (the major source of biographical materials on Charlotte) and Mary Taylor. These were Mary Taylor's first impressions of Charlotte, watching her arrive at school:

> "I first saw her coming out of a covered cart, in very old-fashioned clothes, and looking very cold and miserable.... She looked a little old woman, so short-sighted that she always appeared to be seeking something, and moving her head from side to side to catch a sight of it. She was very shy and nervous" (quoted in Gaskell, 1857, p. 88).

Ellen Nussey arrived at Roe Head a week later. She recounted her first awareness of Charlotte:

"I became aware that... there was a silent, weeping, dark little figure in the large bay-window. I was touched and troubled at once to see her so sad and tearful" (quoted in Fraser, 1988, p. 63). Compounding Charlotte's unhappiness was her "consciousness of her oddity, her utter dissimilarity to the girls around her" (Fraser, 1988, p. 64). Also galling, Charlotte was "considered exceedingly ignorant" and was placed in the lowest grade. Aware of her own intelligence and abilities, this was "an overwhelming humiliation" (p.64).

Charlotte lacked basic knowledge in geography and grammar; however, as Ellen observed, Charlotte had extraordinary knowledge, far more than the other students, in politics, literature, and poetry. Mary Taylor noted that Charlotte "picked up every scrap of information concerning painting, sculpture, poetry, etc. as if it were gold" (Fraser, 1988, p. 64). Her short-sightedness kept her from playing games with the others; "she was considered ... a dreamy, strange creature." Mary noted that while the girls played, Charlotte would often "stand under the trees in the play-ground. ... At Cowan Bridge she used to stand in the burn, on a stone, to watch the water flow by" (Gaskell, 1857, p. 90).

Years later Mary understood that Charlotte had been "nurtured" as an "aesthete, and how she languished" among the girls who did not understand her background. Perhaps Charlotte, the young writer and actor, had chosen to play the role of an aesthete. I imagine that if Branwell knew, he would have roared his approval.

Charlotte's friendship with Mary and Ellen grew. Yet she characterized her good friend Ellen "as 'no more than a conscientious, observant, calm, well-bred Yorkshire girl. She is without romance'" (Fraser, 1988, p. 65). Charlotte's strong critical streak is noticeable in her novels, where she often expressed her grievances in a humorous, sarcastic manner. At school, Charlotte commented that if Ellen "attempted to read poetry or poetic prose aloud, 'I am irritated and deprive her of the book—if she talks aloud of it, I stop my ears'" (p. 65).

Charlotte flourished at Roe Head, but there was an "almost frantic industriousness" in her actions. She worked hard and advanced from the lowest class to the top of her class. "She felt that a great responsibility rested on her; that she was an object of expense to those at home" (Fraser, 1988, p. 66). She often took extra course work. Social class differences were apparent to Charlotte, in the contrast between her background and that of her new friends.

Charlotte was a guest at Mary's home and later at Ellen's. Her exposure to these wealthy and stately homes provided her with material for her books; literal descriptions of these mansions and their environs appeared in her novels. Charlotte's visits to Mary Taylor's home were special. The Taylor family welcomed her; being with them was "one of the most rousing pleasures she had ever known" (Fraser, 1988, p. 70). She felt comfortable socially and was "treated without condescension," finding them to be "kindred spirits.... [They] were as intellectual and argumentative as the Brontës themselves" (Fraser, 1988, p. 69). Charlotte and Mr. Taylor developed a strong relationship: In later years, parcels of books would arrive at the parsonage from him. Charlotte was welcomed by Ellen's widowed mother at Rydings, their spacious home. Although Ellen was "snobbish, extremely conventional and blindly pious," she was also supportive, comforting, and very loyal to Charlotte (Fraser, 1988, p. 72). They maintained a close relationship for years. When Charlotte was in crisis and appealed to Ellen to visit her, almost invariably Ellen would appear.

The "kind-hearted" Miss Wooler, director of Roe Head, enjoyed the companionship of her students. In the evenings, she walked around the room where they gathered, conversing with the girls as they walked together. Charlotte enjoyed this ritual and would repeat it at the Haworth Parsonage with Branwell and her sisters.

Charlotte remained at Roe Head for three terms, making much progress: "she had lost much of her initial shyness and had become quite a figure in her own way" (Fraser, 1988, p. 74). She had become acquainted with a wider world and a different way of life. Her experience at Roe Head could hardly be termed tragic. Ellen, disagreeing with Elizabeth Gaskell's description of Charlotte's morbid character wrote in 1871, in *Scribner's Monthly*:

> The fellowship of the school society knew the secrets of her heart better than did any who became acquainted with her in after life.... The real Charlotte Brontë ... was a bold, clever outspoken girl; ready to laugh with the merriest, and not even indisposed to join in practical jokes. (Fraser, 1988, p. 78)

Charlotte's relationship with Ellen continued after Charlotte returned home; they wrote frequent letters and exchanged visits. Though she discussed many family and personal issues with Ellen, Charlotte's secret writings remained her (and Branwell's) secret. Charlotte generally did not discuss wider social and political issues with Ellen. The content of her letters to Mary Taylor, more of an independent, sophisticated and worldly feminist, is unknown, as Mary subsequently burned all of Charlotte's letters to protect Charlotte's privacy.

Ellen's first visit to the parsonage in 1833 was a mutually enjoyable event. She was warmly welcomed; even Emily, who tended to reject strangers, responded positively to her and wanted her to return. Ellen felt she was special to Emily "because I never *seemed* to mark her peculiarities and I never pained her by treating her as a peculiar person" (quoted in Fraser, 1988, p. 84).

Nature and animals were special to the Brontës; Ellen enjoyed watching the family's "unconventional" recreations: "rambling on the moors... for miles and miles and hours in all kinds of weather" (Fraser, 1988, p. 84). Though the family lifestyle was reclusive, Ellen felt that the Brontës were "completely happy with one another's companionship, because it was 'solitude and seclusion shared and enjoyed with intelligent companionship, and intense family affection'" (Fraser, 1988, p. 85).

Charlotte threw herself into a new series of stories. "High Life in Verdopolis" featured the Duke of Zamorna as its leading character. Glass Town grew into the new Kingdom of Angria, a world in which Branwell and Charlotte immersed themselves. Charlotte wrote chiefly about Zamorna and his complicated love life, which included "mistresses and illegitimate children.... Passion throbs from every line." The vicissitudes of the political life of Angria were also important subjects (Fraser, 1988, p. 88).

When Charlotte was 19, in 1835, Miss Wooler invited her to teach at Roe Head, offering free tuition for one of her sisters. Big plans were being made for Branwell, whose artistic ability and interest had led to his application to the Royal Academy of Arts in London. The thought of teaching at Miss Wooler's school was pleasing to Charlotte, in part because she worried about her father's heavy expenses for Branwell. She wrote: *"Duty—necessity—these* are stern mistresses who will not be disobeyed" (quoted in Fraser, 1988, p. 96). It was comforting that Emily would be going with her.

Adulthood

Teaching at Roe Head

Charlotte's return to Roe Head became a deeply disturbing experience; she was flooded with feelings of depression and guilt and preoccupied with religion and her own "sin." While fulfilling her "duty," she resented the impositions on her time, did not enjoying teaching, and missed her writing and her world of the imagination

(Fraser, 1988). Charlotte also worried about Emily, who could not adjust, and about Branwell, whose life was falling into disarray and chaos. Emily, homesick, stayed at Roe Head for only three months; Anne took her place. Anne, also homesick, made a better adaptation; however, she was later sent home because of stomach illness.

Branwell had shown earlier signs of instability, but now his life markedly deteriorated. Anticipating a spectacular career as an artist, he journeyed to London but never got there, returning home two weeks after he left. Branwell never explained what happened or how his money disappeared. Speculation has flourished, but the mystery still remains. Was he robbed? Did he drink too much? Did he lose his nerve and never apply? Was he rejected by the academy? Did he have a breakdown?

Back home, Branwell, now "frustrated, bored, drinking more," was moving away from his ambition of "being a great artist to being a great writer" (Fraser, 1988, p. 102). His poetry was becoming "increasingly preoccupied with death, his own sinfulness and fear of divine retribution, as well as the hypocrisy of practicing Christians" (Fraser, 1988, p. 102). Charlotte may have felt that he had betrayed the sacrifices she had made for his benefit. Fraser suggests that Charlotte, who had been "so intimately entwined with Branwell" in their fantasies, was now witnessing his religious crisis, which may have "contributed to the intense religious crisis which she herself now began to experience" (Fraser, 1988 p. 102).

Fraser (1988) offers no further explanation of this intriguing hypothesis, which suggests a symbiotic relationship. Whatever the trigger, Charlotte was in serious emotional turmoil, with feelings of depression, anxiety, fear of death, and obsession with guilt and sin.

Ironically, Roe Head now seemed more like a prison—Charlotte felt trapped and burdened with teaching routine lessons to uninspiring girls. Her intense ambition to be a writer was going by the wayside, and the refuge of her imaginative kingdoms was unavailable. She felt deprived of time to write. Her social life was now minimal; her former schoolmates were absent, and their younger replacements were now her "charges," not her friends. Mary and Ellen were free to lead leisurely lives. Could Charlotte accept the inevitable resentment and jealousy this may have aroused?

The Duke of Zamorna had some rather wild affairs; Charlotte's own sexual fantasies may have caused her guilt. Miller (2001) talks of Charlotte's "escaping into vivid voyeuristic daydreams—often erotic" (p. 9). Fraser (1988) noted that her stories about the Duke of Zamorna illustrate "her vicarious life of heterosexual love" through Zamorna's adventures (p. 107).

Miss Wooler treated Charlotte kindly, encouraging her to visit her friends nearby, but Charlotte rejected this possibility. Elizabeth Gaskell (1870) saw Charlotte's depression as a temporary state and compared it to Branwell's depression, noting that "both were not mental but physical illnesses; however, Branwell's depression was 'the result of his faults'" (p. 104).

In the past, Charlotte had looked down on Ellen's simplicity and religiosity; now Charlotte needed Ellen's "calm, conventionally religious attitudes" (p. 107). Some of her letters to Ellen were passionate: "'don't desert me ... don't be horrified at me. ... I wish I could see you my darling, I have lavished the warmest affections of a very hot, tenacious heart upon you ... —if you grow cold—it's over'" (quoted in Fraser, 1988, p. 107).

Some biographers have suggested that these letters point to a "lesbian tendency in Charlotte"; Fraser is dismissive of the idea of an actual "physical relationship" but adds that "perhaps Charlotte was a little in love with Ellen" (1988, p. 107). Ellen was to remain her closest friend; she was now the only person Charlotte could trust, yet even then she could not trust Ellen fully.

Charlotte's reaching out to Ellen now had a desperate quality; she talked of her "increasing desperation and feelings of sinfulness" (Fraser, 1988, p. 107). Charlotte was deeply in need of warmth, closeness, and acceptance. In clinical terms, she needed a *self-object,* a person she could depend on to meet her needs for security, self-esteem, and confidence, her need to be loved. In this instance, Ellen's warmth toward Charlotte was insufficient to dispel her depressive feelings, but Ellen was her only source of comfort. We will see repeatedly how her self-object needs pervade her life and her major romantic crises. Charlotte's need to be loved was a desperate need.

In her novel *Villette,* Charlotte (Brontë, 1893) described Paulina, six years old, who is grief-stricken after her mother's death and her father's temporary abandonment. Paulina develops a strong tie to Graham, her caretaker's 16-year-old son. Her world centers on Graham, who becomes her *self-object* (Kohut's concept, discussed in chapter 5):

> With curious readiness did she adapt herself to such themes as interested him. One would have thought the child had no mind or life of her own, but must necessarily live, move, and have her being in another: now that her father was taken from her, she nestled to Graham, and seemed to feel by his feelings: to exist in his existence. (Brontë, 1893, p. 26).

Brontë had this insight in 1853, in artistic and human terms, over 100 years before Kohut elaborated the self-object concept (Urdang, 2008). Perhaps writing *Villette,* an autobiographical novel, helped

Charlotte, seeing herself in Paulina, gain insight into her own needs for closeness and reassurance.

The concept of self-object is highly relevant in clinical work. Mack and Hickler (1981) wrote a case study that focused on the significance of self-objects, *Vivienne: The Life and Suicide of an Adolescent Girl:*

> Vivienne, 14, took her own life by hanging herself (after several previous suicide attempts). Struggling for a long time with feelings of low self-esteem and depression she felt uplifted when a new teacher provided her with a warm and supportive relationship; he was a critical figure to her (i.e., self-object) in her life in terms of her self-esteem. The loss she felt when he left the school and moved across the country appears to have been devastating. "Well over a year before he left, Vivienne anticipated that she would feel deeply bereaved, and wrote that her "joy will be gone in a year" (Mack and Hickler, 1981, p. 101). The teacher's leaving had "a greater significance than his loss as a person. It struck at the core of Vivienne's psychological vulnerability" (p. 101). The good feelings about herself which Vivienne felt in his supportive presence could not be sustained in his absence. (Urdang, 2008, p. 18)

The concept of self-objects is also relevant to clinical supervision. The following discussion is based on a study of new social work field instructors (Urdang, 1999). It should come as no surprise that supervisors function as self-objects to students who are frequently insecure and anxious in their new and challenging roles. However, it is less well understood that, paradoxically, a student can meet the self-object needs of the supervisor:

While self-object experiences are critical in early child-hood, they are nonetheless important throughout the life cycle. "Indeed, the need for self-object responses is always present, waxing and waning with the ups and downs of the strength and vulnerability of the self" (Wolf, 1994, p. 81). Looking at the new supervisory experience as one of some "vulnerability of the self," it follows that the super-visor may be in need of self-confirming responses from the student, as the parent is in need of acceptance from the child. It is as important for parents to have a child who thrives as it is for a supervisor to have a student who also thrives. (Urdang, 1999, p. 98)

"Mirroring" self-object relationships involve people who reflect back in a joyful, sustaining way our (frequently grandiose) ambi-tions for ourselves" (Young, 1991, p. 75). It was also important to Charlotte, now 21, to have some confirmatory response about her writing ability, hopefully an admiring and mirroring one. She sent her poetry to Robert Southey, the then poet laureate. Southey, however, was a poor choice for Charlotte: He was "was an arch-reactionary, pessimistic, and declining in health and years" (Fraser, 1988, p. 109).

Southey replied after a long delay, conceding that Charlotte had talent but noting that a literary career was difficult for anyone, particularly women (Fraser, 1988, p. 109). Charlotte nevertheless went forward with her ambitions. Southey's negative attitude about women writers was not unique to him. This general sentiment led Charlotte, Emily, and Ann to publish their book of poetry, several years later, under the male names of Currer, Acton, and Ellis Bell.

Although Charlotte and Branwell continued their collabora-tion, they were growing apart. Charlotte's concerns differed from

Branwell's, whose life centered more on his friends and alcohol. Charlotte found Roe Head more intolerable. The school moved to Dewsbury, where Charlotte felt even more isolated. Anne became ill with gastritis and was sent home. Charlotte's own health deteriorated and her depression worsened. She wrote: "'I neither could nor dared stay any longer. My health and spirits had utterly failed me, and the medical man whom I consulted enjoined me, if I valued my life, to go home'" (quoted in Fraser, 1988, p. 113).

In her typical pattern, when removed from an uncongenial and stressful environment to a comforting situation, Charlotte's health and mood promptly improved. Shortly after returning home, she "made a remarkable recovery in her health and spirits" (Fraser, 1988, p. 115).

Branwell, employed as a portrait painter in Bradford, would come home on weekends; initially he seemed to be flourishing, enjoying life and drinking with his artist friends. But when daguerreotypes entered the art world, there was a decreased demand for portrait painting. Branwell's livelihood suffered; he was "gradually reduced to varnishing other painters' canvasses" (Fraser, 1988, p. 116).

Branwell started using opium, which was not then illegal or thought to be dangerous or addictive. De Quincey's book, *The Confessions of an Opium Eater,* written in 1821, popularized the drug (Fraser, 1988). Charlotte, however, could see its negative effects on Branwell. "Her affection for Branwell is mixed with awareness of the feckless nature of his charm" (Fraser, 1988, p. 117). Yet Branwell's presence enhanced her feelings of relaxation.

Quite unexpectedly, on March 4, Charlotte received a marriage proposal from Ellen Nussey's brother Henry, 27, a curate. Charlotte found his proposal humorous. Henry "in due time … should want a wife to take care of his pupils, and frankly asks me to be that wife" (quoted in Fraser, 1988, p. 120). Henry reappears in *Jane Eyre* as St. John, a minister who makes a similar proposal to Jane. Neither proposal was accepted.

Charlotte lived at the parsonage with her family after her return from Roe Head; the girls had sporadic work as governesses. Unexpectedly, it was Anne who found employment as a governess; her tenure of five years and five months was longer than any her sisters ever held. Anne's *Agnes Grey* vividly portrayed the hardships of the life of the governess, as neither a servant nor a member of the family.

Charlotte took a temporary position as a governess, and although it was an unhappy experience, it did furnish her "with novelist's material" (Fraser, 1988, p. 126). At Ellen's suggestion, the two friends spent a vacation at the seashore. It was the first time Charlotte had seen the ocean, which she loved; she returned to Haworth rejuvenated.

In 1840, a new curate, the handsome William Weightman, 25, came to the parsonage. Charlotte became a governess with the Whites in Bradford, and Anne went to Thorp Green Hall, near York. Branwell had some sporadic employment as a tutor, losing one position for neglecting his duties and drinking. He then became a booking clerk on the Leeds-Manchester railway and left home. Although achieving a promotion, "he was now living in greater confusion and disarray than before" (Fraser, 1988, p. 152).

As the family discussed their future, Mr. Brontë and Aunt Branwell suggested that the sisters open their own school. Aunt Branwell volunteered to lend them money to do so; they were enthusiastic about this plan. This proposal evolved into another plan: Charlotte, wishing to travel and to further her education, felt that if she and Emily studied French and Italian, they would be in a better position to start their own school. They decided to enroll at the Pensionnat

Heger in Brussels, recommended by Mary Taylor, now at school in that city.

The Pensionnat Heger

With great anticipation, Charlotte prepared for the trip. Mr. Brontë accompanied Charlotte and Emily to Brussels on February 8, 1842. Charlotte was thrilled about the trip, which included a stop in London to visit the sights she had dreamed about; Lucy Snowe in *Villette* also exulted about visiting London.

The Brontës then traveled to Brussels, which Charlotte found delightful. She described it at length in *Villette* and even named the fictional city Villette. They were warmly greeted at the Pensionnat Heger by Madame Heger, 38, who was "dignified and imposing... the continental woman at her most polished and efficient, while managing to be serenely attractive at the same time" (Fraser, 1988, p. 159). Monsieur Heger, 33, was not present at this meeting.

The school had an excellent reputation, and the Hegers were highly regarded in the community (Fraser, 1988, p. 160). Monsieur Heger was "an incomparable, almost charismatic teacher" and when Charlotte knew him was "at the height of his teaching powers" (Fraser, 1988, p. 159). Fraser observes that Gaskell describes Monsieur Heger "tactfully" as a "'kindly, wise, good and religious man.'" However, Fraser asserts that "this description scarcely does justice to the virile man painted by the distinguished Belgian painter Joseph Gerard... who radiates magnetism and authority" (1988, pp. 159–160).

Monsieur Heger had previously taught at Athenee Royal; his first wife and their young baby died tragically in 1833 during a cholera epidemic. Three years after his wife's death, Heger married his second wife, Claire Zoe Parent, who was five years older. At that time, she was already a respected teacher who had her own school. Monsieur Heger worked primarily at the Athenee Royale but also taught literature at his wife's pensionnat. "Based on mutual physical attraction, devotion to teaching and profound Roman Catholic beliefs, their extremely happy marriage would last over fifty years" (Fraser, 1988, pp. 161–162). They had six children.

Monsieur Heger enjoyed creating "an intimate paternal relationship with students" (Fraser, 1988, p. 162). One student observed "that he almost demanded it, and grew angry if it was denied him." He was supportive and friendly, shared cakes with the girls, and was always eager to engage them in conversation and foster their involvement with literature. Though Monsieur Heger tended to fly into "rages... he was very tender-hearted" (p. 162). He could be "egotistical and vain, [but] was always fascinating. He ruled the Pensionnat like a little kingdom, its impatient, fiery, kindly and slightly absurd god" (p. 163).

At first, Charlotte had little contact with him, but later, as his pupil, she was impressed with his intellect and his passionate interest in French Romantic writers. Charlotte's feelings towards Monsieur Heger became more intense. "Such emotional involvement, such intimacy, such intellectual passion: they were... like a match to dynamite on his fervent, brilliant, emotionally starved pupil, Charlotte Brontë" (Fraser, 1988, p. 162).

Charlotte, 25, and Emily, 23, had some difficulties at first adjusting to life at the Pensionnat. The other students were 15 years old, Catholic, spoke French, and had different cultural backgrounds, and the Brontë sisters were not comfortable with the Catholic influence permeating the school. They lived in a dormitory with 20 girls; Madame Heger partitioned a space for them with a curtain. Emily and Charlotte enjoyed each other's company in this new environment full of strangers. They also had friends in Brussels whom they would visit, including Mary Taylor and her sister Martha, and they became friendly with the English Wheelwright family. Charlotte told Mary, anticipating a visit: "'it gets cold living among strangers'" (quoted in Fraser, 1988, p. 164).

Fifteen years later, when Gaskell visited, Monsieur Heger told her that he felt the sisters had special abilities. He had devised a special program for them. Rather than teaching them grammar and vocabulary, he would read to them French classics, and then together they would analyze and discuss the works. Heger also said that he "rated Emily's genius as something even higher than Charlotte's.... Emily had a head for logic and a capability of argument." He added that a "stubborn tenacity of will, which rendered her obtuse to all reasoning where her own wishes, or her own sense of right, was concerned" impeded her potential (Gaskell, 1870, p. 167). He observed that she had such a powerful "imagination" that if she wrote a "history, her view of scenes and characters would have been so vivid, and, so powerfully expressed, and supported by such a show of argument; that it would have dominated over the reader" (p. 167). He then added that she "appeared egotistical and exacting compared to Charlotte, who was always unselfish (this is M. Heger's [*sic*] testimony); and in [Charlotte's] anxiety... to make [Emily] contented, she allowed her to exercise a kind of unconscious tyranny over her" (p. 167). Charlotte is generally perceived as the more dominant of the two sisters; however, Monsieur Heger, with considerable insight, saw the subtle interplay of their relationship. Charlotte, who felt responsible for her younger sister, allowed Emily to control her emotionally.

This type of interaction, not visible on the surface, is often seen in clinical work in parent-child therapy. For instance, some children, when not getting their way, display psychological or physical symptoms that they know will tyrannize their parents, who then give in to their demands. As a case example, Jimmy, age five, was in therapy because of repeated vomiting without evident physical cause (Urdang, 2008). It was reported during joint sessions with Jimmy and his mother that whenever any separation from his mother had been brought up, Jimmy would later vomit, making his mother anxious and preventing the separation.

Charlotte was content at the Pensionnat: "'I am never unhappy; my present life is so delightful, so congenial to my own nature, compared to that of a governess. My time, constantly occupied, passes too rapidly'" (quoted in Gaskell, 1870, p. 169). She described her initial impressions of Monsieur Heger as "'a man of power as to mind, but very choleric and irritable in temperament'" (Gaskell, 1870, p. 169). Later, more enthusiastically, she noted that "M. Heger was the first teacher... who really understood contemporary literature and was passionately interested in it" (Fraser, 1988, p. 166).

Charlotte was deeply appreciative of Monsieur Heger's teaching and his attention to improving her writing; he helped her see "what was redundant and over-ornamental in her writing" (Fraser, 1988, p. 168). She felt she owed Heger a "debt" for all his teaching and told him "she would like to write a book and dedicate it" to him. He told her that he felt her "French prose style was the language of an artist.... The more time that Charlotte spent with him, the more... she came to admire him" (p. 168). Heger appreciated the sisters and often would read their writings aloud in class.

Charlotte and Emily had made much progress. Madame Heger encouraged them to extend their studies for another half year—they would study French and German and, in turn, teach some classes. This was agreeable to all. In their joint letters to Ellen, "their spirits were high" (Fraser, 1988, p. 170). Mary Taylor wrote to Ellen that the Brontës, "often a prey to melancholia, were thriving" (Fraser, 1988, p. 174).

Unfortunately, this idyll was interrupted by several catastrophes. First, Mr. Brontë's curate, William Weightman, whom everyone adored, died from cholera. Then Branwell was fired from his railroad job and accused of stealing money. The money was actually stolen by a porter, but Branwell, responsible for the office, was dismissed. Back at the parsonage, unemployed and deeply affected by Weightman's death, Branwell became depressed and obsessed with thoughts of death. Also tragically, Mary Taylor's sister, Martha, 23, died in Brussels of cholera.

Then news arrived that Aunt Branwell was gravely ill with an internal obstruction. She died before the girls could leave Brussels. Emily was not upset at leaving Brussels; Charlotte was. Monsieur Heger wrote a letter for her father, stating his hope that they might continue their studies (Fraser, 1988).

The girls felt the loss of Aunt Branwell: "... she was a kindly woman who had been part of their lives since early childhood." Branwell, who was his aunt's favorite, was deeply affected (Fraser, 1988, p. 178). The family now made new domestic arrangements: Charlotte would return to Pensionnat Heger, Emily would help at home, and Anne would continue as governess at Thorp Green; she obtained a position there for Branwell as a tutor.

Charlotte left on January 27, 1843, for her second year at the Pensionnat.

Madame Heger, realizing that Charlotte was now alone, was kind and solicitous. Charlotte felt lonely without Emily and without Mary Taylor, now in Germany. The highlight of her present life was the English lessons she gave to Monsieur Heger and his brother-in-law.

Charlotte wrote to Ellen: Mary "'has nobody to be as good to her as M. Heger is to me; to lend her books, to converse with her sometimes, etc.'" (Gaskell, 1870, p. 189).

> It was obvious that Charlotte was "increasingly emotionally reliant on M. Heger" and "deliberately blinded herself" to this (Fraser, 1988, p. 187). Heger is portrayed as Paul Emanuel in *Villette*. Those who knew Heger "protested that the portrait of M. Paul Emanuel was identical to him until the moment when he falls in love with Lucy Snowe [representing Charlotte]" (p. 187).

Miller (2001) comments that "it seems hard to deny that there was a mutually intense element to the relationship, even though Charlotte felt more romantic" (p. 122). But the nature of the Brontë-Heger relationship remains a mystery. Did Heger's playfulness, his habit of frequently giving her books, lead her to misinterpret his affections? In a letter to Branwell, Charlotte "referred to Monsieur as 'the black swan,' a romantic term that she might... have used about the Duke of Zamorna" (Fraser, 1988, p. 191). Is it possible that Charlotte's behavior "produced behaviour in M. Heger that was a little more tender and more flirtatious than was suitable" (p. 190)? It is possible that some of Heger's "idiosyncratic behaviour" was misinterpreted by a "lonely, excitable and naive young woman" (p. 188) or that Heger might have expressed feelings of love and passion to Charlotte that she could never forget and that he would have been quick to deny.

On July 29, 1913, the *Times of London* printed four newly discovered letters Charlotte had written to Monsieur Heger in 1844–1845, "which caused a storm of controversy" (Miller, 2001, p. 120). Interpretations of these letters multiplied:

The letters have been read as the expression of a conscientious pupil's gratitude toward a teacher; as the culmination of a hysterical schoolgirl infatuation; as evidence of a tragic unrequited *grande passion;* as symptoms of a neurotic father fixation; as an imaginative act of self-dramatization; and as a comment on Charlotte's literary ambition. (Miller, 2001, p. 120)

Charlotte noticed changes at the Pensionnat. Her English lessons with Monsieur Heger were suddenly stopped; Madame Heger was not friendly. Charlotte became convinced that a teacher was spying on her for Madame Heger. She wrote to Emily that she did not understand why Madame had negative feelings to her. Charlotte became more convinced that Madame Heger herself was spying on her. Charlotte often wrote biting, sarcastic pieces about people she was angry at, turning them into fictional characters who were often recognizable by others. In *Villette,* Madame Heger becomes Madam Beck, who runs a French school in Villette (Brontë, 1893): "Madam had her own system for managing... and a very pretty system it was. . . .'Surveillance,' 'espionage,'——these were her watchwords" (p. 86). And a further barb: "She of course had her staff of spies" (p. 88).

Charlotte's unhappiness and depression culminated in August, when everyone at the Pensionnat went on vacation, except for one teacher, with whom she was uncomfortable. Her desperate feelings escalated, leading her to look for comfort in confession in a Catholic church; this scene, described in her letters, is repeated in *Villette.* Lucy, having never been in a Catholic church, let alone to confession, did not know how to proceed. She confessed to the priest: "Mon pere, je suis Protestante" (Brontë, 1893, p. 201). He asked why she had come:

I said I was perishing for a word of advice or an accent of comfort. I had been living for some weeks quite alone; I had been ill; I had a pressure of affliction on my mind of which it would hardly any longer endure the weight. (Brontë, 1893, p. 201).

After assuring her that she had committed no "sin" or "crime," the priest was uncertain how to help. If she were Catholic, the course would be clear. He explained that her present feelings of distress "are messengers from God to bring you back to the true Church. You were made for our faith" (Brontë, 1893, p. 202). He encouraged her to continue their discussion. Lucy had no intention of visiting him again. However, she felt good about this experience: "He was kind when I needed kindness; he did me good. May Heaven bless him" (pp. 203–204).

Charlotte was very unhappy during the remainder of her time at the Pensionnat.

Mary encouraged her to return home. When she did leave, she was surprised by the warmth and "regret" from her students. She received warm wishes form the Hegers and a diploma from Monsieur Heger, "certifying her abilities as a teacher" (Fraser, 1988, p. 201). Charlotte wrote to Ellen that she would not "'forget what the parting with M. Heger cost me; it grieved me so much to grieve him, who has been so true, kind, and disinterested a friend'" (quoted in Fraser, 1988, p. 201).

Return to Haworth

Returning to the parsonage, Charlotte continued to think of Monsieur Heger and of seeing him again. They wrote to each other, but only one letter from this early correspondence remains. In it, she wrote that she is studying French:

> for I am firmly convinced that I shall see you again... for I wish it so much, and then I should not wish to remain dumb before you... Monsieur; as I pronounce the French words it seems to me as if I were chatting with you. (cited in Fraser, 1988, p. 205)

Later, when Elizabeth Gaskell went to Brussels to interview Monsieur Heger, he told her that he was certain Charlotte kept his letters "as they contained advice about her character, studies, mode of life'" (quoted in Fraser, 1988, p. 205).

A breakdown in their communication developed. Charlotte remained as eager as ever to write, but Monsieur Heger held back. He probably felt threatened by her feelings for him. Charlotte refers to a "rebuke" he sent her, asking her to limit her letters (Fraser, 1988, p. 208). What followed then were pathetic letters from her, expressing her pain, longing to hear from him, and begging for a response; he generally did not respond.

The Brontë sisters continued to discuss plans for their school, which would be at the parsonage to enable them to look after Mr. Brontë, who was now almost blind. Although the sisters had a prospectus printed and attempted to recruit students, they had no applicants, and they eventually gave up these plans. Charlotte was depressed and felt isolated. She had no employment and did not write for fear that it would strain her eyes and lead to blindness. Charlotte was worried about her father's loss of eyesight; it may have stirred fears in her about becoming blind herself. Charlotte wrote: "What appears to have been a hysterical form of near-blindness had her in its grip" (Fraser, 1988, p. 206). Charlotte was also upset that Mary Taylor had decided to go to New Zealand. There Mary's brother Waring had established a general store in Wellington. Mary herself was to become a businesswoman, invest in land, and manage a store. Multiple physical, psychological, and social factors were impinging on Charlotte all at once; loss was a major theme in all these factors.

After more waiting and no response from Monsieur Heger, Charlotte wrote to him in January 1845: "If my master [Heger] withdraws his friendship from me entirely I shall be without hope; if he gives me a little . . . I shall be satisfied, happy; I shall have a reason for living on, for working" (Fraser, 1988, p. 213). Charlotte, depressed and feeling desperate, wrote again to Heger. However, beneath her pleading for only "a little" from him and noting how happy this would make her, there is also a punishing, guilt-provoking aspect to this message. His writing would give her a reason to live; conversely, if he does not write, she implies she would have no reason to live, even suggesting the possibility of suicide. This places a heavy emotional burden on him. In clinical practice, it is not unusual to see depressed people and those with suicidal thoughts place blame and guilt on others for their alleged lack of responsiveness and caring. It is also not uncommon for the significant others of a person who has committed suicide to feel intense responsibility and guilt. Apparently, Monsieur Heger "tore up the letter and threw it away as he did with the other letters" (Fraser, 1988, p. 214). However, Madame Heger retrieved the letter from the wastebasket, restored it by sewing it together, and kept it "as a safeguard for the future" (p. 214). This document, with its stitches visible, was preserved and is now at the British Museum.

A tempest struck the parsonage when, according to Branwell's account, he was fired from his job as a tutor to Edmund Robinson, the 11-year-old son of Mr. and Mrs. Robinson. Mr. Robinson discovered that Branwell and Mrs. Robinson (17 years older than Branwell) had been having an affair for the past three years. Branwell said that Mr. Robinson "threatened to shoot me if I returned [to the Robinsons]" (quoted in Fraser, 1988, p. 235). However, "like everything about Branwell, the truth of what happened with the Robinsons is hard to distinguish from his own wild imaginings" (p. 231).

Many versions exist of this affair: It was very passionate; it never happened; it was Mrs. Robinson who seduced Branwell; Mrs. Robinson met Branwell at Harrogate and planned to elope with him. Most disbelieved the story, but subsequent mysterious happenings were never explained, leaving the impression that the story had some credibility: There had been a mysterious visit from Mrs. Robinson's coachman to Branwell at the local tavern; and large sums of money were sent to Branwell, "some definitely from Mrs. Robinson's doctor," which Branwell claimed originated from Mrs. Robinson (Fraser, 1988, p. 231). The entire episode exemplifies the problems of evidence gathering for biographers, including the temptation to fantasize and invent in the absence of hard facts or documentation. Clinicians may be exposed to similar temptations. Charlotte became concerned that Branwell might be engaging in extortion. Branwell was also frequently in debt. When debt collectors arrived demanding payment and threatening imprisonment, Mr. Brontë paid the bill. Branwell "gave himself up totally to his obsession with Mrs. Robinson; this was the final stage in his deterioration" (Fraser, 1988, p. 236). Branwell lived another two years after this.

Charlotte, meanwhile, started writing *The Professor.* Discovering a notebook with Emily's poetry, Charlotte was overwhelmed by the beauty of her writing, "the genius of which [Charlotte] was the first to recognize" (Fraser, 1988, p. 245). Emily resented Charlotte's intrusion into her privacy. Charlotte wrote: "'. . .it took hours to reconcile her to the discovery I had made, and days to persuade her that such poems merited publication'" (quoted in Fraser, 1988, p. 245).

After considerable searching, Charlotte found Aylott and Jones Publishers in London. They agreed to publish the collected poems of the three Brontë sisters if the Brontës paid the costs. They consented, using money from Aunt Branwell's legacy. Concerned about prejudice against women writers, the Brontës chose masculine names: In May 1846, *Poems by Currer, Ellis and Acton Bell* was published. The book received some excellent reviews; special praise was given to Emily's poems. Rumors and speculation spread in London about the identity of the Bells. Although a total of two copies were sold, the praise from the reviews encouraged the sisters, and they made efforts to have their novels published: Charlotte's *The Professor;* Anne's *Agnes Grey,* and Emily's *Wuthering Heights.*

Jane Eyre

Mr. Brontë was now blind from cataracts and seriously incapacitated. Charlotte arranged for William James Wilson, an eye surgeon in Manchester, to remove the cataracts. She rented a house so that she could stay with her father while he recuperated. The operation was successful: He regained his vision and was able to resume work. The morning of the operation, Charlotte heard the bad news that *The Professor, Wuthering Heights,* and *Agnes Grey* had been rejected for publication. She worried that Emily and Anne had the burden of caring for Branwell while she was in Manchester, and she was also in pain from a chronic toothache "related to gum disease" (Fraser, 1988, p. 261). In the midst of these trying circumstances, she began writing *Jane Eyre*.

Charlotte submitted the manuscript the following summer to Smith, Elder and Company, then a little known publishing company. She listed the author as Currer Bell. The publishers were delighted with this intriguing novel, quickly accepted it, and published it on October 16, 1847. The critics praised it and the public loved it: Sales boomed and Currer Bell became a sensation overnight. Thackeray wrote an enthusiastic review, which especially pleased Charlotte.

Jane Eyre was in many ways an autobiographical novel. As already noted, Lowood represented Cowan Bridge, and Mr. Brocklehurst, its headmaster, represented Reverend Cyrus Wilson. Marie's death is reflected in the death of Jane's friend, Helen Burns. Feelings for Mr. Rochester replicated her feelings for Monsieur Heger. Many settings were modeled on her friends' homes and other places she had known. And Jane Eyre "was Charlotte herself, struggling for independence, for recognition and for love" (Fraser, 1988, p. 265).

In her novels, Charlotte highlighted women's roles in society. The "feminine" ideal to which they were expected to conform was in conflict with her emphasis on freedom and independence. Charlotte admired Jane Eyre, her "unorthodox heroine," for her "courage and honesty." In the novel, Jane is happy that Mr. Rochester loves her for herself and does not try to mold her into what she can never be. In a society that frowned on its discussion, Charlotte treated passion as a vital force: Passion "could become the strongest thing on earth" (quoted in Fraser, 1988, p. 264).

Though a best seller, *Jane Eyre* also aroused considerable negative criticism; its controversial messages stirred an outcry. Fraser noted that *The Sunday Times* stated that Currer Bell "'has passed the outworks of conventional reserve,' and that the passages between Mr. Rochester and his wife were too disgusting to quote" (quoted in Fraser, 1988, p. 281). The *Mirror* said: "'*Jane Eyre* was one of the many blows... aimed at our institutions, political and social'" (quoted in Fraser, 1988, p. 281). In a society where there was strong Evangelical influence, "their supporters were quick to see a threat and to sense an unwelcome change of emphasis" (p. 280).

Charlotte was hurt by the attacks, especially accusations that she was antireligious. She protested: "'I love the Church of England. Her ministers, indeed, I do not regard as infallible personages'" (quoted in Fraser, 1988, p. 283). In the preface to the second edition of *Jane Eyre* she strongly criticized her critics, adding: "Conventionality is not morality. Self-righteousness is not religion" (Brontë, 1847, p. 2). Fraser observed: "She was not the daughter of the volcanic Patrick Brontë for nothing" (p. 285).

She received encouragement from her publishers, Smith, Elder, and especially from the editor William Smith Williams, who was the first to "discover" her book. Williams and Charlotte started a correspondence that continued for many years. She also developed a gratifying correspondence with Thackeray, who praised her work.

Overall, pleased with reactions to her book, Charlotte was enjoying the anonymity of Currer Bell. No one, including her publishers, knew her real identity, and speculation continued. Much later Mr. Brontë told Elizabeth Gaskell that he was not surprised to learn that his daughters were writing books, for they spent a great deal of time writing, and it "could not have always have been letters" (Fraser, 1988, p. 287).

Anne's *Agnes Grey* and Emily's *Wuthering Heights* were published during this time. Both sold well and went into second impressions. However, *Agnes Gray* received little attention from reviewers, and Emily received very bad reviews strongly condemning *Wuthering Heights.* Charlotte told Elizabeth Gaskell later that her pleasure at her own success was overshadowed by Emily's distress about her reviews. After Emily's death, five reviews "comparing her book unfavorably to Charlotte's" were found in her desk (Fraser, 1988, p. 292).

The Brontë sisters continued to use the pen name Bell. Taking advantage of this, Newby Publications (publisher of Emily's and Anne's books) spread rumors that Ellis Bell (Emily) was the author of *Jane Eyre;* accusations were made in newspapers that "'trickery' and 'artifice' were used by the [Bell] brothers" (Fraser, 1988, p. 290). This spurred Charlotte to write a prefatory note in her third edition of *Jane Eyre* declaring "that my claim to the title novelist rests on this one work alone" (Brontë, 1847, Preface, p. 4).

Charlotte herself did not approve of *Wuthering Heights.* In a letter to Mr. Williams, she spoke of Ellis's talent and of "his 'strong original mind.'" She felt that Emily wrote wonderful poetry but that her prose included "'scenes which shock more than they attract. Ellis will improve, however, because he knows his defects'" (quoted in Fraser, 1988, p. 292). After Emily's death, Charlotte wrote a preface to *Wuthering Heights,* and just as Gaskell would whitewash Charlotte, Charlotte whitewashed Emily, explaining that Emily's sweet nature was unduly influenced by the harsh, uneducated Yorkshire people.

In the spring of 1848, Charlotte enjoyed the success of *Jane Eyre,* which was now in its third edition and popular in the United States. Anne and Emily were writing new novels, and Charlotte had made a good start with *Shirley.* Then another literary crisis erupted, incited by Newby Publications. Smith, Elder was informed that all the Bell novels were written by the same person. Charlotte was especially incensed that Smith, Elder might believe that the Bell brothers had swindled them.

> Deciding that there was only one way to solve this thorny problem, she and Anne traveled to London to meet her publishers directly and explain the fraudulent behavior of Newby Publishers. They made their way to Smith, Elder and approached the reception desk. They were not expected. They asked to see Mr. Smith but would not give their names. He came to meet them, resenting being interrupted at his work by unknown visitors. When he came out of his office he saw" 'two rather quaintly dressed little ladies, pale-faced and anxious looking' " (quoted in Fraser, 1988, p. 304)One of them came forward and presented me with a letter-addressed in my own handwriting to Currer Bell, Esq. I noticed that the letter had been opened, and said with some sharpness, "where did you get this from?" "From the post office," was the reply. "It was addressed to me. We have both come that you might have ocular proof that there are at least two of us." (quoted in Fraser, 1988, p. 304)

Smith was "simply amazed that this little creature could be the author of that passionate masterpiece *Jane Eyre* . . . . He now had before him the author for whom all London was searching" (Fraser, 1988, p. 304). He excitedly started making social plans for Charlotte and Anne. The Brontës met Mr. Smith's sisters; they all attended the opera together that evening. The next two days were a social whirl. There was also a meeting with Anne's publisher, Mr. Newby, "and [they] attempted to dissuade him from further villainy" (p. 308).

Charlotte returned to Haworth in a happy mood and with books from Mr. Smith. She was "rather relishing her new position with her publishers" (Fraser, 1988, p. 309). Then Branwell unexpectedly died on September 24, 1848—it was known that he had consumption, but no one realized his death was imminent. Charlotte "collapsed" at the funeral. She was ill and "incapacitated for a week" (p. 313). Mr. Brontë was "utterly distraught" (p. 313).

The family tragedies continued. Emily, who had caught a cold at the funeral, now was seriously ill with pulmonary tuberculosis, denying her illness and refusing help "with a power that seemed almost a will to die" (Fraser, 1988, p. 316). Charlotte's attempts to help her were rebuffed; it was painful for Charlotte to deal with Emily's "ruthless stoicism."

Emily died on December 19, 1848. Her funeral service was conducted by Mr. Nicholls (later to be Charlotte's husband) and attended by the family and her beloved dog Keeper, who "walked in the short cortege.... He was taken into the church and the Brontë's own pew, where he sat quietly while the burial service was read, and for the next week he lay outside Emily's bedroom and howled" (Fraser, 1988, pp. 318-319).

Now worried about Anne's failing heath, Charlotte asked Ellen to come to the parsonage. Ellen came. A doctor diagnosed tuberculosis but with some optimism stated that sea air might helpful in the spring. Anne complied with all medical treatments. Charlotte's work on *Shirley* receded to the background as Anne's health failed. Charlotte, accompanied by Ellen, took Anne to Scarborough for sea air. She died on May 28, 1849, and was buried at a cemetery in Scarborough (Fraser, 1988).

Mr. Brontë told Charlotte to stay at the seashore and regain her own strength. She did, with Ellen for company, for most of June and then returned to Haworth alone.

Elizabeth Gaskell

Charlotte and Elizabeth Gaskell first met at Lake Windermere as house guests at the home of Sir James Kay Shuttleworth and his wife. Charlotte was "quite captivated by this warm, impulsive and determined woman, who had all the confidence of great physical beauty" (Fraser, 1988, p. 381). She wrote to Ellen that she had been "'truly glad of [Gaskell's] companionship. She is a woman of the most genuine talent, of cheerful, pleasing and cordial manners and—I believe—of a kind and good heart.'" Gaskell described Charlotte in a letter to a friend:

> She is (as she calls herself) *undeveloped,* thin, and more than half a head shorter than I am; soft brown hair, not very dark; eyes (very good and expressive, looking straight and open at you) of the same colour as her hair; a large mouth; the forehead square, broad and rather over-hanging. She has a very sweet voice; rather hesitates in choosing her expressions, but when chosen they seem without an effort admirable, and just befitting the occasion; there is nothing overstrained, but perfectly simple. (Gaskell, 1896, p. 344)

A warm friendship developed that continued for many years through letters and visits. Gaskell wrote to her friends "defending the author of the scandalous *Jane Eyre,* anxious to convince them that Miss

119

Brontë is a 'nice person' who had 'high noble aims' " (Fraser, 1988, p. 384).

Charlotte, criticized for expressions of passion in her book and her acceptance of unconventional (and immoral) behaviors, must, Gaskell thought, be presented as a pious woman, innocent and influenced by terrible circumstances and reprehensible people in her family and Haworth. Gaskell wrote a "plea for understanding her friend, an *apologia* on her behalf" (Fraser, 1988, p. 384). Her goal was " 'to show her as a very noble, true Christian woman firstly, and an author secondly.' "

Mrs. Gaskell's determination to see her friend in a positive light led to a number of major misrepresentations of her life: Mr. Brontë was a tyrant; her brother Branwell was a dissipated ne'er-do-well; and Haworth was populated by lawless, rough, and uneducated people. All these evil influences purportedly affected Charlotte's writing.

Gaskell described Charlotte's background so that "the reader should be made acquainted with the peculiar forms of population and society amidst which her earliest years were passed" (Gaskell, 1857, p. 9). Arthur Nicholls, who became Charlotte's husband, subsequently commented: "Haworth might be a queer place, but it was nowhere quite as queer as Mrs. Gaskell made out" (Fraser, 1988, p. 25).

The cultural values of Victorian England strongly influenced the lives of Charlotte and Elizabeth Gaskell as well as the public reaction to *Jane Eyre.* Religion, morality, and social convention predominated. Women's rights were negligible; assuming family responsibilities was their primary role. Job opportunities were limited: Becoming a governess was the primary option for educated women.

Miller (2001) suggests that Gaskell distanced herself from the passionate nature of Charlotte's writings, which she found unacceptable: She never "fully engaged with the powerful, intense, and uncompromising side of Charlotte's personality" (p. 33). And for her part, Charlotte was discreet about what she shared with Gaskell. This often has its counterpart in practitioners who avoid dealing with the client's sexual life or who deny manifestations of their clients' erotic feelings (as well as their own). In more recent times, discussions about sex as well as about the sexual orientation of both the clinician and the client have become more open and more frequent. There are also occasions, both for the biographer and clinician, when focus on the subject's or the client's sexuality becomes excessive, even intrusive.

Anticipating Charlotte's visit to her home, Gaskell "felt the sort of tug at her heart strings: 'Poor, poor creature,' she would exclaim, while devising plans for quiet visits for her new friend" (Fraser, 1988, p. 385). Gaskell had strong protective instincts and was involved in reform efforts. "Rehabilitating" Charlotte's image would be compatible with her involvement in social work with Charles Dickens and others.

Mrs. Gaskell was a warm, maternal figure. Charlotte, emotionally needy, welcomed her warmth and sympathy. "In her company Charlotte was able to be almost as relaxed as she was with Ellen" (Fraser, 1988, p. 411). Did she feel comforted sharing the tragedies of her past with a sympathetic listener? The complementarity in their relationship is seen in many therapist-client relationships, where the client's needs for sympathy are matched by the clinician's needs to nurture. This can complicate both the biographer-subject and the therapist-client relationship. For example, the needs of a client for commiseration, when matched by a therapist's need to be benevolent, can interfere with the more disciplined process of difficult emotional exploration. It can also contribute to taking sides with one member of a couple who can successfully recruit the therapist's sympathies. And it can result in the avoidance of necessary therapeutic confrontation.

Gaskell was dominant in her relationship with Charlotte—she would give guidance to the "pitiful" Charlotte. Similarly, some practitioners may be tempted to assume a dominant role by offering "solutions" or premature advice. Gaskell's "solicitous" behavior may also have masked professional jealousy. Charlotte is generally considered a far more brilliant writer than Gaskell. By downplaying Charlotte's literary abilities (which Gaskell openly stated was her aim) while emphasizing Charlotte's suffering and sterling moral character, Gaskell's literary rival becomes less threatening.

Gaskell became an active participant in Charlotte's life in different ways. Charlotte became attached to the Gaskell children, especially Julia, 7, who returned the affection. Julia "reminded Charlotte... of Mrs. Gaskell" (Fraser, 1988, pp. 409- 410). Charlotte referred to Julia in letters to Elizabeth: "'Could you manage to convey a small kiss to that dear, but dangerous little person, Julia? She surreptitiously possessed herself of a minute fraction of my heart, which has been missing, ever since I saw her'" (quoted in Gaskell, 1870, p. 375).

Although Charlotte would not entrust Gaskell with her feelings for Monsieur Heger, she did confide her ambivalence about marrying Arthur Nicholls. Gaskell quite approved of Charlotte becoming a married (and thus more respectable) woman. When Charlotte told her that one reason Patrick Brontë disapproved of Nicholls was his lack of money, Gaskell secretly wrote to a friend, a patron of the arts, asking whether he could offer a pension to Arthur Nicholls to enable Charlotte to marry him. This man met with Nicholls, who was puzzled about this offer. It is unknown whether he accepted it. This kind of interaction can be seen in some practitioners who manifest strong, often unconscious wishes to take over aspects of the client's life.

Gaskell was directly involved twice in Charlotte's professional life: The publication of *Villette* was delayed at Gaskell's request; her own novel, *Ruth,* was scheduled to come out at the same time, and as Charlotte (who agreed to this) explained to Ellen: "Mrs. Gaskell wrote so pitifully to beg that it should not clash with her *Ruth"* (quoted in Fraser, 1988, p. 430). Charlotte could now be a "benefactress to her gracious literary friend" (p. 430). It is striking that Gaskell did not offer instead to give precedence to her literary friend whom she professed to see as pitiful and suffering.

On another occasion of interference in Charlotte's professional life, Gaskell wrote to George Smith, Charlotte's publisher, after Charlotte's death, asking him not to publish *The Professor,* as there were portions Gaskell found objectionable. Even though Arthur Nicholls had edited it, "'I fear he has left many little things . . . likely to make her misunderstood. For I would not, if I could help it, have another syllable that could be called coarse to be associated with her name'" (quoted in Fraser, 1988, p. 491). Nonetheless, Smith did publish *The Professor,* in 1857—with a short preface written by Arthur Nicholls.

Shirley

Charlotte keenly felt the silence and emptiness of her home, with its painful reminders of her sisters—Keeper the dog continued his daily visits to Emily's room. Charlotte worked on a new book during the day, which provided her some comfort, but being alone at night was difficult. Charlotte was taking increasing "pride in endurance" and turning more to religion for solace, although she found it "far from an easy comfort" (Fraser, 1988, p. 328).

Shirley is not considered a great novel. It did not have "the unity of *Jane Eyre*.... It never quite makes up its mind whether it is... a novel of social protest... or a love story, and uneasily combines the two" (Fraser, 1988, pp. 328–329). Charlotte continued to highlight the themes of "feeling and truth" (p. 329). Her two major characters, Caroline Helstone and Shirley Keeldar, typified the limited role of women in society, in which they lacked freedom and autonomy.

The reviews of *Shirley* were less enthusiastic than were the reviews of *Jane Eyre,* but there was also much less condemnation. Although Charlotte preferred good reviews, she "thrived on challenge.... There was never any real question of capitulation to opinion" (Fraser, 1988, p. 341). Charlotte's sense of enjoyment and pleasure was returning; she thought of visiting London and was invited to stay at George Smith's home. Ellen helped her find some special clothes for the occasion.

George Smith had arranged a dinner party for Charlotte, inviting Thackeray, which greatly excited her, for she admired his writings. Her awe of Thackeray initially inhibited her developing a more informal relationship with him, although over time she was comfortable enough to lecture him about his behavior and his writing.

Smith noted that "his mother and sisters had found Miss Brontë rather a difficult guest because of her nervousness.... 'She was very quiet and self-absorbed, and gave the impression that she was always engaged in observing and analysing the people she met'" (Fraser, 1988, p. 350). Mr. Smith and Mr. Williams spent much time entertaining Charlotte, taking her on excursions to the theater, exhibits, Parliament, and other sights. She began developing warm feelings for George Smith.

Returning home, she felt lonely and depressed. She was disappointed that books from George Smith did not arrive as often as she hoped. She realized that she was probably too dependent on the mail:

"I cannot help feeling something of the excitement of expectation till the post hour comes, and when, day after day, it brings nothing, I get low. This is a stupid, disgraceful, unmeaning state of things. I feel bitterly vexed at my own dependence and folly; but it is so bad for the mind to be quite alone." (Quoted in Gaskell, 1870, p. 321)

Charlotte felt especially disappointed when the wished-for letter or books were from someone for whom she had special feelings: In this case, it was George Smith; in the past, it had been Monsieur Heger. As described in *Villette* in the chapter called "The Letter," Lucy pines for a letter from Dr. John (who represents George Smith).

Mr. Brontë, concerned about Charlotte's depressed mood, encouraged her to visit Sir James Kay Shuttleworth and his family. She enjoyed the visit but remained troubled. Then she decided to visit George Smith; this was her most enjoyable visit to London (Fraser, 1988).

She was relaxed, and the "tone of her letters... became increasingly euphoric" (Fraser, 1988, p. 366). Although at times Charlotte could be "off-putting," George Smith found "her personality... was always peculiarly interesting to me"; when with him, Charlotte noticed she was "at her most vivacious" (p. 366). She began to call him by his first name and enjoyed his " 'buoyant animal spirits and youthful vigour' " (Charlotte, quoted in Fraser, 1988, p. 367). "Charlotte was becoming increasingly drawn to George Smith; Mrs. Gaskell heard gossip about it" (p. 373).

Smith arranged for the painter George Richmond to paint a portrait of Charlotte. "They went everywhere together, and sufficient intimacy had arisen, no doubt aided by Charlotte's sparkling frankness, for him to invite her on a trip to Edinburgh" (Fraser, 1988, p. 373). She found this to be "one of the most enjoyable times she could remember" (p. 374). Fraser comments: "A more sensitive, more imaginative, less businesslike man might have seen that he was giving rise to some sort of expectation" (p. 375). Much later, Smith stated that he was "never in love" with Charlotte:

> "The truth is, I never could have loved any woman who had not some charm of grace or person, and Charlotte Brontë had none—I liked her and was interested in her, and I admired her—especially when she was in Yorkshire and I was in London. I was never coxcomb enough to suppose that she was in love with me. But I believe my mother was at one time rather alarmed." (Smith, cited in Fraser, 1988, pp. 373–374)

Mr. Williams suggested that Charlotte edit a new edition of her sisters' works, clarifying the confusion about the Bell identities. Charlotte did, excluding Anne's *Wildfell Hall*. She found a new, inspiring, appreciative review of Emily's *Wuthering Heights,* but editing was often painful, stirring up memories of Anne and Emily.

Charlotte received a number of invitations to visit friends, but she refused them, feeling she must finish her work. "Charlotte wrote to Ellen that her depression of that autumn had entirely lifted" (Fraser, 1988, p. 390). Charlotte's depression often lifted quickly when visiting and surrounded by warmth and stimulation.

Charlotte was finding herself more drawn to George Smith. In January, 1851 he proposed that they take a trip together down the Rhine in the summer. She was tempted but felt it would create complications in their relationship and social disapproval. She explained to Ellen that it was not possible: "'I am content to have him as a friend'" (cited in Fraser, 1988, p. 394). She wrote many letters to him that were "enchanting, whimsical, [and] flirtatious... which impelled him to respond" (p. 394). Charlotte accepted an invitation to visit the Smiths in London in June. As she prepared for the trip, the parsonage buzzed with excitement with all the shopping and sewing.

Villette

Charlotte was warmly received by the Smiths. Mrs. Smith took her to a Thackeray lecture attended by many prominent people. Thackeray, who spread the rumor that "Jane Eyre was in the audience," greeted her at the door. Mr. Smith was working overtime; Charlotte did not see much of him but enjoyed her visit to London. One night, after George and Charlotte went to the theater, it became clear to her that "she could never be more to George Smith than friend and author" (Fraser, 1988, p. 406). Two days later she developed a bad migraine and felt very ill. On June 14, she decided to go back home.

Then, on June 19, Sir James Kay Shuttleworth invited Charlotte to his London house, where she stayed for a week. He arranged for many famous visitors: "she had to confess some pleasure in having some of the great and good lay their tribute at her feet" (Fraser, 1988, p. 407). Her depression faded, and the headache disappeared. George Smith asked her to stay until June 25, as he was to have a holiday.

They had a lot of fun, which included seeing a phrenologist, using the name "Fraser" as a disguise, and saying they were brother and sister. The trip brought them closer together again.

On her way home, Charlotte enjoyed a visit with Mrs. Gaskell. When she returned to Haworth, she felt cheered. Charlotte and George Smith continued to write to each other. She wrote often in her usual "brilliant, intimate, analytical vein," although she refused his frequent invitations to visit London. "'There is the pain of that last bidding good-bye, that hopeless shaking hands, yet undulled and unforgotten.... I could not bear its frequent repetition'" (quoted in Fraser, 1988, p. 414)—this was reminiscent of the way she felt saying goodbye to Monsieur Heger.

The winter of 1852 was bitter: Charlotte was ill with chest pains, insomnia, and depression, and she worried about consumption. Her doctor found no organic disease but thought she had an "irritable condition of the liver" and gave her medicine. She asked Ellen to visit, and with Ellen in the house she slept well. "Her illness seems to have been largely psychosomatic. While Ellen was there, Charlotte recovered remarkably, but she grew worse again immediately on her departure" (Fraser, 1988, p. 418). This depressive spell coincided with her decision that any romance with Smith was impossible.

Charlotte wrote most of *Villette* between August and October, sending the first two volumes to Mr. Smith at the end of October. Asking for his assessment of the book, Charlotte did not mention that she based Dr. John on him and Mrs. Brett on his mother. Deeply hurt that George Smith had not reciprocated her feelings, Charlotte responded in her typical fashion, by skewering the "offenders" in her writings. He "was not so insensitive as to miss the resemblance between his mother and himself." Later he said, "and it's all he said—many of his mother's and his expressions were used verbatim"

(Fraser, 1988, p. 423). Yet the Smith, Elder publishing house, when Charlotte first knew it, was struggling and in financial difficulty. The success of *Jane Eyre* brought them great success as well as a welcome infusion of money. Whatever his personal feeling, it would have been difficult for George Smith not to publish *Villette*.

Charlotte finished *Villette* on November 20, and she accepted an invitation to the Smiths'. In an unexpected turn of events, although Mr. Nichols knew the Brontë family for many years as Mr. Brontë's curate, this was the very first time he made a romantic overture to Charlotte. One evening before her trip, according to Charlotte, Mr. Nicholls

> "... stood before me. What his words were you can imagine; his manner you can hardly realise, nor can I forget it. He made me, for the first time, feel what it costs a man to declare affection when he doubts response.... The spectacle of one, ordinarily so statue-like, thus trembling, stirred, and overcome, gave me a strange shock. I could only entreat him to leave me then, and promise a reply on the morrow. I asked if he had spoken to Papa. He said he dared not. I think I half led, half put him out of the room." (cited in Gaskell, 1870, p. 405)

When Charlotte told her father about this, he became quite agitated; she was distressed by his vehemence and his insistence that she immediately refuse Nicholls. She sent Nicholls a sympathetic note and told him she did not reciprocate his feelings. A major tempest ensued. Nicholls was distraught: He could not eat, could barely function at work, and then resigned. When Nicholls later offered to withdraw his resignation, Mr. Brontë would accept only if Nicholls would never bring up the subject of his feelings toward Charlotte again. Nicholls could not accept this, and in the middle of this stalemate, Charlotte left for London.

Charlotte's visit to the Smiths was pleasant. There she spent time correcting the proofs of *Villette*. George Smith and Charlotte saw little of each other, however. *Villette* would be popular with the public and the first reviews positive. Many praised the book's "remarkable power, freshness and skill in creating such 'living' characters.... It was confirmation of the genius which had written *Jane Eyre*" (Fraser, 1988, p. 434). But there were again negative comments, some regarding Charlotte's criticism of Catholicism and organized religions.

Engagement and Marriage of Arthur Nicholls and Charlotte

Charlotte returned to the parsonage in February 1853, where the tension between her father and Arthur Nicholls continued. "They were like two offended potentates who had the misfortune to share the same kingdom" (Fraser, 1988, p. 439). Although Charlotte felt sorry for Nicholls, they never conversed.

Before Nicholls left for another curacy, he stopped to say good-bye. When Charlotte saw that he remained outside, she went to him. He was leaning " 'against the garden door in a paroxysm of anguish, sobbing....'" (Fraser, 1988, p. 444). Charlotte could not encourage him, but she felt he understood she was not without sympathy for him.

From his new curacy, Nicholls wrote Charlotte five letters to which she did not reply. She did respond to the sixth letter. By fall they were writing regularly to each other.

Elizabeth Gaskell came for a visit that September at Charlotte's invitation.

She was seeing the parsonage for the first time. She admired the cozy house and was impressed that it was "exquisitely clean" (Gaskell, 1870, p. 422). She also was pleased with the decoration, which was "in harmony with, the idea of a country parsonage, possessed by people of very moderate means" (p. 423). They had a mutually enjoyable visit and agreed they should exchange more visits.

Gaskell went home with even more pity. She thought of Nicholls as "'very good, but very stern and bigoted.'" "'He sounds vehemently in love with [Charlotte]'" (Fraser, 1988, p. 450). Mr. Brontë remained resistant: He felt that Charlotte should marry someone with better prospects. Charlotte confronted him:

> "Father I am not a young girl, nor a young woman even—I was never pretty. I am now ugly. At your death I will have £300 besides the little I have earned myself—do you think there are many men who would serve seven years for me?... Yes I must marry a curate if I marry at all; not merely a curate but your curate:... he must live in the house with you, for I cannot leave you." (quoted in Fraser, 1988, p. 455)

Following this confrontation, Mr. Brontë would not talk with Charlotte for a week, but then he slowly accepted this idea. Charlotte still had internal struggles about marrying Nicholls: As she wrote to Mrs. Gaskell, "I cannot deny that I have had a battle to fight with myself" (quoted in Fraser, 1988, p. 456). In some of her letters, she lists Nicholls's good traits, as though to convince herself as well as her audience: he is "affectionate, pure in heart and life" (p. 456).

Ellen Nussey was unhappy about Charlotte getting married and evidently jealous of Nicholls. When she complained to Mary Taylor about Charlotte's marriage, Mary told her to stop complaining—Charlotte had a right to happiness. Ellen agreed to be Charlotte's bridesmaid, and a small quiet wedding was planned. The night before, Mr. Brontë decided that he would not give the bride away; a last-minute decision was made that Miss Wooler would take on this role.

The couple went to Wales and Ireland for their honeymoon. In Ireland, Nicholls took Charlotte to visit his relatives and to see the stately home where he grew up, which surprised and impressed her. Charlotte's bad cold marred part of the trip, but Nicholls remained concerned and involved. Charlotte still expressed reserve about him but was grateful for his affection and care. After the honeymoon, they seemed more comfortable with each other; they could laugh together, found they had a similar sense of humor, and enjoyed the foibles of others. Fraser (1988) argued that Nicholls "deserves much credit for their increasing happiness. Nothing was too much for him" (p. 469).

Charlotte seemed happy in her marriage: Her letters were cheerful and her references to Arthur affectionate; "a new contented Charlotte was emerging" (Fraser, 1988, p. 473). Her health had improved and she was delighted at the absence of "headache, sickness, and indigestion" (quoted in Fraser, 1988, p. 473). "I have a good, kind, attached husband; and every day my own attachment to him grows stronger," she told Gaskell (Gaskell, 1870, p. 437). Nicholls can be said to have met Charlotte's self-object needs at this time, as seen in the conspicuous improvement in her mood, health, and state of well-being. Her life, which she was clearly enjoying, now centered around Arthur Nicholls:

My own life is more occupied than it used to be. I have not so much time for thinking: I am obliged to be more practical, for my dear Arthur is a very practical, as well as a very punctual and methodical man.... I believe it is not bad for me that his bent should be so wholly towards matters of life and active usefulness; so little inclined to the literary and contemplative. As to his continued affection and kind attentions it does not become me to say much of them; but they neither change nor diminish. (Gaskell, 1870, p. 436)

In January 1855, Charlotte began feeling ill with nausea and faintness; the doctor "assigned a natural cause for her miserable indisposition; a little patience, and all would go right" (Gaskell, 1896, p. 450). Charlotte was pregnant. Unfortunately, her illness progressed, and she had a fever. Eating was difficult, and she became emaciated. "Then she took to her bed, too weak to sit up" (p. 450). She died on Saturday, March 31, 1855, before her 39th birthday.

Officially, Charlotte died of tuberculosis; however, there is controversy regarding this diagnosis versus the possibility of a disorder of pregnancy. Gaskell commented that if only she had known about Charlotte's illness, "she could have induced Charlotte to terminate the pregnancy" (Fraser, 1988, p. 488).

Mr. Nicholls, keeping his promise to Charlotte, remained at the parsonage with Mr. Brontë. They stayed together for another six years, until Patrick Brontë's death.

After Charlotte's death, many articles about her, some of which were critical, appeared. As a result, Mr. Brontë asked Gaskell to write an accurate representation of Charlotte's work and life. Gaskell had been thinking along these lines herself and agreed.

Gaskell chose to leave the country temporarily once the *Life* was published: She was concerned in case Charlotte was criticized. In actuality, the book was praised and very popular with the public. But Gaskell faced two lawsuits. One related to her portrayal of Cowan Bridge School and the headmaster Carus Wilson, who was outraged. The second was brought by the former Mrs. Robinson (Branwell's alleged mistress), now Lady Scott; she demanded a revised edition, which was done.

Mr. Brontë made no public statement about Gaskell's negative portrayal of him, but he privately told her that he objected to descriptions of his violent temper. He asked Gaskell to delete some negative (and untrue) comments, such as one section in which he is reported as prohibiting "his children from eating meat" (Fraser, 1988, p. 493). On the whole, though, Mr. Brontë was pleased with the book.

As Charlotte's fame spread, people came to visit her home. Mr. Brontë received many requests for "samples of her handwriting" to the consternation of later biographers, he cut fragments from her letters to send. The fragments were later collected and reassembled.

Mr. Brontë and Mr. Nicholls sent George Smith poems by Emily and Charlotte, along with the beginnings of Charlotte's new manuscript, *Emma*. Although some believed that Nicholls took no interest in Charlotte's writing, "his pride in his wife and reverence for the fame of the family show in his letters; it particularly pleased him that Thackeray was to write an introduction to the *Emma* fragment" (Fraser, 1988, p. 495).

Mr. Brontë wrote to George Smith to thank him for his thoughtfulness, for his "gentlemanly conduct towards my daughter," and to ask him to express his appreciation to Thackeray for his comments (Fraser, 1988, p. 495). He added that if Charlotte's spirit could see Thackeray's introduction, she would feel "'additional happiness on scanning the remarks of her Ancient Favourite'" (quoted in Fraser, 1988, p. 496).

Arthur Nicholls would leave Haworth after Mr. Brontë's death, taking all his wife's possessions with him as well as Mr. Brontë's dog. He returned to Banagher, his childhood home in Ireland, and left the clergy to become a farmer. He married Mary Bell, his cousin, 2 years later. He died at 88 on December 2, 1906.

Charlotte's life was marked by loss. Especially significant was the loss of her mother when she was five years old, which created a sense of emotional insecurity and need for the affection and admiration of self-objects. Although her life at the parsonage has been characterized as tragic, especially by Elizabeth Gaskell, Charlotte's family life was also full of gaiety, reading, and writing. The children grew up in a unique world of narratives of their own creation and a shared imagination that was vibrant and continually evolving. Although experiencing early maternal loss and the death of two sisters, their bonds with each other were very strong and contributed to their confidence and security.

Elizabeth Gaskell wrote an innovative and landmark biography, without the benefit of comparable models or guidance. The more recent adverse appraisal of her personal involvement and bias vis-a-vis Charlotte has come from present-day critics, who have had the benefit of many critiques of biographical works.

Mr. Brontë died on June 7, 1861, and was buried next to Charlotte. In his will, he declared Arthur Nicholls as his sole beneficiary. During Mr. Brontë's final illness, Mrs. Gaskell and her daughter Meta came to visit. Mr. Brontë told them he was happy they had come. He talked about Charlotte and said that Elizabeth Gaskell's book "'would hand her name to posterity'" (quoted in Fraser, 1988, p. 496). In that he was correct.

CHAPTER 4

Ved Mehta: Self-Exploration in Autobiography

Ved Mehta, the well-known contemporary writer, born in Lahore, India in 1934, has written serial autobiographies exploring his life in a self-reflective way to further his self-understanding. There are eleven autobiographies in the series, known as the Continents of Exile Series. The first, *Daddyji,* was published in 1972, and the most recent, *The Red Letters,* was published in 2004. Mehta became totally blind as a result of meningitis when he was almost four years of age; how blindness affected his life is a major theme in his work. Mehta began his series of autobiographies, *Continents of Exile,* in 1972, shortly after completing his psychoanalysis; this enabled him "to write in a whole new autobiographical vein, exploring interior worlds previously inaccessible to me" (Mehta, 2001, p. 345). He wanted to understand the puzzles and enigmas in his life that remained after his analysis. From the viewpoint of *retrospective teleology,* he was seeking a different understanding of his past experiences by revisiting them. This autobiographical series is a journey that he invites the reader to take with him, as he shares his experiences, successes, struggles, and insights.

Mehta discusses his Hindu home, the Indian caste system, and the clashes engendered by cultural differences between his English-educated father, who was a prominent public health doctor, and his uneducated mother, who was influenced by religious superstition. In the series, he examines the impact of his experiences at the Dadar

School for the Blind in Bombay, the Arkansas School for the Blind, Pomona College in California, Oxford University, and the *New Yorker* magazine, where he was a successful staff writer. Mehta gives us a glimpse into his psychoanalysis, and the series follows Mehta to Dark Harbor, on Isleboro Island in Maine, where he builds a new house and settles down happily with his wife and two children.

Unlike some autobiographers, Mehta does not hide or disguise his inner feelings or what he refers to as "shameful" aspects of his or his family's behavior. Arthur Conan Doyle, for example, would not talk about his father's alcoholism, whereas Mehta discusses his father's problems with gambling. He shares his own feelings and conflicts, including his many embarrassments, his self-consciousness and social gaffes, and his struggles with depressions and feelings of inadequacy. He also shares his pride in his accomplishments and how he overcame a myriad of difficulties: accommodating to blindness, adapting to diverse cultural conditions, and coping with loss and loneliness. The first two books in his series were written as biographies of his parents: *Daddyji* (1979) and *Mamaji* (1988). This, too, was an attempt to get to know them and himself more deeply.

Mehta also discusses the process of writing his autobiographies. He wanted to understand more about the onset of his blindness and the ways his parents reacted to it: His biographical "research" involved speaking to them about their recollections of this event. This "allowed my father and mother to talk freely to me, for the first time, about their individual memories of the event." In turn, this led "toward reconciling perhaps them, and certainly me, to the irrelevance of the tantalizing might-have-beens to the reality of my blindness" (Mehta, 2004, p. 10). Engagement in autobiographical writing can stimulate dialogue with significant people in the writer's life. In a similar way, undergoing psychotherapy can also motivate people to understand their lives and relationships more deeply; this often leads to dialogue with parents, children, colleagues, friends, and others, which may help heal past hurts and rebuild relationships. Sometimes, though, these conversations can lead to negative confrontations and a severing of ties.

The autobiographies include letters written by him and about him, such as correspondence between his father and the principals of two of his schools. His teenage diaries, which he had not seen for 30 years, brought back memories. Relevant newspaper articles and others' perceptions of him (which he sometimes solicited) are also included.

Ved Mehta intensely refused to be limited by his blindness and to live in a blind community: In India he would not cane chairs; in the United States he would not be a piano tuner. He thought of himself as sighted and wanted others to think of him in this way. He also struggled with self-doubts, feeling he was "damaged goods" (Mehta, 2004, p. 298), and had deep fears of abandonment and dependency. He aspired to higher education and to a writing career; his books contain much visual detail.

The serious problems blindness presents, requiring physical, social, and emotional adaptations, are compounded in India by the social stigma attached to it. Many blind people become beggars. Mehta's father was determined that Ved should not become help-less—he must be educated. At age five, he was sent to an institutional school for blind orphans in Bombay, 900 miles away from home. This early separation from his family was traumatic, reverberating throughout his life. In his autobiography, he sought to understand how this experience affected him, both then and later in life.

Although Mehta lived away from his parents for long periods of his life, they were very much in his life; when he was five years old and living in Bombay at the Dadar School, he was taught Braille:

> I remember that in order to memorize which dots stood for which letters, I would think of combinations of dots as telephone numbers, and of the letters formed by the combinations as standing for members of my family. When I punched (or dialed) one, three, six, I got "u," for Umi.... When I punched one, three, four, I got "m" for Mamaji. (Mehta, 1987b, p. 82)

Daddyji was supportive and always there for Ved, even when thousands of miles apart. His father wrote to Ved often, made inquiries to his headmasters, and imparted instructions to them about Ved's education and well-being: Ved should not take a woodworking shop; he should not be on the wrestling team. Daddyji shared Ved's aspirations for himself; in fact, it was Daddyji, a successful physician, who set his education in motion. It is not surprising, then, that the first two volumes in his autobiographical series are biographies of his parents, and that the first was on Daddyji (Mehta, 1979).

With regard to the following sections, it should be kept in mind in reading the recountings of his parents' lives that we are seeing them through the prism of Ved Mehta's research and perspectives, his search for himself, and his personal and cultural self. They embody a journey of inquiry for the histories that we may imagine shaped him and his life.

Family Background

Daddyji

Daddyji had a long journey. He went from a small village in the Punjab to medical school to England for advanced training in public health and tropical medicine and then back to India, where he became a respected public health doctor. His career was interspersed with other journeys.

The Mehta family had its roots in the Punjab. Daddyji's father, Bhola Ram (Lalaji), grew up in a relatively well-to-do family (Mehta, 1979). When Lalaji was about 10, he learned to read and to write Urdu, copying the Koran to "improve his calligraphy" (p. 7). Lalaji met the district collector, an Englishman, who was impressed by his personality and his elegant penmanship. Although lacking a formal education, Lalaji was offered a job as a *patwari* for the Department of Canals and Irrigation.

A patwari was a government official who recorded the amount of government canal water the villagers used and assessed landowners' taxes accordingly. To ensure impartiality, the patwari could not work in his home village and every three or four years was required to move to another location. Lalaji was delighted to obtain this position and chose the last name Mehta (his subcaste's name).

When Lalaji was 28, a marriage was arranged for him to a 15-year-old girl.

Negotiations were successful, as the major points were satisfied: The couple came from the same caste, the families had similar economic levels, she was healthy and attractive, and, finally, their horoscopes were "compatible." As was traditional in Hindu marriages,

Lalaji and his bride never met until the marriage ceremony, and even then the bride's face was covered by a veil.

After three days of celebrations, the couple, with some members of the wedding party, went to Lalaji's house, where his bride received the name Bhabiji (Elder Brother's Wife). Her life would now "like that of every other relative ... [be] defined entirely by her role in the family" (Mehta, 1979, p. 11). And, as tradition dictated, "the unquestioned ruler of the household was ... Manji, Lalaji's mother" (p. 16). In the next generation, Daddyji and Mamaji married in the same tradition.

Lalaji was ambivalent about his work. Although it carried a certain amount of prestige, there was some stigma attached to it. He began corruptly accepting money from taxpayers to lower their taxes. This source of extra income was also a source of shame. Perhaps this is why "he was insistent on his own importance" (Mehta, 1979, p. 20):

His bearing was that of a polished courtier, and he was strong, laconic, and dictatorial. He seldom ate with the family, and even preferred to smoke his hookah in solitude. He scarcely ever talked to anyone at home; Daddyji remembers that in Lalaji's entire life-time they had at the most twenty or thirty exchanges. (Mehta, 1979, p. 20)

Education was important to Lalaji. He kept a diary, studied folk medicine, read a newspaper, and had high expectations for his sons. He wanted them to "break away from the superstition and backwardness of village life" (Mehta, 1979, p. 21). He helped his brother, Ganga Ram, receive an education and was thrilled when he became the first college graduate in the family. Following Hindu tradition, Ganga

Ram, in his turn, helped Daddyji, for example, by giving him "lessons from the Urdu primer" and teaching "him English words" (p. 22).

At 10 years of age, Daddyji and his brother, Daulat Ram, then nine, moved to Multan to attend high school. They lived with Uncle Ganga Ram, now the headmaster of the Ayra Samaj High School. At the last minute, Bibi, Daddyji's sister, at her insistence also went along to attend school. The three children and Manji (Ganga Ram's mother and Daddyji's grandmother) took a 24-hour train trip to Multan.

Daddyji found that the evenings at Uncle Ganga Ram's house were "somewhat strained"; his wife "seemed sad and withdrawn" (Mehta, 1979, p. 33). Ved thought maybe it was because after two years of marriage they had no children (being childless was generally "shameful" for Indian women). Whatever was troubling her, it was possible she was unhappy that her quiet married life was suddenly interrupted by the addition of three children and one mother-in-law, whose visit extended for more than one year.

Although Ganga Ram was dutifully carrying out his obligations to his brother's family, interpersonal tensions and conflicts erupted. Daddyji (and Mamaji) later experienced similar tensions, when Daddyji, as the oldest son, had his younger brothers live with his family for an extended time.

Daddyji's new school's headmaster was committed to sports, especially hockey and cricket: "sports were in Daddyji's blood ... he never missed a chance to play" (Mehta, 1979, p. 36) This led to conflict with Uncle Ganga Ram, "who considered all sports a waste of time, a luxury for the idle rich" (p. 37). Another conflict involved choosing a college for Daddyji. Ganga Ram voiced his opinion that Daddyji should go to an engineering or other professional school.

Lalaji wanted him to have a "general education" at Government College, which was Daddyji's wish:

> Neither man liked to have his opinions questioned, and there was a long silence... "Government College!" Bhaji Ganga Ram said at last. "He'll only fritter away his time on hockey and cricket, and ape the British sahibs....
>
> Next he'll want to be a maharaja!" [literally "great king," lord of one of the former states of India]
>
> Lalaji... said, "are we, then, to be less than maharajas?" (Mehta, 1979, p. 41)

Daddyji attended Government College and then went to medical school. He did not do well in his first year—taking sports but not his studies seriously, he failed his examinations. He kept this a secret for 50 years, to "serve as a good example to his younger brothers and, later, to all the Mehta children" (Mehta, 1979, p. 60). His subsequent medical education was successful: He achieved high standing in his class and received academic rewards and scholarships.

Daddyji left for England to complete his medical education in London. His mother's parting words were "Don't come back with a memsahib!" (a respectful or subservient term of address for a white, upper-class woman; the message was to not get married to an Englishwoman) (Mehta, 1979, p. 72). Daddyji arrived in London without having applied to any medical school; he managed to get admitted to University College for a degree in public health and then (without informing the school) was admitted to the London School of Tropical Medicine. He received medical degrees from both schools and returned to India, but Daddyji loved London and hoped to return.

Back in India, Daddyji became the municipal health officer in Rawalpindi, making a major contribution in finding and eliminating the source of the bubonic plague rampant in the area; his innovative discovery was noted in the *British Medical Journal* (Mehta, 1979). He applied for a Rockefeller Foundation Fellowship in the United States. Although he had other relatives to support, "Daddyji could not resist the temptation." Awarded a fellowship, he left for the United States (Mehta, 1979, p. 105). Shortly after he arrived, he learned that his father had died. He "flung himself across the bed and sobbed into his pillow. It was the first time he had cried as a man" (p. 114).

Daddyji received training in malaria control in Virginia and then worked in Virginia and Sardinia. He subsequently spent a year in different British hospitals learning about tuberculosis. He wrote to his brother, now a health officer in Lahore, that he was planning to settle in England. He was planning to go into private practice and was looking for housing. "'Once I have a home in London, all our brothers can come for an education"'; he added: "'if one lives in England there's no harm in taking an English wife'" (Mehta, 1979, p. 116). He then received a "tearful" letter from his brother; Daddyji had created an emotional crisis. Their mother was distraught and had developed physical symptoms: "the doctor says no medicine can help her, for she is grieving." This decision also distressed his brother (p. 118): "What is London, what is worldly success... compared to Bhabiji, and her love for her son... ? Come home at once." And so, "Daddyji knew he had to go back" (p. 118).

Daddyji, a physician, independent and autonomous, with plans to remain in England, gave them all up and dutifully returned home. His mother's guilt-provoking demands, seconded by his brother and strengthened by strong cultural traditions, determined his decision. Family behaviors often appear incomprehensible in purely psychodynamic terms, when answers may lie in the powerful roles of cultural values and rituals at play.

Daddyji returned to India. There he was soon "in great demand in the marriage market" (Mehta, 1979, p. 129). When asked what he was looking for in a wife, he said that a dowry was not necessary but that she should "be presentable, speak English," be "musical... able to give good parties... be modern and free of superstitions." She should accompany him to his clubs and be able to socialize with "the Indian and English wives" (p. 130).

The "courting" and marriage rituals were those followed by his father. It was surprising that Daddyji, with some Westernized values and ideas, did not at least insist on choosing his own wife (as he had been ready to do in England). Daddyji was told by the bride's father (who also showed him a picture of Mamaji) that she had all the attributes he required. Once he received approval from Uncle Ganga Ram (who was now head of the family), his mother and sister were dispatched to talk to Mamaji's father to work out the marriage arrangements.

The wedding itself was also "traditional." The couple never met beforehand (although Daddyji made an unsuccessful attempt to glimpse Mamaji by hiding behind bushes near her house). After the wedding rituals, they became acquainted, and Daddyji slowly came to realize that Mamaji's attributes had been misrepresented to him (for example, she could not speak English), but he handled this in a comforting way. He did not make an issue of it but instead took her to a shoe store to buy new shoes, a new experience in her "cloistered" life. He taught her to swim and to drive. She also often accompanied him on trips he took to different health stations. "Mamaji was observant and ready to learn" (Mehta, 1979, p. 139).

When she realized that she was not pregnant after two months of marriage, she became quite distressed and fearful of being sent back to her parents. Not only was it important to have children, but it was of primary importance to have sons. Daddyji reassured her: "'you're going to be my one and only wife'" (Mehta, 1979, p. 143). They learned that she had an easily corrected gynecological problem. Her daughter, Promila, was born a year later.

Daddyji began spending less time at home and more time at the club, enjoying the companionship there; he soon was playing poker "with a gambler's zeal. Although he was only on a government salary, he thought nothing of risking a month's pay to garner a day's winnings" (Mehta, 1979, p. 154). Mamaji would always wait up for him to return. If successful, he would give her the money, and she "would flush with excitement. If he had lost, the subject wouldn't be broached." She was "terrified" of losing everything (p. 155). Although aware of her anxiety, "the stakes he played for were so staggering that he could not bring himself to reassure her" (p. 155).

Although gambling may begin as an avocation for some, for many it comes to control their lives (Urdang, 2008). As noted by Blume (1992), "The gambler's family life and work situation deteriorate as debt grows and personal possessions, savings, and legitimate loan sources are exhausted" (p. 4). From Ved's account, it does not appear as though the family was devastated by his father's gambling—details about the family's finances are not given. However, it clearly was an ongoing cause of tension between the parents.

Mamaji

Mamaji, born in Lahore on August 16, 1908, was named Shanti Devi. Her father, Babuji, was a lawyer "and a man of consequence in Lahore—in university circles and at the High Court—Babuji went about in a Victoria, a curtained carriage" (Mehta, 1988, p. 102). His first wife died at 27, in 1902, leaving three children. When he married his second wife, Mataji, she became responsible for caring for his children (generally considered an undesirable position by prospective wives). "As a widower's second wife, her position in the family was insecure," Ved noted (p. 81).

Babuji and Mataji's first child, a son, was born in 1906, and Shanti Devi (Mamaji) was born two years later. When Mamaji was about 1 year old, her brother died from diphtheria. Almost every year for the next 10 years, Mataji was either nursing a child or grieving one. Through all seasons, Babuji followed strict routines of daily living: "he liked a certain order to his life, for it provided an anchor in the turbulence of calamity and change that threatened to overwhelm him" (Mehta, 1988, p. 104).

When Mamaji was about seven, she was sent to local school. When Ved interviewed her for his biography, she could not remember much about it—to her it felt like a "foreign place, without purpose, to which she was sent because she was too young to be married" (Mehta, 1988, p. 120). She did recall one highlight: She and a friend were in a short play and received much praise. They "were the stars of their class; Mamaji felt she had never before been so happy" (p. 121).

When she would return from school, Mataji would call her, and she "was immediately put to work picking stones out of the rice or lentils, scrubbing the kitchen floor, or feeding babies. She doesn't remember ever once being asked 'How was your day at school?' or

'What did you do today?' " (Mehta, 1988, p. 120). Shortly after she failed a test, Babuji decided Mamaji should stop attending school. "She is educated enough—she can keep household accounts and write a letter. What use is there to filling her head with more studies?" (p. 122).

Babuji, immersed in his work, was not involved with his family. When the children heard him come, they would usually disappear. Mamaji saw him a "distant awesome figure," and she "developed a *hauwa* (literally fear of a demon)" (Mehta, 1988, p. 124). She was also beginning to have troubles with her domineering half brother, Bhagwan Das, 23, who "discovered he had new power over his father's second family—especially his stepmother and his eldest half sister" (p. 125).

Family discussions of Mamaji getting married had begun. Several proposals were offered and negotiated but rejected. Babuji now gave some thought to Mamaji's education: "he wanted to marry her to a Hindu gentleman." He hired an Anglo Indian woman to give her English lessons, "to drill her in simple English sentences: 'Would you like a cup of tea?' " (Mehta, 1988, p. 122). This type of English fluency was not what Daddyji had in mind when he made his proposal.

Mamaji was concerned about pleasing Daddyji and submitting to his wishes; at the same time, he encouraged her to express her wishes. One day, however, he came home early and found her singing to an idol. " 'Such superstitions don't become you,' he said" (Mehta, 1988, p. 185). From then on she "kept her prayers private" and "redoubled her efforts to become a student of his moods. She extracted information about him from her in-laws." When she learned about the superstitions that ran through his family, she would "quietly remind him" of this (p. 185). Mamaji, strictly controlled by cultural expectations, nevertheless found ways to manipulate Daddyji and the system to gain some control. Although cultural demands can overcome individual desires, in this instance we can see from the clinical perspective ways in which individual and interpersonal dynamics are universal and cut across culture. This is important because of the paradoxical danger of stereotyping the client and assuming that culture alone explains the behavior of every client of a particular cultural affiliation, of believing that clients simply go along with all prescriptions of their culture and that they are shaped by only one culture (Urdang, 2008). The issue of superstitions would flare up later when Ved became blind, and against Daddyji's strong wishes, she engaged in various superstitious rituals and medical practices that she felt were on Ved's behalf but that hurt and frightened him.

After three years, the family moved to Lahore (where Daddyji had always wanted to live), and there he built a new house. When it was ready, they moved in, "and so did all the other members of … [his] family living in Lahore" (Mehta, 1988, p. 149), which included Bhabiji, Daddyji's mother; four of his brothers; three of his sister Bibi's children; and one cousin. "Mamaji began to feel—rightly or wrongly—that in Daddyji's affections Bhabiji was first, then his brothers and close relatives, and then their own children, and that she came last" (Mehta, 1988, p. 215).

Ved's Childhood

Illness

Ved developed well. Then, when he was almost four years of age, Daddyji went on a medical tour of some villages, accompanied by Ved, Mamaji, and Ved's new baby sibling. One afternoon Mamaji and Ved were taking a walk when the weather turned very cold. That night Ved developed a fever of 105, which did not go down. The next day blood was taken. The doctor thought he might have pneumonia. Daddyji suggested a new German drug, Prontosil Rubrum (one of the first sulfa drugs), to bring his fever down, and the doctor concurred; Ved's temperature dropped to 101.

The next day the results of the blood tests arrived. Daddyji suspected cerebrospinal meningitis and wanted a lumbar puncture; the other doctor agreed, but the senior doctor at the hospital felt this procedure was not necessary. This doctor told Daddyji to stop the Prontosil immediately. Daddyji followed his advice about both the medicine and the spinal puncture.

Daddyji became alarmed later when Ved could not tell him what color hat he was wearing. Daddyji called his brother, Daulat Ram, a physician in Lahore, who said that he should bring Ved to Lahore right away. What then followed was later to become an emotional crisis for Daddyji. An important medical commissioner was to arrive that night, and a tennis tournament had been planned in his honor at the club. Daddyji, eager for a promotion, felt he should be there; the trip to Lahore was postponed until the next day.

The next morning they left for Lahore Hospital, where a neuro-surgeon did a lumbar puncture. Ved was sick for two months; his spine was tapped twice a day. Although he was improving, it became apparent that "the optic nerves had been irrevocably damaged. He was left totally blind" (Mehta, 1979, p. 188). As an adult, Daddyji had cried only once, when his father died; now he "broke down again and cried helplessly" (p. 187).

Daddyji feared that in India Ved's blindness would be seen as a punishment "for the misdeeds of his previous life.... Blindness, like leprosy, was the lot of the poor and the cursed" (Mehta, 1979, p.

188). He was worried about the lack of services and schools for the blind. Mamaji thought that Ved's blindness must result from "some misdeed she committed in an earlier incarnation, and she had already set about working towards improvement in her next life by redoubled piety and devotion" (p. 188).

Ved's parents, devastated by the onset of his blindness, were grief stricken and felt guilty. They did not know where to turn or how to educate him. Daddyji heard that there were some schools for the blind and put ads in newspapers in Bombay and Calcutta stating that he was looking for a school for his blind son. A letter arrived from Ras Mohun Halder, an Indian Christian, who had some training working with the blind in the United States and now ran an American mission school in Bombay; he offered Ved a placement there. Mamaji strongly opposed this—she felt he was too young and that his sight would be restored. Nonetheless, the decision was made for Ved to go to Bombay.

Prakash, Ved's cousin, the son of Daddyji's sister, Bibi, was going to Bombay for a job and agreed to accompany Ved on the trip. On a winter morning, Ved, his parents, and Prakash went to the train station. Ved did not want to go; he cried, protesting. He asked Daddyji to go with him. "Ved held on to Mamaji's neck and wouldn't let go.... Daddyji felt weak" (Mehta, 1979, p. 191).

> Now Daddyji heard the whistle—the Frontier Mail was pulling out. He snatched Ved up and handed him, crying, through the window of the compartment to Prakash. The last words Daddyji said to Ved (and the first words I remember hearing) were "You're a man now." (Mehta, 1979, p. 192)

This scene haunted Ved for years: "I would ask my parents to describe that scene to me again and again, as if I needed to relive it and to sort out their contradictory impulses and actions as they waved me off to a brutal boarding school half a world away" (Mehta, 2001, p. 208).

Dadar School

Throughout his autobiographies, Ved refers to this school in very negative terms: Dadar School "was an orphanage-cum-asylum. I was lucky to escape alive after three harrowing years there" (Mehta, 2003, p. 268). Years later he had an unpleasant dream about Dadar but was relieved that "the wretched school in Bombay couldn't touch me now" (Mehta, 1987b, p. 39).

Yet many positive aspects of the school are described in *Vedi* (1987b). There were touching descriptions of the friendship of the boys, the dedication and caring of many of teachers, and the investment in teaching and ingenuity of the headmaster, Mr. Ras Mohun, who arranged for a trip to the seashore and a visit to the zoo and bought Braille chess sets for all the students. Ved loved chess, which became very popular at the school. Ved received special care from Deoji, an older student, who was protective and empathic. Once they talked about Ved's sneezing; Deoji asked him: "You know what it means when you sneeze? . . . It means that someone in your family is thinking about you. I can't tell you who, but someone is surely remembering you" (p. 39).

The school was poor, with primitive facilities, but Ved learned and became more independent in his daily functioning. When he went home on vacations, he missed the routines and felt the loss of some of his independence, such as making his bed and polishing his shoes. He missed telling time; he was reassured at school by Mr. Ras Mohun's bell ringing to mark beginnings and endings of activities; receiving no help with this at home, he devised his own system, by keeping track of activities around him: "When I heard the sweeper washing the drain in the *gulli* in front of the house in the morning, I knew that it was eight o'clock and time to get up" (Mehta, 1987b, p. 129).

Being wrenched from his family at such a young age was traumatic. He was parted from his family, with its daily warmth and attention, underwent two hospitalizations, and had to assimilate to the culture of the orphanage and the loss of all that was familiar. He wrote:

> When I was less than five years old I had been sent away to the first of several substandard institutions, and there I hadn't had anyone to run to or confide in. I had had to learn to be wary. As a consequence, I had become mature in some ways long before my time and had remained infantile in other ways much too long. (Mehta, 1987a, p. 237)

The eating of an egg in the morning, a seemingly trivial act, epitomized Ved's feelings of estrangement and loss. Daddyji had made special arrangements (which he paid for) for Ved to eat with Mr. Ras Mohun and his wife in their upstairs apartment apart from the "poor" boys who ate as a group downstairs. Newly arrived, Ved was served an egg for breakfast.

> At breakfast... Mrs. Ras Mohun put my chair next to her... tied a bib around my neck, and showed me how to eat a

soft boiled egg by myself with a spoon. I tried to get her to spread the egg on the toast, as Mamaji did at home.

"That's how jungly boys eat," Mrs. Ras Mohun said. "You must learn to eat your egg from its shell with a spoon."

I let go of the spoon and got soft boiled egg on the tablecloth and my bib. "Only naughty boys throw their eggs around," Mrs. Ras Mohun said. (Mehta, 1987b, p. 11)

It is understandable that the pain and trauma of feeling "abandoned" by his family may have colored Ved's later memories of the Dadar School. And yet paradoxically, the positive aspects of his experience there derive from what he has written himself.

Perhaps another reason for his later negative attitude toward the Dadar School is related to humiliation that he had attended a school for poor, orphaned, and blind children—he did not want to be defined by his association with this population. At the end of *Dark Harbor* (2003), Ved describes his happy married life on Isleboro, but "that did not stop me from wondering how it was that I ever found myself at the table of the Dark Harbor rich, for whenever I visited India and a beggar approached me... I would weep inside... 'There but for the grace of God go I'" (p. 272). This made Ved "all the more determined to avoid their fate, to erase the traces of Dadar School—to defy the accepted notion that the blind must keep to their pitiful place in a world that is organized and run by the sighted" (p. 272). Ved seemed ashamed of having attended the Dadar School. In India, where caste is so important, to be blind automatically lowers one's social status; to have lived in a poor orphanage lowers it even more. Daddyji advised Ved, before leaving for the Arkansas school, to marry a "Western girl, a nice Christian girl"; in India, Ved could not marry "in our caste group and education group.... Because of your blindness, no parents in our education group would give their girl to you" (Mehta, 1987a, p. 24).

The partition of India occurred in 1947, during the period when Ved lived at home, between his attending the Dadar and Arkansas schools. Ved and his family were caught in the middle of this conflict, as they were Hindu and lived in Lahore, which had now become part of Pakistan. Ved describes the terror, the violence and bloodshed, and the hordes of refugees. "Hindu property was as good as gone" (Mehta, 1984, p. 391). Babuji and Bhaji Ganga Ram were threatened with murder if they did not leave their home. "It was only after we started living in Erneston that we began to understand what the loss of Lahore meant to us. Like all Lahore Hindus, we had lost our property to Pakistan—our life savings and the house Daddyji built" (p. 403). The family's lifestyle and finances changed dramatically after this.

Arkansas School for the Blind

Being back at home was a conflictual experience for Ved: He was happy to be with his family, but there was no school he could attend and no educational or social outlets, although he did learn to ride a bicycle. He wanted to go to school in the United States, but he was rejected by all the schools for the blind he applied to on the basis that it would be too difficult adjusting to the culture. Finally, he received a letter of acceptance from the Arkansas School for the Blind. Ved, then 15, left Lahore for Arkansas.

This state school was not well funded, but Mr. Wooley, its principal, was a dedicated educator and welcomed Ved as a student. Mr. Wooley was understanding and accommodating toward Ved throughout his three-year stay there. Ved had problems initially adapting to the school and its students, struggling as always with his feelings of inadequacy and social discomfort. However, he became absorbed into the student body, was well liked, and was elected president of the student council. He and another student, Oather, became close friends. Ved's conflicts about his blindness continued: He would not accept it nor the limited future that lay in store for his friends at school, content to be piano tuners. He alone had college aspirations.

Mr. Chiles, one of Ved's favorite teachers, taught history and a class in social adjustment. He stated that:

> "Most sighted people shy away from handicapped people.... They are frightened off by anyone who is not like them, so you have to make an extra effort to make them feel that it's worth their while to get to know you.... If you don't prove your worth to the sighted, you will live lonely, miserable lives, without sighted friends, without work, without a useful place in society." (Mehta, 1987a, p. 136)

Ved thought about what Mr. Chiles had said regarding blind people and their differences:

> That remark gave me pause. If difference is what puts sighted people off us... then my blind fellow-students, in turn, must be put off by me. In some way I'd always known that, and... I had taken care to seem like everyone else at the school, and kept my different Indian background a dark secret, instinctively realizing that it would get in the way of my acceptance.... And my wish to win acceptance...

was so strong that to me, often, everything in my background seemed inferior, everything in the backgrounds of the other students superior. (Mehta, 1987a, pp. 136-137)

In fact, Ved found that his being Indian was seen positively. He became a valued speaker to organizations and schools, giving talks about India, and was featured in several newspaper articles in Little Rock. In his journal from that time, he wrote: "Today I gave a talk to an outstanding school in Little Rock. I spoke to the sixth grade class [about India] for twenty minutes successfully and was asked many brilliant questions" (Mehta, 1987a, p. 123).

Ved kept a journal while at school. He typed it himself, which meant he did not have to dictate it first to a reader—he never thought it would be read by anyone. "Typing the journal was for me like talking to my pillow, which could neither remember or repeat one syllable" (Mehta, 1987a, p. 115). Thirty years later, as he looked at old journal entries for his book, he found himself reluctant to know what they said, as well as to let those who read for him know, to confront "what I dimly remembered as my embarrassing adolescent self" (p. 115).

Having readers was a vital matter for Ved: He needed them to read books, review the papers he wrote, and know what was in his correspondence. One kindly school administrator read his letters to him; this meant that whatever he wrote or received was filtered through the eyes of someone else. He appreciated her neutrality when she read, not commenting or judging. One embarrassing exception was a letter he received from Daddyji discussing sex, emphasizing the importance of celibacy. His reader "bit the bullet," making no comments, but Ved was aware that she was reading faster than usual.

Ved Mehta has needed readers and an amanuensis throughout his writing life.

Having money to pay for readers in college was a weighty consideration. Later, in college, when he was writing an early autobiography, his amanuensis was a young woman with whom he was in love. He hoped that hearing his life story would arouse similar feelings in her; this did not happen.

Dating and sexuality were important and conflictual problems for him. The school encouraged dating. Ved struggled with his discomfort but did have some dates. An older male cousin visited him and encouraged him to date because it was part of American culture. When Ved wrote to his father about this, the response was the letter about celibacy—this did not help. "I wish I had someone around whom I could trust with all my confidences" (Mehta, 1987a, p. 236). This is one of the times where Ved might have benefited from supportive counseling. Ved dated in college but had to overcome much discomfort; his difficult relationships with women is what brought him to analysis.

The school held classes in mobility. Ved was initially excited—he felt this would open the door to ability to travel in Little Rock and elsewhere. However, when it came to using a cane, he was resistant and angry: This would call attention to his blindness; he deliberately broke his cane in half. He often felt humiliated and insulted by prejudicial comments sighted people made about his blindness. One of his classmates expressed the sentiment well: " 'We don't give a damn about being blind, but to be blind among people who have eyes, that's what's hell' " (Mehta, 1987a, p. 164). Ved commented that "for the first time, I had an inkling of why so many . . . students talked . . . of go[ing] straight from the school to a sheltered workshop, and pass the rest of their days among their own kind" (p. 165).

In India, Ved was aware of his limited opportunities for school, work, and marriage because of his blindness. In the United States, it was primarily the condescending attitudes of sighted people that he found hurtful. For example, once when waiting to cross a street, with the light in his favor, he waited for the green light to reappear. A man, nearby, told Ved that he had a green light; when he said he knew, the man asked, " 'Why didn't you walk then? Do you need a hand?' When Ved said he would wait for the next light, the man said "in annoyance, 'I won't help *your* kind again!' " (Mehta, 1987a, p. 167).

One night, Ved heard a radio broadcast ending "Good night and good luck," Edward R. Murrow's sign-off of his World War II broadcasts. He was drawn to Murrow, and although he was unable to listen every night, he made it a habit to listen to him Friday nights. Ved had asked Mr. Wooley whether there was any room available for him to write and listen to the radio; Mr. Wooley said there was no extra space. Finally, an empty broom closet was found for him. This was now Ved's space. He learned how to tape-record and then could tape all of Murrow's talks:

> Murrow came to fill a vacuum in my life in Arkansas which I hadn't realized existed until I started listening to him. I came to hear in his broadcasts echoes of servants and neighbors, family and friends of my childhood discussing the crash and bang of the world war, the rumble and tumble of the British Empire.... I realized ... I had been—except for Mr. Chiles's world history class—cut off from world events.... Now ... instead of thinking about my own problems and my own failure, I came to believe that Murrow's ... comments ... were a perfect way to describe the world. I came to honor and venerate him....

After listening to him, I would sit in my broom closet…
wondering how I could become another Murrow. (Mehta,
1987a, p. 289)

Ved missed his family and stayed connected with them through
letters and memories. In one journal he wrote:

Lois cleared her throat [in] English class today. I thought
of Mamajee's *[sic]* cough. Then I heard Mamajee clicking
the knitting needles as she hummed to herself. I heard the
scraping sound of Daddyjee's *[sic]* pumps on the bare floor
as he worked his feet into them. There were raindrops on
the tin roof of our Simla cottage and the hiss and rattle as
the coals finally caught fire in the fireplace. (Mehta, 1987a,
p. 117)

In another journal, he wrote: "I got a record from home that the
family had had specially made by going to a studio. I was able to
hear everyone's voice for the first time in seven months. I couldn't
control my tears" (Mehta, 1987a, p. 128). Ved was usually depressed
when alone, as when everyone went home during school vacations.
"I was afraid that as soon as I was alone the ghosts and apparitions
of my childhood would arrive in the night, along with the haunting,
nettling dreams" (Mehta, 1987a, p. 177). Dreading a lonely upcoming
summer, he proactively made the decision to speak to Mr. Wooley
about working, and a job was obtained in an ice cream plant. He
also found his way to the Boys' Club and developed some warm
relationships there.

Ved did very well academically. At graduation his friend Oather was valedictorian, and Ved was the salutatorian. He reflected on graduating:

> The three years of my life I had spent in Little Rock became sealed in a compartment in my mind which I dread to open, not so much because... they had been unhappy... [but] the near-total submersion in a residential school... seemed to accentuate my blindness, when all along my aspiration had been to be a well-adjusted member of the seeing society outside. (Mehta, 1987a, p. 428)

Reconstructing his life in the process of writing these autobiographies helped Ved undo his "sealing" of his memories in "compartments."

Psychoanalysis

Ved went on to Pomona College in California and then to Oxford University, doing well but bringing with him his conflicts about blindness. He became a successful writer for the *New Yorker,* but his romantic life was not successful, causing him increasing distress. His final breakup with one woman was traumatic, leading to feelings of depression and thoughts of suicide. This motivated him to seek psychoanalysis, which he "hated" but nevertheless pursued.

He did not want to talk to his analyst about his childhood because of his painful memories and was concerned analysis might diminish his ability to write. Writing, he felt, was fueled by his "deprivation and discontent" (Mehta, 2001, p. 276). He finally concluded that this "might be the only way for me to attain my goal of getting married and having children" (p. 276).

His therapist, Dr. Bak, and Ved discussed his fear of authority figures. "Yet the odd thing is that most of them have been very kind to me, and when they are, I become very slavish in my devotion" (Mehta, 2001, p. 281). He spoke of his love for William Shawn, his editor at the *New Yorker*. This led to a discussion of his father: "although my father had a great influence on me, we saw very little of him when we were growing up. Most of the time he was at his club. . . . My sister Umi used to say that we grew up with a great hunger for a father" (p. 281).

The most dramatic breakthrough of his analysis was precipitated by an accident. One day when Mehta arrived at a session, the office door was unexpectedly half open. He hit his forehead on the door's edge; it started bleeding and swelling, but like a "good patient," he went straight to the couch. Feeling that Bak should respond to his distress, he said, "Didn't you see that I hurt myself?" (Mehta, 2001, p. 279). Bak did not say anything, and the discussion turned to Ved's upset feelings about finding that Bak's previous patient was someone he knew. The physical pain increased, but he did not want to "touch [his forehead] because I was ashamed of it. Still, I found myself calling attention to it. 'How can you be so unconcerned? . . . *Don't you know I'm blind?'* (Mehta, 2001, p. 276).

Although Ved had been seeing Bak for some time, the subject of blindness had never come up before; this now led to further exploration and insight. They discussed other related issues such as feeling like "damaged goods" (Mehta, 2001, p. 298) and his deep fear of abandonment and dependency.

Ved's relationship with his mother was also discussed. He became aware that he had been putting her down, deprecating her lack of education and not looking at her positive influence on him. Bak "made me see that there had been a very strong bond between my mother and me when I was a baby, a bond that helped me pull through certain traumas. . . . Bak ascribed my generally optimistic outlook to that bond" (Mehta, 2001, p. 335).

Mehta was in analysis with Bak for four years. He felt that "whatever the pros and cons of analysis, it was thanks to Bak that I learned to face the fact of my blindness squarely and never shrink from discussing it with anyone I wanted to be close to" (Mehta, 2001, p. 344). Mehta also felt that through the "telling and retelling" of his "painful experiences," he "was able to integrate them into the core of my being" (pp. 344-345). "Whatever the reason, I kept everything to myself. . . . But my silence had come at the cost of years of loneliness. . . . What I had considered embarrassing and shameful was instead common human experience" (p. 137).

A joint paper I wrote with Barbara Ceconi on child therapy with a blind clinician serves as a further example of autobiographical as well biographical exploration of an aspect of life. In this partnership, Barbara was the autobiographer and I the biographer. In the process, she was interacting with herself as author and subject, as Mehta was with himself. The tasks of writing such a paper in part mirror those of biography in general. On Barbara's side, it involved articulating a range of experiences, problems, and solutions.

Barbara was a master's in social work student who had become totally blind, as a result of juvenile diabetes, while a second-year student at Amherst College (Ceconi & Urdang, 1994). This was overwhelming: " 'I was mourning the loss of my eyesight. My mood shifted at breakneck speed between anger, depression, fear, and isolation' "; with the help of her family, Barbara came to an "acceptance of herself as a person who is blind" (p. 181). As her comfort increased,

"'I became more adept at making people feel at ease with it'" (p. 181). Unlike Ved, who suffered for many years denying his blindness, Barbara was open in discussing this with others; in fact, she had spoken publicly about blindness to school children, medical students, and doctors. She saw doing so as "part of my coping process" (p. 182).

In her second year of graduate school, Barbara wanted a placement doing play therapy with children. As her faculty advisor at the time, I was intrigued with this possibility, and we decided to write a paper together about both the potentialities and problems in doing this. That Barbara was so open about discussing her blindness directly with clients was a major asset.

In some instances, she turned limitations about her sight into opportunities.

Because, for example, she could not see the children's pictures, she would ask them to describe them, which often extended the therapeutic dialogue. When Sally, a child client, would dress up and want to be admired by Barbara, Sally would first have to describe to Barbara what she looked like:

> Paradoxically, in order to be admired, she first had to admire herself, so that she could share with Barbara the visual impression she was making. In this context, the self-admiration could be perceived as "giving and sharing." Perhaps this acceptable (and "necessary" ...) method added a dimension of taking pleasure in her appearance that was more socially acceptable, than if the observer "could see for herself." (Ceconi & Urdang, 1994, p. 191)

Ved could not "imagine what my life would have been like without analysis"; he also found that he then could write in a different way about himself, "exploring interior worlds previously inaccessible to me" (Mehta, 2001, p. 345). Therefore, feeling there were issues that he wanted to explore further, he chose to write this series of auto-biographies.

About 14 years after his analysis, he fell in love with Linn, about 20 years his junior, whom he had known since she was 11—he was a family friend and for years had an avuncular relationship with her. He later became conscious of Linn as a young, beautiful woman. When he was 49, they fell in love and married.

Ved had been deeply invested in building a house at Dark Harbor on Isleboro Island in Maine. He was totally involved in every aspect of design and building. All the building details as well as his anxieties, but mostly his exuberance about this project, are shared with the reader in *Dark Harbor* (Mehta, 2003).

After Linn and Ved married and had two daughters, the family would vacation at Dark Harbor each summer, and they became part of the community. Ved loved the informality of children running back and forth to each other's homes, which made him think of the hospitality he felt in India. He had never felt that he "belong[ed] anywhere." Now in Dark Harbor, not only had he achieved his objective of having his own family, but with the warm friendships with other islanders, he felt that "they had become our surrogate family." He was now part of a special community (Mehta, 2001, p. 268).

Ved Mehta refused to let his blindness dictate his life course. His fierce determination motivated him to overcome his visual limitations and succeed in the sighted world. The intensity of his denial of his blindness often resulted in anxiety, loneliness, and shutting himself off from others. His psychoanalysis freed him from his self-created "imprisonment" and led to warmer and more open relationships (Mehta, 2001). The therapeutic relationship helped him gain confidence, face his blindness, and examine his life. From a narrative perspective, the *"telling and retelling"* of his story led to emotional growth and happiness (Mehta, 2001).

Ved's story also illustrates the power of his imagination and creative abilities.

The image of Ved sitting in his special closet at the Arkansas School, listening to Edward R. Murrow, and dreaming of being a journalist is unforgettable. Although sometimes struggling with relationships, he did have friendships—there were many adults and peers who cared about him, and he had excellent "recruitment" capacities. His autobiographical exploration and sharing of his feelings about his loss of vision and his fight not to be confined and "stereotyped" offers readers insight into the vicissitudes of blindness.

SECTION II

CONSTRUCTING BIOGRAPHY

CHAPTER 5

Theoretical Orientation: The Biopsychosocial Framework and the Life Course Perspective

Biographical writings provide a unique opportunity to study the portraits of individual personalities, to reflect on how they change (or remain the same) and the ways their vulnerabilities and strengths interrelate. We can watch relationships develop and grow (or deteriorate), uncover themes and ideologies that motivate lives, and learn how will, self-direction, and creativity play out in the life course. We can witness how inner (psychological) and outer (social) worlds are woven together into the tapestry of a person's life. According to Brooks (1984), Rousseau observed that "to understand his characters one must know them both young and old, and know them through the process of aging and change that lies in between" (p. 21).

There have been few formal longitudinal research studies of the life course. Life span studies present numerous technical obstacles, including their cost. Although the biographical quest has its imperfections, this pursuit is readily available and offers the opportunity to become acquainted with many lives amid a panorama of diverse social milieus and historical events. *Bios* is derived from Greek, and one of its meanings is " 'lifetime' or 'the course of a life' " (Olney, 1998, p. 410).

Some people who experience early stability and show "promising" beginnings decline into nonproductive, unsatisfying, and unhappy adulthoods. Others, enduring early loss and trauma, evolve into creative and resilient adults, overcoming pain and deprivation in unique ways. Their adaptations may repair earlier emotional scars, setting in motion self-righting tendencies that further their own personal growth. Life is not a black or white picture of success or failure, happiness or emotional pain. The road to a "happy life" is not without its detours or downward turns. And sadly, external success and relationships that seem stable do not always bring happiness (or remain stable) and may not forestall increasing despair and depression.

If a person becomes resilient in some respects, does this remain a permanent state, or can this strength be "shattered" or overwhelmed under certain conditions?

How solid is the basic core of identity, how "shatter-proof"? To what degree is an underlying fragility held together by special social supports?

In looking for answers to these questions through biographies, we must take into account the author's theoretical framework. Is this theoretical model made explicit? Even when it is not explicit, authors use theoretical constructs in deciding which materials and perspectives to include in their presentation. Biographers are always making choices, as Backscheider (1999) reminded us.

Does the biographer accept and incorporate the concept of an inner world, including unconscious and subconscious processes, or does the biographer prefer to view social and cultural influences as paramount? "The degree to which we believe the unconscious and the subconscious [are] influential and the weight we give cultural versus personal experiences in our everyday lives is translated into perimeters bounding our presentation and interpretation of our subjects" (Backscheider, 1999, p. 101).

> The biographer who believes strongly in the unconscious will look for themes, for repeated metaphors in speech and writing, for patterns that seem to reveal this deep, inner life, while others will just as confidently assign these themes and metaphors to a sense of nationhood, to the influence of a parent, or to the subject's self-conscious attempts to present himself as, for instance, the ideal man to be governor of New York. (Backscheider, 1999, p. 101)

Some biographers use a single theory to explain their subject's development.

For example, one might say that a subject's artistic productions were related to a need to overcompensate for feelings of inferiority or that a subject's writing results from anger at the social oppression of women. However, people and their lives "take so many trajectories, exhibit 'development' or 'regression' in so many ways, and assume (probably not attain) coherence in so many ways that no developmental or personality theory will ever be adequate to the larger purposes of biography" (Backscheider, 1999, p. 122). Today, psychobiography "is intrinsically interdisciplinary" (K. Isaacson, 2005, p. 110), which implies it is open to multiple theories and perspectives.

In the present book, a comprehensive biopsychosocial framework is used to examine biographies of particular individuals in the chapters devoted to them. This synthesizing model interweaves both inner and outer worlds and encompasses psychological development; biological features, physical and mental health issues, as well as interpersonal relationships; and environmental, cultural, and social factors. Emphasis within this framework is given to psychodynamic theory, which incorporates psychoanalytic, ego psychology, object relations (including attachment theory), and self-psychology theories, as these theories concern the vital, dynamic inner life as well as identity development, all critical in individuals' life choices, emotional states, and relationships.

In more recent years, postmodern thought has influenced social work, psychology, and many other disciplines. It challenges the "search for scientific truths, the quests for certainty, objectivity and rationality" (Ornstein & Ganzer, 2005, p. 566) and claims that knowing is subjective in nature. Its underlying framework is constructivism, which states that "there is no fixed reality, only constructed versions of reality determined by the perspective of the one doing the describing" (DeLaCour, 1996, p. 214). Constructivist thinking has also significantly influenced narrative theory. Both are discussed in chapter 7.

Constructivist ideas are reflected in this book, as I examine the biographer's subjectivity and its involvement in every aspect of the biographical enterprise. The constructivist view of the subjective nature of reality also insists that the biographer attempt to understand the subject's construction of his or own "reality." Nathaniel Hawthorne kept two journals of his life: In one he recorded his daily activities, in the other his inner reflections (Spengemann, 1980). The psychodynamic perspective and the constructivist view together are what bring the biographical subject to life for us, illuminating, as stated by Lichtenberg (1985), " 'the mysteries of the soul' [which] remains the core of what great biography *conveys*" (p. 62).

Life course events and nonevents that illustrate that life is dynamic and fluid are also interwoven within the biopsychosocial framework. Included are concepts of change, transitions, and turning points and the role of human agency—that is, that people have the motivation, will, and power to make decisions and ascribe meanings to life events.

We are fortunate that many serious scholarly biographies and autobiographies exist today, often written from a broad biopsychosocial perspective, including exploration of both psychological complexities and the historical and cultural contexts of lives. We cannot, for example, appreciate Rudyard Kipling's life without understanding the impact of his living in India, his struggles with multiculturalism, and the effect of his Indian experiences on his contemporary readers. "He was never less than aware of his privileged access to worlds of which his audience knew little" (Mishra, 2004, p. 11).

Tomalin (2002), in her biography of Pepys, discusses the interweaving of his inner and outer worlds. Pepys, the famous diarist, lived during a period of great historical turmoil, in 17th-century England. Tomalin (2002) integrated this tumultuous time with Pepys's psychological life; she also credits Pepys himself with an appreciation of this comprehensive perspective. He observed "the complex relations between the inner and outer worlds of a man" (Tomalin, 2002, p. 378). Pepys's life "had its ordeals by sickness, passion, fire, bereavement, imprisonment, false accusation and revolution, and it was played out against the most disturbed years in England's history" (p. 377).

The remainder of this chapter reviews the highlights of the biopsychosocial approach and the life course perspective, which provide the basic model for the analysis of lives.

Biopsychosocial Framework

Psychodynamic Bases

Psychoanalytic theory has given us profound insights into the depths of unconscious mental life and into the power of the emotions. Decisions made and paths taken may often be "dictated by strong emotional forces which do not necessarily flow from logic, and may not even be entirely in our conscious awareness" (Urdang, 2002, p. 3). Donald Winnicott, the well-known British psychoanalyst, characterized his patients' emotional problems as being in "the 'swampy lowlands' of messy, confusing difficulties that elude objectively derived solutions, challenge existing theory, and are characterized by uncertainty, ambiguity, and unpredictability" (Applegate & Bonovitz, 1995, p. 18).

Biographies can provide insight into the "swampy lowlands" of emotions, often illuminating emotional states such as passion, depression, grief, inner conflicts, and self-defeating behaviors. Psychodynamic theories shed light on creativity, love, compassion, and adaptation.

Psychoanalytic theory, including such concepts as drives, affects (emotional states), unconscious mental life, and the importance of the past is discussed in the next section. This is followed by discussions of post-Freudian theories, including ego psychology, with its emphasis on ego functioning and adaptation to the external world; object relations theory, with its emphasis on attachment, loss, the internalization of important relationships, and the development of identity; and self-psychology, with its focus on the development of a cohesive self and self-objects. The postmodern theory of constructivism, incorporating narrative theory, is also discussed, including its focus on individuals' interpretations of reality, their philosophies, and developing perspectives.

Psychoanalytic theory. Backscheider (1999) has observed that both Sigmund Freud and Erik Erikson (the psychoanalyst who introduced the concept of the psychosocial development of the ego over the life cycle) have greatly influenced biographical writings. As noted in chapter 1, "readers as well as biographers share what has been called a national *language of psychology*" [italics added] (p. 114). Many psychoanalytic concepts appear in biographical writings.

Freud made lasting contributions to our understanding of the human psyche, including "concepts and clinical findings relating to the significance of the unconscious, dreams, fantasies, the repetition compulsion (often seen in acting-out behaviors), drives, internal psychological conflict, and past experiences." He also introduced the concept of the defense mechanisms, such as denial, counterphobia, rationalization, somatization, and displacement. People use these mental mechanisms to protect themselves from anxiety-producing memories, situations, and relationships, often in an attempt to resolve complex feelings. For example, it can be argued that Charlotte Brontë displaced her conflictual romantic feelings toward Monsieur Heger by creating a fictional professor in her novel *Villette* and that her angry feelings toward his wife were displaced onto the shrewish head mistress in this book.

Freud expanded our understanding of internalized psychological conflict, in which individuals' drives and wishes are engaged in a struggle with their sense of morality and conscience (the superego). *"Superego guilt,* a concept introduced by Freud, was much earlier described by Shakespeare, who created Hamlet, a character brooding with guilt" (Urdang, 2008, p. 11).

For example, Cohen (1996), the biographer of *Alice in Wonderland* author Lewis Carroll, describes Lewis's intense emotional conflicts, as he was torn between his feelings of sexual attraction to young girls (his impulses) and his punishing conscience (his superego):

> Beneath the bubbles and the froth lived yet another force, however, a brooding guilt. . . .He was a good practicing Christian, but he nevertheless saw himself as a repeated sinner. Stern Victorian that he was, he could never give voice or employ pen and ink to record the nature of his sins, but the painful appeals to God for forgiveness that he confided to his diary reveal a man in spiritual pain for transgressions that surely go beyond ordinary failings like idleness or indolence. Lewis Carroll's strong and virile imagination must also have bred sexual fantasies. His dreams probably reached out beyond what he considered accepted terrain and ventured into dangerous precincts. A severe disciplinarian, he never transgressed propriety or violated innocence. He was ... superhuman, in today's terms, in controlling his impulses during waking hours. But the nights brought troubled thoughts for which he saw himself a miscreant. (Cohen, 1996, p. xxi)

Arthur Conan Doyle struggled with his loyalty to his dying wife in conflict with his intense romantic attachment to Jean Leckie, who subsequently became his second wife. He also suffered with depression after his first wife's death (Booth, 1997).

Peter Brooks (1984), a literary scholar, not a psychoanalyst, discusses Freud's emphasis on the vitality of the past. Brooks is particularly impressed with Freud's emphasis on the patient's "need to repeat, rather than simply remember, the past" (p. 98) and relates the relevance of repetition to literary texts:

> ...repetition is so basic to our experience of literary texts.... Rhyme, alliteration, assonance, meter, refrain, all the mnemonic elements of literature and indeed most of its tropes are in some manner repetitions that take us back in the text, that allow the ear, the eye, the mind to make connections, conscious or unconscious, between different textual moments.... An event gains meaning by its repetition, which is both the recall of an earlier moment and a variation of it. (Brooks, 1984, pp. 99–100)

Another dimension of repetition has been termed "acting out": Seemingly inexplicable or illogical actions may be interpreted as a repetition in action and overt behaviors of core inner conflicts. Brockmeier (2001) highlights the concept of *retrospective teleology*—looking back on one's past but with a new understanding or perspective because "the past of a life becomes ordered in the light of the present" (p. 276). Therefore, by retelling the story of one's past, "new meanings may be attributed to past happenings that were not attributed to them at the time of their occurrence" (Freeman & Brockmeier, 2001, p. 82). This concept has special relevance for the autobiographer but also can apply to subjects reviewing their lives with biographers (and patients discussing their past with clinicians). Retrospective teleology and its relation to narrative theory and memory is discussed in chapter 7.

Some psychobiographers have been criticized for placing exclusive reliance on early childhood experiences while "neglecting later formative processes and influences" (Runyan, 1982, pp. 208–209).

The present book, emphasizing the lifespan perspective in its discussion of the six lives examined here, gives the reader the opportunity to explore both childhood and adulthood influences and to note the ebb and flow of development and transformations over the life span. Attention is given to the development of patterns and themes permeating a subject's life. Readers will be able to reflect on the influences of past experiences and judge for themselves whether these experiences do indeed remain alive and color adult emotional states, relationships, and behaviors.

Post-Freudian ego psychology. Heinz Hartmann (1958), the "father of ego psychology," further developed Freud's concept of the ego by observing its adaptation to the external world rather than focusing exclusively on the ego as mediator of the internal battles of the drives and the superego. Hartmann defined *adaptation* as "primarily a reciprocal relationship between the organism and its environment" (Hartmann, 1958, p. 24). He further suggested the concept of the *"conflict-free ego sphere* for that ensemble of functions which at any given time exert their effects outside the region of mental conflicts" (Hartmann, 1958, pp. 8–9).

Ego functions are key components of psychological *development-cognition,* for example, which includes the ability to think, to make good judgments, to learn (and to read), to remember, and to problem solve. Sir Arthur Conan Doyle, Rudyard Kipling, Ved Mehta, Charlotte Brontë, Frederick Douglass, and Ottilie Assing also possessed creative imaginations, alongside their high levels of intelligence, insight, and verbal skills; these they continued to develop through their own reading, writing, and educational opportunities. Charlotte Brontë learned writing techniques from her teacher, Monsieur Heger in Belgium. Under his influence, she came to accept that inspiration and passion were not sufficient for a writer, that technique was needed, and that "the craft of writing could be worked on and improved.... He made her more aware of the needs of writing for an audience rather than as a personal escape" (Miller, 2001, p. 14).

Outer perception is "concerned with the ability to perceive the world in a realistic manner" (Urdang, 2008, p. 64). Great writers, with their finely honed observational abilities, have developed their perceptual capacities to a considerable degree. Rudyard Kipling was placed at age six in a dismal foster home in England. Coping with this oppressive circumstance dramatically increased his perceptive abilities as he adapted to the rigors of his foster home (Kipling, 1937). His hypervigilance served him as a self-protective warning and defense system.

> Nor was my life an unsuitable preparation for my future, in that it demanded constant wariness, the habit of observation, and attendance on moods and tempers; the noting of discrepancies between speech and action; a certain reserve of demeanour; and automatic suspicion of sudden favours. (Kipling, 1937, p. 17)

Biographical exploration offers insight into ways people have coped and adapted, including the development of competence and mastery, the capacity to deal effectively with life challenges and to experience a sense of accomplishment. Harvard psychologists Gordon W. Allport and Robert White, who researched self-actualization (Maluccio, 1980), stressed the motivational importance of competence, "an important force in human behavior" (p. 285).

For Ved Mehta, competence, mastery, and agency were compelling lifelong forces. Mehta (1987a) was determined not to let his blindness be the controlling factor in his life, as he strove to adapt in the sighted world, achieving a good education and ultimately becoming a staff writer for the *New Yorker*. He was determined not to accept the fate of being a blind weaver of chairs in India or a blind piano tuner in the United States.

Object relations theory. Many psychodynamically oriented thinkers turned their interest to the development of relationships and their paramount role in psychological life. Ronald Fairbairn, a Scottish psychoanalyst who was a major figure in the development of object relations and attachment theory, asserted that "the seeking out and maintaining of an intense emotional bond with another person" is the fundamental motivation in life (Mitchell, 1988, p. 27). Biographical studies regularly focus on the subject's relationships, from early attachment experiences to relationships evolving over life, including loss and separation experiences and the impact of relationships on the formation of identity and self-esteem.

Ways of relating to others, for example, openness to people, or rigid repetition of old relationship patterns can be discerned through life course studies. Repetition, an important theme in psychoanalytic theory (as in the development of transference), is also important in object relations theory, seen in patterns of past relationships repeated in everyday lives. "The child learns a mode of connection . . . and these learned modes are desperately maintained throughout life" (Mitchell, 1988, p. 27). Some modes of connection, though seemingly self-protective, can produce painful isolation and conflict. Linda Hogan (2001), a Native American writer, described herself as a "child who cried, hid, escaped, whose entire energy seemed pulled between a need to disappear from others and a human desire for love" (p. 97).

In another time (the 17th century) and place (Ireland), Jonathan Swift (of *Gulliver's Travels* fame), whose father died before he was born, was abandoned by his mother as a young child and grew up under the tutelage of emotionally unsupportive paternal uncles (Glendinning, 1999). Subsequently, he achieved great fame as a political voice, a bishop, a writer, and a satirist, but he never married and was wary of committed relationships. "His prescribed strategy for emotional survival is flight from all risk of grief, pain or disappointment—at the price of fleeing also from the pleasure and sweetness which make life worth living for most people" (Glendinning, 1999, p. 223).

Object relations theorists stress the importance of early attachment, observing how parental love, caring, and physically holding and soothing the infant become internalized so that the infant develops a trust in the parental (or caretaker's) love, which further develops into a love of self. From these beginnings, the child develops ongoing internalized images of self *(self-representation)* and other *(object representations)*. Relationships with others are influenced by these internalized images. "Early attachment experiences are apparently represented and carried forward, setting conditions for seeking, interpreting, and reacting to later experiences" (Stroufe, Egeland, Carlson, & Collins, 2005, p. 67).

Object relations theory emphasizes the process of identity formation, our sense of not only "who we are, but that we are" (Mahler, Pine, & Bergman, 1975, p. 8). The development of identity, and its vicissitudes, is of great interest to narrative theorists as well and is an important interdisciplinary concept (Brockmeier, 2001). Linda Hogan (2001), who has talked of wishing to "disappear from others" as well as her desperate need for love, has described her depressed mother, who, while physically present, had "disappeared" emotionally into her own inner world. To her daughter she was silent and uninvolved. Hogan observed that she herself in turn "became wordless as a child.... I only wanted *not to exist*" [italics added] (p. 101).

Winnicott (Giovacchini, 1993) described a state of "false self" in which, when children's needs are not met, the "solid self" may not develop, and their energies go toward complying with their caretakers' needs and wishes instead. There is a "continuum of the false self— 'ranging from the healthy, polite aspect of the self to the truly split-off, compliant, false self that is mistaken for the whole person'" (Winnicott, quoted in Giovacchini, 1993, p. 254). Biographical writings present an opportunity to study the development of identity, of the "solid" versus the "false" self.

Parents also transmit to their children attitudes toward life and moral consciousness. Rosa Maria, Ottilie Assing's mother, had intense romantic feelings about poetry, ideals of love, and the "perfect partnership," which became central to Ottilie's life philosophy as well. Depression and anxieties experienced by parents can also be transmitted to a child indirectly, nonverbally; this process has been referred to as *intersubjectivity.* "Although the parents may be silent... this does not impede the transmission of anxiety.... Unexplained silences further intensify the affective, fearful power of children's fantasies" (Brown, 1998, p. 267).

Recruitment capacities (Kegan, 1982) develop in infancy. This is the ability of infants to draw others to themselves: "our survival and development depend on our capacity to recruit the invested attention of others to us." Although "nature is nowhere more graceful than in the way she endows each newborn infant with seductive abilities" (p. 17), the ability and motivation to recruit the attention of others varies with each individual. Rudyard Kipling made active use of his recruitment capacities to build and expand his social relationships. Mowbray Morris, the editor of *Macmillan's Magazine,* "was taken with Rud's lively personal charm, and promptly welcomed him into the Macmillan stable. . . . 'He is a most amusing companion, full of life and fun, very shrewd withal' " (Ricketts, 1999, p. 147).

A related concept is the ability to internalize support from others (Vaillant, 1993). One can be receiving support from others but, for reasons such as insecurity or self-hatred, may not be able to internalize this, deflecting support as a duck sheds water from its back. Linda Hogan (2001), whose "fearful" mother wanted to be "invisible and inaudible," observed that her mother did not have the capacity to absorb new relationships, nor did she develop new perceptions about herself. Her mother's perceptions of others (and consequently her attitudes toward them) were grossly distorted by her inner object representations.

Narrative theorists emphasize interpersonal influences on identity development (Brockmeier, 2001). "Self-making is powerfully affected not only by your own interpretations of yourself but by the interpretations others offer of your version" (Bruner, 2001, p. 34). Harre (2001) stressed that the concept of self includes more than self-identity and describes the "multiplicities of the self," whereby people often represent themselves to others in multiple ways; in addition, one's notions of oneself often change over time (p. 60). Biographies can be a rich source of material regarding the vicissitudes of identity development. Although there are many similarities between object relations theory and narrative theory, there is, nevertheless, a major difference of perspective. Narrative theory differentiates itself from object relations theory in narrative theory's emphasis on the interpersonal realm of communication, the so-called *discursive arena*, rather than object relations theory's focus on the "internal workings of the mind" (Brockmeier & Carbaugh, 2001, p.12). Hogan (2001), for example, not only received her mother's communication about how her mother views her (discursive), but she has also internalized her mother's way of being: "I was the daughter who inherited my mother's pain and her fears. Now I know her only because *I study her from inside myself,* and my own inner world of fear" [italics added] (p. 95).

Also affecting inner security and the quality of relationships is the impact of loss. Loss is a universal happening in all lives. It may occur early or late in a person's life, and sometimes major and profound losses accompany the whole life course, as experienced by Rudyard Kipling, Frederick Douglass, Charlotte Brontë, Conan Doyle, and Ved Mehta. The psychological effects of loss may not show up in a person at the time of loss but may appear later. William Styron's deep depression occurring in late life was related to his unresolved loss of his mother when he was 13. The effects of loss throughout peoples' lives can be traced in their biographies.

Analyzing the quality of the relationship of the bereaved child to the deceased parent, prior to death, as well as the subsequent caretaking arrangements for the child is crucial in understanding the effect of loss on a child. "The quality of relationship with a subsequent caretaker may be more influential in determining the risk for later depression than simply the experience of bereavement itself" (Worden, 1996, p. 106).

Edgar Allan Poe's mother died suddenly when he was three years old; earlier he had lost his father, who had abandoned the family. After his mother's death, Poe was separated from his brother (who went to live with his father) and his sister (who was put in a foster home). He was raised by a wealthy family in Baltimore but never actually adopted. He chose "Allan," the last name of his foster family, as a middle name. His insecure family life was exacerbated by an ongoing difficult relationship with his foster father.

Silverman (1991) suggests that the recurring themes in Poe's fiction about people who are dead but not dead reflect his wish for his mother's return to life and for reunion with her. However, "one can only speculate about what might have happened if Poe had been in a family with a better *goodness-of-fit,* if he had been helped to mourn his loss, if he had not also lost his siblings, and if his biological father had reappeared in his life" (Urdang, 2002, p. 559).

A subject's death receives special prominence in most biographies. In general, readers want to know (and be involved) in the death scene, perhaps just as most people want to know about the death of those important in their own lives. Biographers put much thought and effort into describing the death of their subjects: "there is a great deal invested, always, in the death of the subject, in terms of how the death relates to the life, how the subject behaves at their death, and how, if at all, the death can be interpreted" (Lee, 2005, p. 95).

Backscheider (1999) has observed that "we need the death to measure the life. Not until death (and sometimes not even then) is the life complete, the individual's story closed" (p. 91). Some biographies actually start with the death of the subject. Biographies can enable clinicians vicariously to confront this painful area to which they themselves often respond with avoidance.

Self-psychology. Self-psychology, developed by Heinz Kohut, focuses on the development of identity and the attainment of a cohesive self. One of its major theoretical concepts involves the *self-object*. Self-objects essentially refer to others who meet a person's needs for developing and sustaining a sense of self and self-esteem. The presence of positive self-objects (nurturing parents or parent substitutes) during childhood is critical for the development of a cohesive sense of self; however, self-object experiences are needed throughout adulthood. "Along with food and oxygen, every human being requires age-appropriate *self-object* experiences from infancy to the end of life" (Wolf, 1988, p. 11).

Although self-object needs are necessary and normal throughout life, some people are desperate to have this need met in order to survive emotionally; if the self-object is lost, they can experience a "terrible emotional pain, a sense of nothingness, and, potentially, a dissolution in the structure of the self" (Mack & Hickler, 1981, p. 107). In chapter 3, we could see how Charlotte Brontë suffered from unmet self-object needs, looking and often desperately seeking new self-objects. It can be perplexing for clinicians and biographers to assess whether a person's seemingly good functioning and positive feelings about himself or herself are based on the existence of a cohesive self or, to the contrary, dependent on the ongoing support and approval of self-objects.

Societal Factors

Social factors. People live in a social context, and social conditions, including social supports, family, and other relationships, are key factors examined within the biopsychosocial framework. Family relationships, especially the bond between the parents, can affect children's emotional states, their attachment processes, and their overall social development. Severe tension between couples, including spousal abuse, divorce, and its aftermath, can lead to serious psychological repercussions for all family members. In addition, "the contextual factors of work, social support, and marriage can affect parenting both directly and indirectly (through personality)" (Belsky, 2005, p. 80).

Economic conditions (and conflicts about money), as well as the quality of housing and neighborhoods in which a person resides, can affect a person's sense of well-being. The poverty that Conan Doyle's family lived in, exacerbated by his father's alcoholism and the growing number of children, led to many hardships, including a deterioration in the quality of apartments they could afford to rent and a decline in their social status (Booth, 1997).

Franz Kafka's father, Hermann, who overcame extreme childhood poverty, was driven (probably as a result of his experience) to succeed financially as an adult. "From the very beginning, life in this family... focused not on the home but on the store" (Pawel, 1988, pp. 13-14). Hermann developed his haberdashery store into a "thriving wholesale dry-goods business... [and he] set out to succeed, with single-minded, driving determination that left no room and little time for anything else in his life" (p. 14).

Ecological theory focuses on the "continuous reciprocal exchanges or transactions" between people, with each other, and with their environments. During these transactions, "people and environments influence, shape, and sometimes change each other" (Germain, 1991, pp. 15–16). This theory suggests a fluidity of life, a continual movement of actions, reactions, and change. In terms of examining the life cycle, the concept of *goodness of fit* is a particularly important contribution:

It is defined as the rightness of the match between people and their social environments. Rudyard Kipling was made editor of his boarding school's magazine by his supportive headmaster, a "fit" that helped him increase his confidence as well as develop his writing skills.

Historical and political forces affect individual lives, even though, during periods of quiescence, they appear to recede into the background. Freud, for example, was educated in Vienna and Franz Kafka in Prague, during a period of marked decrease in anti-Semitism. Their school experiences were affected positively by the lessening of social restrictions against Jews: "The world that shaped Freud's vision, the rising Jewish middle class in nineteenth-century Austria, was also the world of the Kafka's" (Pawel, 1988, p. 7).

Ved Mehta's family lived through the bloody civil war in India, in which they lost their home and possessions in Lahore (which became part of Pakistan). Frederick Douglass (McFeely, 1991) was prominent during the American Civil War era, a period of great social and political turmoil. His life was intimately entwined with the abolition movement, the war, and Reconstruction. Not only was he affected by events, but he was an important leader and shaper of events.

Cultural factors. Cultural factors are critical in the biopsychosocial approach. As an example, consider that Kipling was born in India to English parents and experienced the indulgent care of non-English servants throughout his early childhood in India: His *ayah* was a nursemaid of Portuguese Catholic background, and Meeta was his Hindu "bearer" (or caretaker). Kipling spoke Hindustani but was instructed by his ayah and by Meeta to speak English to his parents during his evening visits with them.

After his warm, nurturing, and indulged beginning, Kipling, six, and his three year-old sister, Trix, were sent to a foster home in England for six years and did not see their parents, who remained in India during this entire time. The parents' social-cultural context sheds light on this seemingly incomprehensible act of "abandonment." Their behavior was not deviant in their milieu; it was the "custom" for Anglo-Indian families (that is, British families living in India) to send their children back to England for schooling (although generally the children would be older at the time). Edmonia Hill (1936), a longtime friend of Kipling, offered an interpretation of this custom. As an American living in India with her English husband, her observations about raising children in India were partially "sympathetic" yet subtly critical of the English parental attitude:

> It is next to impossible to bring up English children in India, not because they could not have literary advantages here, but on account of the bad influence the close contact with the native servant has on the child. He is a slave to every whim, so Sonny Baba grows too domineering *to suit the fancy of an English parent.* ... Also, once a chi chi accent—as English contaminated by a native tongue is termed—is acquired, it is rarely lost even after years of later life in England, and *pure speech is an essential, according to an Englishman.* ... The hardest choice a woman must make in India is to decide whether it is best to go home with her children or to stay with her husband. [italics added] (Hill, 1936, p. 414)

Cultural conflicts can loom large in individual lives. As already described in chapter 4, the writer Ved Mehta was born into a Hindu family in India. His father, a physician, was strongly influenced by his English education and affinity for British culture, which affected many of his decisions. Ved grew up amid the strict caste system in India. Although his family was upper caste, he would have been stigmatized by his blindness. His education in the United States exposed him to cultural values different from his own as well as the cultural values of the world of the blind, against which he rebelled. His autobiography "explore[s] the boundaries of time and memory, the clash of culture and self, and the meaning of place and exile—as I have experienced them" (Mehta, 2001, p. 345).

Mary McCarthy, raised as a Catholic, was one quarter Jewish. Her references to her Jewishness and to anti-Semitism are often described with feelings of shame. When attending Vassar College, McCarthy "appears to have been ashamed of both her Jewishness and of being an anti-Semite" (Barbour, 1992, p. 155). However, expressing feelings of shame can itself be distressing as "the admission of shame is a confession of weakness or inadequacy, [and so] a person may become trapped in the misery of shame about shame" (p. 155).

Biological Factors

Biological factors, including genetic endowment, neurobiological development, aging, illness, and disability are basic elements of the biopsychosocial perspective. Ved Mehta developed meningitis at the age of three years eight months, which led to the onset of blindness, which in turn profoundly affected his personality and life course. Chekhov, who died at 44, suffered from tuberculosis (beginning in medical school), an ordeal that shaped his life in many respects: "his efforts to ignore and to cope with disease form the weft of any biography" (Rayfield, 1997, p. xvii).

The social network of one seriously ill person can be affected in major ways, including demands for care, fear of loss, and changes in routines and activities. Conan Doyle's first wife contracted tuberculosis; her 13-year struggle with this illness dramatically altered Doyle's life course and had a major impact on their two children.

Whereas biological factors influence psychological development, psychological stress and conflict can also be expressed through physical symptoms. Rudyard Kipling's early childhood trauma probably contributed to his lifelong insomnia; his eye problems were affected by his emotional states (Ricketts, 1999). The centuries-old controversy of whether the mind and body are separate entities (mind-body dualism) continues into the present. Virginia Woolf observed:

> "Literature does its best to maintain that its concern is with the mind; that the body is a sheet of plain glass through which the soul looks straight and clear." Whereas the truth of the matter is that "all day, all night, the body intervenes; blunts or sharpens, colours or discolors, turns to wax in the warmth of June, hardens to tallow in the murk of February." (Fenton, 2003, p. 45)

Illness, pain, and disability can affect a person's physical and social functioning, sense of well-being, self-image, and identity. Samuel Pepys, the 17th-century London diarist, suffered since childhood with intermittent severe pain from a bladder stone; "the sharp pain of the stone was... part of Sam's life" (Tomalin, 2002, p. 27). When he later attended Cambridge University, there were "days and nights when it flared up and he suffered miserably" (p. 40). Finally, the pain "became too bad to endure," and he saw surgery as the only way out of "a condition of constant and dangerous and most painful sickness" (p. 59). Surgery was risky and extremely painful, without anesthesia of any kind, but this was the course Pepys chose. When the stone was removed, and the monthlong recovery proved successful, "his joy was great" (p. 62). This was a turning point in his life; he observed that without the operation, "he could have expected nothing but sickness and poverty" (p. 63).

Congenital malformations, especially disfiguring ones, can damage a person's self-esteem. "Man has an instinctive loathing for these [malformations] and they tend to cause aversion in fellow-beings and an irrational sense of shame in the victim" (Sandblom, 1982, p. 56). A facial disfigurement originating in her later life traumatized Mary McCarthy's maternal grandmother; because of it, she lived in self-imposed social isolation. Mary initially thought that this isolation was caused by her grief over the death of her daughter (Mary's mother). However, she came to understand that her grandmother's distress was related to the disfigurement resulting from unsuccessful face-lifting surgery.

> "Your grandmother's tragedy"—so I first heard the face lifting alluded to ... by one of my friends, who had heard of it from her mother.... It was a tragedy, for [grandmother], for her husband and family, who, deprived of her beauty through an act of folly, came to live in silence, like a house accursed. (McCarthy, 1957, pp. 240-241)

Some people are preoccupied with their bodily health and illness even when not physically ill (hypochondriasis) or may have distorted views of their body (body dysmorphic disorder; anorexia nervosa). The 20th-century Japanese writer Yukio Mishima, preoccupied with his body and its beauty, was desperate over inevitable bodily decline through aging; this theme in fact figured in his later novels (Scott Stokes, 1974).

The sex drive, a cornerstone of psychoanalytic theory, is biologically based. It is exquisitely sensitive to a person's physical health, psychological state, and interpersonal relationships. Psychological conflict can cause sexual dysfunction. For example, Anton Chekhov was sexually impotent only when relationships with women became emotionally significant and veered toward permanency (Rayfield, 1997).

Illness and disability can disrupt a person's sexual life. When Conan Doyle's wife Louisa became ill with tuberculosis she was prohibited from sexual activity, as dictated by the medical practice of the time. We can only speculate how this affected her. We do know that this caused severe frustration and conflict for her husband (Booth, 1997).

Biographers in the 19th century were generally discreet in discussing the sexual relationships of others, as were autobiographers in discussing their own sexuality. This has not stopped modern biographers from trying to unearth as much about their subject's sexuality as they can. Did Charlotte Brontë have an affair with Monsieur Heger? Was Conan Doyle sexually intimate with his second wife-to-be during the long illness of his first wife? Ironically, Freud's apparent assignations with his sister-in-law also have excited the interest of biographers.

Psychobiography has been criticized for its emphasis on psychopathology; however, dismissing psychopathology altogether can limit understanding. Psychopathology, that is, disturbances in thinking and feeling, is experienced by all of us in various degrees throughout our lives. The line between "normal" emotional states and "pathological" conditions is not always easy to draw. Feelings of depression and anxiety, for example, are universally experienced and may range from transient states to fairly persistent and disabling conditions. Backscheider (1999), a biographer, supports the need for clinical understanding by biographers:

> Knowledge of clinical psychiatry can be extremely helpful. By being aware of the differences among personality disorders, clinical syndromes, and adjustment reactions, the biographer has an advantage in recognizing themes and lifelong, unifying tendencies and traits and in interpreting the effects of events on the subject and understanding underlying motives. (Backscheider, 1999, p. 116)

Many biographical subjects suffer (or have suffered) from severe, chronic, debilitating conditions, such as schizophrenia, bipolar disorders, and substance abuse, that often dominate their lives and relationships. Some subjects may be affected by their families or friends suffering from these problems. Frank McCourt (1996) was anguished as a child over his father's serious drinking; Conan Doyle (Booth, 1997) also suffered psychologically in relation to his father's alcoholism and subsequent mental illness; Kipling's sister Trix suffered major mental illness as an adult with serious consequences for her family (Flanders, 2001); and Charlotte Brontë's brother Branwell's drug and alcohol addictions caused great distress to his family (Fraser, 1988).

Graham Greene referred to the reparative function of creativity: " 'Writing is a form of therapy; sometimes I wonder how all those who do not write, compose or paint can manage to escape the madness, the melancholia, the panic fear which is inherent in the human situation' " (quoted in Sandblom, 1982, pp. 44-45).

Some writers present psychological problems as their primary focus, another form of a quest narrative. These vivid, insightful accounts contribute to a deeper experiential understanding of the troubled world of mental illness.

The concept of vulnerability contributes to understanding psychopathology; it is concerned with causality and "the processes that place people at risk" (Ingram & Price, 2001, p. ix). Not every biographical subject is as open and expressive in revealing vulnerability as Hogan (2001) has been. Conan Doyle felt that "there are some things which one feels too intimately to be able to express" (Stashower, 1999, p. 206). Exploring vulnerability that is apparent as well as vulnerability that is hidden can be a rewarding challenge for the reader of biographies.

Vulnerability coexists with strengths, and biographies can shed light on a person's ability to overcome, greatly modify, or succumb to disturbing emotional states. Life circumstances such as positive relationships, ego-enhancing experiences, and psychotherapy may provide a person with the armamentarium to overcome vulnerability factors, enabling the progressive forces of growth to proceed. However, vulnerability may also increase over time, especially if the person is exposed to the same (or new) stresses and situations. This exposure can include, incidentally, people repeatedly placing themselves in self-destructive and unrewarding situations.

A man may achieve "goodness of fit" in a supportive marital relationship that helps mitigate the wounds of early maternal abandonment, and for a period of time he may be less vulnerable to stress. However, if that relationship should break down, perhaps through death or desertion, the vulnerability to abandonment may come to the fore, and psychological breakdown may occur. Edgar Allan Poe married his 13-year-old cousin, Virginia, when he was 30, and lived with her and her mother in a very compatible relationship. However, Virginia contracted tuberculosis and died at 24, the age at which his mother died. Poe, in the wake of this, was overwhelmed, unable to resolve his grief by working it through. His life became disordered.

He had unstable relationships with a number of women at the same time, and his drinking became uncontrolled. He died at the age of 40. His life had been relatively stable during his marriage, but he could not bear his young wife's death and the disintegration of his living arrangements (Silverman, as cited in Urdang, 2008, p. 605).

Poe's unresolved past grief and vulnerability to abandonment led to a breakdown in his functioning. Virginia and her mother served as self-objects for him, enabling him to have a more coherent sense of self. However, this was not enough to build internal structures enabling further growth. Without these self-objects in his life, his inner core was vulnerable to disintegration.

Continued exposure to psychopathological states can itself also increase vulnerability on a neurobiological level. Another aspect of mind-body unity has been called the "kindling" effect (a hypothesis advanced by the neuropsychiatrist Robert M. Post, cited in Ingram & Price, 2001):

> In describing the idea of kindling, Post (1992) has proposed such a process in the area of affective disorders. Post suggests that each episode of an affective disorder leaves a residual neurobiological trace that leads to the development of pathways by which increasingly minimal stress becomes sufficient to activate the mechanisms that result in a disorder. Such a process thus leads to increased vulnerability. (Ingram & Price, 2001, p. 9).

Whether related to biological, environmental, interpersonal, or intrapsychic precipitants, "the locus of vulnerability processes is *within the person*" (Ingram & Price, 2001, p. 10, emphasis added). Even when external stress is involved, the experience is internalized, processed, and experienced by the person. Vulnerability factors are not always directly or immediately observable; "the search for vulnerability markers is thus the search for predictors of the disorder in the absence of symptoms or the disorder" (p. 10). To assess vulnerability and its markers, it is necessary to study individuals over the course of their lives. A life-span perspective becomes essential in assessing vulnerability factors:

> To truly understand vulnerability, theorists and researchers need to adopt a lifespan perspective.... Vulnerability factors, although developed in childhood or adolescence, may nevertheless affect individuals for a lifetime. Understanding the long-term trajectory of these vulnerability factors and their consequences is thus an extremely important quest. (Ingram & Fortier, 2001, p. 52)

The Life Course: Events and Nonevents

The issue of personality change is the subject of major controversy in life-span research: Do individual personalities and identities change or remain the same over the life course? This is often referred to as the problem of *continuous* versus *discontinuous* development (Mortimer, Finch, & Kumka, 1982). There are two important variables to consider in exploring this question: The first is assessing the individual personality itself, including ego functioning, patterns of attachment, and the role of human agency. The second involves assessment of the biological and social factors affecting the individual: health, income, occupation, education, and so forth. In addition, it is important to consider the fluidity of life. As Richard Holmes (1985) discovered following in the footsteps of Robert Louis Stevenson, "life is fluid, not static; people change and their environments and circumstances change" (p. 69).

In examining a life, we need to look at the significant happenings and events in that life. Levinson and Levinson (1996) also gave weight to people's concerns about what does not happen. What Schlossberg (1981) called a "nonevent," Levinson and Levinson refer to as "important *unfilled components:* a person urgently wants but doesn't have a meaningful occupation, a marriage, or a family; and this absent component plays a major part in the life structure" (1996, p. 23). One should also consider the timing of events (that is, how old the person is when an event is occurring, making it "on time" or "off time" in terms of his or her social group) (Hutchinson, 2005). As the individual evolves and advances through life, there can be a fairly smooth progression, a trajectory; there are also transitions and sometimes turning points.

Trajectories and Transitions

A *trajectory* taken by the individual "involves an ongoing, consistent pattern of movement through life.... [It is] the stable component of a direction toward a life destination and is characterized by a given probability of occurrence. A trajectory refers to the tendency to persistence in life-course patterns" (Wheaton & Gotlib, 1997, p. 2).

Transitions are also part of every life course, both from a developmental level (for example, as the infant emerges into the toddler) and from a psychosocial level (as when the adolescent moves away from home and the elderly person adapts to a world of diminished opportunity). Although childhood influences are powerful, later life experiences can substantially influence personality and relationships: "developmentally consequential transitions can and do occur in the adult years" (McAdams, Josselson, & Lieblich, 2001, p. xv). Not every transition has great emotional impact in life. However, some transitions are turning points, events of special meaning and importance to the individual.

Turning Points

Turning points are "turns in the road, changes in the direction or the trajectory of our lives" (McAdams et al., 2001, p. xv). These can be experienced in positive or negative ways, and "sometimes what is experienced initially as tragedy or loss is later emplotted as epiphany or insight leading to growth" (McAdams et al., 2001, p. xvii). While he was in prison, Oscar Wilde wrote *De Profundis,* a conversion narrative in which he described imprisonment as a turning point in his life, observing his "epiphany in prison, a self-realization in which he sees, for the first time, into his true nature" (Schultz, 2001, p. 68). Wilde spoke of the "the curative value of suffering," a phenomenon worth observing in the study of lives. Wilde's turning point is discussed further in chapter 9.

Defining turning points in a given life can be a challenge, both for the biographer (or autobiographer) and the subject. For example, people may be unaware they are going through a turning point when it is occurring. In fact, this is considered by some to be one of its conditions: "they are only recognized to be turning points as time passes and as it becomes clear that there has been a change in direction" (Wheaton & Gotlib, 1997, p. 1). However, is it not possible for people to experience turning points without ever being aware of an event's impact on them? If Oscar Wilde had no introspective capacities, should his prison experience be disregarded as a transformative turning point in his life? Is there ancillary evidence to suggest otherwise? There are other instances, such as the denial of a death or a disability, where no cognitive "meaning making" of the event occurs but in which the emotional consequences can be profound.

Questions have been raised about the durability of a turning point: If a person declares himself or herself changed, has this change endured? According to Schultz (2001), if durability is not present and "if the turning point produces no lasting behavioral outcome, then [a turning point] probably did not happen" (p. 83). However, Schultz (2001) adds, there needs to be room for relapses: "Life is complex. There will be slippage. Even when change is relatively modest or fitful, the turning point concept may apply. It seems important to acknowledge that some turns might be more momentous than others, more sustaining" (p. 87).

Turning points are considered in a broad sense in this book, meaning any event that sets in motion some disruption in the normal chain of events and provides new opportunities and/or a new direction (which can be positive or disastrous). These events have a psychological impact (even if a person is unaware of this). They can be externally triggered (such as being drafted or being laid off from work) or internally triggered (as in deciding to get married or to emigrate). Although most definitions of turning points highlight individual agency, they nevertheless can occur without the input or even the actual presence of the subject, yet still deeply affect the subject's life course.

Conclusion

The biopsychosocial framework guides us in studying lives and appreciating their complexity, as we observe the interweaving of the inner and outer worlds. We also need to be aware that lives are fluid and always in motion. Cohler and Galatzer Levy, cited in Urdang, 2002, took the view that "people change, and personalities are not 'fixed' in permanent patterns; life events (including unpredictable events) play a critical part in personality development" (Urdang, p. 394). However, although personalities may not be "fixed" in permanent patterns, does this mean that no patterns of behavior or attachment are to be found in individuals?

Backscheider (1999) has observed that the question of personality change over time has been "among the most interesting recent developments in biography" and has noted that biographical study can "contribute to our understanding of how changes occur" (p. 116). The biographical presentations in the present book will give the reader an opportunity to reflect on this question.

In the next chapter, we shall look at the life of Arthur Conan Doyle, whose radical shift in midlife to spiritualism and belief in the existence of fairies raised many eyebrows. But determining whether this was a continuous or a discontinuous development for him is not a simple matter.

CHAPTER 6

The Life of Sir Arthur Conan Doyle Viewed through the Biopsychosocial Framework

Arthur Conan Doyle, best known for his creation of Sherlock Holmes, the charismatic and world-famous detective, was a man of intellect and science as was Holmes. Unlike Holmes, Conan Doyle had a warm, generous, gregarious personality. He was well loved by people close to him as well as by the public at large.

Born May 22, 1859, Conan Doyle grew up in obscure, genteel poverty in Edinburgh. He suffered the economic and psychological effects of his father's alcoholism but, with his mother's emotional support, marshaled his considerable intelligence, imagination, and ambition to achieve artistic mastery and great acclaim. Conan Doyle "was a paradoxical character, an enigma, sometimes complex, at others naive and simplistic. He was also dictatorial, doggedly stubborn, rejected all criticism and would never admit he was wrong about anything" (Booth, 1997, p. x).

Conan Doyle resented Sherlock Holmes for overshadowing his other writings, especially his historical novels, which he considered more scholarly and significant. More than once, he attempted (unsuccessfully) to have Holmes murdered, and when he was finally successful, he succumbed to worldwide outrage over Holmes's death and resurrected him.

Conan Doyle was also a physician, athlete, politician, historian, and crusader. His life was a storybook of adventures, and although living out childhood dreams, for most of his life he was a realist—a physician involved in scientific pursuits, scholarship, and political problems, including advocacy for divorce reform. His "crusades" generally championed the downtrodden and promoted justice. During the years he practiced medicine, he was considered a very competent and compassionate doctor.

Those who knew him or followed his life were baffled to find him in his later years committed to the world of the occult, having conversations with dead souls, admiring mediums, believing in fairies, and contributing large sums of money to support these beliefs. His immortality would now come, he felt, by spreading the true message of spiritualism to the world. Does this radical shift in perspective and focus represent a "discontinuity" in his identity and life course, or are there underlying threads and patterns that form a "continuity"?

As we trace Conan Doyle's life, we are struck by his astonishing vitality, exuberance, and optimism. Why he became a writer is not a mystery, but other puzzles remain: He engaged in risky behaviors that at times nearly cost him his life. And how did this scholarly man become involved in the world of fairies and spirits? Surely, Sherlock Holmes would have talked some sense into him.

Following the biopsychosocial framework, we shall examine Conan Doyle's life from his humble beginnings, through worldwide acclaim, to his decline into the labyrinths of the occult (which he viewed as a progression to the highest level of existence). Attachment to his loyal mother, a conflictual relationship with his father, and childhood loss and separation were major underpinnings of his psychological life. Rejection of weakness and the possibility of failing as his father had and overcoming shame were major forces igniting his ambition. His many strengths included great intellect, creativity, self-agency, resilience, and an ability to attract (or recruit) other people to him and to maintain relationships. Influenced by his mother's teachings, he developed a strong moral code, involving chivalry and honor, which permeated his life and writings.

Social and historical forces were prominent in his life. He was both a product of and an important influence on the Victorian and Edwardian societies of his time. His drive for adventure and his crusading spirit were colored by this period, when "value was placed on the dramatic gesture, the romance of insurmountable odds, and the heroic sacrifice to a cause" (Rodin & Key, 1984, p. 84). Society's strong social stigma against alcoholism and mental illness contributed to his feelings of shame regarding his father. That his schooling was under Catholic auspices was decisive in his losing his first race for Parliament. More to his advantage, his involvement in the Boer War and advocacy for its continuation led to his knighthood.

Family Background

Conan Doyle's relationship with his strong, supportive, dynamic (and oft-times controlling) mother, Mary, was both sustaining and character forming. His attachment to her remained strong throughout his life, waning only at the end because of her opposition to his immersion in spiritualism. Mary's own sense of agency, willpower, and adaptation also served as a role model for him. Living in poor (and declining) circumstances in Edinburgh, surrounded by her many young children, and watching her husband descend into alcoholism and mental illness, Mary herself could well have descended into depression, but she did not. She was an "intelligent, imaginative, charismatic and practical" woman who was also "bubbly and gay" (Booth, 1997, p. 10).

Conan Doyle's father, Charles, was a prominent influence in Arthur's life, although Arthur referred to him infrequently in his autobiographical writings. Charles, an artist himself, tended to be withdrawn: "he was serious, sometimes moody and pensive" (Booth, 1997, p. 10). As Arthur internalized his mother's characteristics and values, he rejected and fought within himself against his father's characteristics. His ambition was stirred by a determination to be different from his father, thus complying with a message undoubtedly communicated by his mother. He learned "never to whinge at his lot as, no doubt, she suggested—and Arthur realised—his father did" (Booth, 1997, p. 12). His father, melancholic and low in self-esteem, could not deal with the increasing stresses in his life and retreated into alcohol.

Charles and Mary came from families of a higher social class, whose financial standing and cultural advantages were greater than the circumstances in which they lived as a couple. Charles was a tragic figure, whose social decline from his beginnings was even greater than was Mary's, as his family was socially and artistically prominent. He was to become estranged from his wife and children, whom he loved, and ultimately placed in a psychiatric hospital, as discussed later in this chapter. "He died a lonely and pathetic man, heartsick for his family and believing himself to have been unjustly confined" (Stashower, 1999, p. 153).

Mary's father was a doctor who died when she was a young child, but Mary's competent, strong-willed mother supported her two daughters and sent Mary to a Catholic boarding school in France. Mary Doyle taught Arthur about his family's heraldic background and inspired him to develop a sense of chivalry and honor. Mary, herself a book lover, encouraged Arthur's love of reading. Son and mother were united in their love for each other, in their belief in their distinguished past, and in their hope for a more "glorious" future. As they steeped themselves in heraldry and read together, their tenement apartments in Edinburgh, their struggles against poverty, the ongoing arrival of new babies, and the alcoholism of Charles were blocked out, at least momentarily. Even if unarticulated and unfocused, Conan Doyle's sense of mission was instilled as a child.

Charles Doyle

Charles Doyle was the youngest of seven children (two of whom died young). He grew up in a prosperous Irish Catholic home in London. His father, John Doyle, was a successful artist and a highly regarded political cartoonist (although he carried out his work anonymously for 30 years, using the initials H. B.). John Doyle was "arguably the father of the modern political cartoon" (Booth, 1997, p. 3). Three older brothers were highly successful; all were artists, as well as achievers in other spheres. Charles's life was not the same as that of his siblings, who were raised by both parents. Charles, in contrast, had lost his mother when he was very young.

We know little about Marianna, his mother, who died when she was approximately 44—even when she died is a puzzle. Booth (1997) noted that when Charles was born (in 1832), Marianna was "terminally ill" (p. 5), which would imply that Charles was a baby when she died. According to Lycett (2007), Marianna died in 1839, when Charles was seven. Concerning its likely impact on Charles, the loss of maternal nurturing in infancy, or even at the later age, could have affected him severely. It is also possible that, after Charles's birth, even if his mother had survived, she could have had a long illness, making her unavailable to Charles.

In talking of the family's London home at 17 Cambridge Terrace before Marianna's death, Lycett (2007) described an atmosphere of "energy and sociability" (p. 7).

> Ensconced in his comfortable four-story house, John Doyle was at last able to relax and enjoy the company of his wide circle of friends... including Walter Scott, Thackeray and Dickens.... Benjamin Disraeli was one of many politicians who visited. (Lycett, 2007, p. 7)

This happy atmosphere ended after Marianna's death from heart problems. "Lacking his wife's support, John Doyle reined in his professional... commitments, and devoted more time and energy to the children" (Lycett, 2007, p. 7). Details about Charles' early years are missing.

Charles's early life was probably accompanied by profound feelings of loss, and it is unlikely that these feelings were dealt with: "emotional outpouring was not a Doyle family trait" (Lycett, 2007, p. 7). Charles, at seven years of age, showed artistic ability "but was more withdrawn than his siblings" (Lycett, 2007, p. 7). As a child, he "was prone to emotional outbursts and rages" (Booth, 1997, p. 5), and although these can be attributed to genetic or temperamental factors, they may have been related to anxiety-laden nurturing within a depressive atmosphere. John was described as a good father. "Austere he may have been, and strictly Catholic in the upbringing of his children, but he was also loving and involved himself with them" (Booth, 1997, p. 4), encouraging their artistic abilities. Nonetheless, the nurturing Charles received both before and after his mother's death was probably insufficient for him to develop a solid sense of self, resulting in his inability to sustain the later increasing demands and stress in his life.

The family's economic situation gradually deteriorated, servants were dismissed, and the only daughter, Annette (who was musically talented), became the housekeeper (Lycett, 2007). During the 1840s, Charles's three brothers were successfully employed, but Charles "without their self will, was beginning to lag behind and did not like it" (Lycett, 2007, p. 10). He was encouraged by his family to take a job in Edinburgh "to remove him from London's distractions" and where he "would be subject to the disciplines of a formal office environment" (p. 10), earning an annual salary.

He was led to believe that this employment held possibilities for advancement, as well as potentially leading to his return to England. However, this was never to be: "He was to spend the rest of his working life as a civil servant in Edinburgh" (Booth, 1997, p. 5). Charles was talented in architectural design, his most famous work being the fountain at Holyrood Palace in Edinburgh; however, he was mostly involved in office work, which displeased him. In spite of salary increases, he struggled as his family increased in size; little money was left for luxuries.

Charles supplemented his income by doing art work, including paintings and illustrations for children's books, and working for newspapers as a sketch artist in criminal cases. However, a general decline became evident in his work as well as in his personality (Booth, 1997). As the family moved from home to home, each deteriorating in quality, he drank more heavily. "It is probable that he was never cruel or violent to his children or to Mary yet he was, in all but flesh, an absentee father, who when family life oppressed him deeply, would go off fishing. . . . He also retreated into the bottle and developed into an alcoholic" (Booth, 1997, p. 9).

The biopsychosocial perspective sheds light on the interrelationship of multiple factors affecting Charles's life: economic insecurity, lack of goodness of fit in employment, family stress and demands, and his history of early loss. In addition, depression by its nature can lead to alcoholism. The kindling effect of both depression and alcoholism, with their psychological and physiological consequences (Ingram & Price, 2001), is evidenced by Charles's progressive decline. At a later date, epilepsy was diagnosed.

When the English writer Thackeray visited the family, this occasion became another source of shame for Charles. "Such visitations humiliated Charles who could not afford to wine and dine his callers in a fashionable eating-house: he had to entertain them in his shoddy accommodation" (Booth, 1997, p. 9). There was a marked contrast between Charles's hospitality to Thackeray and the entertainment of Thackeray (and other celebrities) provided by Charles's father in the past.

As Charles continued to drink, as his employment decreased, and as his expenses increased, he probably also felt humiliated at his inadequacy as a provider, disappointing Mary and increasing the stress in her life.

Mary Doyle

Mary's parents grew up in Ireland. Her father, William Foley, who was "easy going . . . not one fired with any great ambition," nevertheless graduated from Trinity College and became a doctor. He married

Mary's mother, Catherine Pack, in 1835. At the time, Catherine and her sister were in charge of a boarding school for girls in Kilkenny, Ireland, that had been established by their mother. Catherine's father was a Protestant landowner. "The Packs were more firmly entrenched in the Anglo-Irish establishment—a position that brought pedigree, responsibilities, and pretensions" (Lycett, 2007, p. 12).

When Catherine married William Foley, who was Catholic, she converted to Catholicism. Six years later, having given birth to two daughters (Mary and Catherine), she found herself a widow; William died suddenly in his 30s. Catherine returned to Kilkenny with her children and started another school. However, the socioeconomic circumstances of the time (especially the severe potato famine) led to the failure of her school, which she then sold before moving to Edinburgh.

In Edinburgh, Catherine established the "Governesses' Institution supplying British and foreign governesses to families and schools" (Lycett, 2007, p. 13). To further supplement her income, she took in a border, Charles Doyle, when Mary was 12 years old. Catherine valued education for her daughters: Mary received a good Catholic education and was sent to a boarding school in France at the age of 12.

Mary returned from her schooling as "a lively and cultivated young woman" (Booth, 1997, p. 6). Charles and Mary married when she was 18 and he was 23. Catherine was an important source of financial and emotional support to Mary; her death, when Arthur was 3, was a hardship for the family.

The little material available about Mary's life suggests a warm, sustaining bond with her mother; we do not know how her father's early death affected her. Mary's mother demonstrated considerable strength, coping alone to raise two daughters and earn an income. Sending Mary to France for a "good Catholic education" was in keeping with the educational status of the family and suggests some financial means and/or perhaps a contribution from family members.

Mary's successful attachment to her competent mother was in marked contrast to the maternal loss experienced by Charles, which was compounded by his feelings of inferiority in relation to his successful father and brothers.

Childhood

Arthur Ignatius Conan Doyle was born in Edinburgh, Scotland, on May 22, 1859, the first son and the third of nine children, seven of whom lived into adulthood. The Doyles' second child, a girl, died as an infant a year before Arthur's birth. Another daughter died at age two, when Arthur was four. Arthur was given the name Conan, after Charles's maternal great-uncle, Michael Conan (the brother of Charles's mother, Marianna), who became his godfather. Michael Conan worked in Paris as a foreign correspondent of the *Art Journal.*

Arthur grew up in an increasingly stressed family. His mother taught him to read and to write; she herself was "cultivated and well read, and … was rarely without a book within her reach. Conan Doyle wrote of her as stirring porridge with one hand and turning the pages of … [a book] with the other" (Booth, 1997, p. 12).

With the exception of Arthur's younger brother, Innes, the other children were girls. Details of their childhood are not known, but they apparently adapted well, were educated, earned livelihoods as governesses, and helped care for the younger children. Conan Doyle described his sisters' contributions as well as his concern for his mother:

My noble sister Annette, who died just as the sunshine of better days came into our lives, went out at a very early age as a governess to Portugal and sent all her salary home. My younger sisters, Lottie and Connie, both did the same thing; and I helped as I could. But it was still my dear mother who bore the long, sordid strain. Often I said to her, "When you are old, Mammie, you shall have a velvet dress and gold glasses and sit in comfort by the fire." Thank God, it so came to pass. (Doyle, 1924, p. 5)

Arthur and his mother shared a world of dreams and aspirations. In contrast, Charles was, to Arthur, "a distant figure with whom he found it hard to relate." His mother protected him from his father's increasing drinking (Booth, 1997, p. 10). Little is known of his early relationship with his father. Arthur maintained intermittent interest in him throughout his life. He hung his father's paintings in his medical office, and the first Sherlock Holmes stories were illustrated by his father. In 1924, he sponsored a posthumous exhibit of his father's work. Charles followed his son's career through newspaper accounts, saving these in scrapbooks.

However, the absence of an ongoing relationship does not mean absence of longings for closeness and inner struggles with conflicting emotions, even if Conan Doyle never wrote of this. Perhaps his conflicts were transmuted into the "inner demons" that would sometimes surface in his work and in his later involvement with fairies and spirituality. Family secrets permeated his Sherlock Holmes stories.

In his autobiography, Conan Doyle, although open about his father's shortcomings, puts them in the context of Charles's creativity, omitting any mention of his psychiatric problems and institutionalization. Mary, in her effort to send Arthur to a good school and keep him at a distance from his father, sent him to live with a friend's family when he was about seven or eight; he stayed with the Burtons at Liberton, about three miles from Edinburgh. According to Booth (1997), Arthur lived with the Burtons for two years while attending school. Little is known of his life with the Burtons or of his contact with his own family during this time. I speculate that Arthur's separation and abandonment anxieties were experienced and then suppressed, reinforced by his mother's "messages" to be brave. This "expulsion from home" may also have intensified feelings of anger toward his father, who was the root cause of this displacement.

It is not possible to learn from Arthur how he experienced his father's alcoholism or how he was affected by it, as he never described his father's alcoholic behavior, let alone admit it existed. A glimpse of Charles's behavior has been provided by a psychiatrist, Allan Beveridge (2006), citing a letter written by Mary Doyle in 1892, which he found while examining Charles Doyle's old psychiatric records. In the letter, Mary described Charles's desperate attempts to procure alcohol: "'Every article of value he or I possessed [he] carried off secretly"'; the family incurred large "'debts... to our trades people... all for goods which never entered our doors, but were at once converted into money'" (quoted in Beveridge, 2006, p. 2).

The children must have known that money was scarce, their mother anxious, and their father frequently absent. One vivid passage that Mary wrote suggests that the children probably experienced some of the resulting tumult: "'He would strip himself of all his underclothes, take the very bed linen, climb down the water spout at risk of his life, break open the children's money boxes. He even drank furniture varnish'" (quoted in Beveridge, 2006, p. 2).

Like Arthur, children of alcoholic parents are often secretive (as their alcoholic parents and spouses or partners often are) about the fact that there is a drinking problem in the family. Children frequently experience shame and endure many distressing experiences (sometimes abuse) when exposed to out-of-control parental drinking behavior.

Although Mary Doyle may not have succumbed to depression (as far as we know), many spouses with alcoholic partners do, and children also suffer from the disruption of family life. Out-of home placements are frequently made as a result of the ensuing multiple problems. Mary Doyle took such a step by "placing" Arthur in Liberton to protect him. In those days, families struggled with these difficulties on their own without the support of clinical services that are available today.

In his autobiography, Conan Doyle makes no reference to living in Liberton, referring only to the school. The reader is led to assume that he attended this school while living in his own home:

> Of my boyhood I need say little, save that it was Spartan at home and more Spartan at the Edinburgh school where a tawse-brandishing schoolmaster of the old type made our young lives miserable. From the age of seven to nine I suffered under this pock-marked, one-eyed rascal who might have stepped from the pages of Dickens. In the evenings home and books were my one consolation, save for week-end holidays. (Doyle, 1924, p. 5)

Arthur was often in fights with other boys, observing that "my comrades were rough boys and I became a rough boy, too" (Doyle, 1924, p. 5). He developed positive relationships with the Burton boys, especially with William, "who became one of his earliest and closest friends" (Booth, 1997, p. 14).

As Charles's alcoholism progressed, Mary decided that Arthur should attend boarding school, away from Edinburgh. This education was paid for by his father's brothers (Booth, 1997; Lycett, 2007; Stashower, 1999). Conan, Arthur's godfather, was instrumental in the selection of Stonyhurst, a Jesuit school. He told Mary that "the Jesuits impressed him not so much for their religiosity as for their emphasis on education" (Lycett, 2007, p. 28).

Conan Doyle (1924) does not concede that the "charity" of his uncles enabled him to attend boarding school; he wrote that his mother paid his way. The Church offered to pay his fees, if "I were dedicated to the Church" (p. 12), but his mother refused to do this:

> When I think, however, of her small income and great struggle to keep up appearances and make both ends meet, it was a fine example of her independence of character, for it meant paying out some £50 a year which might have been avoided by a word of assent. (Doyle, 1924, p. 12)

Arthur was about 10 when he left home for Hodder (Stonyhurst's division for younger boys), traveling alone by train to England. "It was a long journey for a little boy who had never been away from home before, and I felt very lonesome and wept bitterly upon the way" (Doyle, 1924, p. 8). This is a rare example of Conan Doyle admitting to "weakness" and "loneliness." "Arthur found himself, from the best of motives, adopting a habit of glossing over his feelings" (Lycett, 2007, p. 35). Conan Doyle referred to this trip as his first separation from home, "obliterating" the two years he (presumably) lived in Liberton.

Arthur's two years at Hodder were "on the whole . . . happy years" (Doyle, 1924, p. 8). His teachers (who were Jesuit brothers) were young and treated the boys "kindly." Arthur could "hold my own both in brain and in strength with my comrades" (p. 8). His teacher, Francis Cassidy, was nurturing and encouraging. Arthur (1924) had "always kept a warm remembrance of this man and of his gentle ways" (p. 8). Arthur had the capacity to internalize this support and to draw on it in the service of his intellectual growth.

Francis Cassidy, a talented storyteller, encouraged Arthur to write poetry and stories and emphasized the development of memory, "teaching the use of mnemonics, rhymes and linked-image training" (Booth, 1997, p. 21). Experienced in memory training from his mother's lessons in heraldry, Arthur was an enthusiastic learner and further developed his "exacting and prodigious ability to recall facts and details almost at whim" (p. 21). Sherlock Holmes would "inherit" this ability from Arthur.

Arthur remained at school during the school holidays, coming home for 6 weeks each summer. When older, he visited home during the year. Mary Doyle wanted to minimize his contact with his father (Booth, 1997). Arthur and his mother kept up an active correspondence. Arthur continued to write to her throughout his life—at one time, there were "over fifteen hundred extant [letters] in the family archives" (Booth, 1997, p. 31). His mother (a self-object) was "never out of reach"; his internalization of her and their relationship (object representation) helped him feel secure and develop his sense of solid self.

When Arthur was 10, a virulent epidemic of diphtheria swept through the school, and although he was not stricken, many boys died. It is not known how Arthur reacted to this or what worries he may have had about his own survival and the fragility of life. This must have been a crisis for the students, faculty, and staff that inevitably affected the school's atmosphere and functioning. It is not known how bereaved parents were helped (if they were). The children were probably overwhelmed with fears of becoming infected, fears of their own dying, and grief over losing many classmates and friends.

Today schoolwide grief and crisis counseling is generally available to children, their families, and school affected by death through illness or violence. Such work often includes support groups. "Being a member of a group gives an opportunity to decrease isolation, and meet others who are confronting similar situations.... Recent research... confirms the benefits gained by participation" (Sutton & Liechty, 2004, p. 508). Given the close social network of Conan Doyle's school, group crisis counseling might have been welcomed and effective—had it existed.

Although not mentioning this epidemic in his autobiography, Doyle (1924) did discuss his very first memory, which was of his maternal grandmother dying when he was three. Her "death-bed— or rather the white waxen thing which lay upon that bed—is the very earliest recollection of my life" (p. 3). He probably also felt his mother's grief.

However, Doyle makes no reference to the death of his two-year-old sister, exactly 1 year later, when he would have been four. Arthur must have been aware of this loss, as the loss of his grandmother was already imprinted in his memory. In all probability, he witnessed his mother's intense grief, for Mary Doyle was reported to have been "devastated by the death of her daughter Mary" (Lycett, 2007, p. 21).

After two years at Hodder, Arthur was promoted to Stonyhurst, its senior school, where its "Spartan lifestyle" was accompanied by the rigidity and punitiveness of the teachers. He complained of "the soul-deadening quality of the education" (Stashower, 1999, p. 23) and wrote about the "'uncompromising bigotry' of his Jesuit masters and an educational system 'calculated to leave a lasting abhorrence of the subjects' " (p. 23).

Arthur was perpetually in trouble with his teachers, in a school where physical punishments were severe and frequently used. He was "one of those boys who revelled in displaying to his peers how he could take physical punishment, not letting it break or get the better of him" (Booth, 1997, p. 24). This theme of Arthur, the hero, the courageous, as the antithesis of his father, would reappear throughout his life.

Arthur's reading was part of his "anti-authoritarian rebellion" (Booth, 1997, p. 29). He would read using " 'surreptitious candle ends in the dead of night, when the sense of crime added a new zest to the story' " (p. 29). His "delinquencies" were generally "run-of-the-mill schoolboy infractions," such as smoking, and "by his own admission, he went out of his way to be mischievous, to show that he would not be cowed by it [that is, punishment]" (Booth, 1997, p. 24). He did not believe that he suffered negative consequences from these punishments "because he had been 'such an obstinate little mule' " (p. 24).

Arthur, "the street-toughened lad from Edinburgh, believed that authority for authority's sake was wrong" (Booth, 1997, p. 25). Perhaps this rebellion was also a way to act out (in a disguised form) against the absolute authority of his mother and toward his father, whose self-absorbed, dissipated lifestyle led to Arthur's separations from the family. His rebellious and punishment-eliciting behaviors might also be viewed as an assertion of autonomy from his mother's protectiveness.

Arthur had positive relationships with his peers, an important source of social support and a critical developmental need both in middle childhood and in adolescence. According to Kaplan, Sadock, and Grebb (1994), the influential American psychiatrist "Harry Stack Sullivan postulated that a chum or buddy is an important phenomenon during the school years. By about 10 years of age, the child develops a close same-sex relationship, which Sullivan believed is necessary for further healthy psychological growth" (p. 47). Arthur enjoyed his excellent athletic abilities, becoming captain of the school's cricket team. He was an active sportsman throughout his adult life; belonging to a team was also important.

In a similar circumstance, Sir Pelham Grenville (P. G.) Wodehouse, the creator of Bertie Wooster and Jeeves, had little contact with his parents and was brought up by a nanny. His life at boarding school represented important emotional and social experiences (Lane, 2004). Men who did not have parents found sympathy and support from "their schools and clubs," where the atmosphere was "more calmative than oppressive," and where "friendship took the place of love." This was so for Wodehouse, whose love for his school, Dulwich College, lasted through his later years, and he would be "as gripped by the latest rugby and cricket results from his alma mater as by anything else in the world" (p. 141).

Arthur came to appreciate and to "capitalize" on his storytelling abilities and experienced his " 'debut as a story-teller' " around this time (Stashower, 1999, p. 23):

> On a wet half-holiday I have been elevated onto a desk, and with an audience of little boys all squatting on the floor, with their chins upon their hands, I have talked myself husky over the misfortunes of my heroes. Week in and week out those unhappy men have battled and striven and groaned for the amusement of that little circle. (quoted in Stashower, 1999, p. 23)

Arthur's wide-ranging reading was a source of intellectual and creative stimulation. He was fascinated with history, greatly admired the works of Sir Walter Scott, was intrigued by American authors, and at 14 read Jules Verne in French. His godfather, Michael Conan, took an active interest in his education and frequently sent him books.

Doyle finished his studies at Stonyhurst at 16 and spent the following year in a Jesuit School in Feldkirch, Austria. There he founded and edited the school magazine. "In a brazen editorial, Arthur condemned the Jesuit brothers' practice of reading and censoring pupils' letters. The magazine was promptly proscribed" (Booth, 1997, p. 37).

A major literary discovery for Arthur that year was Edgar Allan Poe, whose writings had a profound influence on him:

> It was from these brief tales that [Arthur] learnt to understand, appreciate and assimilate the mechanics of short fiction-writing on which he was not only to build his own considerable literary reputation, and his greatest professional achievements, but also to shape the course of modern English literature. (Booth, 1997, p. 38)

By the end of his year at Feldkirch, Arthur "had matured into a thoughtful, intelligent and lively young man with a wisdom in excess of his years. His friends regarded him as loyal and staunch" (Booth, 1997, p. 40). But he was at a loss as to his future direction when he returned home to a "hassled mother and an increasingly ill, drunk and morose father" (p. 40). Through the influence of his mother and his mother's lodger, the physician Dr. Bryan Charles Waller, Arthur decided to study medicine at the University of Edinburgh.

Waller greatly influenced Conan Doyle and his family. The "mystery" surrounding Waller is worthy of a Holmes investigation and may indeed have inspired some of the family secrets uncovered by Holmes. Initially, biographers thought that Waller was an older man and a longtime friend of the family, but recent research has raised new questions about him, especially about his relationship to Mary Doyle. Conan Doyle does not refer to Waller in his autobiography but noted, "'My mother had adopted the device of sharing a large house, which may have eased her in some ways, but was disastrous in others'" (quoted in Booth, 1997, p. 43). Waller was not an "old" man but a medical student only six years older than Conan Doyle. He eventually assumed responsibility for paying the Doyle's rent, and when he later moved to his family's estate at Masongill, in the Pennines, Mary Doyle lived in a cottage on his estate, rent-free, for more than 30 years.

Although Waller was 15 years younger than Mary Doyle, a romantic attachment between them may have existed. "The exact nature of that bond has excited considerable speculation over the years" (Stashower, 1999, p. 68). Mary Doyle named her youngest daughter Bryan Mary Julia Josephine, "Bryan," of course, being Waller's first name. Did Mary give her this name from friendship and gratitude or, as some have suggested, because Bryan Mary was Waller's child?

Mary Doyle moved to Waller's estate in 1882, where Waller lived from 1882 until his death in 1932. He married a local governess in 1896. Mary Doyle remained at Masongill 21 years after his marriage, leaving in 1917. Even after his marriage, Waller would frequently eat meals with Mary in her cottage, and his wife resented Mary. "There was a real affection between [Waller and Mary] of which the latecomer, Waller's wife, was justly jealous" (Booth, 1997, p. 90).

Waller helped Conan Doyle prepare for entrance into medical school and encouraged his writing. Although Conan Doyle resented Waller and his interference in the family, he nevertheless made frequent trips to Masongill throughout the 1880s and was later married there, with Waller as his best man. Masongill became the locale of some of his stories (Booth, 1997; Stashower, 1999). However, Waller is omitted from all of Conan Doyle's writings and letters, and some have observed that "a number of Holmes stories center around the activities of sinister lodgers in boarding houses" (Chabon, 2005, p. 18), thereby suggesting that Conan Doyle was displacing his resentment of his mother's lodger onto "sinister lodgers" in his books.

Booth (1997) speculated that if Conan Doyle had acknowledged the role that Waller played, he also would be acknowledging his father's alcoholism and admitting that the family survived through the efforts of their lodger. He would also have conceded Waller's great influence over his mother and his own jealousy over this relationship.

Whatever the nature of Waller's relationship with Mary Doyle, he was a major help in stabilizing the family and in dealing with Charles's mental problems and subsequent hospitalizations. "It is almost certain that, had Waller not intervened as he did, the family would have been carted off to the poorhouse" (Booth, 1997, p. 67). Waller's involvement with Mary probably had positive, albeit unacknowledged, consequences for Arthur. As Charles deteriorated, Mary turned increasingly to Arthur to meet her emotional needs; she might have become even more "entwined" with him had there been no Waller to fill the void in her life.

In Charlotte Brontë's family, Tabby, the housekeeper, was a significant mother figure to Charlotte and her sisters, although Tabby had no "formal" role in the family structure. Likewise, Waller, in a similar manner, was not an official member of the Doyle family but was clearly significant in their "informal" family organization. Waller was supportive to Mary, who faced overwhelmingly difficult living conditions. They were strongly attached to one another, but whether it was a romantic relationship remains a constant source of speculation for Doyle enthusiasts. Whether Waller's presence and competence added to Charles's poor sense of self and incompetence by comparison, and perhaps jealousy as well, and whether these were factors in his deterioration cannot be determined.

Conan Doyle had mixed feelings toward Waller. On the positive side, Waller supported Conan Doyle's aspiration of going to medical school, and Doyle presumably appreciated how he rescued the family economically. He may at times have resented Waller's intrusion into family life and Waller's developing relationship with his mother, as suggested by Doyle's failing to mention the fact that Waller was his best man at his first wedding on Waller's estate (Stashower, 1999).

Although the Doyle family was not formally a stepfamily, in its informal makeup it was. Practitioners often work with families with organizations that are unconventional but that involve intense (and often) complicated relationships. Lacking clear evidence, there is much we do not know about the "quality" of the relationship between Mary and Waller. In clinical work, where we do have access to data, it is important to assess the commitments of the partners to one another, the impacts (positive and negative) this arrangement might have on the children, and whether the "outsider" coming into the family is welcomed as a family member or made to feel like a perpetual lodger.

Adulthood

Medical School

Initially, Conan Doyle had no ambition to become a doctor—it seemed a practical course of action. However, he developed a strong interest and motivation and felt he had the required ability. Edinburgh Medical School had an excellent reputation, and Conan Doyle embarked on his career at a key moment in medical history: "doctors educated in the 1880's were the first 'modern' doctors.... Observation was, however, still the key word" (Booth, 1997, p. 48).

The professor who became most important to Conan Doyle was Dr. Joseph Bell, who published extensively in medical journals and texts and wrote poetry as well. Arthur found that Bell was a brilliant "detective," able to tell a great deal about a patient's life from his observations and sharply pointed questions. He was the model for Sherlock Holmes, which Conan Doyle later acknowledged, writing to Bell:

> "It is most certainly to you that I owe Sherlock Holmes.... [Although] I have the advantage of being able to place him in all sorts of dramatic positions, I do not think that his analytical work is in the least an exaggeration of some of the effects which I have seen you produce in the out-patient ward." (quoted in Stashower, 1999, p. 77)

In 1879, Conan Doyle had "a real assistant's position" with Dr. Hoare in Birmingham (Booth, 1997, p. 48). This professional experience developed into a warm, longtime relationship with Dr. Hoare and his wife, who "regard[ed] him as they would their own son" (p. 55).

Before his final year of school, he was offered a yearlong position as a doctor on a whaling boat, the *Hope,* headed for the Arctic.

Hope: The Greenland Whaler

Although warned of the dangers, Doyle "accepted the vacancy with alacrity.... He wanted the adventure just as much as-even more than-the money" (Booth, 1997, p. 56). Relieved that he encountered no serious medical problems aboard the ship, he eagerly participated in the seal and whale hunts, and "became one of the crew" (Stashower, 1999, p. 39).

> He had been raised on tales of knights and their quests. Now he himself was having a modern epic, pursuing a gigantic beast through a strange, otherworldly landscape.... The gloom of Edinburgh fell away under the brilliant midnight sun. His father's illness and his family's penury could not follow him here.... A deeper strain of longing had begun to stir. The Arctic, he believed, had awakened "the soul of a born wanderer." (Stashower, 1999, p. 39)

Accompanying Doyle's sense of adventure was his propensity for risk taking. The captain forbade him to go onto the ice on the first day of seal hunting, but when he realized how determined Doyle was, he rescinded his order. That day, Doyle fell off the ice floes into the water twice "and finished the day in bed" (Stashower, 1999, p. 38). Later on, when he was proficient at jumping to adjacent ice floes, he slipped into the freezing waters. All alone, he felt the waters numbing his limbs; in a hair raising self-rescue, he pulled himself up onto the ice floe.

In another near-fatal accident, Conan Doyle and other crewmen were nearly capsized by a whale. "This brush with death only sharpened Conan Doyle's taste for the adventure" (Stashower, 1999, p. 40). Doyle's "flirtation" with adventure and with risk, a lifelong pattern, can be viewed from the psychodynamic perspective of the defenses as counterphobic in nature—that is, he suppressed frightening thoughts of death with its terrifying ultimate abandonment by engaging in death-defying behaviors to ward off these feelings. Triumphing over death is often the goal of writers who hope to "vanquish death through work honored by posterity" (W. Styron, 1990, p. 81); this was a wish frequently voiced by Doyle.

Clinicians often encounter clients' risk-taking behaviors, and it can be difficult to determine what such behaviors mean. Many times they are overdetermined, arising from multiple motives. These behaviors are seen frequently in adolescents, many of whom are involved with substance abuse and promiscuous sexual behavior, putting themselves at risk for unwanted pregnancies, AIDS, and sexually transmitted diseases. Adolescents are also prone to irresponsible driving: "Most mortality statistics for teenagers cite accidents as the leading cause of death" (Kaplan et al., 1994. p. 55). Adults also display similar at-risk and acting-out behaviors; among these are, increasingly, gambling addictions. Risk-taking behaviors (like Doyle's) can represent counterphobic motivations and in some cases may mask an underlying depression (Slaby & McGuire, 1989, p. 23), which can be a precursor to suicide.

This trip was a turning point in Conan Doyle's life. He "was no longer the gawky, uncertain teenager of old. 'I went on board the whaler a big, straggling youth,' he said. 'I came off a powerful, well-grown man'" (Stashower, 1999, p. 42). His whaling experiences were drawn on in his writings throughout his career.

Medical Career

The Beginning. Conan Doyle received his medical degrees in 1881: the bachelor of medicine and master of surgery qualifications. While looking for work, Doyle also "began falling in love with a regularity that alarmed his mother" (Stashower, 1999, p. 44).

Conan Doyle desperately needed to earn money; having no money also prevented his establishing his own practice. His applications to hospitals were rejected. As a last resort, he became a ship's doctor on the African Navigation Company's ship *Mayumba,* which carried cargo and passengers to West Africa, receiving a salary of £12 a month and living expenses. His shipboard experience was disappointing. The exhilaration of his Arctic trip was absent, and he resigned 4 months later. He disliked the heat, the monotony, the fevers he had to treat, and the unstimulating passengers. He became disillusioned with the Europeans living in Africa: They were "a desultory lot who drowned their sorrows in the time-honoured colonial fashion, with alcohol" (Booth, 1997, p. 72). His own "liberal" alcohol consumption worried him:

> "I drank quite freely at this period of my life, having a head and a constitution which made me fairly immune, but my own reason told me that the unbounded cocktails of West Africa were a danger, and with an effort I cut them out." (quoted in Booth, 1997, p. 74)

Booth suggested that drinking brought up painful memories of Charles Doyle's alcoholism.

Although negative about this African trip, it nevertheless provided Conan Doyle with information about the African landscape and social scene. Photography became a serious avocation, and his articles about photography in Africa appeared in the *British Journal of Photography* (Booth, 1997).

Back in England, Doyle's life "was in crisis" (Booth, 1997, p. 77). Economically unable to establish himself, he found no job prospects and temporarily worked for his former employer, Dr. Hoare. He heard from Dr. George Budd, a former classmate from Edinburgh, who had a successful practice in Plymouth and wanted an associate to handle the overflow. Doyle accepted. However, he would soon find that Budd's practice and ethics were highly questionable; he ran a "slick operation preying upon the poor" (Booth, 1997, p. 81).

At the time, Doyle, being "innocent, naive, and consequently gullible," did not realize the degree of Budd's dishonesty (Booth, 1997, p. 81). He became increasingly concerned about Budd's questionable practices, and Budd, resenting Doyle's critical questioning, asked him to leave. Although Doyle had worked with Budd for only 6–8 weeks, "the swindling doctor's influence was to last much longer. Echoes of Budd's personality were to sound for years down the corridors of his stories" (Booth, 1997, p. 84). Doyle resolved to go out on his own. Without persistence and determination, he might have descended into a downward spiral of defeat. Adversity contributed to his aggressive coping. He did not follow the path of his father's decline.

Medical Practice in Southsea. Resolving "to go it alone," Doyle chose Southsea (although it is not known why): "...the prospect exhilarated him.... What he lacked in material possessions he made up for with self-reliant determination" (Booth, 1997, p. 87). He rented a house at 1 Bush Villas, Elm Grove, and bought £12 worth of medical drugs on credit and a small amount of furniture for the front rooms, which served as his office. The remainder of the house was unfurnished and hidden from the public. His brass nameplate was hung on the front door.

Although Dr. Budd had promised to lend him £1 a week, he failed to do so.

Mary Doyle sent him this money along with his 10-year-old brother, Innes, who, she decided, was now to live with Conan Doyle. Apparently, Doyle was pleased with this arrangement, "as he was feeling lonely in his new home" (Booth, 1997, p. 90).

Establishing his practice was difficult. Money was scarce, and he ate little. In the evenings, he purchased his food in low-priced stores and did his housework, careful not to be seen. Initially, his patients were poor. Conan Doyle appreciated Innes's company and his helpful assistance. They "were more than brothers but friends" (Booth, 1997, p. 95). Conan Doyle arranged for Innes to attend school.

After six months, Doyle's practice improved, and he bought some luxuries and acquired a housekeeper. "A motherly woman, she was to be reincarnated as Mrs. Hudson, Sherlock Holmes's housekeeper" (Booth, 1997, p. 95). "He was respected, considered a good, kind man and a competent general practitioner, and [his] income . . . was acceptable for a successful professional" (Booth, 1997, p. 96). Rodin and Key, in 1984, studied Conan Doyle's case books, which "showed how imaginative and advanced Conan Doyle was in his medical thinking, particularly concerning bacterial infections and methods of immunisation" (Booth, 1997, p. 101). Booth noted that Rodin and Key were resourceful in finding this piece of solid evidence to evaluate Doyle's medical competence. Doyle expressed pride in being a doctor, and medicine was "inextricably entwined with his total being" (Rodin & Key, 1984, p. xx).

Conan Doyle completed his thesis for medical school, passed his oral exams, and received his medical degree from Edinburgh in July 1885. To increase his earnings, he began specializing in ophthalmology, studying at the Portsmouth Eye Hospital, where he learned optics and became proficient at doing eye examinations and prescribing glasses.

Conan Doyle became an active member of sports clubs and organizations. He also actively participated in the Portsmouth Literary and Scientific Society, which "taught him to speak in public, widened his intellect and brought into his life people who were to greatly impinge upon it" (Booth, 1997, p. 98). In 1885, he involved himself in local politics. He became a well-known and popular person in Southsea with a busy social life.

Marriage to Louise

Although attending dances in Southsea, Conan Doyle did not become romantically involved with any of the women he may have met there. In 1885, while treating a young man with meningitis who did not live locally and needed intensive care, Conan Doyle "boarded" him at his house. The patient died within a few days, but during this time he comforted the patient's sister, Louise Hawkins, 27, and her mother.

A relationship developed between Conan Doyle and Louise. "A withdrawn, sweet-natured girl, Louise was grief-stricken. Conan Doyle was strong and protective" (Booth, 1997, p. 99). Mary Doyle traveled to Southsea to meet Louise, and "to everyone's relief, the ma'am found nothing objectionable in [Louise,] noting with evident satisfaction that . . . Louisa bore a passing resemblance to herself" (Stashower, 1999, p. 67). (Note that there is no official documentation of the spelling of Louise's first name; sometimes it is spelled "Louisa." I will use "Louise," except when "Louisa" is cited by an author.)

The engagement was announced in April 1885 and followed by a wedding on Waller's estate that August. After the marriage, Louise's mother lived with the Doyles and was to do so intermittently over the years.

Conan Doyle and Louise had a congenial relationship, and he wrote that "'there was no single occasion when our affection was disturbed by any serious breach or division, the credit of which lies entirely with her own quiet philosophy'" (Booth, 1997, p. 100). Booth observed that "they were very close but there was little passion between them. He doted upon her with the respectful adoration of a Victorian husband" (p. 99).

Booth (1997) does not document his premise that "little passion" existed between them. In general, Victorian writers were reserved on this subject. Conan Doyle might also have been circumspect about Louise in his autobiography, which he wrote when married to Jean, his second wife; "it is possible that his reticence stemmed from consideration for . . . [Jean's] feelings" (Stashower, 1999, p. 68).

Louise was a competent housekeeper and "a perfect doctor's wife" (Booth, 1997, p. 100). She was very accommodating to Conan Doyle's wishes and interests, following him wherever his inclinations led him. They lived in Southsea for five years. Their daughter, Mary Louise, was born there on January 28, 1889. Alleyne (known as Kingsley), their son, was born November 15, 1892, in Norwood.

After his marriage, Conan Doyle wrote that "'my brain seems to have quickened and both my imagination and my range of expression were greatly improved'" (quoted in Stashower, 1999, p. 70). Conan Doyle's interest in writing had begun in early childhood, stimulated by his mother's storytelling. His writing of fiction now began in earnest. His first story, about an adventurer and a Bengal tiger was written when he was six (Lycett, 2007). Conan Doyle was a regular storyteller to the boys at Stonyhurst, and he wrote fiction during his medical training. In April 1886, he completed the novella *A Study in Scarlet,* in which Sherlock Holmes was introduced. The book, illustrated by his father, was well received but not with the acclaim Sherlock Holmes was to receive later.

Conan Doyle wanted to gain a reputation as a "serious literary novelist" (Booth, 1997, p. 126). In 1889, on the basis of extensive, painstaking research, he completed the historical novel *Micah Clarke,* centered on English Puritans in late 17th-century England. *Micah Clarke* received mixed reviews, but it was very popular with the public. Its features "distinguished Conan Doyle's later historical fiction—a strong narrative voice, powerful battle scenes, and a lively personal flavor" (Stashower, 1999, p. 83).

Conan Doyle then wrote a second historical novel, *The White Company.* Set in 14th-century England, "it is a boisterous tale about the bowmen and their love of sport and chivalry" (Booth, 1997, p. 130). Published in 1891, it established his reputation as a serious novelist and is the most widely published historical novel in the English language, apart from *Ivanhoe.*

Leaving Southsea

Conan Doyle had a rich life in Southsea, but he was not satisfied. He needed to achieve more and decided that the

key to this was to leave Southsea. However, before final-
izing this decision, he first visited Berlin, where Robert
Koch, the famous bacteriologist, claimed he had discovered a cure for tuberculosis. Conan Doyle wrote: "A great
urge came upon me suddenly that I should go to Berlin
and see [Koch].... I could give no clear reason for this but
it was an irresistible impulse and I at once determined to
go" (Doyle, 1924, p. 82).

Conan Doyle's" abrupt decision to rush off to Berlin ... speaks more of
a restive spirit than a desire for medical enlightenment" (Stashower,
1999, p. 112). Perhaps Doyle's very contentment in Southsea was a
warning signal: Was he settling for too little? He had earlier written
to his mother: "'We'll aim high, old lady'" (quoted in Stashower,
1999, p. 43). Perhaps the acclaim received by Koch ignited his own
sense of mediocrity by comparison. Conan Doyle published a critical
appraisal of Koch's research at a time when overwhelming medical
opinion favored Koch's findings. However, later medical research
confirmed Conan Doyle's opinion, and he "took great pride in the
fact that his warnings had been justified. This was the first time he had
taken up what might be called a public crusade, and he developed a
taste for it" (Stashower, 1999, p. 113). Conan Doyle might also have
taken pleasure in "dethroning" this "competitor."

Another turning point for Conan Doyle was his conversation on
the train to Berlin with a Harley Street dermatologist, who encouraged him to leave Southsea, study in Vienna for a specialization in
ophthalmology, and then establish a practice in London.

With little thought to the consequences, Conan Doyle
resolved to make a sudden and dramatic change of course.

> Trying to explain his foolhardy swim in the shark-in-
> fested waters of Africa, Conan Doyle had admitted to a
> tendency to do "utterly reckless things" that he had diffi-
> culty explaining afterward. Now, as he surveyed his life in
> Southsea, he prepared once again to take a flying leap into
> murky waters. (Stashower, 1999, p. 112)

Doyle decided to move to Vienna. He wrote that his wife "was
quite willing" to go, and he felt that his daughter, then two, "was
old enough now to be left with her grandmother [Louise's mother]"
(Doyle, 1924, p. 85), who lived on the Isle of Wight. Stashower (1999)
is dubious about Louise's "willingness" to go: ". . . she cannot have
had any choice in the matter" (p. 114**).**

Vienna and London

Conan Doyle and Louise reached Vienna in January 1891. His
German was not adequate to study ophthalmology, and his plans
turned into a disaster. Instead, working on a commissioned novella,
he and Louise vacationed in Vienna. Their intended 6-month visit
ended in two months. They moved to London, rented an apartment
near the British Museum, and reunited with their daughter and
Louise's mother. Practicing as an oculist, Doyle rented a medical
office near Harley Street.

His practice was not successful. Going to his office every day, he
found no patients "'to disturb my serenity'" (quoted in Stashower
1999, pp. 118–119). Two Sherlock Holmes stories had been published
already, and so Doyle decided to write other Holmes stories and seri-
alize them. Thus began a very fruitful partnership with *The Strand*

Magazine, another turning point in his life. "Not only had Conan Doyle made a canny marketing decision, he had also found an especially good showcase for his own talents" (Stashower, 1999, pp. 119-120).

Completing five stories, Conan Doyle decided to end his series with the sixth. " 'I think of slaying Holmes in the sixth and winding him up for good and all.... He takes my mind from better things' " (quoted in Stashower, 1999, p. 120). His mother told him: " 'You won't! You can't! You mustn't' ... Moved by his mother's pleas, Conan Doyle granted Holmes a stay of execution" (p. 126).

In May 1891, Doyle was stricken with influenza and nearly died. As his health improved, he felt he was "at a crossroads" (Stashower, 1999, p. 127). Now in London with a nonexistent medical practice and his career in literature taking off, he decided to leave his medical career permanently. He recalled his " 'delight' " at this decision and felt that " 'I should at last be my own master' " (quoted in Stashower, 1999, p. 127). The Doyles moved to a 16-room house in a London suburb; he referred to this period as "The Great Break" (p. 126). Conan Doyle shared his new wealth with his family: He brought his sisters Connie and Lottie to live with them, and he sent money to his mother, who continued to live at Masongill.

This period became the "most productive stretch of Conan Doyle's career" (Stashower, 1999, p.128), as he wrote two more historical novels, a novel of domestic life and manners, and a new Sherlock Holmes series. It was this new Sherlock Holmes series which "made him an instant sensation" (p.151), but this very success resulted in moodiness and anxiety. "He suffered from bouts of moodiness as his fame grew, which occasionally erupted into bursts of temper. He experienced periods of insomnia, and complained to his mother that he was troubled by nerves 'more than most people know" (p. 151).

He led a life of "frantic activity," traveling, giving lectures, writing extensively, and participating in sporting events. Stashower (1999) believed that Doyle's distress related to the fact that his detective stories, rather than his works of higher artistry and scholarship, were so acclaimed. Perhaps, however, this distress also resulted from "excelling" anything his father had ever done, a goal that was always before him but that, once achieved, may have produced guilt. Finally, Doyle decided that the best solution was to eliminate Mr. Holmes:

> "I was in danger of having my hand forced, and of being entirely identified with what I regarded as a lower stratum of literary achievement. Therefore as a sign of my resolution I determined to end the life of my hero.... I am weary of his name." (quoted in Stashower, 1999, p. 145)

Holmes met his death in combat with the archvillain Moriarty, both falling into the Reichenbach Falls in Switzerland. Conan Doyle wrote in his diary: "'Killed Holmes'—and moved on to other matters" (Stashower, 1999, p. 148). In a speech, he later stated: "'I have been much blamed for doing that gentleman to death ... but I hold that it was not murder, but justifiable homicide in self-defence, since, if I had not killed him, he would certainly have killed me'" (quoted in Stashower, 1999, pp. 149-150).

There was an immense public outpouring of protest in response to Holmes's death. Newspapers around the world headlined it on the front page.

> No one, least of all Conan Doyle, anticipated such a furor. In London, black mourning bands were seen. The detective's passing, in 1893, was discussed in language usually

reserved for state funerals. Members of the royal family were said to be distraught. (Stashower, 1999, p. 149)

Narrative theory emphasizes the interactions between narrators and listeners, the *dialogic* connection. Just as the boys at Stonyhurst sat "with their chins upon their hands," fascinated with Doyle's story-telling, the world was now his audience. They communicated their loss and sense of betrayal, to which Doyle later responded, and Holmes was resurrected.

The demise of Sherlock Holmes coincided with two personal tragedies. Charles Doyle, 60, died at the Crichton Royal Institution on October 10, 1893. The second tragedy involved his wife, Louise, who had become seriously ill.

Louise and Tuberculosis

Louise was diagnosed with advanced tuberculosis. The previous year, Louise had given birth to Kingsley and had been unwell during this pregnancy. After she developed a cough and pains in her side, a "particularly virulent form of [tuberculosis] known as 'galloping' consumption" was diagnosed (Stashower, 1999, p. 150). Louise was expected to live only for several months.

Louise's illness "had a galvanizing effect" on Conan Doyle (Stashower, 1999, p. 151). Giving up his activities, he devoted himself to her care and placed her in a sanitarium in Davos, Switzerland. She survived for 13 more years. Louise's illness "marked a deepening of his personal unhappiness. Louisa, as he had baldly stated, was now an invalid rather than a wife; a patient rather than a companion" (Stashower, 1999, p. 152).

An earlier interest in spiritualism revived more strongly and urgently. Conan Doyle's first exposure to spiritualism was a lecture he attended in 1880, before his trip to the Arctic. Initially skeptical, Conan Doyle became more interested in exploring spiritualism as well as mesmerism and telepathy, attended seances, and had other spiritualist experiences. However, spiritualism did not dominate his active professional and literary life as it did in later years (Booth, 1997). Now, living in Davos, "surrounded by the sick and dying, it was natural that his thoughts should have returned to the subject of 'life beyond the veil'" (Stashower, 1999, p. 161). His father's death probably also affected him, although he may have sealed off these feelings. Sherlock Holmes was also recently dead. Conan Doyle struggled with his conflicts about religion and an afterlife:

> "…my soul was often troubled within me. I felt that I was born for something else, and yet I was not clear what that something might be. My mind felt out continually into the various religions of the world. I could no more get into the old ones, as commonly received, than a man could get into his boy's suit." (quoted in Stashower, 1999, p. 161)

Stashower (1999) observed that "it cannot be entirely coincidental that he chose this moment to join the Society for Psychical Research" (p. 161). Conan Doyle was not unique in this interest: Spiritualism had gained much popular support throughout Europe and the United States during this time, and the Society for Psychical Research had many prominent members. Doyle's feeling that he "was born for something else" suggests that the seeds of his messianic mission, his ultimate ambition, had been sown.

Conan Doyle spent considerable time in Davos with his wife; the children and other family members joined them later. As Louise improved, he worked on new literary projects and became interested in skiing, then a new sport, which he had a significant role in popularizing. In 1894, Conan Doyle wrote the *Stark Munro Letters* (an autobiographical novel) and a collection of medical stories. He also developed a new series character, Brigadier Gerard, who lived in the Napoleonic era.

In September 1894, Conan Doyle went on a lecture tour to America with his brother Innes, now 21. This highly successful tour "offered a respite from his troubles and self-recriminations, though he would not have admitted as much to himself" (Stashower, 1999, p. 154). When Conan Doyle returned to England in December, he moved Louise to Hindhead in Surrey, which had a good climate for her health, and he commissioned a mansion to be built.

Jean Leckie

In 1897, seven months before moving to his mansion, Undershaw, Conan Doyle, then 37, met Jean Leckie, 24, and fell in love. They would marry, in 1907, a year after Louise's death. Jean, the daughter of wealthy Scottish parents, was very attractive. "Quick-witted and widely read, she was also a skilled horsewoman and a trained mezzo-soprano" (Stashower, 1999, p. 206). Conan Doyle wrote that he met Jean 10 years later than he actually did. This "cover-up" is understandable, as his romance with Jean occurred while he was married to Louise.

> The early years of his romance with Jean Leckie had been the most wrenching period of his life. He claimed to have fallen in love with Jean the moment he saw her; but at the time, he was still very much a married man. His rigid sense of honor, the code of chivalry that guided his life and shaped his fiction, now faced its sternest test. (Stashower, 1999, pp. 205-206)

Because sexual activity was medically prohibited for patients with tuberculosis, Conan Doyle also became celibate. He was in a moral dilemma, as he remained faithful to Louise, while his relationship to Jean was platonic but intense; "…the conflict between duty and desire became a torment" (Stashower, 1999, p. 206). Sexuality, even now, removed from Victorian constraints, is a topic not always discussed with patients who suffer from disabling conditions and illnesses. "A key issue is the absence of discussion about sex and disability. Texts on sexuality barely acknowledge disability…. Conversely, it is startling how many books on disability do not discuss sexuality" (Olkin, 1999, p. 226).

Stashower asserts that "there is every reason to suppose that Conan Doyle remained celibate for the rest of Louisa's life" (1999, p. 206). However, a letter from Doyle to his brother Innes, found in the newly released Doyle archives, appeared to validate that the couple had had a premarital sexual relationship (Grann, 2004).

Conan Doyle confided to his mother, telling her that Jean "'kept my soul and my emotions alive'" (quoted in Stashower, 1999, p. 204). He "was confident that his mother would approve of the virtuous path he had chosen" (p. 207). According to his way of thinking, he was being faithful to Louise by having a platonic rather than a sexual relationship with Jean, while remaining very attentive to Louise's needs. He also felt that his behavior with Jean was honorable because he was open with her and told her that she should leave him and marry someone eligible, as he had no idea when he would be free. She nonetheless chose to remain in this relationship.

During this time, Doyle:

> ...maintained a very full social life, keeping his thoughts and frustrations well out of sight. Living near London... he attended literary societies, [had] lunch in his club, took on a busy public speaking commitment and played sport.... He was never lax in taking any opportunity to get away from Undershaw and his wife's sick room for a day or two. (Booth, 1997, p. 215)

The Boer War

During this tumultuous time in Doyle's life, the Boer War broke out in Africa, and he decided to enlist in the army. "At forty, he knew that this would be his last chance to see action on a battlefield" (Stashower, 1999, p. 219). Although rejected by the army, a friend who was sending a 50-bed hospital unit to South Africa offered Conan Doyle a medical position with this unit. Doyle accepted and sailed for Africa on February 28, 1900. Jean sent flowers to his room but stayed anonymously among the well-wishers on shore.

In Africa, Conan Doyle worked "to the point of exhaustion." Most of his patients had diseases related to contaminated water supplies, and a "full-blown epidemic of enteric, or typhoid fever, ripped through the British forces" (Stashower, 1999, p. 221). The sanitation conditions within the hospital were deplorable, and the death rate among troops was high; staff also sickened, and three died. "All the while, Conan Doyle stayed at his post, bending to his task with a grim determination" (p. 222). The severe epidemic lasted about one month, abating when sanitation conditions improved. Conan Doyle then traveled with the soldiers, which left him with "few illusions about war, but he retained his admiration for the 'splendid stuff' of the fighting man" (Stashower, 1999, p. 223).

Conan Doyle became ill with fever when he returned to the hospital but continued to work. He probably had typhoid, and it was "another ten years before his digestion 'recovered its tone.' . . . [His] ribs also took a beating in a staff football match" (Stashower, 1999, p. 224).

In June 1900, when England seemed to be winning, Conan Doyle returned home to write a history of the war (Stashower, 1999). He "was anxious that his book should be the first history of the war to appear. . . . [He] saw himself in the role of a war correspondent sending a dispatch from the front" (Stashower, 1999, p.224).

Conan Doyle ran for Parliament in the election of 1900. Both the Conservatives and Liberals indicated interest in him. He ran with the Liberal-Unionist Party (allied with the Conservatives) and chose Central Edinburgh as his district. Motivating his decision to run was a "nagging sense that he had not yet found his mission in life. . . . 'Deep in my bones I felt that I was on earth for some big purpose,' he wrote, 'and it was only by trying that I could tell that the purpose was not political'" (Stashower, 1999, p. 228). He ran a very vigorous campaign, and although he lost the election, he had received much popular support.

Two years later, Conan Doyle was knighted by King Edward VII for his services in the Boer War. Initially, he planned to decline as Kipling and Chamberlain had before him because he felt that accepting knighthood would not be an "honorable" action. (Stashower, 1999). His mother, however, had other ideas about this subject, and "in the end she wore him down" (Stashower, 1999, p. 247).

Return to Undershaw

In August 1900, Conan Doyle was back at Undershaw, resuming his regular activities and secretly seeing Jean Leckie. Doyle intended that Louise "should never know of his divided affections" (Stashower, 1999, p. 207). He told others about Jean, including Jean's parents and brother; even Louise's mother "condoned her son-in-law's behavior" (Stashower, 1999, p. 207). Jean received heirloom jewelry from Conan Doyle's mother and forged a positive relationship with his children.

Conan Doyle again ran for parliamentary elections and again did well but lost. He decided to give up politics but still was "'deeply convinced that public service was waiting for me somewhere'" (quoted in Stashower, 1999, p. 253).

Although Conan Doyle's "affair," which was known to others, was kept secret from Louise, she suspected an extramarital relationship. Just before her death, Louise told her daughter Mary "not [to] be shocked or surprised... if her father should marry again. If he did, the dying woman insisted, he would have her blessing" (Stashower, 1999, p. 254). Stashower concluded that "there is no reason to suppose that Louisa knew of her husband's attachment to Jean" (p. 254). Louise's statement, however, could very well suggest that she had some level of awareness of this relationship. Her response seems typical of her loyalty to her husband.

As Conan Doyle's relationship with Jean continued, their tensions increased. "Whatever pleasure they found in each other's company was shadowed by an unspoken truth: their hopes for future happiness constituted a deathwatch for Louisa. The strain took its toll on both of them" (Stashower, 1999, p. 253). Louise died on July 4, 1906, at 49, "with her husband and mother at her bedside" (Stashower, 1999, p. 254). Doyle was devastated by Louise's death:

Tortured by insomnia, he grew weak and listless. His work ceased. The intestinal complaint of his South Africa days returned to plague him. He carried flowers to his wife's grave and spent dark hours alone with his thoughts. It would be months before he roused himself. (Stashower, 1999, p.254)

With other crises in his life, Conan Doyle always "rose to the occasion"—he was challenged by adversity. With Louise's death, he may have been tortured by the guilt surrounding his wished-for freedom. However, presumably the loss of Louise was itself painful to him. Dear, gentle Louise had been his companion, his support, the mother of his children. In her selfless manner, she "was always there for him," and now he was abandoned by her. He may also have come closer to fears of his own mortality.

In a sense, Doyle's modus vivendi was to confront threatening situations head on, through action. However, given the emotional storm of conflicted feelings Louise's death probably unleashed, such coping mechanisms probably could not work. Feelings of helplessness are often experienced by the bereaved; in a parallel manner, the clinician may also feel helpless to relieve the client's pain and suffering. The pain expressed or sensed can stir up clinicians' own feelings about loss, and because "action" or "solutions" alone are not what is demanded, they may feel incompetent to help, as this is one problem they cannot "fix."

This fact can be especially difficult for students who have no experience in working with bereavement. As an example, consider Erik, a master's-level student whose field placement was in a nursing home, where Erik was assigned to Mr. W., an elderly patient whose wife had recently died. Erik made four attempts to actually walk into Mr. W.'s room before he felt ready to talk to him.

> When Mr. W. did start talking about his wife's death, Erik began talking about discharge planning to help "distract him." "What do I have to offer Mr. W. I can't make his wife come back.... I don't know how to console him.... At least if I can help him make plans I am doing something!" (Urdang, 1991, p. 129)

During his mourning, Conan Doyle read a newspaper account about George Edalji, a man he felt was falsely accused of a crime. He chose to defend Edalji, and after his successful investigation, his depression lifted, and he resumed his normal activities. He became energized by the case; now he could again become involved and active and be a protector of the vulnerable, as he had protected Louise.

The George Edalji Case

An outbreak of cattle mutilations had occurred near an English village where George Edalji lived with his Indian family. Edalji was convicted of the crime and imprisoned. Although subsequently released, he wanted to prove his innocence. A public outcry about his conviction and imprisonment stressed that community prejudice against the family led to his conviction on faulty evidence. Conan Doyle, feeling an injustice had been done, wanted to correct the matter.

During their first meeting, Conan Doyle noticed that in the waiting room, Edalji was having difficulty reading the newspaper, " 'proving not only a high degree of myopia but marked astigmatism. The idea of such a man scouring fields at night and assaulting cattle while avoiding the watching police was ludicrous to anyone who can imagine what the world looks like to eyes with myopia of eight diopters' " (quoted in Stashower, 1999, p. 257). Thus, the former oculist, in a truly Sherlockian manner, began his analysis of the case. Conan Doyle also discredited other evidence, receiving much publicity for his work.

> Most of the facts had been assembled by others, but Conan Doyle used his narrative gifts to cast the evidence into a compelling and seemingly unanswerable argument. He began with a letter-writing campaign in the newspapers and then, in late January 1907, published an eighteen-thousand-word pamphlet called "The Story of Mr. George Edalji." (Stashower, 1999, p. 258)

The case received worldwide publicity. Paradoxically, having annihilated Holmes, Conan Doyle had now assumed his mantle.

Marriage to Jean Leckie

Conan Doyle and Jean Leckie married on September 18, 1907, and moved to a new home, Windlesham, in Sussex. Kingsley and Mary, now teenagers, had a close relationship to Jean, and family life was harmonious. Jean gave birth to their sons, Denis, in March 1909, and Adrian, in November 1910. A daughter, Jean, was born in December 1912.

Conan Doyle's writing was not prolific during this period, as he was happily engaged in home activities and family life. However, Doyle also turned to outside interests, which included uncovering evidence of serious police ineptitude in the case of Oscar Slater, a man wrongfully accused of murder. He also turned his attention to writing plays, and even produced some. The staging of Sherlock Holmes, starring William Gillette, was very successful.

Conan Doyle also worked for the Divorce Law Reform Union and wrote *The Crime of the Congo,* expressing opposition to Belgium's oppression of the natives in the Belgian Congo. Returning to fiction, he wrote *The Lost World* to great acclaim. In this book, he created the character of Professor Challenger, who traveled to an unexplored region of the Amazon and found a living prehistoric world. "His high spirits and sense of humor are evident on every page." However, his "influence as a writer of science fiction is seldom acknowledged" (Stashower, 1999, p. 275).

Children

Mary Louise and Kingsley had a less secure and a more disruptive family life than did Doyle's children with Jean. Mary was four when Louise's tuberculosis was diagnosed, and Kingsley was only a baby, "so they had never really known their mother as anything but an invalid" (Booth, 1997, p. 215). The children were often cared for by relatives and did not see their mother for periods of time. Although frequently away from home, "there is no doubt that Conan Doyle loved his children. Kingsley, a handsome, well-built child with fair hair, was his favourite" (Booth, 1997, p. 215). Louise's illness, which took its toll on Doyle, also affected his relationship with his children.

> Conan Doyle loved his children and had been an attentive, affectionate father when he happened to be at home. In this period [of Louise's illness], however, as the strain of his suppressed desires took its toll, he became distracted and quick-tempered.... [He was] away often. When he returned, he behaved in a gruff and distracted manner. . . .For Kingsley and Mary.... who had known great warmth and affection in happier times, the change would have been unsettling. (Stashower, 1999, p. 208)

Mary Louise and Kingsley developed an attachment to Jean during their mother's illness; "now... [during Conan Doyle's and Jean's marriage, they] were greatly attached to Jean, and their father's new happiness marked a warming of their relationship with him" (Stashower, 1999, p. 261). Kingsley later went to medical school, leaving to enlist in the First World War. Although surviving the war, he died of influenza shortly afterward. During the war, Mary Louise worked in a factory; she later became a spiritualist, working in her father's spiritualist store.

Arthur and Jean's children grew up in a more stable atmosphere, and Conan Doyle was very involved in their lives. When his last three children were born, Conan Doyle was in his early 50s, of "grandfatherly" age, and had a more relaxed and indulgent attitude toward them:

> These children had an altogether different upbringing from that of Mary and Kingsley. Their parents were very

close, very much in love and involved in each other and their children's lives. Conan Doyle was no longer the strict authoritarian but an approachable, affable father who rarely lost his temper with them.... His sons were later to say of him that he was the best pal they had ever known. (Booth, 1997, p. 215)

In 1923, Doyle wrote *Three of Them: A Reminiscence,* which described the childhood of Doyle's three children with Jean: "by modern standards [it is] a somewhat sugary and sentimental volume" (Booth, 1997, p. 281). Owen Dudley Edwards, a Doyle scholar, was not impressed with Doyle's youngest sons. The three children from Doyle's second marriage were his "literary heirs... the two boys were playboys... Denis, was... utterly selfish... Adrian, was a repulsive crook. And then there was an absolutely wonderful daughter" (quoted in Grann, 2004, p. 65). Lycett (2007) observed: "Because neither man [Denis or Adrian] ever did anything useful in his life, they both took pleasure in making things difficult for anyone who tried to write about their father" (p. 464).

When World War I broke out, Conan Doyle was rejected for service; instead, he organized a group of civilian volunteers, which was active in Britain. He also published pamphlets defending British involvement in the war and wrote a six-volume history of the war, which "he hoped would be a definitive history of the war" (Stashower, 1999, p. 309).

Involvement with Spiritualism

Conan Doyle's interest in spiritualism began when he was a young man. Initially a skeptic, his developing interest culminated in his total devotion to this movement. Spiritualism promulgates the belief that the soul exists after death, on a higher plane, from which spirits can communicate with people remaining on the earthly plane.

> In doing so, it attempted to establish links between the physical and metaphysical, leading to such famous spiritualist phenomena as rapping noises coming from beyond, movement by poltergeist, the emanation of auras, telepathy and clairvoyance, most often induced or conducted through a medium. The absence of scientific proof of the cause of paranormal phenomena resulted in a spiritualist philosophy... known... as spiritualism. (Booth, 1997, p. 120)

Spiritualism was very popular in England and in many parts of the world during Doyle's life. This strong interest increased during World War I because of the horrific death toll and vast personal losses. However, Conan Doyle's devotion to this cause ultimately became so fanatical that many spiritualists shunned him, and he was ridiculed in the popular press.

He emphasized that his interest in spiritualism was not sudden but a buildup of interest over his adult life. "It was crucial to Conan Doyle that his views be taken as the culmination of a lifetime's deliberation" (Stashower, 1999, p. 334).

"It is the thing," he would write, "for which every preceding phase, my gradual religious development, my books... my modest fortune... my platform work... and my physical strength... have each and all been an unconscious preparation. For thirty years I have trained myself exactly for the role without the least inward suspicion of whither I was tending." (Stashower, 1999, p. 332)

In 1917, he stated that he "was now prepared to declare himself publicly as a dedicated spiritualist" (Stashower, 1999, p. 333), referring, as he did so, to the passage of time:

"Every now and then as one jogs along through life some small incident occurs to one which very forcibly brings home the fact that time passes and that first one's youth and then one's middle age is slipping away." (quoted in Stashower, 1999, pp. 333-334)

Conan Doyle spoke of finding "great spiritual peace, an absence of fear in death, and an abiding consolation in the death of those whom we love. It is, I repeat, this religious teaching which is the greatest gift that has been granted in our time" (Stashower, 1999, p. 335). Although many religions affirm an afterlife, Conan Doyle concretized this belief by "direct communications" between the living and the dead and was convinced that conversations he had witnessed at seances were authentic.

Automatic writing is a procedure in which mediums, in a trance state, "automatically" write the "ethereal" messages they are "receiving." Initially skeptical, Conan Doyle had a critical experience convincing him of its validity. At the time, a practitioner of automatic writing and a good friend of Jean's was living with the Doyles. She received a "message" for Conan Doyle from Jean's brother, Malcolm, who had died in the war. The message related to a past private conversation between Doyle and Malcolm that Doyle felt no one could have known about. "If any single incident can be said to have crowned Conan Doyle's progress from acolyte to missionary, this would be it" (Stashower, 1999, p. 338). It did not occur to him that Malcolm could have told Jean or someone else about it. For this astute man, such a blind spot suggests the operation of the twin defenses of compartmentalization and denial.

At the time of his "conversion," Conan Doyle's son Kingsley and brother Innes were still alive, but Doyle related his own deep interest in spiritualism to the many losses in World War I. The more Doyle felt that this was his mission, the less he felt the need for scientific evidence, and the more he propounded his strong beliefs, the more he came under criticism. One *New York Times* headline declared: " 'Credulity Hard to Understand' " (Stashower, 1999, pp. 342–343):

> "Admirers of Sir Arthur Conan Doyle as a writer of detective stories... have reason for a peculiar grief because of the strange, the pathetic, thoroughness with which he has accepted as realities the 'spiritualistic' interpretation of the phenomena of trance speaking and writing.... This well-educated and intelligent man-with not a little of the scientific and the philosophic, too, in his mental furnishings—talks much as did the followers of the Fox sisters fifty years ago." (quoted in Stashower, 1999, p. 343)

In the following years, Doyle's spiritualist writings became more prolific and fanatic; he traveled to many countries, giving lectures.

During one trip, he received a telegram that his son Kingsley had died; although overcome, he decided to proceed with his lecture. "My duty," he declared, "is to other sufferers" (Stashower, 1999, p. 345). He told his audience that Kingsley still existed. Four months later, his beloved brother Innes died, followed in two years by his mother. He later described receiving messages from these special people during seances.

Fairies

In another bizarre turn of events, Conan Doyle, in 1920, declared his belief in fairies. "This, for many people, was the last straw" (Stashower, 1999, p. 349). Suddenly, Conan Doyle "became the spiritualist movement's greatest liability" (p. 351). In what was later admitted to be a hoax, a 16-year-old girl and her younger cousin claimed that they saw fairies in Cottingly, a village in the Yorkshires, and took photographs of them. Conan Doyle felt that these photographs were conclusive evidence that fairies existed. In 1922, he published *The Coming of the Fairies,* declaring that fairies might exist as a separate race. The book was ridiculed, and many spiritualists worried that his views would bring down their movement. He then disavowed the connection between fairies and spiritualism while maintaining his belief in fairies.

Several theories have sought to explain Conan Doyle's fascination with fairies: Culturally, Conan Doyle's Celtic background exposed him to stories involving fairies and leprechauns. His paternal uncle, Richard, illustrated children's books with fairies, and his father also drew many fairies. When Conan Doyle arranged an exhibition of his father's work in 1924, the critic William Bolitho related Conan Doyle's affinity for fairies to Charles Doyle's predilection for them.

> "Charles Doyle reveled in this miniature world.... His elves and fairies are Dresden figurines come to life and able ceaselessly to amuse themselves." This subject matter, he noted, opened a suggestive field for speculation: "Sir Arthur's own fairies, one realizes with a start, which have puzzled the world, and convinced part of it, are of the same race as these his father has drawn; identical in fancy, dress, psychology. One feels that the acute Sherlock, examining the evidence for fairies from his creator's own book, would have noticed this striking resemblance between the father's playful and the son's serious revelations." (quoted in Stashower, 1999, pp. 360-361)

Finally, Conan Doyle might have wished to prove that his father was not mentally ill. If fairies existed, then his father would be vindicated and perceived as "a man of sensitive genius" (Stashower, 1999, p. 361). Conan Doyle "lived in the shadow of his father's madness, dreading the thought that this madness... might be transmitted to him"; if his father were not insane, then "he was not likely to go insane" (Booth, 1997, p. 323).

Lady Jean as Medium

Jean was initially resistant to spiritualism, until 1921, when she herself developed the "gift" for automatic writing. Initially, the messages she received were from members of the family, although "Louisa

Conan Doyle, who had been dead for fifteen years... never said a word" (Stashower, 1999, p. 366). Messages were later received from a wide source of dead souls. The following year Jean came under the influence of the long-dead Pheneas, a "spiritual guide" who had lived in 3,000 BCE. Conan Doyle was impressed by the accuracy of information Jean "received," and Pheneas became a voice encouraging Conan Doyle's worldwide crusades.

Conan Doyle's mother, Mary, died at 83 in 1921, while he was on tour in Melbourne. Doyle was "very distressed that he had not been with her at her passing" (Booth, 1997, p. 320). His mother "rejoined" him after her death, sending positive messages about his new vocation through Jean.

Around this time, Houdini, the master magician and illusionist, became "the world's most outspoken anti-spiritualist crusader" (Stashower, 1999, p. 380). During Conan Doyle's 1922 tour of the United States, Houdini and his wife visited the Doyles in Atlantic City. Houdini attended a seance conducted by Jean, with the intent of contacting Houdini's deceased mother. Jean gave Houdini a message from his mother, which Houdini declared unconvincing.

> Two facts did not fit. The first, perhaps of little consequence, was that 17 June [the day of the seance] was Houdini's mother's birthday, yet she made no reference to it. The second was more crucial. The message "came through" in English but Houdini's Jewish mother had only ever spoken Yiddish fluently and she always wrote in German.... Conan Doyle dismissed the anomaly by saying that spirits often became more educated in the after-life. (Booth, 1997, p. 328)

By 1924, Conan Doyle had not produced a novel for nine years but had authored a history of World War I and seven spiritualist books. He also published his autobiography, *Memories and Adventures,* in which he discussed giving up his creative writing in favor of spiritualism. He gave large financial donations to the spiritualist movement and was involved in major spiritualist organizations. One colleague, Price, observed that Conan Doyle's " 'extreme credulity … was the despair of his colleagues, all of whom, however, held him in the highest respect for his complete honesty. Poor, dear, lovable, credulous Doyle! He was a giant in stature with the heart of a child' " (quoted in Stashower, 1999, pp. 359–360).

Death

In 1929, Conan Doyle's health declined, and although suffering heart problems, he insisted on keeping his speaking engagements. After a serious attack, bed rest was ordered, and although restricted mostly to home, he continued to write and to take an interest in world affairs. He knew he was dying but expressed no fear.

After a serious heart attack on July 6, requesting not to die in bed, he was taken to the living room and sat in "an armchair facing the window, looking out over the Sussex countryside, resplendent in high summer. Seated there, surrounded by his family, he died at 8:30 on the morning of Monday, 7 July 1930. He was 71" (Booth, 1997, p. 353).

Conan Doyle's life was full and rich; he spoke of the happiness he had experienced. In an obituary, *Strand Magazine* noted: " 'He lived and enjoyed his life to the full' " (Booth, 1997, p. 35). Conan Doyle's death was reported in newspapers throughout the world.

Two days after his burial, a memorial service at Albert Hall was attended by 8,000 people. The family sat on the stage by an empty chair for Doyle's presence. After eulogies and hymns, a medium declared she had seen Conan Doyle entering Albert Hall and gave Jean a message from him. For several days after this, mediums throughout the world reported receiving his messages. "In death, as in life, it seems he kept up his busy routine of correspondence" (Booth, 1997, p. 354). Jean was to hear his voice in seances until her death in 1940.

Reflections on the Life and Clinical Implications

Conan Doyle was a great narrative artist, a doctor, reformer, politician, and humanitarian. He grew up in a poor neighborhood in Edinburgh, in a large family facing many stresses, including a father with a serious alcohol problem and mental illness. It would have been understandable if Doyle had developed a dysfunctional lifestyle. But he did not. He was highly successful and popular, a friendly, outgoing, and enthusiastic person, who enjoyed exploring new ideas and new experiences. The biopsychosocial perspective enables us to examine the complex contributions of his personality, his family and social world, and strong constitution to his successes and perplexing late-life obsessions.

A psychodynamic orientation is a vital component of the psychological assessment. If we examine Doyle's life exclusively in terms of his external behaviors, we will have only a superficial understanding. As noted in chapter 5, such psychodynamic concepts as attachment, a solid sense of self, and internalization come to life in the present chapter, illustrated by Doyle's attachment to his mother and his internalization of his mother's love and aspirations.

The importance of early attachment of children to loving caregivers and of their positive regard of the child have been emphasized by object relations theorists. Conan Doyle was deeply loved and valued by his mother; his confidence and inner strength in large measure stemmed from this.

He could respond to the warmth and interest of others. He also had "good recruitment" capacities. He was able to internalize the positive regard of others for him; he did not need to reject this. Unlike Linda Hogan's (2001) "fearful" mother, he did not have a "depressive" core. She wanted to be "invisible and inaudible" and did not have the capacity to absorb new relationships, nor did she develop new, more positive perceptions of herself. Conan Doyle had many supportive people in his life, such as his teacher at the Hodder School, Francis Cassidy. He had the capacity to internalize this support and benefit from it.

It is not unusual to find that children who have had distant or frightening relationships with their parents turn away from and reject the overtures of therapists. Clinicians often find themselves in the difficult situation of supportively reaching out to troubled children, only to be rejected by them. These children need support as much as Arthur did, but for them it is not comforting but threatening. Therapists may find it difficult not to feel rejected.

The psychological development of the child, from the very beginning, takes place within a relationship with parents or other caregiving persons. Object relations theory stresses the importance of secure early attachments for the development of a secure sense of self. As the child grows, the social world expands and includes others. Conan Doyle was involved in social networks, which included, as he grew older, teammates in his athletic pursuits, the crew of the Greenland whaler *Hope,* his friends, members of clubs, and others.

Conan Doyle also was involved with his extended families: When financially able, he took in his sisters to live with the family in their home. .He was also solicitous of Louise's mother, who lived with them for long periods of time. In his turn, he received support that helped him cope with the crisis of his attachment to Jean while Louise was ill. In particular, he received approval from both his mother and Louise's.

Conan Doyle's intense preoccupation in later life with spiritualism most likely had roots in his early life related to deep-seated anxieties about death, loss, and abandonment. Therefore, the turn to spiritualism can be seen as a continuity, even though on the surface it may appear to be a discontinuity in his life course. Messianic impulses also represent a major theme in his life: " 'Deep in my bones I felt that I was on earth for some big purpose,' " he said (Stashower, 1999, p. 228).

Conclusion

Paradoxically, Conan Doyle has gained immortality, not through his spiritual messages, nor through his histories, but through his nemesis: Sherlock Holmes. Holmes, one of the most popular figures in English literature, is still read and has been read continuously for over 100 years. Holmes, seen by many as a real person, along with his colleague Dr. Watson, lives on through books, plays, film, and television. Writers have added their own inventions of later adventures to the original "canon." The Baker Street Irregulars (a present-day organization devoted to the lore of Sherlock Holmes, named for the street urchins regularly employed by Holmes to assist him in his cases) remains active, with members meeting to study and celebrate the life of Sherlock Holmes. Holmes's methodologies and insights have become part of everyday discourse: "When all other contingencies fail, whatever remains, however improbable, must be the truth" (from *The Adventure of the Bruce-Partington Plans, 1912)*.

I like to think that Arthur Conan Doyle, if he exists in the beyond, might have mellowed toward Sherlock, chuckling over the pleasure he has given to so many. Perhaps there is a barely perceptible twinkle in his eye as he reflects on the numbers of people Holmes, his creation, has outwitted.

Conan Doyle was a storyteller from an early age, with his mother as his audience. They became collaborators, together weaving stories of family heraldry and her aristocratic forebears and the glorious future that awaited him. The telling of stories and the listening to them will be discussed further in the next chapter, on narrative theory.

CHAPTER 7

The Role of Narrative Theory in Constructing Biography

Narratives are inescapable; they come at us from everywhere—academic and professional writings, politics, newspapers, business, advertising, and personal conversations. Poniewozik (2009), writing in *Time Magazine* about the controversial Sarah Palin, asks: "So how does a reality star regain control of her narrative?" (p. 28). Scott Rudin, the producer of the movie *It's Complicated,* comments that the movie's sets, "don't serve merely as well-appointed backdrops; they convey essential details of character. 'Everything-the silverware, the food in the fridge—is part of the narrative'" (Merkin, 2009, p. 44). In a *New Yorker* cartoon, an analyst tells his patient: "Look, making you happy is out of the question, but I can give you a compelling narrative for your misery" (Mankoff, 2007, p. 92).

The telling of stories and listening to them can be traced back thousands of years, going back to oral traditions (such as sagas): "every culture of which we know has been a story-telling culture" (Brockmeier & Harre, 2001, p. 42). Telling stories appears to be a basic aspect of human nature, possibly an intrinsic part of mental development (Stern, 1985). "We order and reorder our life experiences through stories. We give disconnected moments of experience an ongoing form and meaning. Using stories, we begin to distinguish self and nonself" (Coleman, 1999, p. 238).

Narrative theory, with its focus on storytelling, has blossomed into a field of interdisciplinary interest. Although it has roots in literary theory, writers from a range of disciplines, including literature, anthropology, and psychology (and even those within the same discipline), approach the subject from different orientations, drawing on various perspectives of narrative theory. They do, however, have in common an "orientation that aims at examining the nature and role of narrative discourse in human life, experience, and thought" (Hinchman & Hinchman, 1997, p. 10).

Narrative theory, in its most commonly held meaning, refers to people telling their own stories, presenting their own views and perspectives and creating their own meanings. It assumes that only individuals themselves can know their own lives and feelings because interpretations by others are bound to be inaccurate as well as intrusive.

> We are living in the age of the Narrative Turn, an era when narrative is widely celebrated and studied for its ubiquity and importance. Doctors, lawyers, psychologists, business men and women, politicians, and political pundits of all stripes are just a few of the of the groups who now regard narrative as … an essential component of their work. These groups acknowledge narrative's power to capture certain truths and experiences in ways that other modes of explanation and analysis … cannot. Phrases such as "narrative explanation," "narrative understanding," "narrative as a way of thinking," and "narrative identity" have become

common currency in conversations inside and outside the academy. (Scholes, Phelan, & Kellogg, 2006, p. 285)

Narrative theory places a high value, perhaps excessive from the perspective of objectivity, on the narrator's subjectivity and experiential description of events. The readers (or listeners) are invited into the world of the storyteller, to understand what he or she is experiencing and what meanings the narrator draws from this. W. Styron (1990), for example, in *Darkness Visible: A Memoir of Madness,* shares with the reader his profoundly depressive feelings, suicidal inclinations, and his insights into their origin.

Role of Constructivism

Narrative theory in general is related to *constructivism,* which emphasizes the subjective nature of knowing, rejecting the modernist "search for scientific truths, the quests for certainty, objectivity and rationality" (Ornstein & Ganzer, 2005, p. 566). This concept fits under the umbrella framework of *postmodernism,* which is generally opposed to formal theories and ideologies, especially in relation to the arts.

Constructivism encompasses diverse points of view, but its underlying premise posits "that there is no fixed reality, only constructed versions of reality determined by the perspective of the one doing the describing" (DeLaCour, 1996, p. 214). Individuals are viewed as active agents in their own lives with the capacity to change and to create meaning; this ability is termed *self-agency.* Observers are always involved in their observations. The "act of observing inevitably affects what is being observed" (Lee & Greene, 1999, p. 24).

Thus, it is held that the "intrusion" of biographers into the life of the subject (whether or not the subject is living) and of therapists into their client's self-narrative means that the "portrait" of the subject is filtered through the inquirers' own experiences, values, and subjectivities.

Although ascribed to postmodernist thinking, constructivism's philosophical underpinnings have a long history, starting with the philosophies of Lao Tzu and Buddha in the fifth and sixth centuries BCE. Buddha observed that we fully participate "in the construction of our worlds by means of our thoughts, fantasies, and all manner of imaginings" (Mahoney, 2003, p. 3).

Piaget, who was not a philosopher but a psychologist whose primary work centered on cognitive development, also used constructivist principles, albeit in a somewhat different context. He studied the ways in which children perceive their worlds, how this develops over time, and how they come to construct their sense of reality, meaning, and morality. Although emphasizing cognition rather than subjectivity, he realized that reality did not exist for children in a holistic, absolute, and concretized manner; instead, reality was a construction in process that needed to be perceived, cognitively processed bit by bit.

However, adhering to a strictly constructivist perspective can present therapeutic difficulties. Given that it asserts that the client's narrative of his or her experiential world is an accurate representation, then, for clinicians to question that narrative would be contraindicated. This would tie practitioners' hands, making it difficult if not impossible to objectively evaluate the "severity of crises, potential of danger, etc." (Northcut & Heller, 2002, p. 219). The clinician needs to "negotiate the dance between believing all and believing nothing" (p. 222).

For example, if bound by the constructivist approach, the clinician would be at a loss when facing a puzzling Munchausen syndrome by proxy case. In such cases, a child (usually young) is brought into a hospital, by parents who seem overly eager to cooperate, telling a compelling narrative of their child's illness (Sadock & Sadock, 2003, p. 884). The child has generally had a number of prior hospitalizations, during which a medical diagnosis could not be made because of atypical, "peculiar or puzzling" physical symptoms (p. 884). Further exploration reveals that the parent or parents have caused the problem "by injecting toxins or by inducing the child to ingest drugs or toxins to cause diarrhea, dehydration, or other symptoms— and then eagerly seeks medical attention" (p. 884). The adult denies doing this or even knowing that this has happened. It has been noted that "symptoms quickly cease when the child and the perpetrator are separated" (Mercer & Perdue, 1993, p. 75). One major aid in evaluating this problem has been the hospital secretly videotaping the interactions of the parent and child, a strong evidence-based approach. Simple unquestioning acceptance of the narrative would lead the clinician down a false path.

Role of Culture

Constructivism also gives important standing to social and cultural events and experiences that affect individuals and in turn are affected or altered by individuals. These perspectives are often highlighted in biographies. Pepys's diaries, for example, offer a firsthand account of the great London fire of 1666. His description of the fire "is one of the most famous set pieces in the Diary" (Tomalin, 2002, p. 222). In the stories of the lives of Frederick Douglass and Ottilie Assing, presented in chapter 8, we see slavery, the Civil War, and Reconstruction through their eyes. Conversely, Douglass's impact on the history of these times is not inconsequential. Diedrich's (1999) presentation of Assing's early experiences in a 19th-century German Jewish community makes that aspect of history come to life. These biographical dimensions can sensitize clinicians to the impact of major social and political events on individual lives and to consider such dimensions in the lives of their clients.

The concept of culture "incorporates all the symbolic meanings-the beliefs, values, norms, and traditions... shared in a community and [that] govern social interactions among community members or between members and outsiders" (Longres, 1995, p. 74). Culture is utilized in narrative theory in several ways. First, attention is paid to ways in which culture is interpreted by people-the meaning it has in their lives. Narrative understanding "'gives "voice" to social relations and locally embedded cultural meanings'" (Hymes 1996, quoted in Brockmeier & Carbaugh, 2001, p. 7). When Lia Lee, a Hmong child, developed epilepsy, her parents perceived this condition as an "honor.... 'They felt Lia was kind of an anointed one.... She was a very special person in their culture because she had these spirits in her and she might grow up to be a shaman.'" (Fadiman, 1997, p. 22). A hospital social worker with a strictly medical perspective, unaware of or failing to consider the cultural dimension, whose primary and reasonable concern is to keep Lia's epilepsy under control, could find him or herself in conflict with Lia's parents, who may want to hold on to the special status conferred by the epilepsy.

Role of Narrative Techniques and Memory

Narrative discourse, a fundamental aspect of narrative theory, goes beyond the storytelling and meaning making of the narrator. It maintains that an intended or actual audience is involved. The narrator tells his or her story to someone (explicitly or implicitly, even if the someone is momentarily unseen). Who is the "shadow" reader of the diary in process? The narrator thinks (consciously or unconsciously) about how he or she wants the audience to hear and react to this story. As Scholes and colleagues (2006) remind us, it is ". . . the relationship between the teller and the tale, and that other relationship between the teller and the audience . . . (which forms) the essence of narrative art" (Scholes et al., 2006, p. 240). Tellers do not impassively recount their tales; they "seek to engage and influence their audiences' cognition, emotions, and values" (p. 297). The "greatest advances [in narrative theory] in the past forty years have been in the study of narrative discourse" (p. 314).

Narrative theory is also attentive to the *point of view* of the narrator and the different ways this is expressed, such as the style of the artistic medium (writing, performance, etc.), the presentation of the characters, and the ensuing plot and dialogue. The *voice* of the narrator permeates the narrative. Writers vary in their awareness of their own subjectivity and point of view and mayor may not make this awareness explicit to their readers.

The *plot* is an important aspect of all narratives, as it provides the structure of the narrative, its story line, and meaning; it is "the dynamic, sequential element in narrative literature" (Scholes et al., 2006, p. 207). Brooks (1984) refers to plot as "the design and intention of narrative, what shapes a story and gives it a certain direction or intent of meaning" (p. xi).

From its beginnings, narratives have been concerned with *character*. Early narratives often included descriptions of character but generally in an external way that excluded the inner development of its personages. "The notion of peering directly into the mind... seems to arise quite late in most literatures" (Scholes et al., 2006, p. 175). Characters do undergo changes in early narratives, but their inner struggles or thought processes are generally not presented to the reader; these actual character changes represented a "plot formulation rather than a character formulation" (p. 168).

The remembrance of things past is intrinsic to most narrations, but can these *memories* be accepted at face value? Assuming a subject's intention to present "honest" memories, how reliable are they? Watching the painful struggles of people with serious memory deficits, we are struck by the fragility of memory itself. But even when memory is robust, how accurate are memories and to what extent do we have total recall of the past? Have other memories been "fused" onto these earlier memories, reinforcing or perhaps distorting the original memory? And to what extent are our memories influenced by the responses of our listeners? In clinical work, the influence of therapists—sometimes subtle, sometimes not, and sometimes unwittingly—on "repressed memories" of child abuse claimed by clients has been debated.

Childhood sexual abuse of any degree is traumatic for all children—even more so when it occurs in a context of extreme terror, including kidnappings, physical torture, and threats of death to the victim (or those close to the victim). Children abused by a parent feel betrayed and helpless; in some cases, they are further violated by the other parent (or partner of the abuser) participating in the abuse. Depending on the nature of the abuse, the child's relationship to the abuser, the personality of the child, and availability of emotional support, a variety of immediate and long-term reactions are observed.

Some children can discuss the abuse openly; others, feeling shame and fearful of repercussions, may be unable to share the experience, denying the abuse. Sometimes, perplexingly, a child may narrate a story of being abused where no abuse had occurred. This could represent a child's fantasy or sometimes result from the child being pressured by an adult, perhaps by one parent in divorce proceedings accusing the other parent of abuse. Sometimes a therapist has covertly suggested the abuse narrative to children, who then adopt the narrative. There have also been controversial cases, sometimes involving multiple children (for example, in a nursery school), where it is been asserted that no abuse occurred. Assessing the veracity, accuracy, and/or the distortion of the memory narrative in these situations requires a high level of clinical skill.

The nature of narrative discourse, the development of character, the role of memory, and the narrative's place on the truth-deception spectrum are intertwined with the author's point of view, forming an integral part of the biographical enterprise. These concepts are highly relevant to clinical work; the discourse between the narrator and the listener, for example, has parallels in the relationship of the client and the clinician:

> Psychoanalysts, as well as clinicians of other theoretical orientations, incorporate basic narrative precepts in different ways; "it is part of the appeal of the narrative metaphor that it does not prescribe procedure ... but this new language does provide us with new ways to think about old problems (Josselson, 1995, p. 337)." (Urdang, 2008, p. 152)

As there is no prescribed procedure, this philosophy has been adapted by clinicians to enhance their own particular type of clinical meaning making. Those who are cognitively and/or family systems oriented find a rationale in this philosophy, as do those who are psychodynamically and psychoanalytically oriented. All "narrative therapists" emphasize the storytelling and meaning making of the client-narrators; the role of the clinician in this framework is to enable clients to "co-create" or "re-author" a new narrative of their lives. How "narrative therapists" go about attaining this goal varies with their underlying practice orientation; this is discussed further at the end of the chapter.

Narrative Discourse

Narrative theory is not only about the storytelling and meaning making of the narrator. Its *discursive* nature is one of its essential components: An audience is necessary, whether physically present or as fantasized listeners. Here the term *discourse* is used in the broad sense of communication through spoken or written language in a social context. Bakhtin introduced the term *dialogic,* which emphasizes the speaker-listener connection. This notion "has captured the imagination of scholars in a multitude of disciplines" (Josselson, 1995, p. 332). It lends support to the concept of *intersubjectivity,* that is, the interactive exchanges (oftentimes only in thought and emotion) between the speaker and the listener. This point is highly relevant when applied to the incorporation of a narrative approach into psychotherapy, although some narrative therapists emphasize the storytelling and meaning making of the client and omit its discursive, intersubjective aspects. A therapist, for example, might tell his supervisor, at great length, the story the client has told about his unhappy marriage; nevertheless, he left out how the client told it: Did he keep blaming his wife for the problems, perhaps in order to sway the therapist to his side of the story? What type of response might the client have been trying to elicit from the therapist? Indeed, what type of response did he receive from the therapist? And how then did the client respond to this response? Did the therapist's omission of the intersubjective aspects reflect some discomfort he was feeling about his interaction with the client? And could this omission further reflect anxiety about sharing his own feelings with the supervisor?

Illustrating the dialogic principle, Brooks (1984) cites a direct writer-reader dialogue involving the mid-19th-century writer Eugene Sue. Sue had been writing his novel, *Les Mysteres de Paris,* as a newspaper serialization for 16 months but had not yet completed it. Readers would let Sue know their thoughts about his book, and he would incorporate their ideas into his ongoing novel. "The result was a dialogue that shaped both the ideology and the form of the novel" (Brooks, 1984, p. 163).

It is not uncommon for the reader to be so drawn into a story or a conversation that once this involvement has started, it can be difficult to withdraw:

> The intersubjective and reversible pattern of dialogue has been created. *Why are you telling me this?* the interlocutor may want to ask—but by the time he comes to make such a response, it is already too late: like the Ancient Mariner's Wedding guest, he has been made to hear. If a number of nineteenth-and twentieth-century narrative texts present sophisticated versions of traditional oral storytelling, it

is because this gives them a way to force the reader into transferential relationship with what he may not want to see or hear. [italics added] (Brooks, 1984, p. 261)

The oral narrator was essential in Native American narrative discourse: Stories and poetry were of necessity conveyed in the oral tradition, as there had been no written language or alphabet. Stories and poems were considered the cultural property of the tribe, and individual artists were not recognized. Even if the poet were contemporary, he or she would not acknowledge authorship. Conversely, the teller of the tale or reciter of the poem, the *conveyer,* puts his or her own individualistic spin on it, no matter how traditional the material. Tedlock (Krupat, 1985) explained how, in the Zuni culture, "the 'conveyer' is always an 'interpreter' as well" (p. 12):

> The interpreter may suddenly realize something or understand something for the first time on this particular occasion. The teller is not merely repeating memorized words; nor is he or she merely giving a dramatic 'oral interpretation' or 'concert reading' of a fixed script. We are in the presence of a *performing art,* all right, but we are getting the *criticism* at the same time and from the same person. (Tedlock, quoted in Krupat, 1985, p. 12)

Tellers do not impassively recount their tales; they "seek to engage and influence their audiences' cognition, emotions, and values" (Scholes et al., 2006, p. 297). We must, however, consider the possibility that even if an "impassive" narrator delivers a tale, his or her basic impassivity is also a form of communication. This leads to the profound insight of Watzlawick, Beavin, and Jackson (1967), psychologists whose writings have been influential in the field of systemic family therapy. One of their major axioms states that it is impossible not to communicate. Are not depressed or psychotic persons (who may be mute) communicating (by their behavior and affect) how they are feeling and how they are feeling about communicating?

> It appears that the schizophrenic *tries not to communicate.* But since even nonsense, silence, withdrawal, immobility (postural silence), or any other form of denial is itself a communication, the schizophrenic is faced with the impossible task of denying that he is communicating and at the same time denying that his denial is a communication. The realization of this basic dilemma in schizophrenia is a key to a good many aspects of schizophrenic communication that would otherwise remain obscure. (Watzlawick et al., 1967, pp. 50–51)

The use of objects as symbols is also not unknown to the novelist. Flaubert illustrated inner thoughts and feelings through the symbolic usage of physical objects by Emma in *Madame Bovary,* "using her dog, her bridal bouquet, Binet's lathe, and other physical objects to symbolize Emma's mental states" (Scholes et al., 2006, p.196).

How one represents oneself to others is a complex amalgam of how one perceives oneself and how one wishes to be (or thinks that one is) perceived by others. People may present unrealistic aggrandized pictures of themselves as well as unrealistic negative self-portrayals; they may have the capacity to present an "outward appearance," which can be dramatically different from their inner self-image (or self-representation). Kafka was positively regarded by his teachers, but this was not congruous with his negative self-image.

Narrative theorists emphasize interpersonal influences on identity development: "Self-making is powerfully affected not only by your own interpretations of yourself but by the interpretations others offer of your version" (Bruner, 2001, p. 34). As we navigate through life, we often protect ourselves from our own thoughts and feelings and worry about how we present ourselves to others and how we are regarded by others. We may wish to be open and honest, and yet we may hold back.

In the biographical realm, some subjects present images of themselves to the public and future biographers (and in their own autobiographies) that range from major deception (such as presenting a fictional life as their own) to less severe distortions, including omitting painful or "shameful" personal memories. Some subjects, as Dickens did, take great pains to burn or otherwise destroy many of their private papers.

Conan Doyle presented himself in his autobiography as a courageous, chivalrous hero and a "spiritual" leader, promising immortality through communication with dead souls; his personal anxieties and family conflicts were omitted. Frederick Douglass and Ottilie Assing were concerned with their public persona and how they represented themselves to others. Within the therapeutic context, it is not unusual to find factors within the patient-therapist relationship itself that may also impede authentic discovery, such as "masking, pretending, and denying so that the self-estrangement in the end cannot be fully overcome" (F. Wyatt, 1986, p. 207). And this can occur on both sides of the therapeutic dyad.

A patient might present as defensive and avoidant, claiming, for example, that "nothing is really bothering me; my wife thought I should come." Underneath, however, he may be scared and lonely but feels too vulnerable to admit this. The therapist, in turn, might wish to impress the patient with his professional competence but is hiding his natural compassion by his formal responses.

An MSW student who was having difficulty developing her therapeutic skills agreed to do some video role-play, playing the clinician in an interview, with her friend, also an MSW student, as the client. The faculty advisor would observe, and together the three would try to understand the difficulty. When the "interview" was over, the friend said to the student: "What's the matter with you—you sound like a robot!—But that's not the way you are!" The student said: "But I'm being professional!" In this illustration of the "public persona," the student's notion of the way a "professional" acts and her evident anxiety about the client's perception of her (a common problem for students) was inhibiting her more natural responses and therefore paradoxically impeding her professional effectiveness.

Point of View

The narrator's or biographer's point of view is reflected in everything from selection of the subject to choice of data to present and the attempt to influence the audience's appraisal of the subject. Sometimes it is clear that the writer's own voice is present, as when he or she overtly narrates and comments on the story. At other times, the author's voice is expressed indirectly through voices of the characters and the dialogue he or she creates for them.

In a more complex variation, the author introduces a narrator who tells the story (with his or her own point of view), which may be different from the point of view of the characters, and the "invisible" author may cunningly manipulate all these voices from behind the scenes. In *Gulliver's Travels,* the reader can notice that a "major disparity of viewpoint seems to lie between Gulliver and Swift, with the audience aware of the disparity and sharing Swift's view" (Scholes et al., 2006, p. 256).

Henry James attempted to eliminate the voice of the author by deleting the narrator from his novels and by emphasizing the centrality of the characters; this proved impossible.

> In a Jamesian novel all the language is annihilated to Jamesian thoughts in a Jamesian shade. The result of the disappearance of the narrator is not the refining away of the artist but a continual reminder of his presence—as if God were omnipresent and invisible, yet one could continually hear Him breathing. (Scholes et al., 2006, p. 270)

The autobiographer, too, has a point of view and an "authorial voice"—but can an autobiographer be the authority on his or her own life? The constructivists would declare that the autobiographer would be the only authority on his or her life. Saint Augustine might question this: "How can the self know itself?" (Spengemann, 1980, p. 32). But even if the self knows itself (that is, how one feels and experiences the world), does the self always know how one is perceived by others and the effect he or she has on other lives? Furthermore, even if the author is self-reflective, how much of this self-understanding does he or she wish to share with the reader?

Narrative biographers (and autobiographers) would not be satisfied with presenting the subjects' lives (or their own lives) through a chronological history of dates, events, and accomplishments. They want their readers to see their biographical subject (or themselves) as a living, breathing person with thoughts and feelings who has special relationships and who moves about in a world shaped by social, economic, and political happenings. Artistry, creativity, and rhetoric also play roles in making this life come "alive," engaging the reader's interest. To what extent can the account of this life be dramatized, with "dull" aspects disregarded? Not all biographical (or autobiographical) writers choose to stick to the unadorned facts.

> The impulse to shape, to improve, to present not what was said or what did happen but what should have been said or ought to have happened, inevitably makes itself felt. Narrative art is the art of story-telling, and the more literate and sensitive a man is, the more he feels creative pressures which drive him to seek beauty or truth at the expense of fact. Narrative art is an art of compromise, in which gains are always purchased at the expense of sacrifices. The story-teller is often faced with the choice of being either a bore or a charlatan. (Scholes et al., 2006, p. 258)

Likewise, the point of view of the clinician is also of central importance in clinical work. Clinicians make a diagnosis and select a treatment approach based on their conceptual frameworks; they have subjective reactions to each client, which may color their treatment. Spence (1986) considers *narrative smoothing,* whereby clinicians choose certain facts but leave out details which do not support their theories; this "allows interpretation to masquerade as explanation... which effectively prevents the [clinical] reader from making contact with the complete account... [or] coming up with alternative explanations" (pp. 212–213).

Clinicians may face or be unaware of the temptations of narrative artistry as they prepare to narrate the stories of their patients to their colleagues in oral or written reports. They may be hesitant to reveal their own involvement in their work and reluctant or unwilling to record the detailed process of what actually transpired in the therapy. Spence (1986) uses the term *unpacking* to denote this incomplete processing and has observed the resistance by some analysts to "unpack the session more fully ... [because they] often choose to protect themselves from too detailed an awareness of how they function—in part for narcissistic reasons" (p. 230).

However, this situation may be more complex than issues of countertransference and resistance. When clinicians present their cases to an audience, they are addressing a specific group of listeners, whose presence can influence the narrative. Is the audience composed of a friendly ongoing support group of peers? Does the audience have the "power" to give the presenter a grade, or admit the presenter to (or graduate him or her from) an institute of advanced training? Kernberg (1965) has observed that the requirements and policies of the psychoanalytic training institute can affect the clinical work of the analytic candidate; this would, in turn, impact the candidate's case presentation.

Plot

The plot provides the structure of the narrative, its story line, and intended meanings; it is "the dynamic, sequential element in narrative literature" (Scholes et al., 2006, p. 207). The plot is "the design and intention of narrative, what shapes a story and gives it a certain direction or intent of meaning" (Brooks, 1984, p. xi). Brooks asserts that plot is also related to time and to our sense of mortality: Plot "develops its propositions only through temporal sequence and progression. Narrative [helps us understand] the problem of temporality; man's time-boundedness," and awareness of death. And plot is the "principal ordering force of those meanings that we try to wrest from human temporality." (Brooks, 1984, p. xi).

Autobiography, by its nature, cannot include the author's "final" ending, but its plot evolves through the sequence of the subject's life events. The autobiographer delineates how he "comes to terms with himself, realizes his nature, assumes his vocation" (Scholes et al., 2006, p. 215). In looking at Ved Mehta's autobiography, we see that the plot revolves around his blindness, the social problems this presented to him, the prejudices he experienced, and how he finally achieved "his quest"—his acceptance and achievement in the sighted world—and in addition, how he gained self-acceptance of his blindness and greater comfort with himself and others.

Character and Identity

The term *character* has been used in various ways, such as an individual's personal sense of morality ("he's of good character") or as a description of personality characteristics ("she's obstinate, strict, and orderly"). Today character is generally used more comprehensively, incorporating a sense of identity, and often synonymously with personality: Character "consists of the totality of objectively observable behavior and subjectively reportable inner experience" (Campbell, 1989, p. 119).

Identity encompasses a person's sense of self, and although experienced in a deeply subjective manner, it develops through early interactive experiences with care-givers and other figures and is closely related to the development of language, to stories one hears about oneself, and stories one begins to tell about oneself. We are interested in exploring our personal histories, and in the process we develop a sense of "autobiographical consciousness" that contributes to our development of a sense of identity (Freeman, 2001, p. 287).

The concept of identity can include more than a singular picture of self. Andrew O'Hagan (2009) refers to Samuel Johnson's "multiplicity":

> Johnson's glory lives in his multiplicity. He was never one thing. He was Janus-faced but also Janus-souled: investing as much of himself in the opposite of rancor and enmity as he did in rancor and enmity, and sometimes within the same half-hour. It is the main reason why James Boswell was able to make him the subject of the best biography ever written: the two minded biographer met his four-minded subject and a form of literary intimacy was born that time has neither breached nor weathered. (O'Hagan, 2009, p. 7)

Biographers often struggle to ascertain the accuracy of their subject's self-representations. Diedrich (1999), in her biography of Ottilie Assing, discussed her difficulties with understanding Ottilie, as Ottilie was perpetually concerned with how she represented herself to others, needing to "invent" a portrait of herself that was acceptable to her.

Early narratives often included descriptions of character. In the Norse sagas, description of character is fundamental, but only brief descriptive character sketches are presented; later actions of the characters are predicated on this introductory description. "But the sagas never attempt to penetrate inside the character. Only words and actions are described; thoughts are never analyzed" (Scholes et al., 2006, p. 172). However, this does not mean that all early narratives treated inner life as nonexistent: "...the inward life is assumed but not presented in primitive narrative literature" (Scholes et al., 2006, p. 166).

One of the techniques used in early narratives to reveal the thoughts of characters is the use of supernatural forces, such as the "*dei ex machina*...to open up the minds of their characters" (Scholes et al., 2006, p. 175). Homer, rather than describing Achilles's inner struggle with his angry feelings, presents the goddess Athena, who has a private discussion with Achilles. Subsequently, because of her influence, Achilles decides to express his anger verbally rather than through action. Later, as Christianity developed, the devil appeared as a "*deus ex machina* who assists in the dramatizing of motivation and the revelation of character" (p. 177).

The development of the *interior monologue* was another step toward presenting a person's thoughts to the reader. In its specific use in narrative literature, interior monologue refers to "a direct, immediate presentation of the unspoken thoughts of a character without any intervening narrator" (Scholes et al., 2006, p. 177). In early narratives, they appeared infrequently and generally were related to a specific plot goal.

The concept of interior monologue is differentiated from the more modern psychological notion of *stream of consciousness,* which generally is the "illogical, ungrammatical, mainly associative pattern of human thought" (Scholes et al., 2006, p. 177). Scholes et al. (2006) believed that it was Homer who first introduced the interior monologue to the narrative tradition. Homer used the interior monologue at key dramatic moments in the *Iliad.* One important line recurs: "'...but why does my own heart *[thymos]* dispute with me thus?'" (quoted in Scholes et al., 2006, p. 179). It is not uncommon to hear a client say something like "I know it doesn't make any sense to leave college right now, but something inside is pushing me to do this."

Freudian concepts of the ego, id, superego, and their psychic conflicts would not be formulated for well over 2,000 years after Homer, and yet Homer intuitively understood that the human psyche had its struggles:

> The *thymos,* which can mean something like heart or something like mind, is seen as disputing *(dielexato)* with the will of the individual. The psyche has been divided into two parts which dispute for mastery, often in a manner hinting at a concept of the ego, which cares for its own preservation, and a superego, which drives the individual toward acceptable action. Some such concept of the divided psyche seems essential for the development of the interior monologue technique. (Scholes et al., 2006, p. 180)

Although Homer did make use of the interior monologue, he was primarily interested in action. The advance of interior monologue has been attributed to Apollonius of Rhodes, who used it when a character such as Medea was in painful psychological conflict (Scholes et al., 2006):

> Medea . . . is torn between her newly acquired passion and her loyalty to her father. There is no one to whom she can confide all her thoughts. She attempts to resolve her dilemma in a debate with herself. Apollonius treats her inner struggle at length, combining narrative analysis with

a long passage of interior monologue. (Scholes et al., 2006, p. 182)

In the footsteps of Apollonius, Virgil uses the interior monologue to narrate Dido's story in the *Aeneid*. It is the women, in these early narratives, who experience the greatest passion and its ensuing conflict. They often lack confidantes and therefore have a greater need to express themselves through monologues. "The inner life of the female ... contemplating her erotic situation has been a focal point of narrative concern with the psyche from Medea and Dido to Anna Karenina and Molly Bloom" (Scholes et al., 2006, p. 183). A distinction has been made between stream of consciousness and interior monologues whose purpose and organization are rhetorical. Earlier interior monologues were dominated by rhetoric—that is, "words artfully deployed so as to move the reader or audience by focusing on him and his responses.... The monologue became a set piece, an opportunity for display of verbal virtuosity" (Scholes et al., 2006, p. 185). In modern psychological monologues focusing on thought and character, stream of consciousness has often prevailed— that is, spontaneous thoughts, freely flowing and not subjected to systematic organization. It is similar to the idea of patients' free association in psychoanalysis. Its use in literature is an attempt to depict the mind at work.

Modern novels such as *Ulysses* by James Joyce and *Mrs. Dalloway* by Virginia Woolf lean heavily on the use of stream of consciousness. Some authors combine this approach with interior monologue as rhetoric. Scholes et al. (2006) note that one excellent example of this is Anna's interior monologue toward the end of Tolstoy's *Anna Karenina* "just prior to her suicide" (p. 194). They add that Dostoyevsky's writings also notably exemplified this development.

The plays of Shakespeare and the development of Elizabethan drama contributed both to the development of characterization and the use of monologues. These "hover between the rhetorical and the psychological in characterization" (Scholes et al., 2006, p. 188). Hamlet's "To be or not to be" soliloquy is one of the best-known examples of an interior monologue; it is also one of the best examples of eloquent rhetoric.

The dilemma of whether to include or eliminate the author's "voice" becomes especially troublesome when considering how the voice of the subject should be presented. With respect to biographical writings, authors are omnipresent, even if trying to be invisible. Their point of view pervades all aspects of the work. Should the author actually quote the subject? Is it proper to "invent" words the subject might have said? Is the writer sufficiently attuned to the subject's inner world to adequately convey it to the reader? Does the writer (or the practitioner) make assumptions about the subject's thoughts and feelings and then present them as facts?

Making assumptions about a client's thoughts and feelings is a frequent occupational hazard for clinicians. This can occur for various reasons, including theoretical orientation and reductionism. For example, a clinician assumes that the cause of Mildred's present distress about her female supervisor must be the fact that she had had a poor relationship with her mother. Or practitioners can overidentify with clients: For instance, I know how she must have felt when she contemplated divorce, because that is how I felt. Or fear of dealing with a client's expression of strong feeling may lead to cutting off discussion without sufficient exploration, while making assumptions about what is troubling the client.

Backscheider (1999) referred to the writer's perspective as one determinant of presenting the subject's voice:

By the perspective of the biographer I mean the movement in and out of the mind of the subject, the freedom assumed to interpret the subject's actions and thoughts, the degree of the commitment to let the subjects speak for themselves, and the extent to which biographers are willing to insert their own voices and sensibilities into the narrative. (Backscheider, 1999, p. 90)

Richard Holmes (1985) is a biographer who places great value on entering the experiential world of his subjects; he declares, however, that he must attempt to be aware of the boundaries between his own interpretations and his subject's actual thoughts. Barrell, a critic of Holmes, raised questions about Holmes's possible "boundary" transgressions in his writing on Coleridge:

> It's [Holmes's] extraordinary gift for "speaking for" his subjects that has recently provoked some doubts in his critics: Barrell is skeptical about "the ventriloquial *[sic]* magic of the free indirect style, which allows him to pass off his own thoughts as the thoughts of Coleridge... [as if] he can speak Coleridge's mind for him." (Lee, 2001, p. 53)

In addition to authenticity, the biographer is concerned about the aesthetic and artistic aspects of his or her work—a biographer wants to engage the reader. Biographical writers have experimented with new techniques, accompanied by ensuing debate (Holroyd, 2002). For example, whether it is "legitimate for a biographer to borrow from the techniques of the fiction writer," such as the creation of dialogue between the subject and others (Backscheider, 1999, p. xix). And is it permissible to let the reader in on the writer's thoughts about what the subject was thinking at a given time?

The artistically minded historian or biographer, even before he writes a word, is looking for esthetically satis-fying patterns in the people and events he considers as potential subjects for his work. And every historian or biographer who hopes to reach an audience beyond his fellow professionals is to some extent artistically minded. (Scholes et al., 2006, p. 217)

Autobiographers, it can be argued, have in fact been there—they should be capable of remembering what they thought and what they said. But how much do autobiographers remember about the actual details of conversations held, and how accurate can they be in their memories about what they were thinking about years earlier? Autobi-ographers, too, are concerned about narrative style and withholding their audience's interest. "A diarist who makes a second draft of his diary, as Boswell did and as even Pepys may have done, is moving toward fiction already" (Scholes et al., 2006, p. 258).

Narrative theory offers insights that are highly relevant to both biographers and clinicians into the development of character and identity and the dilemmas entailed in presenting such portrayals to an audience. Clinicians are required to interpret their findings to others, including colleagues and students. How do they convey a sense of their client's thoughts and feelings? Do they simply literally quote the client's words? And if they do so, do they understand fully what these words mean? How do they "narrate" the client's feelings and omissions? If practitioners assume the liberty to interpret their clients' stories, are they, like Holmes, "speak[ing] Coleridge's mind for him?" Are clinicians prone to influence the audience regarding their own theoretical perspective—what Spence (1986) referred to as "narrative smoothing"? And to what extent, in an effort to make case presentations interesting to their listeners, are they being "artistically minded"? The possibilities for such "narrative smoothing" were imagined by Muriel Spark in her 1981 novel, *Loitering with Intent*. The book contains a depiction of an organization called the Autobiographical Association, a discussion group made up of people working on their autobiographies. The secretary of the association suggests that autobiographers might wish to take artistic liberties with the facts a bit, just to "liven" up the narratives for readers. Clinicians may be tempted to do the same when reporting on their cases.

Memory

Memory can be "partial, self-serving, or faulty," and "we always manage to turn our memories into good stories-even if those stories aren't quite true" (Mendelsohn, 2010, p. 74). Conan Doyle commented that "'the vivid stories which [my mother] would tell me stand out so clearly that they obscure the real facts of my life'" (quoted in Stashower, 1999, p. 22). Further, to what extent have later memories been "fused" onto earlier memories, reinforcing or perhaps distorting the original memory? In his autobiography, Nuland (2003) puzzles over whether an early memory of his father is accurate or whether it is distorted by his history of conflict with his father. He recalls that once, when a toddler, he stuffed his father's watch and chain into a wall socket, experiencing both an electric shock and the shock of his father exploding with rage at him.

> How can I be so sure about my father's rage on that day? Is it really possible that at two and a half I could already have learned to anticipate such an excessive response, or

am I looking back on the entire episode reflected in the mirror of so many subsequent paroxysms of self-righteous outrage? (Nuland, 2003, pp. 14–15)

Nuland (2003), struggling to understand whether his memory is accurate, shares his uncertainties with the reader; he is processing his experience of remembering.

Saint Augustine gave much thought to the phenomenon of memory. He observed that the capacity for memory is one of the conditions for creating continuity of the self throughout life (Olney, 1998). Augustine does not claim that everything he "remembers" is derived only from his own memories; he includes experiences that he may "have heard from others" or "believed on the basis of experience" (Olney, 1998, p. 20).

Saint Augustine saw memory as an active, ongoing process. He discussed this phenomenon in his *Confessions,* observing that there is a "present of the past, in the form of memory, and a present of the future, in the form of anticipation or awaiting" (Brooks, 1984, pp. 328–329). Using the metaphor of weaving, Augustine described this integration of memories:

"There are all the things I remember to have experienced myself or to have heard from others. From the same store too I can take out pictures of things which have either happened to me or are believed on the basis of experience; I can myself weave them into the context of the past, and from them I can infer future actions, events, hopes, and then I can contemplate all these as though they were in the present." *(Confessions* 10.8, 218–219, quoted in Olney, 1998, p. 20)

Augustine's notion of "weaving, as a characteristic metaphor for the operation of memory," is a core concept of life writings (Olney, 1998 p. 20). Memory and weaving are not static but in motion, and just as weaving will produce changing forms, the process of active recall will "bring forth ever different memorial configurations and an ever newly shaped self" (Olney, 1998, p. 20). Telling a story of one's life, then, becomes a dynamic process; this would be different from using rote memory, such as the repeating of a memorized psalm. And yet, perhaps reciting a psalm may not be as rote as it initially appears, as when Hegel noted " 'that the old man repeats the same prayers he learned as a child but now altered, weighted, given entirely new coloring by the experience of a lifetime' " (quoted in Olney, 1998, p. 21).

Writing about the past, as in memoirs, can actually enhance memory and the development of recall; it may also help the writer gain a new perspective on the past. The dynamic process of the narrator recalling the past while developing a new understanding has been termed *retrospective teleology* (Brockmeier, 2001). Marcel Proust's *À la Recherche du Temps Perdu* (1919) illustrated vividly how recalling and reliving the past can produce remembrances of life experiences of "a richness and depth that was impossible to grasp and to evaluate when they were experienced originally" (Freeman & Brockmeier, 2001, p. 80). Ved Mehta (1987b), reflecting on the writing of his autobiographical *Vedi,* discussed how his memories expanded in the writing, making the writing an active aid in the process of recall:

> I had realized that memory expands by some kind of asso-
> ciative process, so that a remembered scene that at first
> seems hardly worth a line grows in the act of thinking

and writing into a chapter, and this full-blown memory uncovers other memories, other scenes, which in their turn expand and multiply. (Mehta, 1987b, Preface)

Life events can trigger recall of buried memories and feelings. The death of Thomas Hardy's first wife, Emma, from whom he had been emotionally estranged for years, brought forth a flood of his old passionate feelings for her, which he expressed in poetry. "He had become a lover in mourning" (Tomalin, 2007, p. xviii):

> He began at once to revisit their early love in his mind with an intensity that expressed itself in a series of poems. "One forgets all the recent years and differences," he wrote to a friend, "and the mind goes back to the early times when each was much to the other—in her case and mine intensely much." (Tomalin, 2007, p. xviii)

In the opposite direction, acquiring new knowledge (or "brooding" on old knowledge) can negatively color past memories that were essentially positive. Tomalin (2007) speculated that Hardy "reinvented" a childhood that in reality was not as unhappy as he later implied (p. 258). (Rudyard Kipling has been accused of the same, as discussed in chapter 10.)

> Hardy appears to be reinventing his childhood and making it worse. This prompts the question as to whether he had only lately learnt the facts of his own conception and birth, and become aware that he had been an unwanted child whose existence forced his parents into a marriage neither desired; or only lately brooded on the implications of this

knowledge. A retrospective blight cast across his life is a very Hardyesque possibility. (Tomalin, 2007, p. 258)

Clinicians frequently focus on past experiences with their clients, and they, as well as biographers, search through the fog of murky memories to help recover the conflicts, fears, traumas, and realities of the past. Sometimes it is memories of happiness that have been forgotten, as Hardy may have forgotten the happiness of his childhood. The narrative lens of retrospective teleology often enables the gaining of a new perspective and the construction of a new narrative. Reading biographies critically can enable clinicians to appreciate the vicissitudes and complexities involved in reconstructing life stories.

Authenticity and Deception

Narrative theory presents us with a paradox: When narrators convey their experiences and interpret events, they construct reality; however, narrative theory insists that an audience's reactions to a narrated story become part of the dynamic intersubjective transaction between the audience and the narrator. We are left to wonder whether narrators are telling their story purely from their inner experiential world or whether the purity of the telling is contaminated by narrators' concerns about their listeners and how they might react to the narration. The listener may be left to ask, as Brooks (1984) has asked, "Why are you telling me this" (p. 261)? Therapists might also ask themselves this question when listening to a patient's story. Perhaps the question "Why are you telling me this now?" should be considered.

In searching for authenticity in biographical material as well as in the clinical experience, we have to accept that we may never have the absolute truth, the full story of anyone's life. We must consider the many distinctions and gradations within the authenticity-deception spectrum and the range of self-representations within every individual. For example, Joan has applied for a job and presented herself in a favorable light in the interview, emphasizing her motivation and positive attributes. Later, when talking to her therapist, Joan observed that she felt fraudulent in that interview—she herself had not believed one word she said to the interviewer. A few weeks later, Joan learned that she had a dangerous health problem. She did not tell her therapist the diagnosis. Not wanting to cause the therapist any sadness about her health, she provided the therapist with a light-hearted account of her illness. Was she authentic or deceptive in these situations?

In the recent novel *The Guernsey Literary and Potato Peel Pie Society* (Shaffer & Barrows, 2008), Juliet, a writer, sends a letter to Sidney, her publisher and friend, and discusses her observations about two different parts of herself:

> Sidney, in these past two or three years, I have become better at writing than living.... On the page, I'm perfectly charming, but that's just a trick I learned. It has nothing to do with me. At least, that's what I was thinking [on the boat when]... I had a cowardly impulse to throw my red cape overboard and pretend I was someone else. (Shaffer & Barrows, 2008, pp. 159–160)

Biographers have the daunting task of getting to know their subjects in their various personalities and presentations. This is never easy, but some biographers have more of a struggle when their subjects are elusive. Although Norman Sherry was authorized by Graham

Greene to be his biographer, Greene's secretive lifestyle complicated the task:

> Greene was given to writing two versions of a diary entry
> to conceal a visit to a prostitute . . . and to sending two
> postcards to his mistress, a chaste version addressed to
> her and her husband at home, and a more intimate one for
> her to collect elsewhere. . . . He once wrote . . . "If anybody
> ever tries to write a biography of me, how complicated
> they are going to find it and how misled they are going to
> be." (Franklin, 2004, p. 100)

Although autobiographers speak with their own voices, we cannot always assume that their presentations of their lives or descriptions of other people are accurate; degrees of truthfulness, self-awareness, and sometimes deception are at play. Some authors, like Gandhi, emphasized the importance of telling the truth, and "his autobiography is a self-conscious endeavor to test his capacity for the truth" (Barbour, 1992, p. 12). This does not necessarily mean that he was more successful at it than anyone else. In any event, not all writers can reasonably assert this moral claim, as some take great pains to conceal the "truth."

Margery Allingham (1988), in *Dancers in Mourning,* introduces the reader to Mr. William Faraday, who is writing his memoirs. In the process, he becomes progressively uncomfortable with the lack of drama in his life, so he proceeds to edit his life in the service of the memoirs:

> When Mr. William Faraday sat down to write his memoirs
> after fifty-eight years of blameless inactivity he found the

work of inscribing the history of his life almost as tedious as living it had been and so, possessing a natural invention coupled with a gift for locating the easier path, he began to prevaricate a little upon the second page, working up to downright lying on the sixth and subsequent folios. (Allingham, 1988, p. 7)

Mr. Faraday is a fictional character; however, many have created their own supposedly candid memoirs that have been pronounced fictional and fraudulent upon publication. Writing fraudulent auto-biographies is not a rare aberration. One of the most sensational cases occurred in 1969, when Clifford Irving, a novelist, decided to take a turn at biography, choosing the wealthy and reclusive Howard Hughes as a subject. He wrote this as an autobiography with the help of his collaborator, Richard Suskind, receiving an advance of $750,000 from McGraw Hill (Yagoda, 2009). Hughes found out about the scam and informed the press, As a consequence, Irving was sent to prison for 17 months. Although other fraudulent autobiographies have been written, Yagoda stated that Irving was "the only autobi-ographical faker, as far as I have been able to determine to do time for the offense" (2009, pp. 247-248).

A fascinating debate about authenticity and deception revolves around Helen Keller: Were her autobiographies authentic or were they plagiarized? Accusations were frequently leveled at her: "...the charge of expropriation, of both thought and idiom...dogged her at intervals during her early and middle years" (Ozick, 2003, p. 193). One critic, Thomas Cutsforth, a blind psychologist, wrote in 1933 that her descriptive use of colors, such as " 'a mist of green,' " was not honest: it was " 'implied chicanery,' and 'a birthright sold for a mess of verbiage' " (Ozick, 2003, p. 194).

Helen Keller's history, by now legend, was dramatized in the play and subsequent movie *The Miracle Worker.* Keller was born in 1880 with normal hearing and vision but suddenly became completely blind and deaf after a severe, undiagnosed illness when she was 19 months old. When Helen was seven years old, a teacher, Annie Sullivan, herself partially blind, arrived to help Helen.

The famous breakthrough came when Helen acquired her first word: *water.* With Annie Sullivan's guidance, Helen was able to make the association between the word water and the substance water. One of the criticisms leveled against Helen was related to the influence of Annie Sullivan on her thinking and writing: Were these Helen's thoughts or Annie's thoughts? Was Helen "the puppet of an ambitious teacher" (Shulevitz, 2003, p. 731)?

Early accusations of Helen's plagiarism resulted from her first publication, *The Frost King,* when she was 11 years old; it was subsequently discovered that this greatly resembled *The Frost Fairies* by children's author Margaret Canby. Annie Sullivan had .spelled out this story into Helen's hand three years earlier. It remained there in her "prodigiously retentive memory; she was entirely oblivious of reproducing phrases not her own" (Ozick, 2003, p. 194).

On a number of occasions, Helen described the richness of her world and how much she could perceive: " 'Blindness has no limited effect upon mental vision,' she argued again and again" (Ozick, 2003, p. 196). She once commented: " 'The bulk of the world's knowledge is an imaginary construction' " (p. 195).

In another context, during a visit to Mark Twain, she commented that her "strongest impression of him was that of sorrow. There was about him the air of one who had suffered greatly. Whenever I touched his face his expression was sad, even when he was telling a funny story' " (quoted in Herrmann, 1998, p. 169).

Helen Keller and her achievements are indeed inspirational. Yet beyond her personal struggles and triumphs, her life and her narratives do raise perplexing questions about the nature of experience, reality, authenticity, and imagination—"she stands for enigma" (Ozick, 2003). What she contributed to posterity, however, "is an epistemological marker of sorts: proof of the real existence of the mind's eye" (p. 196).

Clinicians also attempt to find the balance between authenticity and deception in their clients' narratives. In seeking psychotherapy, the patients want relief from psychological pain; surely they are willing to share their troubles with a sympathetic clinician who is ready to help. But the narrator-patient is also concerned about self-image "and how he is coming across to . . . the analytic listener" (F. Wyatt, 1986, p. 205). Patients want to conceal parts of their narratives even from themselves—they may not be able to bear the pain or the shame of remembering, and sometimes their memories are not in their awareness. There is a "measure of deception and evasion to be found in almost all stories, mixed in with what seems to be the stuff of authenticity." In fact, "all storytelling tries to deny and be silent about just as much as it strains to convey" (p. 208).

Clients may deliberately distort their stories in order to "deceive" the therapist because of "instrumental" concerns, such as having child custody restored to them; or for "psychological" reasons, such as a need to manipulate and control, a wish to be admired, or a fear of censure. The recognition of deception in the therapeutic context is a commonly neglected phenomenon; when deception does occur in therapy, the therapeutic interaction is affected (Gediman & Lieberman, 1996).

If narrative theory-oriented therapists operate on the premise that there are only subjective versions of the truth, assessing deception can be problematic. A particularly complicated problem is assessing accuracy and distortions in the recall of more remote past events.

Listening to the details of the client's life story can help the clinician gain insight into the experiential and feeling states of patients, as well as serving other therapeutic purposes, such as helping the client remember important events and experiences. Ved Mehta's autobiographical writing was an active aid to him in the process of recall; his memories expanded as he wrote. The recollection of past memories also occurs frequently in therapy, in the active telling of past events to an interested listener. The therapeutic dialogue can also be fostered by asking specific questions to stimulate the recovery of additional thoughts and memories. For example: Has this happened at other times? What comes to mind when you think about this? You haven't talked about your college days: what was that time like for you?

Eliciting details can also help the client evaluate his or her own perception of events and become aware of possible distortions. For example, after several sessions of therapy, a woman said that her minister told her not to come anymore. The therapist asked: "What did he say?" The client responded: "He said that if I didn't feel I was being helped, I didn't have to go." The therapist asked: "What if I complained to you that I bought a pair of shoes—but the color wasn't right and they were too tight?" The client responded: "Do you mean I got him to say that?" This awareness opened the door to discussion of the client's discomfort in telling the clinician directly that the treatment did not feel like a "good fit" for her.

Narrative Theory and Clinical Work

Narrative theory, with its chameleon-like adaptability, has been used by therapists of many different persuasions and in work with diverse client populations. *Reminiscence,* or telling their life stories, enhances self-esteem, memory, and coping and improves social relationships in the elderly (Spira, 2006). Child welfare workers help foster children compose life books, which narrate and illustrate the story of their fragmented lives. In *reciprocal storytelling,* children tell their own stories to the clinician, who responds in terms of the feelings and content present in these stories (Brandell, 2004).

Homework assignments for clients, such as journaling, is popular with cognitive-behavioral and constructivist therapists. Working with addicted clients, Diamond (2000) suggested that in addition to journaling, they write letters to significant others and a good-bye letter to alcohol. Writing about oneself can be therapeutic; sometimes it becomes "the defining moment and healing encounter in a person's life" (p. 337). Autobiographical writing can lead to ongoing personal growth (Barbour, 1992).

> Autobiography ... requires that one take stock of one's past, seizing it as something to be weighed, assessed, and evaluated in the light of a normative model of life. Autobiographical self-construction thus requires self-distancing; it is a "second-reading" of experience ... guided by the demand that one confront oneself "honestly" and own up to the trouble spots of one's history. As such, it is the way we make sense of our lived lives in order to face the possible lives we envision. (Freeman & Brockmeier, 2001, p. 80)

Some clinicians find that narrative approaches enable them to better understand people from diverse cultures. Laird (cited in Freeman & Couchonnal, 2006) emphasized that in examining a narrative, one should take into account "not only the facts of the story but also the meaning the narrator makes of the events and the narrator's worldview, or belief system" (p. 200). Some narrative theorists have adopted a *social constructionist* position: Narratives, they believe, are determined primarily by social customs and values. Others, opposing this theory, have argued that although shaped by their cultures, people can also "transcend their cultural horizons" (Josselson, 1995). The American psychologist, George Rosenwald, who investigated the case study method for interpreting life stories,

> ...takes issue with the social constructionists who profess that life stories are only a reflection of social conventions. Although Rosenwald agrees that narratives are shaped within a social situation and told in an interpersonal context, there remains the tension between subjectivity (desire) and social necessity. The interplay between them is the ultimate "plot" of a life course. (Josselson, 1995, p. 339)

When narrative theorists discuss the role of the therapist, the clinician (generally referred to as the *co-author*) is described as facilitating the writing of a new narrative jointly with the client. It is in the process of this rewriting that the theoretical schools so widely diverge. The cognitive-behavioral and systemic approaches emphasize helping clients gain a different cognitive perspective, based on a reframing of their stories.

In discussing the application of narrative theory to systemic family therapy, for example, Josselson (1995) described the approach of White and Epston, which includes family members writing letters to each other, the therapist writing letters to the family, and members role-playing, all with an emphasis on breaking through the family's present negative patterns of interaction and discovering new ways of being together.

Freeman and Couchonnal (2006) applied narrative theory to clinical social work, noting in particular that it highlights the strengths perspective and can be integrated with "family systems, task-centered, solution-focused, and crisis intervention models" (p. 201). One recommended technique is using the stories told by other people, including personal stories told by the therapist "or the stories of other clients" (p. 204).

> Another aspect of this affirmation strategy involves co-constructing alternative narratives with clients about other people's experiences.... The steps include not only identifying other people's stories that have meaning to clients' lives ... but also developing life lessons based on an analysis of the co-constructed narratives.... An important step ... involves the practitioner's affirmation of their [clients'] efforts to transform their self-images. That step can be accomplished by asking solution-focused questions such as, "how are you different as a result of this session?" (Freeman & Couchonnal, 2006, p. 204)

In contrast to cognitive-behavioral and system approaches, psychodynamic therapists explore the client's inner world more intensively and use the discursive concept at a deeper level. Psychodynamically oriented therapists are not only "coauthors" of the client's new stories but are also actively engaged in the client's reenactments of past conflicts, as they bring the past into a highly emotionally charged present. The dialogic, intersubjective component of the psychodynamic therapy demands an interpersonal intensity and involvement from both participants, and the inner worlds of both the client and the therapist are examined and drawn on.

Many compatibilities exist between psychodynamic models and narrative theory. F. Wyatt (1986) observed that psychoanalysis has always incorporated aspects of narrative theory: "we are dealing in stories and with stories all the time." (p. 193). Although Freud has been criticized by many, including present-day constructivists, as a "positivist," with a drive-dominated, mechanistic framework, others see him as an excellent narrative therapist. Brooks (1984) refers to psychoanalysis as a "primarily narrative art, concerned with the recovery of the past through the dynamics of memory and desire" (p. xiv).

Freud saw an analogy between detective work and psychoanalysis, as both look for "explanations" (Brooks, 1984, p. 270). Freud's famous patient, the Wolf Man, in his memoirs, commented on Freud's interest in Sherlock Holmes. He thought Freud would dislike this kind of literature. To the contrary, Freud was quite intrigued: "The fact that circumstantial evidence is useful in psychoanalysis when reconstructing a childhood history may explain Freud's interest" (quoted in Brooks, 1984, pp.269-270).

Edelson (1993) also found narrative and psychoanalytic theory compatible. Major ideas in psychoanalysis and psychotherapy are found "in language about telling and enacting stories" (p. 294). He focuses on the experiential and feeling states of patients; trainees are taught to "eschew the vague and general, and instead to pursue the particular" (p. 316)—that is, the details of their patients' narratives, which should not be interrupted by therapists supplying labels or interpretations. Edelson quoted himself in words that many biographers would applaud:

> Out with conceptual labels summarizing or classifying experiences! Out with vagueness!… Ask yourself as you listen to the patient: Can you see a scene in your mind, a particular time and place, particular characters? Can you see what they are doing? Hear what they are saying? (pp. 316–317)

Edelson also focused on the intersubjective encounter of the patient and the therapist—the discursive aspect of narration. He referred to the "microprocess: 'the *immediacy of the therapeutic moment'* " (Edelson, 1993, p. 317, quoting Shapiro). Therapists need to be attuned to the ongoing interpersonal and affective interactions between the patient and the therapist. This close examination of the therapeutic hour highlights the "moment-by-moment dynamic… the blips and perturbations, the minute changes of affect and emphasis" (Edelson, 1993, p. 317).

Narrative theory offers us a lens and a framework for considering life stories, narrators, and audiences that can enhance our insights into both biographical writings and clinical work. Biographers strive to engage their readers to "tune in" to the experiential world of their subjects. Tuning into the client's subjectivity, unfortunately, is not always the goal for clinicians. Today, with managed care and evidence-based practice, the emphasis is often on the reduction of symptoms. However, for clinicians who want to "know" their clients as people with unique lives, relationships, and experiences, one path to achieve this is to become a good audience to the client as story-teller, to deepen one's listening skills. Biographies offer an opportunity to experience the depth of others' experiences, their inner and outer worlds, to understand the plot of their lives as they traverse their life course.

Realization of the discursive nature of narratives can also expand the scope of the clinician's professional development, altering the focus from exclusive concern with the surface narration itself to its intended effect and actual effect on the listener. As clinicians exercise this awareness in practice, they gain insight and skills by understanding therapy's intersubjective nature.

CHAPTER 8

The Narratives of Frederick Douglass and Ottilie Assing in the Construction of Their Biographies

While planning was proceeding for the National Museum of African American History and Culture in Washington, DC, a controversy erupted about the museum's message: "What story will it tell?" (Taylor, 2011). Would the pain and suffering associated with slavery and racism be emphasized, or would black achievements and resilience be highlighted? In relation to Frederick Douglass's life, both narratives are necessary: His pain and suffering as a former slave were interwoven with his resilience and strength throughout his development as a prominent leader in the abolitionist movement, the Civil War, and Reconstruction.

Frederick Douglass's well-known odyssey, from slavery, escape, and emancipation to international renown, is heroic; yet the narrative of his personal and family life remains in the shadows. Douglass presented himself through his three autobiographies as he wished to be perceived by his audiences. "Most of what we can learn about him is what Frederick Douglass chose to tell us" (McFeely, 1991, p. 7).

Ottilie Assing, a half-Jewish German journalist for the German newspaper *Morgenblatt,* though relatively unknown to history, was an important figure in Douglass's life. At 33, fascinated by American society, she immigrated to the United States. Her interest in racial conflict and Frederick Douglass's autobiography led to their meeting. The relationship they subsequently formed was to last 25 years (McFeely, 1991).

This chapter presents the lives of these two self-willed personalities. Their fervor in promoting equality and justice existed alongside their own self-promotion. Narrative theory, with its emphasis on storytelling, self-representations, deceptions, and memories, lends itself to an understanding of these two vital people. Historical and social forces, central to narrative theory, are intertwined with their lives; conversely, their actions, activities, and writings also influenced American history.

William S. McFeely (1991), the primary Douglass biographer referred to, assessed Douglass, his life, and influence. His narration is well researched; occasionally he dramatized scenes and added people's thoughts.

Maria Diedrich (1999), Assing's biographer, emphasizes Assing's own narrative style, including her self-representations and her representations of Douglass and their relationship. The story of the Douglass-Assing relationship is "of necessity a difficult balancing act between narrative and interpretation, between fact and fiction" (p. xxi).

Diedrich (1999) documented her sources and impressions, differentiating ascertainable fact from opinion. She does acknowledge including "novelistic" touches, describing scenes as she imagined them, while noting that this "liberty" is based on factual data. Excerpts from the novel *Aphra Behn* (1849), which Diedrich believed influenced Assing, are presented. In Diedrich's numerous annotations, she sometimes used narrative drama, reflecting what she believes Ottilie was thinking when it seems "to fit."

I, too, am an active participant in this chapter, with my own reactions to Douglass, Ottilie, and their biographers, and in the process, I have made choices about what to emphasize and what to omit. I have also been touched, inspired, and at times angered by these two lives. Moreover, I have worried about "tarnishing" an icon—Douglass. Backscheider (1999) observed the biographer's "inclination to protect the image of a race's hero or heroine and of the race itself" (p. 221). I present not an encomium but, rather, "portraits" of two significant people who were also flawed, as all people are.

Frederick Douglass speaks in this chapter; his three autobiographies are cited. Ottilie also speaks, primarily through her letters. The most significant collection of Ottilie's letters were those written to her sister Ludmilla, who remained in Europe. A subtext can often be discerned in these letters: The sisters had a long-standing conflictual and competitive relationship. Ottilie told Ludmilla stories of her successful life in America and her successful relationship with Douglass. Was her account a realistic picture of the relationship, Ottilie's view of it, or an attempt to impress Ludmilla? Diedrich (1999) noted that her "book is filled with questions I cannot possibly answer" (p. xxii).

Frederick Douglass's Autobiographies

Douglass's dignity and humanity pervade all three of his autobiographical texts. The first, *Narrative of the Life of Frederick Douglass, an American Slave,* was published in 1845. It describes his slave experiences, his escape, and an abolitionist meeting in Nantucket, the start of his speaking career.

Douglass's audiences developed "the growing disbelief… that this articulate, charismatic black man had ever been a slave" (Weissman, 1975, p. 132). His first autobiography purposefully demonstrated the authenticity of his slave experiences—he documented names, places, and dates. It also demonstrated his literary talent to those who believed that others wrote his speeches.

Mcfeely (1991) suggested that Douglass was "determined to be something far beyond a curiosity.… He [would]… write a story of his life that would make the world pay true attention" (pp. 114-115). And the world did pay attention: The *Narrative* was translated into many languages and sold more than 30,000 copies (Weissman, 1975).

Douglass's second autobiography, *My Bondage and My Freedom,* written in 1855, includes a more detailed and nuanced picture of his experiences and relationships. He adds his successful lecture tour of Great Britain, where his British friends purchased his freedom. The first book presented the unmitigated harshness and cruelty of life in slavery; the second included scenes of joy and warmth. Mcfeely (1991) noted that *My Bondage* offers "deeper reflections on slavery" (p. 7). Weissman (1975) observed that Douglass had made a "spontaneous recovery of early memories.… Experiences are recalled with more richness and complexity" (p. 741). Could his modifications also have been influenced by his concern with its impact on the audience, his dialogic connection? Douglass was known to alter events in his orations "to make his story better" (McFeely, 1991, p. 159).

In the clinical context, it is not uncommon to find clients presenting different versions of their life narratives. The client might feel increasingly secure with the therapist, "safe" enough to share painful and "shameful" memories. Conversely, he or she might feel insecure, needing to present him or herself in a positive light to gain approval.

Douglass's final autobiography was written in 1893, when he was 75. His early life and slave experiences are included, along with a discussion of his later life.

Multiple narratives are found in Douglass's story. It is a historical work, encompassing the Civil War period, Reconstruction, and the pervasiveness of racism. Lloyd Garrison, John Brown, Elizabeth Stanton, and President Abraham Lincoln are among the prominent people Douglass portrays.

This is also a narrative of Douglass's life course—the plot of his odyssey to personal freedom. When seven years old, Douglass asked: *"Why am I a slave?"* (Douglass, 1855). He remembers being *"even then,* most strongly impressed with the idea of being a freeman someday" (p. 179). This conviction remained strong throughout his youth, and even when he was a free man, the importance of freedom, both for himself and others who were still slaves, remained a powerful motivating force.

Douglass also conveys (sometimes directly and sometimes subtly) his belief that he is a "special" person with a mission—it was his destiny to lead his people to freedom, "never forgetting my own humble origin, nor refusing, while Heaven lends me ability, to use my voice, my pen, or my vote, to advocate the great and primary work of the universal and unconditional emancipation of my entire race" (Douglass, 1855, p. 406).

Weissman (1975) discussed Douglass's self-presentation as "an unconscious hero myth," his defense against his multiple rejections, and his sense of superiority to other slaves:

> Embedded in the account are the other classic features
> of the unconscious hero myth: the extraordinary percep-
> tiveness of the child hero, the extraordinary feats of the

young hero, and the sense of being specially chosen by fate with signs of divine favor. . . . It is also developed by implicitly contrasting himself to the other slaves who are characterized as docile, unassertive, and, most importantly, unaware victims of slavery. He writes in this version [the first autobiography] as if to suggest that he grew up in a world in which no one else saw the inequities of the system or protested against them by either defiance or escape. (Weissman, 1975, pp. 739–740)

Early Life

In Douglass, resilience and vulnerability existed side by side. He had strong convictions, self-determination, and a drive to be free and to be educated. He endured highly destructive and oppressive life circumstances, sometimes feeling despair and suicidal depression; at other times, these circumstances only increased his defiance and determination to be free.

Douglass experienced positive social opportunities, far greater than those experienced by the "average" slave. Although considered "property," with no autonomy with regard to his life choices, he also experienced an unusual amount of autonomy at many critical junctures in his life.

Douglass knew that he was born in Tuckahoe, Talbot County, Maryland, but not when he was born. "I suppose myself to have been born about the year 1817" (Douglass, 1882, p. 26); according to later researchers, he was actually born in February 1818 (McFeely, 1991).

> I have no accurate knowledge of my age, never having seen any authentic record containing it. By far the larger part of the slaves know as little of their ages as horses know of theirs, and it is the wish of most masters . . . to keep their slaves thus ignorant. (Douglass, 1845, p. 9)

So begins Douglass's first autobiography. He was born Frederick Bailey but changed his name to Frederick Douglass after he escaped from slavery, by which name he is almost universally known. He barely knew his mother, Harriet Bailey; they were separated when he was an infant. He has no memories of her during the first six years of his life. After that, he saw her four or five times before she died when he was about eight or nine years old.

His father's identity remained a mystery that puzzled and troubled him throughout his life. He knew that his father "was a white man, or nearly white" (McFeely, 1991, p. 151). "It was sometimes whispered that my master was my father" (p. 151). His father was "rumored among slaves to have been his master, Aaron Anthony, born 1767" (Gates, 1996, p. 1049). Anthony, who owned both Douglass and his mother, died in 1826, when Douglass was about eight. At that time, Douglass was given to Lucretia, Anthony's daughter. Lucretia was married to Thomas Auld; when she died young a few years later, Douglass remained as Thomas Auld's slave. He and Frederick had a complex relationship; Fredrick suspected that Auld was his father. Thomas and Lucretia were actively involved in Frederick's life and seem to have provided him with an unusual degree of special protection when he was a young boy. This could argue for a blood relationship based on Auld's paternity. Conversely, if Anthony was in fact his father, Lucretia would have been his half-sister. What is especially puzzling to biographers is how the relationship with the

Aulds evolved: Did this bright boy appeal specially to them, or if they knew (or suspected) that they were related to him, did this make him special to them? There is no conclusive evidence one way or the other. Frederick very much would have wanted the answer to this puzzle.

Grandmother

The most important early figure to Douglass was his grandmother, Betsey, who raised him "on the outskirts of the plantation, where she was put to raise the children of the younger women" (Douglass, 1845, p. 14). Douglass portrays her as an extremely competent and capable woman who was "held in high esteem, far higher than is the lot of most colored persons in the slave states" (Douglass, 1855, p. 35). She, too, had a surprising amount of personal freedom and autonomy in her daily life.

This positive picture of Douglass's grandmother has been corroborated by others (McFeely, 1991). Gates (1996) noted that she worked as a "midwife for pay" (Gates, 1996, p. 1049). In his second autobiography, Douglass introduces his grandfather, Isaac Bailey, a free man who worked as a woodcutter. Betsey, although a slave, was permitted to live with him apart from the slave quarters. Douglass speaks positively of Isaac; he and Douglass's grandmother "were the greatest people in the world to me" (Douglass, 1855, p. 38). However, Douglass says nothing else about him, omitting the fact that his grandfather was probably Douglass's first role model of a freed slave. Perhaps he de-emphasized this so as not to diminish his own hero image, asserting that freedom evolved in his own thinking as a child.

Douglass (1855) described a happy and carefree life for his first six years: "It was a long time before I knew myself to be a slave" (p. 38). He played with other children, running through the woods, swimming, and fishing:

> [Grandmother] took delight in having [her grandchildren] around her, and in attending to their few wants.... The notions of family, and the reciprocal duties and benefits of the relation, had a better chance of being understood than where children are placed—as they often are-in the hands of strangers, who have no care for them, apart from the wishes of their masters. (Douglass, 1855, p. 38)

Douglass had a special bond with his grandmother; he felt she contributed in many ways to his development. He felt fortunate not to be farmed out to strangers.

Today kinship foster care is increasingly used for children unable to live in their own homes. The Adoption and Safe Families Act of 1977 mandates that children should, if possible, be placed with their relatives as a priority (Cole, 2006). Grandparenting is one of the most frequently used forms of kinship care today, especially in African American (Beaucar, 1999; Hollingsworth, 1998) and Latino communities (Burnette, 1999). Maluccio (2006) discussed the need for supportive services for these grandparents, who face age- and stress-related health problems, the emotional problems of their grandchildren, and financial difficulties.

Grandmother's nurturing and Douglass's attachment to her were decisive in his own psychological development. Grandmother was also a role model in terms of her competency, mastery, and caring for others. Frederick was free to play and explore his environment;

this contributed to his evolving coping abilities, autonomy, and sense of mastery.

It was only later that "clouds and shadows... [began] to fall upon my path" (Douglass, 1855, p. 39). He heard frightening stories about the "old master": When old enough, children were removed from Grandmother and taken to live in the master's big house. "Grandmammy was, indeed, at that time, all the world to me; and the thought of being separated from her, in any considerable time, was more than an unwelcome intruder. It was intolerable" (Douglass, 1855, p. 39).

In his second autobiography, Douglass describes his abandonment: "my grandmother, knowing my fears... kindly kept me ignorant of the dreaded event about to transpire" (Douglass, 1855, p. 45). Douglass and Grandmother walked 12 miles to the plantation, where he found himself surrounded by unknown children, strange houses, and people working in the fields. "All this hurry, noise, and singing was very different from the stillness of Tuckahoe" (p. 47). Douglass sensed that this "boded no good to me. Grandmamma looked sad.... The shadow fell from her brow on me, though I knew not the cause" (p. 47). Grandmother told him to play with the children, but he was afraid that "grandmother might leave without taking me with her" (p. 49). While watching the children play, one boy shouted to him that "grandmammy gone!"

> I ran into the kitchen, to see for myself, and found it even so. Grandmammy had indeed gone, and was now far away, "clean" out of sight.... Almost heartbroken at the discovery, I fell upon the ground, and wept a boy's bitter tears, refusing to be comforted.... I had never been deceived before; and I felt not only grieved at parting—as

I supposed forever—with my grandmother, but indignant that a trick had been played upon me in a matter so serious. (Douglass, 1855, p. 49)

This painful abandonment was Douglass's "first introduction to the realities of slavery" (Douglass, 1855, p. 50). Years later, he wrote: "I cannot withhold a circumstance which at the time affected me so deeply ... and which I still remember so vividly" (Douglass, 1882, p. 33). Douglass implies that he never saw his grandmother again, but later he comments: "My home at my old master's ... was not home, but a prison to me .... My grandmother was far away, so that I seldom saw her" (Douglass, 1855, p. 135). Douglass had no preparation for his new world.

Child welfare social workers have the emotionally wrenching task of removing children from their homes and placing them elsewhere. Although intended for the good of the child, it is not easy to prepare a child for this. Like Douglass's grandmother, some practitioners might think it less painful not to talk about it and to avoid good-byes. But not facing it brings the pain of abandonment without explanation, reinforcing fears that this is a "punishment" and giving the child no opportunity to mourn the past and prepare to cope with the new present. Douglass's (1855) memories of his mother, Harriet, were few "but very distinct" (p. 52): "Her personal appearance and bearing are ineffaceably stamped upon my memory. She was tall, and finely proportioned; of deep black, glossy complexion; had regular features, and among the other slaves, was remarkably sedate in her manners" (p. 52).

Harriet worked on a farm 12 miles distant, sometimes visiting Frederick at night. He vividly remembers his mother rescuing him from Aunt Katy, his nemesis, who was in charge of the kitchen and the children. Katy's "favorite mode of punishing me . . . [was] making me go without food all day—that is from after breakfast" (Douglass, 1855, p. 55).

One night, hungry but under punishment, Douglass went to the kitchen. While he was roasting a few grains of Indian corn in the fire, his mother came in.

> The friendless and hungry boy, in his extremist need . . . found himself in the strong, protecting arms of a mother. . . . I shall never forget . . . [her] indescribable expression . . . when I told her that I had had no food since morning; and that Aunt Katy said she "meant to starve the life out of me." . . . [Mother] took the corn from me and gave me a large ginger cake, in its stead, she read Aunt Katy a lecture she never forgot. . . . That night I learned the fact that I was not only a child, but *somebody's* child. The "sweet cake" my mother gave me was in the shape of a heart, with a rich, dark ring glazed upon the edge of it. I was victorious, and well off for the moment. . . . But my triumph was short. I dropped off to sleep, and waked in the morning only to find my mother gone. (Douglass, 1855, pp. 56–57)

This is the last time Douglass remembers seeing his mother. She subsequently became ill and died: "I was not allowed to visit her during any part of her long illness. . . . Her grave is, as the grave of the dead at sea unmarked, and without stone or stake" (Douglass, 1855, p. 60). Douglass, eight or nine years old when she died, remembers having "no strong emotions of sorrow for her" (p. 60).

Slavery had "converted the mother that bore me, into a myth; it shrouded my father in mystery, and left me without an intelligible beginning in the world" (Douglass, 1855, p. 60). With time, Douglass began to appreciate "the value of my mother" (p. 60) and took "few steps in life, without feeling her presence; but the image is mute . . . and I have no striking words of hers treasured up" (p. 57).

Douglass lost his mother, of whom he had only dim memories, yet he remembered her throughout his life; he must have had confused feelings when she died. In addition to his loss, he was alone and could not mourn her with others; he was without close support in his plantation life. Grandmother, who would have mourned with him, was absent, and he also could not mourn the traumatic loss he experienced when Grandmother herself "disappeared." That his mother was buried in an unmarked grave further distanced him from any contact with her memory. This is a powerful, vivid image of the dehumanization of slave life.

There are many situations in which people are unable to mourn loss because of an absence of social approval to do so. This has been termed "disenfranchised grief." "Disenfranchised grief can be defined as the grief that persons experience when they incur a loss that is not or cannot be openly acknowledged, publicly mourned, or socially supported." (Doka, 1989, p. 4).

A woman, for example, comes to a family agency seeking help for feelings of sadness and uncontrollable crying. She has been having a secret affair with a married man, who had died the week before. She feels she cannot attend the funeral or share in any of the mourning rituals; there is no one with whom she could share her grief. Similarly disenfranchised grief can occur in lesbian or gay relationships where the partners have kept their sexuality hidden and consequently keep their grief hidden.

Years later, Douglass learned that his mother could read: ". . . she was the only one of all the slaves and colored people in Tuckahoe who enjoyed that advantage. How she acquired this knowledge, I know not" (Douglass, 1855, p. xxx). Were his thoughts about her literacy part of this myth? Is the memory of his mother's visit also a fantasy turned myth? Considering the poor quality of slave rations, could his mother have acquired a special cake?

McFeely (1991), accepting Douglass's version, varies it with details never mentioned by Douglass: "right there in the tyrant's own kitchen, she made her son a sugar cake" (p. 19). The ginger cake is transformed into a sugar cake. It is not unusual that biographers may be "willing to insert their own voices and sensibilities into the narrative" (Backscheider, 1999, p. 90).

Whatever the literal truth of this experience, the emotional truth rings through: Douglass longed for a loving, protective mother. Years later, Douglass, 63, would visit "the kitchen where he had last seen his mother" (Gates, 1996, p. 1072).

Father

Mother had an existence, but Father remained a mystery. Probably Douglass's father was a slavemaster of his, but as noted above, which one is not certain. Douglass was inclined to believe that Thomas Auld was his father. "I say nothing of father, for he is shrouded in a mystery I have never been able to penetrate. Slavery does away with fathers, as it does away with families" (Douglass, 1855, p. 51). However, two men were to become important father figures to Douglass; "Father Lawson," whom he knew as a teenager in Baltimore, and the abolitionist William Lloyd Garrison, whom he knew later in life.

Frederick was troubled by not knowing his father's identity. He had an "almost obsessive search for his lost paternity" (Diedrich,

1999, p. 174). He was certain, however, that his father was white. He remained "torn between two races, tortured by his double consciousness of being both and neither" (p. 174). Though a strong voice for black freedom, he identified with white people; his closest friends, as he grew older, were white.

Childhood at Wye House

Frederick lived at Wye House, part of the immense Lloyd Plantation, owned by Edward Lloyd, "a former governor of Maryland and noted United States senator" (McFeely, 1991, p. 12). Lloyd's chief lieutenant was Aaron Anthony. "On his thirteen farms, covering approximately ten thousand acres, his 550 slaves raised sufficient wheat to make him one of the largest producers of grain in the country" (p. 14).

Douglass describes a predominantly carefree existence at Wye House, with time for play and only some small chores. Frederick attracted others to him. He developed a friendship with Daniel Lloyd, the youngest son of Colonel Edward Lloyd. Douglass (1845) recalled that Daniel "became quite attached to me, and was a sort of protector of me" (p. 30).

Douglass wanted to know about life in the "big house," asked questions, and learned. He noted that why "so little of the slave accent [appeared] in my speech . . . is in some measure explained by my association with Daniel Lloyd" (Douglass, 1882, p. 49). Douglass witnessed brutality, including whippings of other slaves. He was seldom whipped, "although Aunt Katy would give him an 'occasional cuff'" (Douglass, 1882, p. 83). He suffered from being cold, both during the day (without adequate clothing) and at night (without a bed). Douglass rarely had enough to eat. His major source of nutrition was "called *mush*" (Douglass, 1845, p. 30), a "coarse corn meal boiled" (p. 27). Frederick's unhappiness increased, compounded by hunger, cold, his observation of the oppression of the slaves, and Aunt Katy's punitiveness. At times, he wished he had never been born (Douglass, 1882, p. 86).

When Frederick lived at the plantation, he ran errands for Lucretia. She "bestowed on me such looks and words as taught me that she pitied me, if she did not love me (Douglass, 1882, p. 83). When Frederick received a head injury, Lucretia's sympathetic aid increased their bond. "I have no doubt that the simple act of binding up my head, did much to awaken in her mind an interest in my welfare." Lucretia's interest "seldom showed itself in anything more than giving me a piece of bread... but this was a great favor on a slave plantation, and I was the only one of the children to whom such attention was paid (p. 84).

Baltimore: Hugh and Sophia Auld

When Frederick was eight years old, Thomas and Lucretia Auld sent him to Baltimore to a very benign family situation away from the vicissitudes of plantation slavery. He lived with Thomas's brother, Hugh Auld, and Hugh's wife, Sophie, and helped care for Tommy, their two-year-old son.

Why was Frederick, then 8, chosen to go to Baltimore? Douglass, pondering this question, concluded: It must be God's decision.

> I was not the only boy on the plantation that might have been sent to live in Baltimore.... I may be deemed super-stitious and egotistical, in regarding that event as a special

interposition of Divine Providence in my favor; but the thought is a part of my history... Slavery would not always be able to hold me within its foul embrace.... This good spirit was from God. (Douglass, 1855, p. 140)

McFeely (1991) also reflected on the reasons that Lucretia and Thomas chose Frederick to have this experience. He described Lucretia and Thomas as "perplexed and limited people struggling to respond to the needs of an unusual boy who was also a slave. He inferred that "Somehow, that boy had made them feel that he must be specially provided for"; perhaps Thomas and Lucretia wanted "to give Frederick Bailey a different home, a different life" (p. 24).

McFeely (1991) presented no evidence that this was what the Aulds were thinking or of how they felt toward Frederick. If Aaron Anthony had been Douglass's father, Lucretia might have been his half-sister—could this have been a factor in Lucretia's feelings for him? Lucretia died when Frederick was about 10. He remembered her fondly and years later had several moving encounters with her daughter, Amanda.

Douglass realized how critical this opportunity to live with the Auld family in Baltimore was for him. It would prove to be a major turning point in Frederick's life:

> ...it is quite probable that, but for the mere circumstance of being thus removed before the rigors of slavery had fastened upon me; before my young spirit had been crushed under the iron control of the slave-driver, instead of being today, a FREE-MAN, I might have been wearing the galling chains of slavery. (Douglass, 1855, p. 139)

Arriving in Baltimore, Frederick was moved by the warmth of his welcome from Sophia Auld and her two-year-old son, Tommy. Little Thomas was affectionately told by his mother that "'there was his Freddy,' and that Freddy would take care of him; and I was told to 'be kind to little Tommy'—an injunction I scarcely needed, for I had already fallen in love with the dear boy" (Douglass, 1855, p. 138). Frederick responded to Sophia's warm nurturing:

> If little Thomas was her son . . . she . . . made me something like his half-brother. . . . If dear Tommy was exalted to a place on his mother's knee, "Feddy" was honored by a place at his mother's side. (Douglass, 1855, p. 143)

Hugh Auld, minimally involved with Frederick, was "a very sour man, and of forbidding appearance," but he was "never very cruel to me" (Douglass, 1855, pp. 143–144). Frederick was pleased with his improved living conditions. "I had been treated as a *pig* on the plantation; in this new house, I was treated as a *child* now" (Douglass, 1855, p. 142).

Frederick's idyllic experience was abruptly interrupted when his owner, Aaron Anthony, died in November 1826 without a will. Considered merely property, Douglass was returned to Tuckahoe a year later, when Anthony's 29 slaves were distributed among his heirs. Heartbroken, Frederick left Baltimore.

> That was a sad day for me . . . for little Tommy, and . . . for my dear Baltimore mistress. . . . We, all three, wept bitterly that day; for we might be parting, and we feared we were parting, forever. (Douglass, 1855, pp. 174–175)

At the conclusion of the slave valuation and division, Frederick was awarded to Lucretia, "thanks to a kind Providence, in accordance with my wishes" (Douglass, 1855, p. 178). Discrepancies appear in this narrative: The division was in October 1827, but Lucretia had died earlier, in July, 1827. Frederick was therefore awarded to her widower, Thomas Auld; it was Thomas who sent him back to Baltimore.

Reading and Writing

Back in Baltimore, Douglass asked Sophia to teach him to read. Soon he was "master of the alphabet, and could spell words of three or four letters" (Douglass, 1855, p. 145). Proudly, Sophia told Hugh, which would prove a mistake: "Here rose the first cloud over my Baltimore prospects," Douglass recalled (p. 145).

> Mr. Auld promptly forbade the continuance of her instruction . . . that the thing itself was unlawful . . . and could lead to mischief. . . . "He should know nothing but the will of his master. . . , [Next] he'll want to know how to write; and, this accomplished, he'll be running away with himself."
> (Douglass, 1855, pp. 145–146)

Hugh Auld's prohibition increased Frederick's determination, as he came to understand that reading would lead to freedom. "From that moment I understood the direct pathway from slavery to freedom. . . . *He wanted me to be a slave;* I had already voted against that on the home plantation of Col. Lloyd" (Douglass, 1855, p. 147).

Frederick, in defiance and determination, carried a *Webster's* spelling book with him and creatively involved his friends in teaching him. "I generally paid my *tuition fee* to the boys, with bread, which I also carried in my pocket. For a single biscuit, any of my hungry little comrades would give me a lesson more valuable to me than bread" (Douglass, 1855, p. 155).

Frederick engaged his friends in writing games. He would make the letters which I had been so fortunate as to learn, and ask them to "beat me if they could." With play-mates for my teachers, fences and pavements for my copy books, and chalk for my pen and ink, I learned the art of writing. (Douglass, 1855, p. 171)

Using the *Webster's* spelling book and Tommy's discarded school copy books, Frederick practiced his penmanship. He arranged a "study" in the kitchen loft, where he slept. Frederick was not subject to the daily restrictions experienced by peers living in severe conditions of servitude. And Baltimore was a special city.

Life in Baltimore

Baltimore was a thriving shipbuilding center and a major arrival port for immigrants. A large black population, both slave and free, worked in diverse occupations. Black churches and black social and cultural centers flourished. Frederick benefited from this stimulating atmosphere, reading newspapers, socializing with young men, and discussing slavery and abolition. "In Baltimore, I could . . . get into a Sabbath School, among the free children, and receive lessons . . . but having already learned both to read and to write, I was more of a teacher than a pupil" (Douglass, 1855, p. 199).

When 13, Frederick's interest in religion led to his special rela-tionship with Lawson, an older free black drayman who "was my spiritual father, and I loved him intensely" (Douglass, 1855, p. 168). Lawson told Douglass that the "'Lord had a great work for me to do;' and I must prepare to do it; and... that I must preach the gospel. His words made a deep impression on my mind" (p. 168). Hugh Auld prohibited Douglass from visiting Father Lawson, but Douglass continued to see him.

Return to the Auld Family

Douglass was suddenly told to leave Baltimore because of a conflict between Hugh and Thomas Auld. Thomas Auld had sent Douglass's cousin Henny to Baltimore to do housework for Hugh's family. As Henny's crippled hands were "permanently closed," Hugh and Sophia found her useless and sent her back to Thomas. Thomas took this "as an act of ingratitude" and demanded that Frederick be returned to St. Michael's, where the Auld family was living, "saying, if he cannot keep 'Hen,' he shall not have 'Fred'" (Douglass, 1855, p. 182).

McFeely (1991) suggested that Frederick's return may have been precipitated by anxieties about Nat Turner, a well-educated slave and preacher who had led an unsuccessful but bloody slave rebellion in Virginia two years earlier, in 1831. Douglass had similarities to Turner, who was "not under a master's direct discipline, and, what is more, [was] a preacher, self-educated and eloquent" (McFeely, 1991, p. 37). The Aulds "may have reasoned that... [Douglass] would be safer out of Baltimore and back on the Eastern Shore, living like any other ordinary field-hand slave" (p. 39).

Frederick now was mourning the loss of his social life and opportunities: "here was another shock to my nerves, another breaking up of my plans, and another severance of my religious and social alliances." He would miss "those to whom I *imparted* instruction, and to those little white boys from whom I *received* instruction. There, too, was my dear old father, the pious Lawson" (Douglass, 1855, p. 183). Douglass reflected on his own behavior as it affected the family's relationships, for "I was no longer the light-hearted, gleesome boy, full of mirth and play."

> I have no doubt that my state of mind had something to do with the change in the treatment adopted, by my once kind mistress.... I can easily believe, that my leaden, downcast, and discontented look was very offensive to her.... She had changed; and the reader will see that I had changed, too. We were both victims to the same overshadowing evil. (Douglass, 1855, pp. 161–162)

Frederick, 15, returned to Thomas Auld in March 1833. Thomas was now married to Rowena, "an ill-tempered woman... [who was] imperious with her slaves" (McFeely, 1991, p. 36). During the nine months Douglass lived with Thomas Auld, the incompatibilities and tensions between them increased (McFeely, 1991). Douglass (1855) noted that "the boldness with which I defended myself against his capricious complaints, led him to declare that I was unsuited to his wants; that my city life had ... had almost ruined me for every good purpose" (p. 202). Consequently, "Master Thomas ... resolved to put me out—as he said—'to be broken' " (p. 219).

Covey the Slave Breaker

In 1834, Frederick was sent to Covey, a poor man who rented a farm and had the "reputation, of being a first rate hand at breaking young negroes" (Douglass, 1855, p. 203). Recalcitrant slaves worked on his farm, but Covey, in return for his service, paid their owners nothing for this labor. Living conditions were poor, work was hard, Covey spied on his workers, and Douglass endured many beatings: "I was sometimes prompted to take my life, and that of Covey, but was prevented by a combination of hope and fear" (Douglass, 1855, p. 219). He continued:

> I suffered bodily as well as mentally. I had neither sufficient time in which to eat or to sleep, except on Sundays.... [I had] that ever-gnawing and soul devouring thought—"I am a slave—a slave for life—a slave with no rational ground to hope for freedom." (Douglass, 1855, p. 221)

One day, Douglass, after collapsing with sunstroke, was beaten and kicked by Covey. Bleeding from his head, Douglass ran to Thomas's house for help, which Thomas refused. "Frederick never forgave Thomas's ridicule of his claim that if he returned to Covey he would be killed, nor did he forgive [Thomas's] grudging permission to stay the night—without supper or breakfast" (McFeely, 1991, p. 45).

Douglass, painfully making his way back through the woods, met the slave Sandy Jenkins, who took Douglass home. Douglass, citing his own specialness, comments that Sandy and his wife felt it was "a privilege to succor me" (Douglass, 1855, p. 237), for "I was loved by the colored people, because *they* thought I was hated [by slaveholders] for my knowledge, and persecuted because I was feared. I was the *only* slave *now* in that region who could read and write" (p. 237).

Douglass continues to develop his narrative of his specialness, which he believes made other people proud to befriend him. His self-representation is incorporated into the plot of his life: He will be a free man one day, and he has been chosen because of "a special interposition of Divine Providence in my favor." And finally, he will be a leader instrumental in freeing all slaves.

When Frederick returned, Covey initially responded benignly. The next day, however, Covey attacked him, and Douglass fought back. Covey called for help. When Covey's cousin Hugh came, Douglass hit him, too. Hugh left in pain. Covey then asked Bill, the hired hand, for help; "Bill refused.... 'My master hired me here, to work, and not to help you whip Frederick.' ... Bill walked off" (Douglass, 1882, p. 175). Caroline, Covey's slave, also refused to help. She "was in no humor to take a hand in such sport. We were all in open rebellion, that morning" (p. 176). Covey stopped fighting after two hours and never hit Douglass again.

To Douglass, this fight "was the turning point of my *'life as a slave'*" (Douglass, 1882, p 177):

> It rekindled in my breast the smoldering embers of liberty; it brought up my Baltimore dreams, and revived a sense of my own manhood. I was a changed being after that fight. I was *nothing* before; *I was a man now.* It ... inspired me with a renewed determination to be a *free man*.... I had reached the point, at which I was *not afraid to die.* This spirit made me a freeman in *fact,* while I remained a slave in *form.* (Douglass, 1882, p. 177)

Douglass had made a further advance in shaping his life plot: He was not yet free in reality, but he had now internalized the image of being a free man. McFeely (1991) asserted that Douglass overlooked an important point, however. In this fight with Covey, he had help from Bill and Caroline: "They, not he alone, bested Covey" (p.47).

Freeland Farm

When Frederick's yearlong contract to Covey was fulfilled, Thomas hired Douglass (now 17) out as a field hand to William Freeland, a benign slaveholder. Douglass adapted well to farm life, proud of becoming "large and strong." He preferred being a field hand "to the enervating duties of a house servant" (Douglass, 1882, p. 184). He developed close relationships with his "brother slaves. . . . I must say, I never loved, esteemed, or confided in men, more than I did in these" (p. 601).

Douglass started a secret Sabbath school, with 40 highly motivated men. All participated at great personal risk to learn to read.

Although positive about many aspects of his life at Freeland Farm, Douglass still felt that "the slaveholder, kind or cruel, is a slaveholder still," and his determination to run away increased; he plotted with his fellow slaves on the farm (Douglass, 1855, p. 269):

> I was the youngest but one of the party. I had, however, the advantage of them all in experience, and a knowledge of letters. This gave me a great influence over them. Perhaps not one of them, left to himself, would have dreamed of escape as a possible thing (Douglass, 1882, p. 197)

Here we can see that Douglass continues his self-representation as a special person who was superior to other slaves; he is also "announcing" his awareness of his leadership potential.

Before their escape plan was actualized, the five men were betrayed and arrested. Four were released, but Douglass remained in jail for a week. Thomas decided to return him to Hugh in Baltimore. Douglass (1882) wrote, "…he feared for my safety if I remained there [in St. Michael's]" (p. 221). Thomas wanted Douglass to "learn a trade…. If I behaved myself properly, he would *emancipate me at twenty five*" (p. 218). Thomas Auld, in this instance, was protective toward Douglass. While Douglass was in jail, Master Thomas received substantial offers from slave traders to buy him, but he accepted none. Douglass observed that "money could not tempt him to sell me to the far south" (p. 221). Not too long before this incident, Thomas grudgingly offered Douglass a temporary sanctuary when he fled Covey's cruelty, but then insisted he return to Covey; Douglass accepted, but resented this. During Douglass's later imprisonment, Thomas could have insisted on punishing Douglass for attempting to escape, by sending him to the more severe conditions of slave territory further south. Instead he sent Douglass back to a benign setting in Baltimore. Here Douglass presents Auld to the reader sympathetically.

The conflictual relationship between Douglass and Auld is marked by ambivalence. Ambivalence, seemingly opposed feelings and attitudes, is a core concept in clinical work and a phenomenon regularly encountered in practice situations.

Adulthood

Return to Baltimore and Escape

Douglass, now 18, found changes in Baltimore after his 3-year absence: "the loving relations between me and Mas' Tommy were broken up.... The time had come when his *friend* must become his *slave*" (Douglass, 1855, p. 307).

Frederick, apprenticed as a caulker at Gardiner's shipyard, received no training; there he was victimized by racist conflict and viciously beaten. Hugh Auld, outraged at Douglass's treatment, instead arranged for Douglass to be an apprentice caulker in the shipyard where Auld worked. Douglass was happy with his employment; he earned a good salary and continued with his learning. The other black caulkers "could read, write, and cipher.... I owe much to the society of these young men" (Douglass, 1882, p. 231). Douglass at this time joined the East Baltimore Mental Improvement Society.

Douglass arranged to work and live independently; he gave Hugh his salary and kept some for self-maintenance. Douglass now had vocational success, some independence, a rich social life, and educational opportunities. However, "it was not long before I began to show signs of disquiet with slavery.... I was living among *freemen*.... *Why should I be a slave?*" (Douglass, 1882, p. 231). He also resented giving his (good) wages to Hugh. Douglass's life's plot reasserted itself; he could not be content with a fulfilling, comfortable life if he were not free. In a similar manner, we saw Conan Doyle suddenly leaving a fulfilling existence in Southsea to pursue his "higher" goals.

A major altercation occurred with Hugh when Douglass was once two days late in paying him. "I could hire my time no longer" (Douglass, 1882, p. 238). Three weeks later, Douglass escaped from

Baltimore. In his earlier autobiographies, Douglass omits details of his escape to protect himself and others. In his final volume, he described how he obtained identity papers from a free seaman and made his arduous trip by trains and boats to New York.

Douglass also omits any reference to meeting his wife, Anna Murray, at the Baltimore Improvement Society. He mentioned her for the first time (an example of his tendency in his various narratives to downplay his wife and her role in his achievements) after his escape to New York on September 3, 1838, when he wrote to "my intended wife" to tell her of his safe arrival. Anna (a freeborn woman) then traveled to New York; they married 2 weeks later. Douglass never refers to her again in his autobiographies despite the fact that they were married for 44 years and had five children.

The family's narrative relates Anna selling "a featherbed to finance [Frederick's] journey, and . . . [how she] altered his clothing to make it look like a seaman's" (McFeely, 1991, p. 70). Neither Anna nor her featherbed appear in Douglass's narrative presumably for the following reasons: His self-representation rested on being considered a special person; if Anna were to be given credit for aiding his escape, he might have felt his heroism would be diminished. Anna was very dark-skinned and also illiterate, two factors that shamed him (discussed in greater depth later in the chapter). There is insufficient evidence to judge the quality of their early relationship, but as time went on, she became the "invisible" wife, yet clearly the "visible" housekeeper.

In marital counseling, it is not uncommon for each partner's narrative to ignore the contributions and strengths of the other; this is often a source of bitterness. In Douglass's case, his wife was not in a position to publicly assert her own side of the story.

After a few weeks, Frederick and Anna moved to the thriving black community in New Bedford, Massachusetts, a safer location than New York, with its "slave catchers." As a further precaution, Fredrick changed his name from Bailey to Douglass.

New Bedford

Douglass had difficulty finding work; they were very poor their first winter. Living conditions later improved when Douglass found steady work for three years as a day laborer. Their daughter Rosetta was born on June 24, 1839, and a son, Lewis Henry, on October 9, 1840; Douglass does not refer to either event in his narratives.

Douglass (1855) reported that he "supplied my wife—who was unable to work—with food and some necessary articles of furniture" (p. 350). Diedrich (1999), however, reported that the family managed because Anna also worked. Anna was:

> a strong, determined partner, and there was all the loyalty and support imaginable, but little romance in their life together.... The feelings that bound Anna Murray and Frederick together were defined by their daily struggle for bread, the demands of their growing family, their apprehensions of racial discrimination and violence, and their nagging fear of Frederick's reenslavement. (Diedrich, 1999, p. 176)

Frederick says nothing about his feelings for Anna. This relationship would seriously deteriorate later, but its basic quality and evolution remain unknown.

Douglass subscribed to William Lloyd Garrison's *Liberator.* He noted, "I loved this paper and its editor" (Douglass, 1882, p. 264). After joining the Black Zion Methodist Church, Douglass "was soon made a class leader and a local preacher" (Douglass, 1855, p. 353). Having heard Douglass speak at an antislavery meeting, William C. Coffin, a prominent abolitionist, invited him to an antislavery convention in Nantucket.

Orator for the Abolitionists

Douglass spoke at the Nantucket meeting of the Massachusetts Anti-Slavery Society on August 16, 1841. His talk was widely reported to have been electrifying. Garrison followed with a powerful oration based on Douglass's speech. This was another major turning point in his life:

> Frederick Douglass was not the first former slave to be brought forward to arouse concern for his brothers and sisters, but this night on Nantucket, it was clear that a powerful new voice had been raised, one that demonstrated how high a former slave could stretch in a demonstration of his humanity. (McFeely, 1991, p. 89)

Douglass accepted a position as a (paid) agent and orator for the Massachusetts Anti-Slavery Society's lecture circuit. "A great career in the anti-slavery movement was born that evening" (McFeely, 1991, p. 89). Douglass toured for almost four years, receiving a regular salary and a house. Although Douglass had not yet achieved freedom, his self-concept of specialness was enhanced, and he took a significant step toward achieving his goal of becoming a leader. That he would now be a paid orator for the Antislavery Society was a dramatic turning point, the beginning of a new career, bringing him much fame.

Most antislavery meetings were well attended and peaceful. Sometimes mobs objected; "…the throwing of rotten eggs… [was] commonplace" (McFeely, 1991, p. 102). Douglass was popular within the antislavery movement, and he was "gaining an increasingly strong and independent voice" (McFeely, 1991, p. 104). Douglas also protested Northern racism, seeing racism and slavery as inseparable issues.

Douglass's first autobiography, *Narrative of the Life of Frederick Douglass, an American Slave,* was published in 1845, with the aims of "authenticating" his life story and expressing his own thoughts and opinions. However, in documenting his history as an escaped slave, he risked discovery by "slave catchers."

To protect Douglass, as well as to encourage Britain's strong anti-slavery sentiment, the Abolitionist Society sent Douglass to Britain as a speaker, where he toured for two years while his family remained in Lynn, where they had moved from New Bedford in 1841.

Douglass's tour of Great Britain was a great popular success. With his "impressive appearance, [and] great powers of oratory," he attracted large audiences and was often entertained by influential abolitionists and politicians (McFeely, 1991, p. 124). He experienced no racism in Britain. He wrote,

> "[Britain] is so different here from what I have been accustomed to in the United States. No insults… no prejudice to encounter…. I am treated as a man and equal brother.

My color instead of being a barrier to social equality—is not thought of as such." (quoted in McFeely, 1991, p. 132)

In Ireland, the relationship he developed with Isabel Jennings was "the first in a long succession of woman confidants with whom he corresponded.... The path of some of his friendships may have led to a bed" (McFeely, 1991, p. 125). In Newcastle on Tyne in England, his friendship with the abolitionist Julia Griffiths became "intense and lasting" (McFeely, 1991, p. 145). Griffiths later traveled to the United States to assist Douglass with his newspaper.

The Richardsons, his friends in Newcastle, raised money to pay for his freedom; the agreed upon price was £150 sterling or about $1,250 (in 1846 dollars, or about $4,625 in today's values). Thomas Auld legally sold Frederick to Hugh Auld; Hugh then registered a deed of manumission in the Baltimore County. Douglass became legally free on December 12, 1846. The legal documents were printed in his second autobiography, an excerpt from which follows: " 'I Hugh Auld... have released from slavery, liberate, manumit, and set free, MY NEGRO MAN, named FREDERICK BAILEY, otherwise called DOUGLASS, being of the age of twenty-eight years, or thereabouts' " (Douglass, 1855, p. 375).

Some abolitionists objected to the purchase of Douglass's freedom: "it was a violation of antislavery principles—conceding a right of property in man—and a wasteful expenditure of money" (Douglass, 1855, p. 375). Douglass, however, felt that this was his only guarantee against capture. "I had a duty to perform... to labor and suffer with the oppressed in my native land" (p. 376).

Once a free man, Douglass published his newspaper, the *North Star*. On the 10th anniversary of his escape, he printed an open letter in his newspaper to Thomas Auld. (Douglass, 1855, Appendix). The letter ends:

> There is no roof under which you would be more safe than mine, and there is nothing in my house which you might need for your comfort, which I would not readily grant. Indeed, I should esteem it a privilege to set you an example as to how mankind ought to treat each other. (Douglass, 1855, p. 428)

Elsewhere, in his writings and lectures, Douglass would continue his attack on the Aulds, often exaggerating their misdeeds. "And yet his attacks on them only partially disguise his complex and ambiguous relationship to all four" (McFeely, 1991, p. 23).

A final meeting between the two men occurred when Thomas Auld was old and dying. Douglass (1882) described a moving encounter: "The circumstances of his condition affected me deeply, and for a time choked my voice and made me speechless. We both, however, got the better of our feelings, and conversed freely about the past" (p. 536). Douglass asked Thomas what he thought about Douglass running away from him. Frederick recounted Auld's response:

> "Frederick, I always knew you were too smart to be a slave, and had I been in your place, I should have done what you did." I said, "Capt. Auld I am glad to hear you say this. I did not run away from you, but from slavery." (Douglass, 1882, p. 536)

Auld told Douglass that he "'never liked slavery,' and that he meant to emancipate 'all of my slaves when they reached the age of twenty-five years'" (Douglass, 1882, p. 537). Douglass asked Thomas whether he knew Douglass's birth date: "It had been a serious trouble to me, not to know when was my birthday. He said he could not tell me that, but he thought I was born in February, 1818" (p. 877). We might infer that what Douglass really wanted to ask Thomas was: Who is my father? But this remains forever unanswered.

Thomas Auld died shortly after this meeting. "His death was … announced in the papers, and the fact that he had once owned me as a slave was cited as rendering that event noteworthy" (Douglass, 1882, p. 538).

The North Star

A rift developed between Douglass and Garrison, formerly close friends and colleagues, when Douglass, returning to the United States, decided to publish his own newspaper. Garrison and the Anti-Slavery Society resented this competition and wanted Douglass to remain an orator. In defiance of their wishes and with funds raised by his English friends, Douglass launched the *North Star* in 1847 in Rochester, New York (the North Star, used as a reference point to follow the path northward to freedom, was found by runaway slaves in relation to the "drinking gourd" or the Big Dipper). Douglass later changed its title to *Frederick Douglass's Paper*. Although successful, the *North Star* was beset by financial difficulties. Douglass appreciated the financial help from friends and assistance from Julia Griffiths, who moved to the United States in 1849 to work at the newspaper.

Julia Griffiths lived for a time at Douglass's home, exacerbating marital tensions. Gossip spread about their relationship, fueled by its interracial nature. This "scandal" was even publicized by the Anti-Slavery Society as a way of attacking Douglass. In response to increased pressure, Griffiths returned to England in 1855. She continued her lifelong correspondence with Douglass and regularly contributed articles to his paper. He visited her twice in England.

Anna Murray and Her Relationship with Douglass

Anna, seven years older than Douglass, had been a domestic servant for Baltimore's postmaster and had "a reputation as an excellent housekeeper" (Diedrich, 1999, p. 175). We never get to hear Anna's voice. She was ostensibly illiterate, and no biographies of her life exist other than a brief "sketch" written by her daughter, Rosetta, long after Anna's death (McFeely, 1991, p. 66).

Douglass barely referred to Anna in his autobiographies. He also rarely mentioned his three sons and two daughters, other than in references to racial, social, or historical issues. For example, he made reference to his sons' service in the Civil War. He did share his deeply felt loss of his daughter Annie, who died at 11.

Anna was happy in Lynn, participated in community life, attended meetings of abolitionist women, and was proud of her achievements (Diedrich, 1999). Douglass did not consult with Anna about moving to Rochester, and this change was difficult for her. According to Rosetta, this was "mother's 'greatest trial'" (Diedrich, 1999). She "never forgave" Douglass for making these plans without her and "was bitter about having to leave Lynn" (pp. 179-180). Anna never forgot her old friends in Lynn and talked about them throughout her life.

Anna and Douglass were both involved with the Underground Railroad. However, in his writings, Douglass does not mention her involvement in this effort.

Observers noted that Anna was a perfect housekeeper and hostess, but Douglass's guests were not her friends. She would socially withdraw. "Visitors to the Douglass home … reported that she behaved more like a domestic servant than mistress of the house" (Diedrich, 1999, p. 150). Rosetta said: "'Father was mother's honored guest'" (quoted in Diedrich, 1999, p. 180).

Whatever marital incompatibilities existed, tensions were aggravated by Douglass's involvement with white, educated women. Soon after Griffith's departure, Ottilie Assing arrived.

Ottilie Assing

Ottilie Assing's background was the polar opposite of Douglass's, yet they had much in common: fierce convictions about freedom and self-autonomy, a love of learning, and atheistic leanings. Both believed in racial and ethnic integration, in every sphere of life, including love.

Early Life

Ottilie lived her own narrative, designed and revised as needed. Combining a strong romantic spirit with a radical political outlook, she was dismissive of social conventions. She was politically astute and sensitized to German anti-Semitism as well as to American racism. She experienced prejudice from both conservative Germans and Orthodox Jews.

Romantic poetry and ideals of love and the "perfect partnership," had been essential to Ottilie's mother, Rosa Maria. Intermarriage was Ottilie's heritage: Her father, an Orthodox Jew, had converted to Lutheranism to marry Ottilie's Lutheran mother. Rosa Maria lived a life of romanticism, creativity, intellectual development, and independence. She taught her daughters that class and race were irrelevant when love was based on a physical, intellectual, and moral compatibility—always provided that "the lower-order lover be willing and able to educate her or himself into the higher rank" (Diedrich, 1999, p. 30). This belief was central to Ottilie's philosophy.

Rosa Maria "fell passionately in love" with Justinius Kerner, a doctor and aspiring poet, as evident in her poetry about their romance and sexual relationship (Diedrich, 1999). When her feelings were not reciprocated, her poetry emphasized images of suffering. Kerner introduced her to David Assing, whose Orthodox Ashkenazi parents were wealthy merchants and highly respected in society and who enjoyed the company of renowned intellectuals such as Immanuel Kant. David was given to depression, brooding, and self-doubt, often isolating himself in his lab.

David and Rosa Maria became lovers and married in 1816. They knew they were confronting social obstacles but faced them with strength from the belief that "tolerance and mutuality defined their union" (Diedrich, 1999, p. 17). It was a happy marriage. "For once in his life the deeply troubled Assing seemed happy." On February 11, 1819, Rosa Maria gave birth to Ottilie, and two years later, her sister, Ludmilla, was born. The passionate love and intellectual commitment between Ottilie's parents continued throughout their marriage.

An intimate bond existed between Rosa Maria and the girls, "more like that between sisters than between mother and daughters" (Diedrich, 1999, p. 19). Both parents believed in equal education and rights for women; the girls were prepared to live independently and work professionally. Rosa Maria tutored the girls: "... her daughters' education was [Rosa Maria's] life mission" (Diedrich, 1999, p. 23). They were precocious, and their education, which included traveling, exceeded the attainments of most girls their age (Diedrich, 1999). Ottilie's "excursions with her mother generated a passion for traveling that never died" (p. 28).

Ottilie received "constant praise and attention" from her parents. Diedrich (1999) suggests that the ensuing development of her "inner strength ... enabled her to defy convention" (p. 20). Ludmilla struggled for equal recognition and deeply resented Ottilie; their conflict persisted throughout their lives.

Rose Maria held an outstanding salon with "Jewish and German intelligentsia" (Diedrich, 1999). Gatherings were lively and stimulating (Diedrich, 1999).

Rose Maria, at 57, developed cancer and died soon after. Ottilie, 21, and Ludmilla, 19, were "devastated by their mother's death," and David became very depressed (Diedrich, 1999, p. 38). Soon after editing a book of his wife's writings, David became ill and died at 55, one day before their 26th anniversary.

Only days after David's funeral, Hamburg was destroyed by fire, although the Assing house was spared. Ottilie and Ludmilla moved to Berlin to live with their 57-year-old maternal uncle, Varnhagen, now a widower. Constant conflicts flared between the sisters in Varnhagen's home: "Fierce arguments were exchanged almost daily, and sometimes it came to blows" (Diedrich, 1999, p. 49). Varnhagen tended to side with Ludmilla (p. 50).

Tensions between Ottilie, Ludmilla, and Varnhagen increased. After one intense quarrel, in which Varnhagen "slapped Ottilie...she ran from the house in a rage" (Diedrich, 1999, p. 56). The following afternoon, Ottilie appeared at her friend Clara Mundt's home, bleeding from "three deep wounds in her chest" (p. 56). Her doctor commented that "it was a miracle she was still alive" (p. 56).

Ottilie had gone to a large public park and, concealed by bushes, stabbed herself with a knife. After being unconscious all night, she managed to get to Clara's house. There are similarities between this attempt and her successful suicide 40 years later (Diedrich, 1999):

> Her suicide attempt had a performance quality-performance as a way of constructing an identity that is threatening to dissolve.... Had not her mother taught her that in certain situations suicide was an act of courage and self-determination? Had not the Romantics glorified suicide as self-elevation and self-purification? Had not some of the greatest writers... chosen this path? And... was not suicide the most powerful way of punishing those who were responsible for her pain? (Diedrich, 1999, p. 57)

Suicide indeed punishes survivors. In addition to grief, many survivors feel guilty, often obsessing about what they did "wrong." In a sense, clinicians may also be survivors of a client's suicide and are not exempt from these feelings.

To avoid a scandal, Varnhagen suggested having Ottilie "declared insane! For this, Ottilie never forgave him" (Diedrich, 1999, p. 57), and she returned to Hamburg. In Hamburg, Ottilie tutored children and wrote articles on literature, art, and cultural events. Ottilie did not seek friendships with "conventional" women, "who, in turn, rejected her as eccentric, arrogant, unwomanly" (Diedrich, 1999, p. 54). She found friends with similar intellectual and political interests.

Ottilie became involved with the Hamburg theater and with Jean Baptiste Baisson, a famous actor and a married man. Ottilie's biography of Baisson, written after his death, shows that he trusted her with intimate details of his life. Baisson was Ottilie's ideal hero: He had progressed against great odds, including poverty and an alcoholic father. He " 'owed his success only to his own talent and to the recognition of the audience' " Ottilie and Baisson had "an intense and dynamic working relationship, just as Ottilie would later work... with Frederick Douglass" (Diedrich, 1999, p. 67).

> Ottilie Assing's relationship with Baisson... anticipated her relationship with Frederick Douglass. [His] social background made him exotic—a man already married and a father... a public figure and celebrity. She.... enjoyed the spotlight of scandal. Yet once the radical step was taken, her conduct was conservative, for she accepted the responsibilities of a legitimate wife, although she lacked her rights. She was faithful, for her liberation was not for free love but to give herself freely to the man she loved. (Diedrich, 1999, p. 75)

In 1847, Baisson became ill. "Soon he was suffering from violent headaches, continuous indisposition, and shortness of breath" (Diedrich, 1999, p. 74). Ottilie "devote[d] herself totally" to his care. He died in January of 1849. During the terminal phase of his illness, Baisson's wife, Carolyn, and Ottilie together nursed him. Their relationship, however, ended on a negative note because Carolyn refused to pay Ottilie money she had borrowed.

Ottilie immersed herself in writing Baisson's biography, a family tradition.

Her mother had documented her life and relationships in her poetry, and upon her mother's death, her father published a collection of his wife's poetry. During this time, she also read the novel *Aphra Behn* (1849), written by her friend Clara Mundt. In this novel about a slave rebellion in Surinam, Aphra, a white woman and the royal slave Oronoko (a married man) develop a romantic relationship. "When her lover hero incites his fellow slaves to rebel... Aphra stands by him" (Diedrich, 1999, p. 85). In an interesting narrative device, Diedrich excerpts passages from this book that she feels parallel Ottilie's life and motivations, especially as they relate to Douglass.

In 1851, Ottilie began writing for the *Morgenblatt,* "one of Germany's most distinguished journals." Upon immigrating, she would continue working for the journal as its American correspondent over the next 14 years. Ottilie was becoming disillusioned with Germany: "its narrowness stifled her" (Diedrich, 1999, p. 80). Ottilie's decision to immigrate to America, however, was not just to escape; it was a pilgrimage to "a desirable place," a country that was full of hope. "She believed that the laboratory experiment in which the future of humanity was being tested would be successful.... And she was sure enough of herself... to believe that she could make important contributions to the New World" (p. 83). Ottilie, now 33, sailed for America on the *Indian Queen* in August of 1852.

Life in America

Ottilie arrived in New York on September 27, 1852. "In less than a year she had found people she wanted to be with, and she was confident that eventually she could make a decent living" (Diedrich, 1999, p. 101). Ottilie "had fallen in love with New York City" (p. 102) and wrote about it for the *Morgenblatt*. She loved the street life and walked through all parts of the city. Ottilie continued her ongoing search for definitions of herself. When she arrived in the United States, "she was no longer a 'half-Jew' from Hamburg but … a German woman" (Diedrich, 1999, p. 95).

> The category crisis that had burdened her all her life would cease. She was free to reinvent herself. Gradually she would begin to take on the perspective of the German-American reporter, using the identifying "us" and "we" as she delineated American events. Ottilie would become Otillia. (Diedrich, 1999, pp. 95–96)

In her newspaper writings, she alternated between a male and female persona.

"So she crossed back and forth, passing and transgressing, inventing and performing in her quest for a self she would always define as a self in motion" (Diedrich, 1999, p. 103).

Ottilie was concerned with "designing" her own self-representation. She kept trying on new ones for size, always aware of an audience. She had strong leanings toward independence, creativity, and not conforming to restrictive societal expectations. She had confidence in herself as a writer, and when she left for New York, she felt able to "make important contributions to the New World," but without the drive of Douglass's determination to change the world, especially in regard to emancipation.

One aspect of Ottilie's life plot involved establishing a romantic relationship with a man who was special, "a public figure and celebrity." That this relationship might be unconventional did not concern her; in fact, it would have an extra appeal, as she "enjoyed the spotlight of scandal." The relationship she developed with Douglass seemed to fit the script she envisioned.

After two years, she began writing about the evils of slavery and how racism permeated American society. "What rendered her work exceptional from the start . . . was her awareness of the importance of race in the American experience" (Diedrich, 1999, p. 118). Ottilie read Frederick Douglass's *My Bondage,* which "threw a magic spell over her" (Diedrich, 1999, p. 127). "Even before she met him, she decided he was special" (p. 127).

Relationship with Douglass

Ottilie interviewed Douglass in Rochester in 1856 and was impressed by him. She wrote that he " 'shows himself to be both learned and ingenious and highly cultivated' " (quoted in McFeely, 1991, p. 183). They agreed that she would translate his autobiography into German and planned to meet again. They corresponded frequently, and Douglass invited her to stay at his home the following summer.

In the winter of 1856–1857, Ottilie moved to Hoboken to be near her new friends, "an exclusive order of German intellectuals" (Diedrich, 1999, p. 112). She also "needed a place to give her the . . . privacy into which she could invite the man she was beginning to love" (p. 143). Assing lived there until 1865, "with Frederick Douglass as a frequent guest" (p. 143). Assing's German friends often socialized with the couple.

Ottilie's first Douglass article (which was not published) was incorporated into the introduction of her translation of his autobiography. This article "leaves little doubt that she was completely taken by Douglass's powerful male presence and determined to have her audience see him through her eyes" (Diedrich, 1999, p. 137).

> Assing discovered in Douglass a man for whose respect and perhaps even friendship she was willing to go a long way, and she had made a decision she would never revise in the twenty-six years that followed: She would focus all her attention on Fredrick Douglass. She would ignore his spouse to the utmost limits of common politeness. (Diedrich, 1999, p. 136)

Assing returned to the Douglasses' home the next summer to work on the translation. She "would present herself as Germany's Negro expert" (Diedrich, 1999, p. 148). Ottilie and Douglass spent time together reading; she taught him German and accompanied him on the piano while he played the violin. She developed relationships with Douglass's five children: Rosetta (18), Lewis (17), Fredrick Jr. (15), Charles (13), and Annie (8). Over the years, a special relationship with Rosetta developed.

Anna Murray, the "invisible" woman, was, nevertheless, very much a presence. Rosetta remembered that her mother "remained aloof and reserved" (Diedrich, 1999).

The Douglass Family. Ottilie believed that the Douglass marriage had been "over long before she entered the scene" (Diedrich, 1999,

p. 175). Douglass's marriage "was a form of bondage"; Ottilie's involvement with Douglass "became an act of heroism, the adulteress reinvented herself as a liberator" (p. 185). Meanwhile, in her journalistic writings, Assing mentioned Anna only once, noting: "'Douglass's wife is completely black'" (quoted in Diedrich, 1999).

Douglass expressed no awareness of the humiliating position into which he had placed Anna. He hinted at marital problems in letters to friends. Ottilie "installed" herself in the Douglass home several months every summer; Douglass visited her in Hoboken; she attended his lectures; and they took trips together. Ottilie called herself his "natural wife" and wrote of their intimate "sensual" relationship (Diedrich, 1999). She expected them to marry when slavery ended, but it is unknown whether they ever discussed their mutual expectations of how this relationship would evolve.

Ottilie and Douglass had radically different conceptions of family. To Ottilie, marriage was a convention often imposed on partners for social and economic reasons. It became "a radical move to assault marriage, an expression of an emancipated mind; for American slaves it was a rebellious, seditious act to demand the right to marry" (Diedrich, 1999, p. 187). Ottilie did not understand how important family was to Douglass and that slavery had degraded and often prohibited the establishment of a family. Abolition would give black people the freedom to have families.

Ottilie Assing and Anna Murray. Ottilie gave herself credit for achieving peace between herself and Anna; she did not understand that Anna "had agreed to a truce with her" (Diedrich, 1999, p. 185).

Mrs. Douglass had similarly treated Julia Griffiths with cold politeness... even having a cup of tea and a chat with her when Griffiths deigned to visit her in the kitchen.... The way she conducted herself suggests ... that she was not just a passive chess figure, allowing her husband to move her around. By establishing a truce with the "other woman" she maintained at least a semblance of control and affirmed her sense of self. The inner struggle she fought must have been fierce, and her life story suggests that she paid an enormous price. (Diedrich, 1999, p. 185)

Why did Anna remain illiterate? Paradoxically, Anna met Frederick at the Baltimore Improvement Society, and she encouraged his learning. Anna was involved with the Lynn Abolitionist Society with politically active, literate women. She was not "'indifferent to the world of ideas'"; her children read to her, and she listened and commented (Diedrich, 1999, p. 181).

Douglass was critical of Sojourner Truth, the famous woman abolitionist, who chose to remain illiterate and "disdained print culture" (Diedrich, 1999, p. 178). Douglass stated that she was a "'genuine specimen of the uncultured Negro'" (p. 177). Anna, like Sojourner, may have "shared a skepticism about literacy which many people raised in oral traditions ... develop" (p. 177). Diedrich reasoned that "Douglass associated literacy with freedom; [Anna], with a silencing of God's voice" (p. 178). Religion was a source of conflict between them: Anna was concerned that abolitionist work would increase Douglass's old antireligious fervor (which it did). Anna and Douglass had very divergent narratives about the meaning of literacy, one of the many sources of their marital conflict.

Was Anna's illiteracy a "rebellion" against Douglass and his values or perhaps her expression of resistance to Douglass's relationship with educated white women? Two teachers who were unsuccessful with her were Griffiths and Assing. Douglass seemed totally oblivious of Anna's humiliation at being put in an inferior position to her two rivals to whom he had given preferential status. Her resistance to being "educated" by them at her husband's instigation is entirely understandable as a displacement of anger toward him.

Ottilie became involved with the Douglass children: "Her presence radiated happiness when their mother was often morose" (Diedrich, 1999, p. 194). Anna's moroseness probably increased as she observed her children's attachment to Ottilie.

> Seventeen-year-old Rosetta, Ottilie's favorite, was a "shy, sensitive teenager, eager to please, unhappy at the conflict between her parents, and somehow lost in adolescent loneliness" (Diedrich, 1999, p. 194).

> Her relationship to her mother was warped. The oldest child and for a long time the only daughter, she had been expected to take care of her siblings and help with household chores even in her earliest childhood. Anna Murray had been a demanding taskmistress, slow to praise. Even as a grandmother, Rosetta could not really forgive her mother for her lack of warmth. She was a "strict disciplinarian." ... Then, as her education seemed to elevate Rosetta to a level above her mother's, the normal tensions between mother and teenage daughter intensified. (Diedrich, 1999, pp. 194–195)

Rosetta felt trapped by parental conflict. In a letter to her father, 30-year-old Rosetta commented on her parents' conflicts, implying that Douglass may have been indifferent or oblivious to his daughter's feelings.

> You say you are a lonely man[;] no one knows it better than myself and the causes. I have been in a measure lonely myself but would not allow myself to analyze my feelings as I was the daughter and had duties to fulfill in that relation. I knew where my sympathies were[.] I do not know whether you ever thought about it[,] having so many things to occupy your mind[,] but my position at home was anything but pleasant.... I never dared to show much zeal about anything where you were concerned.... I could readily bring a storm about [her] ears if I endorsed any of your sentiments about matters pertaining to the household. (Diedrich, 1999, p. 195)

Rosetta felt caught in the middle of parental conflict and that her emotional needs were not being met by either parent. Her dilemma is like that of children caught in family conflict who are powerless to resolve their parents' strife and so instead react with resentful resignation.

Political Shifts in a New Era

Douglass unexpectedly had to flee to England a second time to protect his life. The crisis looming at that time was precipitated by John Brown's raid on Harper's Ferry, which ended with John Brown being hanged by the government. Douglass was not involved in the actual raid or in planning for it. However, Brown, a longtime friend of Douglass, had spent several weeks at Douglass's home before the attack, leaving behind incriminating papers.

When Brown was captured, along with several prominent people, Douglass received a telegram from a friend "saying that we were all to be arrested" (Douglass, 1882, p. 376). Escaping to Hoboken, he contacted Ottilie, who sent a telegram at his request to his son Lewis asking him to "secure all the important papers in my high desk" (Douglass, 1882, p. 378). Douglass then fled to Canada and, on November 12, sailed to England. Ottilie remained in the United States.

Douglass successfully lectured in England and Scotland and visited friends. Prior to this crisis, Douglass and Ottilie had talked of visiting Paris together; however, before arrangements could be made, his daughter Annie, almost 11, died on March 13, 1860. Douglass, overcome by grief and guilt, decided to return to his family (McFeely, 1991, p. 207).

> I should now have gratified a long-cherished desire to visit France . . . had not news reached me from home of the death of my beloved daughter Annie, the light and life of my house. Deeply distressed by this bereavement, and acting upon the impulse of the moment, regardless of the peril, I at once resolved to return home, and took the first outgoing steamer for Portland, Maine. (Douglass, 1882, p. 394)

Douglass arrived in Rochester in July 1860 and, to his surprise and relief, found he was now safe: Congress had ended its inquiry into the John Brown Raid, rather than "pursue possible accomplices and create more martyrs" (McFeely, 1991, p. 208).

Douglass was now in the midst of vibrant political activity, and "for the first time in his life, he was in the political mainstream" (McFeely, 1991, p. 208). The Republican Party was opposed to extending slavery; Lincoln was expected to win the election.

The year 1860 was momentous for Ottilie: Her translation of Douglass's *My Bondage and My Freedom* appeared in Germany, and she became an American citizen on July 20. This was her "pledge of faith to Frederick Douglass... like a marriage vow.... His gift to her was a little red kitten" (Diedrich, 1999, p. 230). Did Douglass's gift signify to him a "marriage vow"? We do not hear his voice.

Ottilie was becoming more a part of the Douglass household, assisting with the Underground Railroad. She was increasingly open about her relationship with Douglass and his family and wrote about this in letters and articles.

"Slavery and race moved center stage in her commentaries, which became part of a unified abolitionist discourse" (Diedrich, 1999, p. 206). The few African Americans Ottilie knew were generally well educated; she had little involvement with uneducated black people such as "black domestics, field laborers, sailors" (Diedrich, 1999, p. 205). Apart from slavery, the special problems faced by poor, black, uneducated people were not addressed in her work.

Changing Political Landscapes:
The Civil War and Reconstruction

Lincoln and the Civil War

Both Douglass and Assing advocated "transform[ing] the Civil War... into a war on slavery" (Diedrich, 1999, pp. 236–237). When Lincoln's

Emancipation Proclamation was delivered on January 1, 1863, Douglass (1882) wrote: "It was one of the most affecting and thrilling occasions I ever witnessed" (p. 430). During the war, Douglass was instrumental in the inclusion of black soldiers in the Union Army and later advocated for more humane treatment of them as soldiers.

Douglass's two private meetings with President Lincoln in the White House were important events in black history. Douglass was impressed with Lincoln's personal and leadership qualities, and when with him, "I was never in any way reminded of my humble origin, or of my unpopular color" (Douglass, 1882, p. 436).

During the Civil War, Douglass and Ottilie spent much time together: "[She] stood by his side, served as his secretary, ghostwriter, and inspiration, unconditionally and unwaveringly.... [This] won her an unprecedented degree of support and devotion from Douglass" (Diedrich, 1999, p. 253).

Reconstruction: The First 10 Years

The liberation was poorly managed, leading to massive social upheavals and further oppression of and injustice toward the black population. The new reactionary Southern state governments enacted the restrictive Black Codes, removing freedoms given to blacks. The Ku Klux Klan was permitted to continue its violence and terror.

Douglass's new mission was obtaining the vote for black people. He was elated when on March 30, 1870, President Grant announced the 15th Amendment to the Constitution, "granting suffrage rights to all citizens regardless of 'race, color or previous condition of servitude'" (Diedrich, 1999, p. 292). He did not recognize that the right to vote "might be insufficient in the face of the murderous intimidation of black voters" (p. 256).

Douglass was moving away from the pressing concerns of the black working class, not giving sufficient attention to the damage slavery had inflicted and the need for special services: "Wary of missionaries, he insisted that his people needed 'rights more than training to enjoy them'"; black people should rise above their present status (McFeely, 1991, p. 242). "He liked to see himself not only as an exceptional, self-made man, but also as a personification of all his race could achieve, of the potential of his race" (Diedrich, 1999, p. 265).

When the war was over, Douglass, then 47, felt that his mission had ended. "'I felt that I had reached the end of the noblest and best part of my life'" (quoted in Diedrich, 1999, p. 254). Though uncertain about the future, Ottilie was buoyant and anticipated being with Douglass. Writing to Ludmilla, she expressed not the "slightest doubt...that this could only mean separation from Anna Murray and a legalization of their liaison" (Diedrich, 1999, p. 255). But, Diedrich asks, "Did it occur to her that her and Douglass's visions might not be compatible?" (p. 258).

From a narrative perspective, Douglass "had reached the end" of his story; the plot of his life course had been achieved. No longer a slave, he had played a leading role in emancipation. He retained his self-image as a "chosen" individual, revered by many. He now felt he had no special mission. Ottilie had almost fulfilled the plot of her life course, her romantic relationship with a "special" man. Her relationship with Douglass fit the script she envisioned. But she was disappointed in her wished for ending, to be this man's wife.

A romance with a happy ending was not part of Douglass's narrative. Readers are left in the dark—his autobiographies say nothing of his feelings about Ottilie.

For the many years that Douglass and Ottilie's relationship flourished, their narratives were compatible. Even before she met Douglass, Ottilie had decided that he was a special person. Their relationship was complementary: Douglass needed to fulfill his destiny; Ottilie needed to be his companion and helpmate. When he had fulfilled his, she had not yet fulfilled hers. The fulfillment of her envisioned destiny never happened. There were to be no shared narratives beyond this point. Instead there was a gradual dissolution of their relationship.

Ottilie idealized Douglass, who was " 'a true elite' of the human race" (Diedrich, 1999, p. 166). They were both special people, and their relationship was unique and special.

> The discourse she constructed to justify their conduct was unassailable in its circularity: her and Douglass's exceptionality freed them for and justified their actions, while their actions manifested and validated their exceptionality.... They had not only the right but the duty to defy those norms... [of] conventionality. (Diedrich, 1999, pp. 166–167)

In the meantime, "with her children gone, with few friends and no fugitives, Anna Murray withdrew to the kitchen and the garden" (Diedrich, 1999, p. 254).

On June 2, 1872, Douglass's home in Rochester was burned to the ground by arsonists; the suspects were never identified or found (McFeely, 1991). Anna, Rosetta, and her family, who were living there, escaped safely. Many of Douglass's possessions were saved, but the complete runs of his newspaper (which he planned to donate to Harvard University), as well as personal letters, probably many from Ottilie (Diedrich, 1999), were destroyed.

Ottilie was now frustrated and angry, having expected to live with Douglass in Washington, DC, while Anna stayed in Rochester. Douglass's family moved to Washington; Douglass invited Ottilie to move in:

> She arrived in a house full of too many people, and she took up a comfortable room, which only made things worse. She seems to have been ruthless in her conduct toward the Douglass family, her ruthlessness matched only by Douglass, who sent for her regardless of his wife's wishes or condition. (Diedrich, 1999, p. 307)

Douglass remained in the public eye, holding a series of positions, which failed, in one way or another, to either enhance his image or advance his people; he drifted away from the mainstream black population. Although he was an "absentee" father when the children were younger, he was now deeply involved in their adult lives. Family difficulties escalated into major financial, health, and relationship problems, and Douglass made continual efforts to "rescue" his family.

Douglass "became irritable, discouraged, and withdrew even from friends and family." In August 1873, he wrote to Rosetta that " 'I was little fit to visit any body and did well to hide myself at Old Orchard Beach' " (quoted in Diedrich, 1999, p. 310). Douglass became apprehensive about aging: " 'I find my continuous working power, in some measure failing me . . . and my health rather uncertain as I grow older' " (p. 311).

Ruptures appeared in the Douglass-Assing relationship: Ottilie was increasingly critical of the demands placed on Douglass by his family. Anna's health was deteriorating, and "her smoldering resentment of her husband grew" (McFeely, 1991, p. 297). Concurrently, Ottilie "was making greater and greater emotional demands" on Douglass; "... she was unwittingly undermining their relationship. It happened slowly, one step at a time, imperceptibly to both" (Diedrich, 1999, p. 297).

Ottilie herself was emotionally stressed—"she seemed near breakdown" (Diedrich, 1999, p. 308). Douglass could not meet her emotional needs; to do so "would have meant becoming engulfed by her overpowering distress. Instead, he increasingly withdrew, which only made her the more eager to have him respond" (McFeely, 1991, p. 298).

In December 1872 (six months after the fire that destroyed Douglass's home), Ottilie experienced a cold and incessant ringing in her ears; she wrote that "this makes it almost impossible to do any kind of intellectual work and often almost drives me to despair" (Diedrich, 1999, p. 308). The following May, Ottilie's friend and physician, Dr. Frauenstein, wrote to Douglass:

> [Dr. Frauenstein] also saw that it was becoming harder for [Ottilie] to cope with this depression; perhaps this was worsened by her going through menopause. "Her self-slaughterous tendencies remain unabated, notwithstanding her improvement, and it is useless, to reason with her on that nonsense; for it is nonsense in itself, to reason on nonsense." (Diedrich, 1999, p. 309)

Ottilie nevertheless carried on with a heavy workload "to compensate for the loss and disappointment" (Diedrich, 1999, p. 310). She worked with Douglass at the *New National Era* and joined the American Society for the Prevention of Cruelty to Animals. Although Ottilie "was a strong woman," her "many hopes" had been "crushed [and] too many new problems were emerging" (p. 310)

Ottilie and Douglass were also diverging in their political views. She was skeptical about Grant as president and disillusioned with American politics and the Republican Party. The result was that "her skeptical pragmatism became a source of contention between them" (Diedrich, 1999, p. 272).

In March 1874, Douglass became president of the Freedman's Savings and Trust Company, in which many hard-working black people invested. Prior to Douglass's presidency, the bank was heading toward insolvency. In spite of Douglass's strenuous efforts, the bank closed. Douglass was also frustrated and despondent about the political situation in Washington. Ottilie, although stressed herself, tried to be supportive.

Distance and Dissolution

Assing's Brief Return to Europe

Ottilie was conflicted about visiting Europe because she did not want to leave Douglass. He promised they would meet in Paris that spring, so she decided to go in the winter of 1875–1876. She met Ludmilla in Hamburg, "but it was a cold reunion." Although they had been apart for 23 years, they now "resumed their feud" (Diedrich, 1999, p. 323).

Living alone in Rome, Ottilie's letters to Ludmilla and Douglass told of being "surrounded by people who cherished her company" (Diedrich, 1999, p. 326). Ottilie "was punishing him with detailed accounts of the joy he was missing" (p. 326). Her last months in Europe were filled with "incessant activity, movement, physical exertion to the point of collapse," her typical way of overcoming depression (p. 328).

Douglass never met her in Paris. When Hayes became president in 1877, Douglass was appointed marshal of the District of Columbia. "Once again, his public triumph was defeat for her private ambitions" (Diedrich, 1999, p. 327).

Ottilie left Europe in September, eager to return to Douglass and to the United States, which she felt was her home. Ottilie and Douglass "faced many challenges after... [her] return from Europe, yet each held on to the other" (Diedrich, 1999, p. 354).

Douglass remained a loyal Republican even though the government would not protect black Southerners or prevent the rise of white supremacy; he did not acknowledge the plight of Southern disenfranchised black people (McFeely, 1991). "The *Redeemers,* as the white leaders liked to think of themselves, had quickly regained control of Southern state and local governments" (McFeely, 1991, p. 299). When many black people from Louisiana and Mississippi (the Exodusters, as they were known) decided to go west, Douglass asserted that they should stay in the South and work for better conditions and equality.

McFeely (1991) commented that "the stances on various issues Douglass was to take between 1877 and 1881 were the least honorable and least helpful to his fellow former slaves of any in his long life" (p. 291). That Douglass was determined to pursue his agenda only "strengthened [Ottilie's] determination to help him see the direction he was drifting in"; however, he did not wish to hear this and "began to dodge her" (Diedrich, 1999, p. 349).

Their relationship did revive, when Ottilie stayed with the Douglasses at their new spacious home in Washington. "Assing and Douglass experienced a sense of healing and rejuvenation in their relationship during the two months they spent together at Cedar Hill that fall" (Diedrich, 1999, p. 339). However, Ottilie returned to Hoboken and personal problems in November 1878. After she lost $4,000 on a bad real estate investment, she moved to New York to room with her former landlady, finding herself in limbo. "On returning to the United States she had realized... that post-Reconstruction America violated her most sacred political and social beliefs. She was left with no place she could possibly love as her home" (Diedrich, 1999, p. 342).

Ottilie's frustration with Douglass increased, regarding their ideological differences and his overinvolvement with his family. However, her major worry was his interest in "younger women.... At the age of 59, he was dreaming of rejuvenation. The problem had become acute in late 1878, when Helen Pitts first came to Cedar Hill" (Diedrich, 1999, p. 350). Helen Pitts, who was to become his second wife six years later, was well educated, lively, and 20 years younger.

Assing could not overlook the eroticism in the air. The more she saw of the younger woman, the more she feared her. She was enormously relieved when Douglass wrote to her... that Pitts's visits had ceased. What he didn't tell her was that he continued to correspond with Pitts and even to visit her when possible. (Diedrich, 1999, p. 350)

Ottilie's sadness at the end of 1878 "developed into another full-blown depression, Assing once again trying to escape... by burying herself in work" (Diedrich, 1999, p. 350).

In March 1880, Ottilie learned that Ludmilla had been diagnosed with "insanity" after contracting meningitis and that she died in a coma in a "mental asylum" (Diedrich, 1999, p. 354). Ottilie was distressed, however, that Ludmilla had totally disinherited her. She decided to challenge Ludmilla's will by proving that her sister "had been mentally incapacitated" (Diedrich, 1999, p. 355). Ottilie's decision to revisit Europe in August 1881 was precipitated by her legal actions. "Ottilie conveniently forgot that ... as early as 1871 [she] had disinherited Ludmilla" (Diedrich, 1999, p. 355).

Before leaving, Ottilie reported an enjoyable visit with Douglass, but what they may have discussed about their relationship is unknown. "This time there were no promises to Ottilie that they would meet somewhere in the Old World" (Diedrich, 1999, p. 361).

Assing's Final Years

Ottilie, unsuccessful in retrieving money from Ludmilla's estate, turned her visit into a pleasure trip. A year later she learned that Anna Murray had died on August 4, 1882. Ottilie's reaction to this news, and whether Douglass told her, is unknown.

> She disappeared completely "for months, telling nobody where she was.... [Her] German publisher ... became so anxious that he published a search inquiry" (Diedrich, 1999, p. 363).

She was both surprised and pleased that her absence had caused concern.

Anna, 69, had had a paralytic stroke in July, leading to her death. Douglass struggled with feelings of grief and depression. "In the summer of 1883, Douglass appears to have been depressed almost to the point of a breakdown" (McFeely, 1991, p. 313). Six months later, on January 24, 1884, he married Helen Pitts.

Diedrich (1999), doubting that Douglass told Ottilie about his wedding plans, notes that one day before his wedding, she wrote a letter to her friend, Amalie Koehler "full of travel plans and gossip, relaxed in tone." If she had known, "this composure was remarkable indeed" (p. 369). After Douglass's marriage, Ottilie "withdrew into complete silence."

In August 1884, Ottilie wrote to the Koehlers from Paris about her proposed visit to Spain. She always ended her letters to them by drawing a cat, her favorite animal. "This time she drew a snake" (Diedrich, 1999, p. 371). Ottilie now used a snake as a signature, which seems very much at odds with her long-standing use of the cat. Perhaps her choice of new signature was benign; perhaps it was an indication of something ominous. She seemed to be trying to communicate something to the Koehlers. If this was hinting at her emotional state, it was ambiguous, and was belied by the future-oriented tone of the letter.

In clinical practice, we often see people making use of symbols and metaphors; this is a form of indirect narrative, allowing them to communicate something, without "giving themselves away," revealing and concealing at the same time. An elderly lady complained at length to a social worker about the demolition of the old parts of the city: They were still valuable but not appreciated. Realizing the woman was alluding to how she felt she was being treated, the therapist did not address this directly, feeling it would be too threatening. She worked with the woman within the metaphor, talking about how much the old parts had added to the city (Wasser, 1966).

What the snake in Ottilie's letter might have been intended to convey was her increasing feelings of desperation and despair. This might also represent her anger at Douglass, who had treated her in a ruthless, underhanded manner. On August 21, 1884, dressed "elegantly," Ottilie went to the Bois de Boulogne, in Paris. "Seating herself on a bench somewhat removed from the park's main walks, she carefully uncorked the little vial she took from her purse and swallowed the potassium cyanide it contained" (Diedrich, 1999, p. 373). When her body arrived at the Paris morgue, an autopsy was not necessary—"the vial they found told it all" (p. 373).

Toward the end of her life, Ottilie told people she had breast cancer, presumably incurable. Douglass and others believed this was the cause of her suicide. This is a plausible explanation, considering that Ottilie had memories of nursing her mother through cancer and would not have wanted to suffer in this way. Diedrich, however (1999), questioned whether this cancer was a fact or Ottilie's fabrication: "there is no reliable documentation of this medical diagnosis" (p. 371).

> We should also consider the possibility that this, like so many other events and relationships in her life, was an invention. It might have been a final gesture of love and generosity to Douglass, to protect him against the charge of being responsible for her death, or... an invention she needed to maintain her pride and integrity, an act of defiance against the man who had betrayed her. (Diedrich, 1999, pp. 371–372)

Douglass wrote to a friend: "'I have been made inexpressibly sad . . . by confirmatory news of the death of my dear friend Miss *N*'" (quoted in Diedrich, 1999, p. 375). Ottilie wrote her last will on April 7, 1883. She left $13,000 in a trust for Douglass. This money was to be

> ". . . safely invested at interest for and during the term of the natural life of Hon. Frederick Douglass . . . to pay over the net interest and income therefrom by equal semi-annual payments to the said Frederick Douglass for and during the term of his natural life . . . and upon and after his decease, to pay over unto the American Society for the Prevention of Cruelty to Animals . . . the whole of said principle sum of Thirteen Thousand (13,000) dollars." (quoted in Diedrich, 1999, p. 379)

Diedrich (1999) commented that Ottilie's "need to protect and control him extended beyond the grave. . . . [She] always refused to believe in ghosts; perhaps she simply devised a more substantial way of haunting Frederick Douglass" (pp. 379-380).

Ottilie made a provision that "'all the letters which will be found in my possession, are to be destroyed immediately'" (quoted in Diedrich, 1999, p. 380); this was done. She had not requested this action in an earlier will. Diedrich suggested that, perhaps earlier, she had wanted these letters included in her memoirs about her relationship to Douglass. Dr. Kudlich, her executor, found a large number of her letters, filed and neatly arranged. "'They constituted a treasure in themselves and bore the signatures of eminent men and women and I was reluctant to permit these precious documents to disappear in smoke'" (quoted in Diedrich, 1999, p. 381). But he followed her instructions.

Remarriage

Helen Pitts had many of Ottilie's qualities, "without the bitterness, without the obsession that kept breaking through Assing's amiable surface" (Diedrich, 1999, p. 367).

A year and a half after Anna's death, on January 24, 1884, Douglass and Helen (then 45) were married in a private ceremony. Douglass's children opposed the marriage, exacerbating family tensions. Douglass had married "someone not their mother," a woman who was not black. "Marrying a white woman seemed a public confirmation of his children's heretofore private grievance, their sense that they, being darker than he, were of less value." There were also "many black Americans who felt betrayed" (McFeely, 1991, p. 320).

Helen's family objected to the marriage. Helen's father (a former abolitionist) would "not give them his blessing" and did not allow Douglass in his home (McFeely, 1991). Helen's mother and other family members later reconciled with the couple.

In September 1886, Douglass and Helen toured Europe and Egypt. Douglass described their trip in his autobiography: He enjoyed his travel and encounters with interesting and prominent people. He says nothing about his feelings for Helen but did express resentment at prejudice about his marriage.

Douglass's Final Years

Over the next two years, Douglass was busy campaigning for Harrison. In 1889, he was appointed minister to Haiti. He was caught in power struggles within Haiti as well as a conflict within the U.S. government about its Haitian policies and resigned in 1891. Douglass published his third autobiography, *Life and Times of Frederick Douglass,* recapitulating his earlier work and updating it. This book did not sell well.

Conditions for black people in the South deteriorated; lynchings were frequent.

Ida Wells, a black editor and orator, became a strong voice protesting lynchings, and Douglass "was driven back into the fray by Wells" (McFeely, 1991, p. 377). Douglass "delivered what was to be his last great speech" (McFeely, 1991, p. 377) in Washington, DC, in 1894, addressing lynching and other oppressive acts inflicted on black people.

Douglass remained politically active until the end of his life. On February 20, 1895, he was honored at a women's rights rally. Upon returning home to prepare for a meeting in a black church, he suddenly collapsed and died.

There was a tremendous outpouring of grief and public memorialization. He was buried in Rochester near his wife Anna and daughter Annie. A statue (one of many memorials) was erected near his former residence in Rochester.

Conclusion

Narrative theory illuminates key aspects of the lives of Frederick Douglass and Ottilie Assing. It was Frederick Douglass's narrative skills that first brought him public acclaim; his powerful, and eloquent speeches about the injustices, exploitation, and losses experienced by slaves moved many audiences. Douglass personalized his narratives by speaking of his own odyssey toward freedom. When audiences began to doubt the authenticity of his slave background, because he was so well spoken, Douglass, to give evidence of his literacy, wrote his life's story in three autobiographies. These became American classics. His narrations were a political tool, contributing to the success of the abolitionst movement; they were also a means of self-representation.

Ottilie Assing, using her background as a journalist, contributed her impressive narrative skills to the fight for abolition. Her German translation of Douglass's autobiography *My Bondage and My Freedom* advanced worldwide recognition of the cause; she gave her dedicated assistance to Douglass in his struggle for many years.

Self-representation and responsivess to one's audience are other aspects of narrative theory. Both Douglass and Ottilie were concerned with their self-representations, and often changed these to suit their audiences (or their perceptions of their audiences). Ottilie and Douglass supported each other's validation of their specialness; their "exceptionality . . . justified their actions" (Diedrich, 1999, pp. 166–167), sometimes with unfortunate consequences. For example, Douglass distanced himself from average black and *unexceptional* working people during Reconstruction and failed to respond initially to their suffering.

Over the years Ottilie had developed her own romantic narrative about a special relationship she would develop with a gifted and heroic self-made man. Her romanticization and idealization of her relationship with Douglass blinded her to its realistic limitations and led to her despair when he abandoned her.

Frederick Douglass has his place in history as a major leader in the abolition of slavery. Ottilie Assing has a less well known but significant place in American history. Although not receiving the attention accorded Douglass, she did have her own voice and her own writings.

Together, by their tireless work, they made major contributions to the achievement of freedom and human rights. Their intertwined narratives illustrate the complexity of lives and relationships in a historical setting.

CHAPTER 9

Gathering, Evaluating, and Interpreting Evidence

Gathering biographical evidence is never a purely objective and straightforward process. Biographers continually make decisions about selection, evaluation, and interpretation of evidence. In deciding what evidence to include, what to delete, what to highlight, which sources to quote, and how to interpret it all, the biographer (even one whose voice seems unobtrusive) is always pulling the strings. "The biographer is explorer, inquirer, hypothesizer, compiler, researcher, selector, and writer; none of these is a neutral act" (p. 119).

Even such "hard" facts as dates of birth or death may not exist or can be disputed. No record exists of Frederick Douglass's birth, as was typical for many slaves. Biographers may also delete factual data that they decide is irrelevant. Furthermore, as a "hypothesizer," the biographer's theoretical, social, or political orientation can be critical (whether explicit or implicit). Is the author representing the life of the subject in a particular way to emphasize societal discrimination and oppression or to validate a psychological theory?

Feminist biographers may reject evidence that presents women in a negative light (Backscheider, 1999). Sometimes psychoanalytic theory is overemphasized, as in Rosamond Langbridge's biography of Charlotte Brontë (Miller, 2001). Psychodynamic and developmental factors can also be minimized. Andrew Carnegie's biographer initially disregarded the impact of the death of Carnegie's young sister on him. Upon later reflection (with a psychiatric consultant), the biographer realized that this tragic event reverberated throughout Carnegie's life (Wall, 1985).

The autobiographer, recording his or her own life, can hardly qualify as a disinterested observer. Motivations and intentions vary considerably, as do the ability and commitment for self-awareness and disclosure.

The parallels between the biographer's evidence-gathering activities and those of the clinician are striking. Every step of the clinical process, including the collection and assessment of "objective" data, has subjective implications. The clinician with a behaviorist orientation may ignore developmental details essential to the psychodynamic clinician. Some clinicians, focusing on the patient's inner life, may minimize the client's sociopolitical and cultural life.

This chapter discusses the varieties of evidence sought by biographers, the vicissitudes of this search, and, finally, the challenges faced when analyzing and integrating the evidence into a comprehensive life story. The parallel issues in clinical practice are addressed. My own psychodynamic orientation within a biopsychosocial framework colors this presentation.

The Evidence

Exploring the Subject's Social and Physical Milieu

Biographers examine the subject's life through multiple sources, including official documents, newspaper accounts, interviews, and the subject's own writings and speeches. Rodin and Key (1984) studied Conan Doyle's medical casebooks and other medical writings and found him to have been a competent practitioner who made a "valuable contribution to both the scientific and nonscientific aspects of medicine of the late 19th century" (p. xxi).

Biographers often visit "the places that bred and mattered to the subject....

The places we live, the landscape we see each day, the weather that provides the rhythm of our year shape the soul and the sensibility" (Backscheider, 1999, p. 72).

Robert Caro (1983), writing about Lyndon Johnson, described the hill country of Texas where Johnson grew up, because, as Caro explained, an understanding its perils was needed to understand Johnson. "The hill country was a trap-a trap baited with grass" (p. 8).

> The tall grass of the Hill Country stretched as far as the eye could see, covering valleys and hillsides alike.... To... [the settlers] the grass was proof that their dreams would come true. In country where grass grew like that, cotton would surely grow tall, and cattle fat—and men rich. In country where grass grew like that, they thought, anything would grow. How could they know about the grass? (Caro, 1983, p. 11)

Newly arriving settlers did not know that the soil was inhospitable to agriculture. Succeeding "required... a pragmatism almost terrifying in its absolutely uncompromising starkness" (Caro, 1983, p. 26). And the Johnsons "were... particularly unsuited to such a land" (p. 26). They lost their agricultural investment and lived a life of genteel poverty. These economic circumstances and resulting family interactions played a large role in Lyndon Johnson's psychological development (Caro, 1983).

Norman Sherry, Graham Greene's authorized biographer, faced a formidable task when writing Greene's biography. Sherry had agreed to Greene's demand that he " 'follow in his footsteps' " by traveling to scenes of his important books, many of which were unsafe. In complying, his biographer "contracted gangrene, which required the removal of part of his intestines" (Franklin, 2004, p. 100).

Reading biographies can enhance clinicians' sensitivity to the influence of clients' social and physical milieus on their lives. Some clinicians make home visits, which are an integral part of the intervention, in settings such as child welfare, public health, schools, hospice, or outreach programs to the mentally ill. In outpatient mental health clinics or private offices, clinicians rarely visit the client's environment.

In a personal communication, E.B. Urdang, MD (November 12, 1964) reported that to take into account the effect that the home environment can have on clients, a child psychiatric training program in a university hospital mandated that therapists working with children and their families invite themselves to have a one-time dinner with the family in the family home. This provided trainees with special insight into the family's problems and interactions as well as their way of life, interests, and strengths.

When circumstances are not conducive to exploring the client's environment, awareness of the relevance of environmental factors can motivate therapists to inquire about their client's lives outside the therapy room and learn about their housing, work, recreation, and so forth. The person's experiential world has outer as well as inner dimensions. Moving to new social environments can also create stress, whether the move is within one's own country or involves emigration.

For example, for refugees, the traumatic aspects of their experiences may be paramount; however, they may have memories of their country and experiences (besides trauma) they want to share. An immigrant may have had "to give up familiar food, native music, unquestioned social customs, and even one's language" (Akhtar, 1995, p. 1052).

Witnesses and Social Involvements

Biographers make decisions about interviewing people (if still alive) who were involved in the subject's life and milieu. If witnesses are no longer living, decisions must be made regarding who and what merits further inquiry (for example, evidence such as the subject's writings). In addition to selecting witnesses, decisions need to be made about their reliability. Boswell interviewed "bishops, actresses, philosophers, booksellers, blue-stockings, childhood friends and household servants" for Johnson's biography (Holmes, 2000, p. 369).

Wendy Moffat (2010), biographer of the novelist E. M. Forster, explored how Forster was perceived by others, noting that he had been described as looking "impeccably ordinary, like 'the man who comes to clean the clocks'" (Moffat, 2010, p. 11). Forster (who went by his middle name, Morgan) often remained "quietly at the edge of the conversational circle. This mousy self-presentation was no accident" (p. 11). Besides being "naturally quite shy," Forster, a closeted gay man, was uncomfortable with the flamboyance of Oscar Wilde or Lytton Strachey.

Forster instead chose to draw people inward, to reveal themselves to him as he remained enigmatic. To speak with him was to be seduced by an inverse charisma, a sense of being listened to with such intensity that you had to be your most honest, sharpest, and best self. Morgan's steadfast scrutiny tested his friend's nerves. Siegfried Sassoon found it "always makes me into a chatterbox." He always had to suppress an urge to act the clown, to "amuse" Morgan to dispel the moral weight of his stillness and empathy. (Moffat, 2010, pp. 11–12)

The perceptions of family members can likewise be informative, adding important perspective on the subject's life. However, their own biases or agendas need to be factored into the analysis. Erik Erikson's daughter, Sue Erikson Bloland, was motivated to write about her father and her relationship with him after reading *Identity's Architect: A Biography of Erik H. Erikson* by Lawrence J. Friedman, published in 1999. Though complimentary about Friedman's scholarship, she felt he did not convey the intricate family dynamics: "his description cannot possibly reflect my own experience" (Bloland, 1999, p. 51). She felt a special urgency about this because her father had been so idealized that his weaknesses and flaws had been passed over.

Bloland (1999) perceived her father as an insecure man, who was far from fulfilling the role of "perfect" father that others ascribed to him. Furthermore, she always felt pressure to be "the ideal daughter that one would expect a perfect father to have" (p. 60). Erikson, she reported, had problems meeting the emotional needs of his children, often evoking in others a need to comfort and reassure him, relying on his wife to meet both his own needs and the children's. Bloland needed to "protect him from any feelings of mine that might bring that pained expression to his face, and continued to do so for the rest of his life" (p. 53).

She observed that "the public image reflects what the private person most longs to be. It represents an ideal self" (Bloland, 1999, p. 54). She believed that underneath her father's insecurity was a strong sense of shame that stemmed from his childhood and especially his being born out of wedlock in Denmark. When his mother later married his stepfather, Erikson had a conflictual relationship with him. Never learning who his biological father was remained a source of pain (and shame) to him throughout his life; he fantasized that his father was a member of the Danish royalty (which was not altogether an unrealistic possibility).

In another family, William Styron's daughter, Alexandra, wrote a memoir about him and her childhood. *Reading My Father,* published in 2011 and excerpted in the *New Yorker* (A. Styron, 2007), shed light on the idyllic public image of her family life in a charming country setting. She discussed her father's inner conflicts, drinking problems, and external conflicts with the family and other people.

One reviewer observed that Alexandra wrote a credible account: "As tough as she is on her father, she sees clearly the better man he could sometimes be.... This is a grown-up memoir, taut and true" (Garner, 2011, p. C4). Alexandra also did research in the archives of Duke University, where her fathers' papers were stored, and interviewed people who were significant in his life.

She discussed her father's famous book, *Darkness Visible,* a vivid portrayal of the crippling depression he experienced. This book, followed by his public speaking on depression, conveyed a positive message to people: One could recover from such despair. Alexandra praised her father's memoir and presented information about his later life.

Unfortunately, A. Styron, after 15 years of remission, suffered a relapse. At 75, when "depression struck again, it found an older, softer, and much less defensible target. The last six years of my father's life were an ongoing disaster" (A. Styron, 2007, p. 58). Alexandra poignantly described his decline and her visits with him: "My father was dying and I wanted to know him better" (p. 60).

People's outward presentations can be at odds with their inner self-image. Franz Kafka thought poorly of himself as a child and was convinced he was a poor student and that his teachers shared his negative estimation. Pawel (1984) found evidence to the contrary:

> Whatever misgivings Kafka may have had about his scholastic abilities, the evidence of his grades suggests both ample talent and application. He was, in fact, a star pupil throughout the first four years, popular among his classmates and exceedingly well liked by his teachers. (p. 33)

Clinicians likewise can gain insights about their patients by interviewing people significant in the client's life, sometimes actually observing clients in interaction with others, such as in couples counseling or parent-child therapy. Their decisions about involving others in assessing and treating the client depend on many factors, including treatment goals and the receptivity of the "other." However, even if not physically present, "significant" people can be brought into the therapeutic dialogue, through reflective discussion with the client.

Archival Material

Details of a subject's life are often found through painstaking archival research of documents and public files; sometimes extensive travel is involved. Paula R. Backscheider (1999) searched in many locations for details about the author Daniel Defoe, who lived from 1660 to 1731, "weeding" through reams of official records and other source material until she found meaningful "nuggets." She learned, for example, that Defoe was arrested for "seditious libel" after she searched many old documents for detailed information.

> Because this was a state offence, the office of the Secretary of State was involved, and there was new information in the State Papers and in the Secretary's Entry and Treasury Books.... The Undersecretary of State charged with monitoring the press left notes about it. Defoe appeared before the Queen, and Privy Council minutes about that survive.... His family was greatly affected, and, by analysing that aspect carefully, I was the first biographer to notice that Mary Defoe was pregnant. (Backscheider, 1999, p. 69)

It is not uncommon that old material hidden away is discovered years later. Many of Boswell's papers, long dormant in an attic, are now in a special collection at Yale University. During his 12 years of psychiatric hospitalizations, Charles Doyle (Arthur Conan Doyle's father) had written and illustrated *The Doyle Diaries,* a sketchbook accompanied by personal annotations. This work remained unnoticed for years unpublished.

Michael Baker (1978), "intrigued by reading *The Doyle Diaries,*" began his "personal odyssey" of exploring Doyle's life: "Who *was* Charles Doyle?" (p. vi). Reading the *Diaries* with Doyle's accompanying illustrations, mostly of a "fantastic" world populated by fairies and birds, he observed that Doyle "had a distinct penchant for puns and whimsy, appeared to be afraid of birds, believed in fairies, and was of an unworldly and careless disposition" (p. vii). Baker wanted to learn more about Doyle's psychiatric hospitalizations, but little information was available to him in 1978; his search of public documents yielded only a few pertinent facts.

However, "a hunt through the *Scotsman* for 1893 turned up an obituary notice," in which however, " Charles's "celebrated family" was mentioned, as was Charles's "illustrative work." His character was described in positive terms, but "its bland good-naturedness was as unrevealing as most obituaries. There was no mention of a mental institution," only a simple statement that he "died at Dumfries" (Baker, 1978, p. xxii).

Baker received more satisfactory information from Charles's death certificate, registered at the Edinburgh Records Office. Doyle, the document revealed, had died at four in the morning on October 10, 1893, in the Crighton Royal Institution, Dumfries. The cause of death was given as epilepsy of "many years" standing (Baker, 1978, p. xxii).

Medical and Psychiatric Records

Beveridge (2006), a psychiatrist, had read Baker's (1978) account and wanted to learn about Charles Doyle's last years. He was able to professionally access medical records unavailable to Baker, including

Charles Doyle's first admission to "an institution for inebriates" (Beveridge, 2006, p. 1). Beveridge explored Charles's psychiatric diagnoses, his experiences during his several hospitalizations, and his creative work during this period. He examined Charles's frequent complaints that he was "wrongfully confined" as well as Charles's "suggestion that his family were instrumental in having him committed" (p. 1).

Charles, in defense of his "sanity," had written, on March 18, 1889, at the beginning of *The Doyle Diaries:*

> ...keep steadily in view that this Book is ascribed wholly to the product of a MADMAN. Whereabouts would you say was the deficiency of intellect? Or depraved taste. If in the whole Book you can find a single Evidence of either, mark it and record it against me. (Doyle, quoted in Baker, 1978, p. 1)

Charles's alcoholism had increased over the years. His work declined, and the family's financial state deteriorated. In 1876, Charles was "forced into early retirement because of his alcoholism" (Beveridge, 2006, p. 2). The Census Records of 1881 noted that he was "resident in a home for 'dipsomaniacs' at Blairerno" (p. 2). According to Mary Doyle's comments (recorded in his medical record), he frequently attempted to escape in pursuit of alcohol.

Four years later, Charles was committed to the Montrose Royal Asylum, where he continued to deteriorate: "...the years of repeated drinking had resulted in brain damage with subsequent impairment of memory. His asylum physicians describe problems with short term memory, which suggest that Doyle suffered from what today we would call Korsakoff's psychosis" (Beveridge, 2006, p. 5).

Four months after his admission, Charles experienced his first epileptic attack.

"Whatever the true nature of his disorder, his repeated fits were accompanied by a further deterioration in his memory and intellectual abilities" (Beveridge, 2006, p. 5). Beveridge reported that "a recurring preoccupation [was] . . . the notion that he was about to die" (p. 5). "Death, religion and the after-life were major concerns of Doyle's during his asylum days" (p. 6). Arthur Conan Doyle's later preoccupation centered on these three issues as well; spiritualism was to become Arthur's religion.

The medical records "make several references to [Charles's] creative pursuits." The doctors found Doyle "a most interesting man to talk to" (Beveridge, 2006, p. 6). Six years later, when transferred to the Royal Edinburgh Asylum, he was described as "suffering from epilepsy, alcoholism and enfeebled memory" (p. 6).

About a year later, Doyle was transferred to the Crichton Royal in Dumfries and admitted as a private patient, at a cost of £40 "paid by Conan Doyle" (Beveridge, 2006). Although Charles's condition deteriorated, he was "described as contented." Seven days before his death, the following note was made by one of Doyle's doctors: "'Pleasant and easily pleased. Solemnly presented me with an empty paper which he assured me contained gold dust & was a reward for professional attendance. He said he had collected it in the sunlight on the bed'" (Beveridge, 2006, p. 7).

Charles Doyle died on October 10, 1893, at the age of 61, after being institutionalized for 12 years. Through the presentation of this psychiatric evidence, Beveridge (2006) was able to conclude that Charles indeed had a psychiatric illness that merited hospitalization. This negated speculation that he was "wrongfully confined" by his family. Beveridge noted that the records suggested that the family infrequently visited Charles.

There are legal and ethical issues surrounding the use of a subject's medical and psychiatric records: Should psychiatrists share their clinical notes with biographers? Should they write their own books about patients who are well known or who can be identified?

Similarly, clinicians may find valuable material in a client's former case records and medical and psychiatric files. "Archival" (and dense) old child welfare and psychiatric records can often yield important "gems" hidden in long reports. Details may reveal important emotional patterns, relationships, and concerns. Ulrich (1991), in writing *A Midwife's Tale,* mined the mundane details of the midwife Martha Ballard's life to present a portrait of her life and social context.

In an anecdotal report, the case was discussed of a young child with poor school performance and behavioral problems whose acts were sometimes inexplicable, often to himself: "I don't know why I did this," he would say. Finding "hints" in the record of an earlier electroencephalogram with some atypical findings, a child psychiatrist searched for the original neurological report and then diagnosed epilepsy. The boy was given appropriate medication; his improvement was dramatic. His mother, walking by his room one evening, found him praying: "Thank God, they believe me now."

Interpreting Later Evidence

The discovery of new evidence is one reason multiple biographies are written about the same subject. Rayfield (1997), Chekhov's biographer, spent 3 years traveling throughout Russia looking through

Chekhov's archives and finding an abundance of unpublished materials. His use of this knowledge added to the understanding of Chekhov's life. Even so, Rayfield did not feel his biography was complete: "To write a full biography would take a lifetime longer than Chekhov's own" (1997, p. xvii). In this vein, he adds:

> Not all the mysteries in Chekhov's life can be solved, and much evidence is missing.... It is... possible that the hundreds of letters Suvorin wrote to Chekhov are mouldering in an archive in Belgrade: their discovery would force Chekhov's life, and (because of what Suvorin knew and confided to Anton) Russian history, to be rewritten. (Rayfield, 1997, p. xviii)

Van Gogh ended his life by suicide in 1888, dying two days after shooting himself in the abdomen. However, Lacayo (2011) reported that in a new Van Gogh biography, the authors, Naifeh and Smith, offer the" 'hypothetical reconstruction' " that Van Gogh was actually shot accidentally by his friend's brother. This would explain many puzzles surrounding Van Gogh's death. Why did his doctor believe that the lethal bullet was fired from a distance? Why was his painting kit never found in the wheat field? And what to make of Van Gogh's odd words to the police, "Don't accuse anyone else." (Lacayo, 2011, p. 66) There has even been new evidence suggesting that Van Gogh did not cut off his own ear (Gopnik, 2010).

New theories as well as new knowledge can also modify our understanding. For example, the "madness" of King George III (in the late 18th century) has been variously diagnosed over the years, as Runyan (1982) observed, citing Macalpine and Hunter:

"His own physicians puzzled what bodily disorder had caused his mind to become deranged; in the asylum era of the middle of the nineteenth century it was simply called mania, and in the descriptive era of classification, manic-depressive psychosis.... When psychodynamics entered the field, it was ascribed to stress and conflict and with it the King's personality and character were denigrated. Reviewed in the light of modern medical knowledge... it emerges as Porphyria, an inborn error of metabolism." (Macalpine & Hunter, quoted in Runyan, 1982, pp. 133–134)

Clinicians also discover new evidence as they work with their clients, which can modify their assessments and treatment plans. In one case, a clinical social worker was seeing Eileen, 15, and her family to help her overcome her school phobia (Urdang, 2008). Aware that school phobia was often a symptom of separation anxiety, she explored this with the family members, but no traumatic events such as losses or similar crises that could have precipitated such anxiety were reported. Treatment went on for some months with no noticeable progress. Sensing that she was up against a brick wall, the clinician finally asked whether they had left anything out, whether there was anything else going on that had not been mentioned.

The family initially denied that there was anything else. After some hesitation, the parents acknowledged that the mother was soon to undergo a hysterectomy. Although there was no basis for their extreme and pervasive anxiety about this upcoming surgery, for them it was as though the mother's life was in imminent danger. Yet within the family the issue had been avoided, rather than openly discussed. In the background was the fact that the mother's father had left her family following a divorce when she was 15, the same age that Eileen now was. Eileen's paternal grandmother had died of cancer when her father was the same age. The parents' unresolved experiences of loss and the accompanying fears were transmitted to their daughter, now at the age they had been when they had suffered their losses. Thus, from their perspective, Eileen, now 15, was in great emotional jeopardy against which she had to be protected. She had no idea what a hysterectomy was, nor did she know that the uterus was not essential for life (Urdang, 2008). After this additional evidence was discussed with the family, the symptoms of school phobia quickly vanished, and Eileen flourished in school and in her social life.

Posthumous Release of Personal Data

Subjects sometimes bequeath their personal data and writing to be released after their death. Mark Twain declared a moratorium of 100 years for his autobiography to be published, as it was so "explosive it would need to be embargoed for a hundred years" (Keillor, 2010, pp. 1, 6). He chose to "speak from the grave . . . so that he can speak freely-'as frank and free and unembarrassed as a love letter'" (p. 6).

Journalist, satirist, critic of American life and culture, and scholar H. L. Mencken left a "diary and other autobiographical manuscripts not to be opened until he had been long dead" (Baker, 1978, p. 10). Some of the revelations, especially his self-proclaimed anti-Semitism, had a devastating effect on his fans in his hometown of Baltimore. "Nowhere was the disappointment more painful than in Baltimore.... A man of Mencken's stature should have only magnificent defects. In mythologizing him, Baltimore had come to think of him as superior to the common country-club bigot" (Baker, 2003, p. 10).

E. M. Forster kept his homosexuality secret from most people (especially his mother) for years. When friends encouraged him to follow Gide's model and go public, he refused, responding: "'But Gide hasn't got a mother!'" (quoted in Moffat, 2010, p. 17). Sharing his secret with trusted friends, Forster also poured his feelings and conflicts into his diaries and into fiction with homosexual themes; these were kept from public view until after his death, as he willed it. Rather than authorizing that his personal papers be destroyed, he wanted them published to increase public understanding and acceptance of gay men.

During his lifetime, Forster had "lived in a world imprisoned by prejudice against homosexuals. He was sixteen when Oscar Wilde was sent to prison, and he died the year after the Stonewall riots" (Moffat, 2010, p. 21). In his 80s, he commented: "'How *annoyed* I am with Society for wasting my time by making homosexuality criminal. The subterfuges, the self-consciousness that might have been avoided'" (quoted in Moffat, 2010, p. 18).

Forster believed in romantic love and commitment between men. Experiencing this love with a man for the first time, he confided his feelings to Florence, a trusted female friend:

"When I am with him smoking or talking quietly... I see beyond my own happiness and intimacy, occasional glimpses of the happiness of 1000s of others whose names I shall never hear, and I know that there is a great unrecorded history." (quoted in Moffat, 2010, p. 162)

Forster's contribution to "recorded history" includes his novel, *Maurice,* a story of two men in love. Written 60 years earlier, only a few trusted friends had seen it. His revisions of *Maurice* were included in the posthumous literary material sent to his friend, Christopher Isherwood. *Maurice* was published in 1971 and made into a movie in 1987.

Charlotte Brontë's parents had written many letters to each other during their courtship. Patrick Brontë showed them to Charlotte when she was an adult; she was moved by them and wished she had known her mother. It is not uncommon in clinical work for clients to receive or discover letters from important people in the past. Such letters are in some instances saved in agency archives for the agreed purpose of showing them to the child at a later time. Thus, a former foster child may read for the first time letters from her birth mother expressing the pain she felt when putting the child into a foster home, her love for her daughter, and how special her daughter was to her.

Writings by the Subject

The biographer makes decisions regarding the inclusion of the subject's writings, which include both fiction and nonfiction, works written for publication, and personal writings, such as diaries and letters. Debate about using subjects' fictional work to illustrate and interpret their lives is ongoing: Are these artistic representations reflective of the subject's life and psychological experiences? Sylvia Plath's *The Bell Jar* is generally accepted as an autobiographical novel and has been much drawn on in biographies of Plath's life.

The relationship between fiction and the fiction writer's life is not always so straightforward, however. How much of Ernest Hemingway's "fiction" is actual fiction and how much is based on his real life is much debated (Phillips, 2011). Hemingway himself "blurred the distinction between his life and his fiction" (p. 9).

Hemingway's personality and life, a source of fascination to many, sometimes attracted more interest than his fiction; this related to the undeniably adventurous and outsize details of his tragic life; his intentional cultivation of celebrity... and... that he wrote fiction so closely tied to the actual places, people and details of his life. (Phillips, 2011, p. 8)

After experiencing a sudden and nearly suicidal depression, William Styron (1990) speculated about whether his depression had "earlier origins" (p. 78) and about its possible relationship to his literary work:

I began to see clearly how depression had clung close to the outer edges of my life for many years. Suicide has been a persistent theme in my books—three of my major characters killed themselves.... I was stunned to perceive how accurately I had created the landscape of depression in the minds of these young women. Thus depression, when it finally came to me, was in fact no stranger.... It had been tapping at my door for decades. (W. Styron, 1990, pp.78–79)

Rudyard Kipling's short story, "Baa-Baa Black Sheep," is a vivid fictional portrayal based on his traumatic experience in an English foster home. Some biographers insist this story is pure fiction and that Kipling's own autobiographical depictions of his foster home as horrendous is in itself fiction. This controversy is explored in the following chapter.

Many foster children have no sense of their own history; they do not know their "autobiographical selves." By seeking details of the child's history with accompanying photographs (when available), child welfare clinicians frequently compose life books for (and with) these foster children to help them put together the chaotic story of their lives. These books can also be used to help children explore and work through painful parts of their life and disappointing relationships.

On occasion, clients give their therapists samples of their "formal" written work, such as fiction, poetry, and essays. This can be a rich opportunity for mutual exploration. In some instances, where the client may be aware of the work's connection to his or her own life, a deepening of self-awareness can occur. If clients defend against examining their lives, then discussing their written work within its own frame of reference, that is, working within the metaphor, may help them get in touch with warded-off feelings.

Personal Communications: Letters and Diaries

Letters. Biographies often rely on letters written and received by the subjects (or by third parties who knew the subjects). Some extraordinary sets of letters are published as "Collected Letters." It is no small wonder that biographers are distressed when they learn that letters have been deliberately destroyed by subjects or their families, as when the executor of Ottilie Assing's papers, in compliance with her wishes, unhappily destroyed her treasure trove of correspondence (Diedrich, 1999). Kafka's executor "defied" a similar request, preserving Kafka's papers and works (Pawel, 1988).

Selecting, validating, and interpreting correspondence is a challenge. Narrative theory (see chapter 7) addresses the motivations and self-presentations of letter writers and diarists. Even when authentic, letters may not be reliable. "The list of ways letters may be misleading, deadening, or worse is very long" (Backscheider, 1999, p. 74). We saw in chapter 8 how Ottilie Assing's letters to her sister, Ludmilla, were colored by their competitive relationship, as she "boasted" about her special romance with Douglass (Diedrich, 1999).

Victoria Glendinning, preparing to write about the marriage of Harold Nicolson, British diplomat and politician during both world wars, and Vita Sackville-West, a novelist and herself a biographer, remembered for her affair with Virginia Woolf, read their correspondence, which conveyed the impression that their marriage "'was a miracle of sustained romance—as in a sense it was, except that Vita was writing love-letters of a different kind to other people as well, nearly all the time'" (quoted in Backscheider, 2001, p. 74). These letters were published in 1992 in *Vita and Harold: The Letters of Vita Sackville West and Harold Nicolson* by their son, Nigel Nicolson.

Letters generally are considered a major resource for "knowing" the subject directly, however flawed some may be. But in the cybernetic age, e-mail has largely replaced letter writing. Is letter writing becoming a lost art? Are biographers being deprived of this source material? Are e-mails composed with the eloquence and reflectiveness found in letters written in an earlier time? Are those e-mails that are saved selected by writers, as the American novelist and essayist Jonathan Franzen suggested, for "'the most flattering possible narratives'" (quoted in Donadio, 2005, p. 15)?

Do editors save their e-mail correspondence with their authors, as previous publishers tended to save such written correspondence? If they do, are only specially chosen ones saved? And where are they stored? These problems are being addressed by some writers, publishing houses, and libraries, but the issues remain unresolved (Donadio, 2005).

Diaries. Diaries need to be analyzed with care. What is the writer's focus? Diaries can emphasize political activities, current events, and details of the narrator's social life and daily schedule. Some diarists reflect on their thoughts and feelings. Nathaniel Hawthorne kept two journals of his life: In one he recorded his daily activities, in the other his inner reflections (Spengemann, 1980). Samuel Pepys reflected on both his inner and outer worlds in his diaries (Tomalin, 2002).

Ulrich (1991) creatively utilized the diaries of Martha Ballard, a midwife in Maine, who began her diary in 1785 and continued writing entries for 27 years. The diaries were sparsely written and focused on such matters as her schedule, the birth dates of the babies she delivered, her fees, and details about her weaving and planting beans. Historians who knew of this book's existence found it lacking. One history of midwifery, published in the 1970s. "repeated the old dismissal: 'Like many diaries of farm women, it is filled with trivia about domestic chores and pastimes'" (Ulrich, 1991, p. 9).

However, in writing *A Midwife's Tale,* Ulrich mined the "mundane" details of Ballard's life for its rich nuggets. As archaeologists, excavating bits of bones and cloth, reconstruct pictures of lives and a culture from these fragments, so Ulrich was able to reconstruct Ballard's life, midwifery practice, and times. She extensively researched documents and newspapers of that time, integrating this with her insights from the diaries.

> Yet it is in the very dailiness, the exhaustive, repetitious dailiness, that the real power of Martha Ballard's book lies.... To abstract the births without recording the long autumns spent winding quills, pickling meat, and sorting cabbages, is to destroy the sinews of the earnest, steady, gentle, and courageous record.... Martha was not an

introspective diarist, yet in this conscientious recording as much as in her occasional confessions, she revealed herself. (Ulrich, 1991, p. 9)

Focusing attention in clinical practice on the so-called mundane details of people's lives can illuminate much about their values, personalities, and relationships. Listening to details about how a mother and her autistic child spend the day can provide rich insight.

Diaries raise questions about the motivation of the diarist and the audience for whom the diary is written. Is it only meant to be the author's private recollections? Does the writer imagine that these diaries will be read by "significant others" in the present or by a different public in the future? And in the very act of writing, is there someone looking over his/her shoulder—a fantasized audience?

Diaries are frequently kept in adolescence, especially by girls. "Daydreams, events, and emotions which cannot be shared with real people are confessed with relief to the diary" (Bios, 1962, p. 94). The diary also provides the teenager with a "surrogate friend" (Seiffge-Krenke & Kirsch, 2002, p. 402). The friend is usually female and often given a name (Bios, 1962; Dalsimer, 1982). Anne Frank addressed her diary to a fictional "friend" called Kitty. Do some adults also write with a "surrogate friend" in mind?

Challenges of Constructing Biography

Resistant Subjects and Families

Some subjects have expressed an unwillingness to have biographies written about them at all and have gone to great lengths to destroy their personal papers and instruct their relatives to protect their privacy. Others, who may have expressed an apparent willingness for this task to be undertaken, have nevertheless exercised control over what was written and what was deleted. J. .D. Salinger, for example, "sued [his biographer] Hamilton successfully for invasion of privacy and forced debilitating revisions of Hamilton's biography of him" (Backscheider, 1999, p. 78). In one rather unique "solution," Thomas Hardy wrote his own biography, under the "authorship" of his wife (Tomalin, 2006).

Some families (often after the subject has died) assume tight "editorial" control over the biography's content. Legal issues, such as copyright laws, and ethical concerns, including violation of privacy, complicate the biographical enterprise.

Copyright Laws and Privacy

Beginning in the 1990s, the passage of stringent copyright laws meant that living writers, other celebrities, and their heirs could withhold materials from potential biographers. In one of the more notorious examples, biographical work on James Joyce was impeded by Joyce's family, who exerted pressure to conceal the long psychiatric institutionalization of Joyce's daughter, Lucia.

When Joyce died, correspondence concerning Lucia was destroyed by those close to him. Joyce's grandson "actually removed letters from a public collection in the National Library of Ireland" (Acocella, 2003, p. 13l). While Brenda Maddox was completing her biography of Joyce's wife Nora, she "was required to delete her epilogue on Lucia in return for permission to quote various Joyce materials" (p. 131). In 2004, when a special exhibition on James Joyce and *Ulysses* was being planned by the National Library of Ireland, Stephen Joyce withheld permission for Joyce's work to be read aloud, and his refusal prevailed (Hamilton, 2007).

The "rights" of the public to know and the "rights" of subjects and their families to privacy underlie the ongoing struggle and dialogue between the two interests. Decades after Sylvia Plath's suicide, conflicts and controversies continued to erupt over interpretations of her life, death, and the role Plath's estranged husband, poet Ted Hughes, had played in her suicide. In *The Silent Woman,* Janet Malcolm (1994) defended Hughes against the considerable public criticism and scorn he was subjected to after Plath's suicide (Hamilton, 2007). Malcolm's book was a virulent attack against "intrusive contemporary biography," which had reached its great popularity because of its "'transgressive nature'" (quoted in Hamilton, 2007, p. 275).

In a poignant and tragic coda to this story, Plath and Hughes's son, Nicholas Hughes (who was a one-year-old when his mother took her own life) also committed suicide, in April 2009, when he was 47. Nicholas had carved out an independent life for himself in Alaska as a highly respected marine biologist. Many of his colleagues did not know about his parentage, and those who did respected his privacy. A memorial service was held for him at the university where he worked; the service was not noted in the local newspaper. A columnist for the newspaper had been aware "for at least a decade that the son of Sylvia Plath and Ted Hughes lived in town"; he "wrote Mr. Hughes' obituary," but, wishing "to give him his privacy," "simply did not feel right to intrude on the memorial service."

Clinicians may also find themselves in the middle of legal disputes regarding breaches of confidentiality and face difficult decisions regarding sharing client information. A clinician, for example, may be refused permission by a client to obtain his or her past psychiatric record or history of former psychotherapy. A particularly troublesome problem occurs when clients themselves are in the middle of legal disputes, such as custody issues, and a clinician's records are subpoenaed by the court. What clinicians believe is written "in secret" for their own files suddenly becomes a public court record, which the client might find offensive—and which in turn may become an incitement to sue the clinician.

Subjective Experience of the Biographer

Evidence is often thought of as "hard" when it draws on facts, documents, and the written record. But subjectivity, intuition, and imagination can also be important evidence. Detectives in mystery books often analyze their own subjective reactions to suspects, to interviews, to the murder scene, puzzling over the "something" that just "doesn't feel right."

Holmes (1985), a prominent biographer himself, declared that biographers, after studying the factual aspects of subjects' lives, must form their own subjective impressions. This is discussed in chapter 2.

Francine du Plessix Gray (2000) observed that ambivalence toward one's subject aids in the development of biographical objectivity. In the following commentary on a biography of Simone Weil, she explained:

> I shall always look harshly on Weil's way of ending her brief life, and persist, like many of her readers, in my mercurial pattern of alternately loving and hating her. And I might add that this ambivalence toward a subject of biography, which I share with many a chronicler of lives, can actually

be a beneficent, if not a treasurable, attribute. It keeps us from falling into either hagiography or pathography. It helps us to maintain that objectivity, that ironic distance, that blend of severity and compassion, which should be the goal of all honest biographers. (du Plessix Gray, 2001, p. 11)

The clinician also struggles with the polarity between the need to develop empathy, compassion, and attunement with the client and the opposing need to hold to strict objectivity, maintain personal boundaries, and become "severe" in imposing therapeutic discipline on oneself. Mrs. G., a new clinician, decided that if she expressed empathy and caring about Ms. D., her client, she would be considered by colleagues to be overidentifying. Therefore, she stuck only to the facts in Ms. D.'s life, moving away from affective material and offering intellectual explanations for her symptoms. She could not understand, then, why Ms. D. was not getting better as she had explained everything to her.

Evaluating and Analyzing Evidence

Biographers continually evaluate evidence for its relevance to understanding the subject and for its reliability. Ultimately, they must synthesize and analyze their research materials to create a portrait of a life. Lee (2005) asked: "How do [biographers] nose out the personality and life of the writer? ... Where do biographers start from and how do they know when to stop?" (p. 4). Which material is especially noteworthy, and which "deserve special emphasis—episodes or events of unique saliency?" (Schultz, 2005b, p. 42).

Frederick Douglass's abandonment by his grandmother was a uniquely salient catastrophe for him and had repercussions throughout his life. Psychological salience can also be found in the themes permeating a life, including a person's repetition of thoughts, behaviors, and relationships, which often form patterns. "It is in the patterns that the evidence forms that the most important truths are usually found" (Backscheider, 1999, p. 88).

In addition to analyzing existing evidence, nonexistent evidence (of all kinds)—that is, what has gone missing—can also be significant. "Error, distortion, omission, and negation might also signify the presence of psychologically salient material" (Schultz, 2005b, p. 47). Conan Doyle never discusses his father's alcoholism and psychiatric hospitalization. Henry Adams completely deleted his wife, Clover, from his life story; the fact that she committed suicide may have motivated this omission. Commenting on Adams's autobiography, Thornton Wilder said: "'It's possible to make books of a certain fascination if you scrupulously leave out the essential'" (quoted in Wineapple, 2012, p. 19).

Sometimes biographers share with the readers their perplexity in evaluating certain facts and theories. The reader is then in a position to analyze both the evidence and the biographer's interpretations. The following four examples, relating to Jonathan Swift, Charles Dickens, Vincent Van Gogh, and Oscar Wilde, are presented to illustrate problems biographers and researchers have faced in interpreting and analyzing the evidence.

Jonathan Swift

Victoria Glendinning (1999) shared with the reader her dilemmas about "knowing" Jonathan Swift. She cited the presence of conflicting evidence, lack of data, and the fact that "it is all so long ago" (p. 2). Many "mysteries" in his life remain, including the nature of his relationship to Stella, his young pupil. Stella became a lifelong friend and a subject of his poetry, but whether she was also a lover or even a wife is uncertain. Glendinning added: "There is no such thing as a definitive biography" (pp. 276–277).

> [The] same man is not always the same man. The living, breathing, joking, suffering Swift remains a lost original. Biographical writers can do their utmost to avoid saying, to quote his Houynhnhnms, "the thing which was not." To say the thing which *was* is harder. (Glendinning, 1999, p. 277)

Glendinning (1999) read "the one fragment of his autobiography which has been found," which she judged to be "poorly written and not reliable. Swift would never have wanted the public to see it" (p. 3). He wrote that he was born in 1667 in Dublin, but Glendinning could find little information about his early childhood. His father died before he was born ("if he was Swift's father"), and Swift was abandoned by his mother, who moved to England when he was a young child, leaving Swift to be brought up by his paternal aunt and uncle (p. 4).

Glendinning analyzed an excerpt from this autobiography, sharing her skepticism about its veracity with us. Swift had described how, when he was a year old, his nurse "stole him away from his widowed mother and his uncle, and from Dublin ... and took him over the sea to her home town of Whitehaven [in Cumbria, England]" (p. 3). Swift wrote this autobiographical excerpt in the third person.

> The nurse, he says, was "under an absolute necessity of seeing one of her relations, who was extremely sick, and from whom she expected a legacy." The nurse was "extremely fond" of Swift; and when his mother realized what had happened, "she sent orders by all means not to hazard a second voyage, till he ... could be better able to bear it. The nurse was so careful of him, that before he returned he had learnt to spell; and by the time he was three years old he could read any chapter in the Bible." (Glendinning, 1999, p. 3)

Glendinning (1999) could accept the fact that the nurse took him to Whitehaven; however, she could accept Swift's assertion that at three he could read the Bible. She observed that "such prodigious claims were frequently made, in his day and later, for children who turned out to be exceptional in later life" (p. 4).

Glendinning (1999) also found it difficult to believe he was taken to England without his mother knowing about this and that he was not brought back because she was afraid of the trip. "This sounds like a comforting fable. ... The most farfetched interpretation of adult behavior is preferable to the possibility that your mother finds your constant presence inconvenient" (p. 4).

Looking at statements from witnesses who had heard Swift telling variations of this tale to his friends, Glendinning (1999) found that Swift often embroidered this story with whimsical exaggerations.

Then, referring to Swift's own writings, she observes how, in *Gulliver's Travels,* he described (note that she adds "I think"):

> Gulliver, a finger-sized manikin among the giant Brobding-nagians, being parted from his giant nurse-girl, wafted in his carrying box over the sea by an eagle, and dropped into the water to float on till he was rescued. I think, when he wrote that, *the Whitehaven story was in the back of his mind.* (Glendinning, 1999, p. 5)

If Glendinning (1999) were Swift's therapist, she could ask directly about this: Was he thinking of the Whitehaven story when he wrote this? Or she could ask, indirectly: Did this story make him think of anything in his own life? Stories clients tell and dreams they share often have themes and plots related to their own lives. Probing the deeper (latent) levels of clients' narratives can elicit important insights.

In a clinical scenario, Ms. J, a client, one day narrated a story at length about a woman next door who was being abused by her husband. The clinician chose not to respond to this story as Ms. J's resistance to talking about herself. Instead she probed the story as presented, asking about the neighbor, what was happening, what Ms. J thought the neighbor should do about this, and so forth. When Ms. J felt safe in knowing the clinician's attitudes, and therefore safe in being more open, she then directly discussed the abusive situation she was living in herself.

Charles Dickens

Even if an event is known to have occurred, differing interpretations can be made of that event. Charles Dickens's marriage offers such an example. Dickens appeared to have had an initially positive relationship with his wife, Catherine Hogarth. Over time, he took a mistress, separated from Catherine, and treated her cruelly. In the early years of the Dickens marriage, the couple traveled together to the United States. Dickens's description of his wife's behavior during this visit was seen by biographers as a precursor of his growing resentment toward her.

Dickens wrote letters to his English friends describing his journey and its frustrations, which included his wife's "clumsiness" in coping with their transportation:

> Catherine " 'falls into, or out of, every coach or boat we enter... and makes herself blue with bruises.' " These passages have been "cited extensively to prove that Catherine Dickens was unusually clumsy, and that Dickens was irritated by her as early as 1842" (Rose, 1984, p. 158).

Rose (1984), however, observed that Dickens also describes Catherine's fortitude and positive attitude about the trip and notes that this account was often deleted by biographers. His letter "as a whole is grateful, appreciative, and affectionate" (p. 158). Rose cited more from Dickens's letter:

> "She really has, however, since we got over the first trial of being among circumstances so new and so fatiguing, made a *most admirable* traveler in every respect. She has never

screamed or expressed alarm under circumstances that would have fully justified her in doing so ... has never given way to despondency or fatigue, though we have now been traveling incessantly, through a very rough country, for more than a month ... ; has always accommodated herself, well and cheerfully to everything; and has pleased me very much, and proved herself perfectly game." (quoted in Rose, 1984, p. 158)

Spence (1986) would probably refer to the earlier "incomplete" description as "narrative smoothing," seen also in clinical work, where the clinician chooses certain facts but leaves out others in the service of a coherent narrative (pp. 212–213). For example, Mr. Smith, a clinician, talked at length with his supervisor about his client, Ms. C, who had had a series of unsuccessful relationships with men, with whom she would become involved sexually before getting to know them. She would then become depressed when they abruptly rejected her. In supervision, he focused on how her past family relationships were affecting her current behavior. What he somehow left out of his narrative was that he was troubled by his own erotic feelings for the client and that in the last of their therapy sessions, she asked him whether they could meet for dinner one evening so they could get to know each other better. This exemplifies "narrative smoothing," which covers up a serious issue in a clinical situation.

Vincent Van Gogh

Runyan (2005b) grappled with the question of alternative explanations of the same event. He explored an incident in which Vincent Van Gogh cut off part of one ear and gave it to a prostitute named Rachel for safekeeping. This legendary event was immortalized in Van Gogh's painting, *Self Portrait with Bandaged Ear and Pipe* (Gopnik, 2010). There have been many conflicting theories explaining this event (Runyan, 2005b). "What sense can be made of such a variety of interpretations? Is one of them uniquely true, or are all of them true in some way, or perhaps, are none of them true? And how can we know?" (Runyan, 2005b, p. 96).

Runyan (2005b) discussed 13 of these theories, which include Van Gogh's interest in bullfights, in which the matador presents the bull's ear to a chosen lady, and an effect of the case of Jack the Ripper, who was then on his murder-mutilation rampage. Possibly Van Gogh was motivated by his belief that his auditory hallucinations were caused by a diseased ear; therefore, eliminating the ear would eliminate the hallucinations. Runyan also noted that "the ear was a phallic symbol. (The Dutch slang word for penis, *lui,* resembled the Dutch word for ear, *lei)* and the act was a symbolic castration" (p. 96).

Runyan (2005b) observed that not all these theories "stand up under critical examination (p. 101). He used the following six criteria to examine each hypothesis: "logical soundness; comprehensiveness; survival of tests of attempted falsification; consistency with [other] relevant evidence; consistency with… general knowledge about human functioning or about the person in question; and… credibility relative to other explanatory hypothesis" (p. 100).

Runyan (2005b) commented that the "most strongly supported explanatory factor in Vincent's breakdown" was related to the impending "loss" of his brother. His brother Theo, who was also his primary caretaker, had just become engaged. Van Gogh's later breakdowns occurred at the time of Theo's marriage and when Theo's first child was born. "A masochistic response under situations of rejection or loss of love was not alien to Van Gogh" (p. 100).

Runyan (2005b) found that the most satisfying resolution of this conundrum related to the ongoing pattern of Van Gogh's relationship with Theo. Van Gogh was dependent on Theo, who assumed a protective role in relation to him; that Van Gogh was about to be "abandoned" by Theo threatened his security. That his breakdowns were precipitated at times when faced with the prospect of abandonment and loss supports this explanation in relation to the self-mutilation.

In clinical cases, it is not uncommon for clients in dependent relationships with others to also display various signs of distress when they are abandoned, even self-injurious acts. Such acts should prompt exploration of the motivations and feelings underlying them.

While speculation about Van Gogh's motivation in cutting off his ear proliferated, this act became an important legendary historical artistic event—a "talisman of modern painting" (Gopnik, 2010, p. 48). Then, in 2009, a book was published that turned this theory on its ear, so to speak: *Van Gogh's Ear: Paul Gauguin and the Pact of Silence,* [Original title (no English version available): *Van Goghs Ohr. Paul Gauguin und der Pakt des Schweigens]* written by Hans Kaufmann and Rita Wildegans, two highly respected German academicians. They make the case that Van Gogh's ear was actually cut off by Gauguin, who had been living with him at the time (Gopnik, 2010). Gauguin inflicted this wound with his sword following an argument; the two men kept this a secret due to Van Gogh's "shame" and Gauguin's "guilt" (p. 50).

According to this new version, Gauguin, becoming increasingly irritated by Van Gogh's incessant talking, argued with him. In anger, Gauguin took out his fencing sword (which he often carried) and made several fast moves with it in Van Gogh's direction. Van Gogh's ear was cut off, apparently accidentally, when he suddenly turned his head. Showing his amputated ear to Gaugin, Van Gogh says: " 'You are silent. Indeed, I will be, too' " (Gopnik, 2010, p. 53).

The seeming surgical precision of the slice is offered as one piece of evidence that it could not have been self-inflicted. In addition, self-mutilations generally are done to the "arms and hands and legs and chests, but… [not to] ears" (Gopnik, 2010, p. 53). Another piece of evidence is found in the veiled comments written later by both men.

Finally, great weight was given to how the word *ictus* is interpreted. Van Gogh and Gauguin frequently used this word with each other, in person, and in writing, sometimes accompanied by a picture of a fish. *Ichthys* means fish in Greek and was used symbolically by old Christian communities. But Kaufmann and Wildegans asserted that it is also a Latin word, used frequently in "French fencing, meaning a blow or hit" (Gopnik, 2010, p. 53). Gopnik concluded that this revised version of events "is suggestive without being entirely convincing" (p. 54). He added: "We accept an ambiguity" in the narration of this event "because the act is itself ambiguous" (p. 55).

Oscar Wilde

Schultz (2001) critically examined the controversy concerning Oscar Wilde's famous work, *De Profundis*, describing the epiphany Wilde experienced while in prison: "a self realization in which he sees, for the first time, into his true nature" (p. 68). Debate relating to its "sincerity" has swirled about this writing. Was he using his narrative skills to represent this new image of himself to the public? Richard Ellmann, a biographer of James Joyce and Oscar Wilde, implied that "Wilde's insights were more rhetorical than real" (Schultz, 2001, p. 83), but Schultz argued that this epiphany was genuine and presents evidence supporting his point of view.

Wilde had the reputation of being flamboyant and a "dandy." Married with two sons, Wilde had an affair with Lord Alfred Douglas, the son of the Marquess of Queensbury. The Marquess was unhappy about the relationship and made an unsuccessful attempt to stop his son from seeing Wilde. The Marquess then sent a letter to Wilde's club "accusing [Wilde] of 'posing' as a 'sodomite' (*sic*)" (Schultz, 2001, p. 69). Wilde sued the Marquess for libel, and in the course of the legal proceedings, Wilde was convicted of "gross indecency" and sentenced to prison for "two years hard labor" (p. 69).

The changes in Wilde's life were catastrophic: Prison conditions were harsh; he performed hard labor, for which he had no stamina. He was ruined financially. His wife divorced him, and he could no longer see his sons. His mother also died. When transferred to Reading Gaol, he was permitted to read some books and to write "one page of prose a day" (Schultz, 2001, p. 69). He used the opportunity to write a letter to Lord Alfred Douglas, later titled *De Profundis* and published after Wilde's death.

The letter began with an expression of his anger at Douglas because he felt that Douglas should look critically at himself. Wilde acknowledges that this letter will be difficult for Douglas to read, but, he adds, " 'it will be all the better for you. The extreme vice is shallowness. Whatever is realised is right' " (quoted in Schultz, 2001, p. 69).

411

Wilde then narrates his own story, focusing on "the triumph of the soul" (Schultz, 2001, p. 70). He stresses that imprisonment is one of the two "turning points" in his life. The first was "when his father sent him to Oxford, an episode of great achievement." This time "'Society' sent him to prison, an episode of great shame" (p. 70). But this shame produced the "'starting point for a fresh development'" (p. 70). He speaks of "suffering" and notes that "'Sorrow, then, and all it teaches me ... is my new world'" (p. 70). Wilde described the experiential nature of this state: "seeing into the essence of things. 'It really is a revelation. ... One discerns things one has never discerned before'" (p. 70).

Schultz (2001) noted that Wilde's statements are congruent with the literature about turning points, which purportedly produce changes in a person and his or her life course. Turning points are often precipitated by the loss of important relationships or a major disruption of one's life course. In addition, a turning point "'must include a self-reflective awareness of, or insight into, the significance of the change'" (Wethington, Cooper, & Holmes, quoted in Schultz, 2001, p. 73). J. A. Clausen, who did research on psychological turning points, emphasized changes in "perceived identity" and life philosophy (Schultz, 2001). Wilde displayed considerable self-reflectiveness about his changes: He is self-critical about his past life and discusses his "postprison identity committed to forgiveness, love, sorrow, and humility" (p. 74).

Wilde referred to the "'inevitability'" of finding himself in prison and attributes mystical qualities to this. "'I am conscious now that behind all this beauty ... there is some spirit hidden ... and it is with this spirit that I desire to become in harmony'" (quoted in Schwartz, 2001, p. 71). Wilde also stressed the subjectivity and individuality of his experience—it is not possible to analyze this experience scientifically or philosophically. It is an emotional, not an intellectual experience.

Wilde presents two differing viewpoints of his own about the nature of his change. He finds that he is completely different from his former self (discontinuous life change). " 'Now I am approaching life from a completely different new standpoint' " (quoted in Schwartz, 2001, p. 71). Wilde also refers to the continuity and the " 'evolution' " of this change over time (p. 71). Although just discovering "suffering, . . . he, at some level always understood this. . . . 'All this is foreshadowed and prefigured in my books,' through which a 'note of doom' runs 'like a purple thread' " (p. 72). This is similar to W. Styron's (1990) retrospective observation during his depression that he now could see a depressive core in his earlier fictional characters *(retrospective teleology)*.

Schultz (2001) suggested that a major factor operating in Wilde's case is his strong sense of guilt, apparent throughout the text. " 'As I sit here in this dark cell in convict clothes, a disgraced and ruined man, I blame myself' " (quoted on p. 75). Being in prison gave him time for reflection. Schultz added that imprisonment has "produced a virtual genre of self-reflective writing" (p. 75).

One cause of skepticism about the "authenticity" of Wilde's conversion relates to his background as a writer and playwright. Wilde wrote *De Profundis* "very much like a play, right up to his enlightenment and catharsis" (Schwartz, 2001, p. 76), raising such questions as "Is the turning point really sudden, or is it just convenient to depict it that way?" (p. 81). Bruner, thinking about his own research subjects, asked: " 'Did the people involved actually experience their lives in this way, or is this just in the telling? . . . or as Henry James once put it, 'Adventures happen to people who know how to tell it that way' " (Bruner, quoted in Schultz, 2001, p. 82).

Schultz (2001) asserted that the most important issue in establishing the authenticity of a turning point is its durability: whether it lasted and whether it produced any "lasting behavioral outcome" (p. 82). Schultz then examined Wilde's life after prison. "No one doubts that Wilde emerged from prison a broken man" (p. 83). Some skeptics, such as Gide, however, did not accept that this was a truly spiritual experience, conceding only that "'His will had been broken'" (p. 83).

Wilde's literary production diminished; he produced three works after prison that were published. One was the poem "The Ballad of Reading Gaol." Two published letters expressed sentiments that were the diametrical opposite of his earlier work; now his topics included the mentally ill and the need for prison reform (Schultz, 2001).

Wilde was very poor after his release but gave some money to men he knew in prison. In personal letters to friends, he stressed the values he had developed of "gratitude, humility, and friendship" (Schultz, 2001, p. 84). He wrote: "'I am not really ashamed of having been in prison . . . , But I am really ashamed of having led a life unworthy of an artist'" (p. 84).

Schultz (2001) noted that Wilde rejoined Douglas about a year after he left prison (to the consternation of Wilde's former wife and his friends). Although it has been argued that this behavior suggests a lack of atonement for his behavior, Schultz pointed out that Wilde had advocated "forgiveness and love as opposed to retaliation and hate." Schultz added: "Wilde's willingness to stand by Douglas, despite all the obstacles, suggests that he *did* live his new truth, not that he exposed its falsity" (p. 85). I would add that although repentant for his past behaviors, of which he was ashamed, he may not have felt remorse for his deep feelings of love for Douglas, even though society felt he should. I would conjecture that the shame he felt was for other aspects of his earlier lifestyle. Schultz concluded: "On balance, then, it appears Wilde's epiphany endured" (p. 85).

The gathering and evaluation of evidence is a complicated task. The point of view of the biographer (and the clinician) in large measure determines what should be given the weight of evidence, what is relevant, and what should be discarded. In practice situations, the theoretical orientation of the clinician can also determine the scope of evidence sought and the focus of treatment.

Given the above information, one essential tool for biographers and clinicians is self-awareness—to know how one's feelings and theoretical orientation are affecting the biographical or the clinical slant. For example, why does one feel perhaps protective of, or resentful toward, the subject or client? What in this person is evoking these feelings in me? The evidence of one's feelings can temper the interpretation of "objective evidence."

In the next chapter, the life course of Rudyard Kipling is presented, incorporating a discussion of the gathering and evaluation of evidence critical to understanding his life story.

CHAPTER 10

Rudyard Kipling:
The Challenge of Using Evidence
to Construct a Life Story

When he was six years old, Rudyard Kipling's parents placed him and his sister Trix, three, whom they had raised in India, in a private English foster home. For six years they never saw their parents, who returned to Bombay. The children suffered intensely from loss and abandonment; their experiences in the foster home itself were devastating. Kipling called it the "House of Desolation" and referred to Mrs. Holloway, the foster mother, as "the Woman." This was "an establishment run with the full vigour of the Evangelical as revealed to the Woman. I had never heard of Hell, so I was introduced to it in all its terrors" (Kipling, 1937, p. 8).

Rudyard not only survived but developed resilience and creativity—it was his creativity that helped him survive. In this chapter, I examine how evidence regarding his life course was gathered and interpreted and consider controversies about the validity of the evidence. Some have questioned whether Kipling exaggerated the misery of this experience. Kipling's "abandonment has now gained the status of a myth" (Seymour-Smith, 1989, p. 19).

An important source of information is Kipling's (1900) autobiographical short story, "Baa-Baa Black Sheep," in which Punch and Judy serve as mirrors of Rudyard and Trix. The skeptics argue that this was an exaggerated and fictionalized account. That Kipling was a prolific letter writer has been useful to biographers. Although his correspondence often conceals his deeper emotions, some letters to trusted friends and relatives are more revelatory. Letters were also written about him by those who knew him, including Henry James, Robert Louis Stevenson, and family members.

Complicating the biographers' task was Kipling's strong need to guard his personal privacy. His autobiography, written a few years before he died, told a fragmentary story of his life; some painful episodes and significant relationships were omitted. Family letters became fuel for his fireplace. When the Kipling Society was formed in his late life, of which his good friend Dunsterville was president, Kipling wrote to him: "'As to your dam [*sic*] Society—how would you like to be turned into an anatomical specimen, before you were dead' " (quoted in Ricketts, 1999, p. 361).

Kipling was often present in his own creative writings: He "wrote a good deal more about his own experiences and emotions than he appeared to be doing" (Dillingham, 2008, p. 2). He had the skill of "getting into another person's skin without getting out of his own, the technique of writing about himself while appearing convincingly to be writing about someone else" (p. 9).

Family Background

Kipling's mother, Alice, born in 1837, was one of six surviving children. Her father, George McDonald, was a Methodist minister. Although not a wealthy or socially prominent family, later in life the four McDonald sisters and their families became prominent: Alice, as the mother of Rudyard Kipling; Georgie, as the wife of the painter Edward Burne-Jones; Louisa, as the mother of Stanley Baldwin, the future prime minister; and Agnes, as the wife of Edward Poynter, president of the Royal Academy (Flanders, 2001). Alice, who wrote poetry, was described as "lively, witty, and talented" (Ricketts, 1999, p. 1).

Lockwood Kipling, Rudyard's father, was born in 1837. His father was a Wesleyan minister. Lockwood studied art, apprenticed as a sculptor, and developed expertise in ornamental art and in pottery. He was a "gentle and kindly man."

Lockwood Kipling and Alice met in 1863 through her brother, a minister in Burslem, where Lockwood was living. Their first meeting was at a picnic near Lake Rudyard in Staffordshire. Their "temperaments contrasted and at the same time did not clash" (Flanders, 2001, p. 92).

> Instead Alice's quickness found a response from the rarely excited but always comprehending Lockwood. Alice had a "sprightly, if occasionally caustic, wit, which made her society always desirable, except, perhaps, to those who had cause to fear the lash of her epigrams" [from *Kipling in India* by Kay Robinson] Lockwood could soothe her when she was overwrought, and match her when he chose. (Flanders, 2001, p. 92)

Lockwood and Alice were able to marry when he received a remunerative position in India as director of an art school. They married in England on March 18, 1865, and went to their new home in Bombay three months later.

Childhood

The First Six Years

Rudyard was born in Bombay on December 30, 1865. Lockwood and Alice spent little time with Rudyard and his younger sister, Trix, leaving their care to servants.

Life in the "House of Desolation" was in marked contrast to Kipling's first six years in Bombay, where he lived a secure existence with both parents and doting servants. Kipling remembered these "years of indulgence and magic as overwhelmingly wonderful" (Shengold, 1981, p. 212). In his autobiography, written in his 70s, Kipling (1937) described this early idyllic life, referring to his *ayah* and to Meeta, his beloved caretakers:

> My first impression is of daybreak, light and colour and golden and purple fruits at the level of my shoulder. This would be the memory of early morning walks to the Bombay fruit market with my *ayah* and later with my sister in her perambulator.... Meeta, my Hindu bearer, would sometimes go into little Hindu temples where... I held his hand and looked at the dimly seen, friendly Gods. (Kipling, 1937, pp. 3–4)

Kipling continued: "In the afternoon heats... [ayah] or Meeta would tell us stories and Indian nursery songs *all unforgotten*" (p. 4, emphasis added). They spoke in the vernacular. In his daily visits with his parents, we were sent into the dining-room after we had been dressed, with the caution "Speak English now to Papa and Mamma." So one spoke "English," haltingly translated out of the vernacular idiom that one thought and dreamed in. The Mother sang wonderful songs at a black piano and would go out to Big Dinners. (Kipling, 1937, pp. 4–5)

Rudyard was loved by his ayah and Meeta; his early bond with them seems to have been very strong. Evidence to support this contention is Rudyard's development of language. English was not his first primary language; the children spoke the vernacular Indian language with Ayah and Meeta; it was also the language Rudyard "thought and dreamed in." Stern (1985) asserted that "language is potent in the service of union and togetherness" (p. 16). However, they had to be instructed to speak English with their parents when they "visited" them in the evenings. When he was left in foster care in England by his parents, his separation from them also entailed a painful separation from these two beloved caretakers.

Little is known about Rudyard's first six years. His biographers stressed that he was indulged; he also acknowledged this, making references to indulged children in his short stories. In "His Majesty the King," "his majesty" is a little boy with a governess named Miss Biddums.

The only early descriptions of Rudyard were recorded in family papers, when Rudyard, two, and his mother visited her family in England in 1868. Alice, pregnant with Trix, came to England to deliver her baby, because she had had a difficult childbirth with Rudyard. They stayed with Alice's family. Accounts written by Alice's disgruntled relatives were critical of Rudyard's disruptive behavior.

> The indulged Anglo-Indian child was quite uninhibited and rather aggressive; his behavior was not what was required of an English child of those days. He is remembered as charging down the streets of a country town, yelling: "Out of the way! Out of the way, there's an angry Ruddy coming." (Stewart, quoted in Shengold, 1981, p. 212)

Kipling biographers eagerly seized this rare source material: "Countless biographers of Kipling have dissected his grandmother's diary entries about his stay" (Flanders, 2001, p. 116). They accepted these descriptions at face value, without examining the witnesses' biases and social context of Kipling's experience. If researchers had examined the evidence more carefully, looking at the details related to his separation from his mother, as noted below, they would have had a more accurate picture of his behavior and what motivated it.

Rudyard had left his father, his ayah, and Meeta, and his home in India. He spent time with his mother until May 10, when Alice went to her sister Georgie, leaving Rudyard in the care of Alice's mother and sister Louie. Alice remained at Georgie's for one month. Trix was born June 11 following another difficult birth (Flanders, 2001, p. 9). Alice remained at Georgie's home for another month while Rudyard stayed with his grandparents. It is not known whether Rudyard visited with mother during this time. When Alice returned to her parents' home with Trix, her sister Louie found that Rudyard was now " 'good and 'nice,' and that for the first time she felt 'very fond of the child' " (Ricketts, 1999, p. 9). The reunion with his mother undoubtedly restored his security. At the age of two, Rudyard was in the midst of the "rapprochement" developmental phase, of which separation—individuation crisis is a part; tantrums are common at this age.

During his stay with his grandparents, Rudyard's grandfather was dying, and the family's anxiety probably permeated the home. Flanders (2001) comments: "It is difficult to imagine in what way he could possibly have behaved that would have won the approbation of his distracted grandmother" (p. 116). His aunt Louisa's comment, " 'Ruddy's screaming tempers made Papa so ill,' " places the blame for her father's illness on Ruddy, but Rudyard's grandfather was seriously ill before the visit (Shengold, 1981, p. 212). He died on November 13, several days after Alice and Rudyard sailed for India (Ricketts, 1999).

Rudyard was probably distressed at leaving because it meant another separation and another change. Ricketts's research (1999), using a range of evidence from grandmother's diaries, effectively refutes the characterization of Rudyard as a "toddler from Hell," this two-year-old who was "staying in unfamiliar surroundings among strangers" and whose mother was "absent a good deal and preoccupied" with a new sib (p. 10). The letters from Louisa and her mother suggest that Alice's visit was an imposition; other family tensions (unrelated to Alice) had also surfaced. Alice perhaps sensed her family's resentment, which may have been decisive in her later selection of a foster home for Rudyard and Trix, away from her family.

Returning to India, life resumed as it had been for Rudyard, until, when he was six, the serenity and security of his life was shattered by his removal to England.

Paradise Lost

Sending children to England was not uncommon for Anglo-Indian parents: It was often done to prevent children from acquiring illness prevalent in India, to give them an education, and to help them acquire an English accent (as opposed to a native Indian dialect). Generally, however, placements occurred when children were older. Alice and Lockwood traveled with the children to England and placed Rudyard, six, and Trix, three, in the Holloways' home. They did not know the Holloways in Southsea; they had chosen them from a newspaper ad. The children did not know this would happen and were unprepared. After taking them to the Holloways, Alice and Lockwood "disappeared," returning to India. The children did not see them for the next five years and three months. They were even more deeply affected by this abandonment as it came without explanation or goodbyes.

Parental Motivations for Placement. Why did the Kiplings place their children in private foster care at such a young age? The children did not seem to be "burdens" to their parents, as their daily care was provided by domestic help; parental involvement in their children's lives was minimal. Arguably, the parents may have perceived them as burdens. No evidence exists as to marital problems precipitating this removal; to the contrary, Lockwood and Alice (from their accounts and those of others) had a warm and close relationship throughout their 45 years of marriage.

A "third child was born and died in India when Rudyard was five, shortly before his exile" (Shengold, 1981, p. 212); this was a still-birth, according to Flanders (2001). However, according to Diaz de Chumaceiro (2005), the baby, named John, lived for several days after being born prematurely. She asserted that both Rudyard and Alice were deeply affected by this event. She cited Andrew Lycett, one of Kipling's biographers, who noted that "for Alice . . . the loss of her child was a devastating experience, also suffered by her sister Georgie six years before" (Diaz de Chumaceiro, p. 1). Again citing Lycett,

Diaz de Chumaceiro added, that for Rudyard "this disturbing event [was] *one that he buried deep in his unconscious and never mentioned*" [italics added] (p. 1), later motivating him to write "Little Tobrah" as "an attempt to master this traumatic event" (abstract). No solid evidence is presented to substantiate this speculation.

Was the decision not to place the children with Alice's family related to her earlier stressful visit? Perhaps now that her sisters had their own families, caring for Rudyard and Trix would be an extra burden. Edith Plowden, Alice Kipling's friend, said that she "'had never thought of leaving her children with her own family, [because] it led to complications'" (Green 1965, p. 29, quoted in Shengold, 1981, p. 213).

The choice of the Holloways is questionable in terms of their general suitability: Their educational attainments were not high; they provided no opportunities for the children's cultural enrichment; Rudyard did not learn to read, nor did he attend school for his first year; and Trix was homeschooled by Mrs. Holloway. Her social involvement with others was minimal.

Life in the House of Desolation

Rudyard and Trix were affected by the sudden departure of their parents. Presumably, the parents thought that just disappearing would be a kinder way to leave. Kipling talks little about his abandonment in his autobiography. He speaks of being taken to a "new small house smelling of aridity and emptiness, and a parting in the dawn with Father and Mother" (Kipling, 1937, pp. 6-7). In "Baa-Baa Black Sheep," more detail is given as he expresses his emotions. Ayah and Meeta are honest with Punch about this upcoming move; his parents are not.

In "Baa-Baa Black Sheep," Kipling describes the fictional "Papa" and "Mama" making preparation for the trip and talking to each other about their difficulty letting the children go; however, the children are not told about this directly by the parents. Mama in a "passionate appeal" to Punch asks him "never to let Judy forget mama" (Kipling, 1900, p. 31). Punch "could not understand what mama meant" (p. 31). However, he would keep reminding Judy to remember Mama. "So Judy promised always to 'remember Mama' " (p. 32).

Papa tells Punch to quickly learn to write, "'and then you'll be able to write letters to us in Bombay' " (Kipling, 1900, p. 32). Punch, still uncomprehending, tells Papa he will "'come into your room.' Hearing this, Papa choked. Papa and Mama were always choking in those days" (p. 32).

Kipling needed to believe that his parents grieved for him and did not wish to abandon him. "The old man [Rudyard] could not take the truth—the 'unexpectedness' still hurt too much" (Shengold, 1981, p. 213). When the family arrives at the Holloways, Punch has an immediate negative impression. " 'Let's go away,' said Punch. 'This is not a pretty place' " (Kipling, 1900, p. 33).

> For six days Mama wept at intervals, and showed the woman in black all Punch's clothes—a liberty which Punch resented "But p'r'haps she's a new white *ayah,* he thought. "I'm to call her "Antirosa What is Antirosa?…" Neither… Uudy] nor Punch had heard anything of an animal called an aunt. Their world had been Papa and Mama, who knew everything, permitted everything, and loved everybody. (Kipling, 1900, pp. 34–35)

Their parents "roused Punch and Judy in the chill dawn of a February morning to say Good-by"; both parents were crying (Kipling, 1900, p. 35). The children went back to sleep, thinking that their parents were going out on a short visit: "... assuredly they would come back again" (p. 36).

When the children awoke, the fictional Harry, Antirosa's son, informed them that their parents had gone to Bombay, and Punch and Judy would be staying with them "forever" (Kipling, 1900, p. 37). Antirosa only confirmed this fact, offering no explanation. Kipling later wrote of his despair: Desertion, he observed, is devastating even to a grown man, but a child "cannot very well curse God and die. It howls till its nose is red, its eyes are sore, and its head aches" (p. 37).

Thinking that his parents must be on a boat, Punch tells Judy that maybe they can find them: " 'they didn't mean to go without us. They've only forgot' " (Kipling, 1900, p. 38). They frantically run to the nearby sea. Judy tires. "They climbed another dune, and came upon the great gray sea at low tide ... but there was no trace of Papa and Mama, not even of a ship upon the waters—nothing but sand and mud for miles and miles" (Kipling, 1900, p. 39).

The children were later found "very muddy and very forlorn" (Kipling, 1900, p. 40). Recalling this experience as an adult, Trix recollected:

> I think the real tragedy of our early days ... sprang from our inability to understand why our parents had deserted us. We had no preparation or explanation; ... They doubt-less wanted to save us, and themselves, suffering by not telling us ... but they left us, as it were, in the dark, and with nothing to look forward to We felt we had been deserted, "almost as much as on a doorstep," and what

was the reason? [Debating and dismissing various possible excuses, Trix then concludes:] But there was no excuse; they had gone happily back to our own lovely home, and had not taken us with them. There was no getting out of that, as we often said. (Fleming, 1939, p. 171)

Their foster home would be a disastrous experience. A lack of warmth and cheer permeated the house, symbolized by the damp basement playroom. Trix described its "rusty grate ... but never a fire, or any means of heat, even in the depths of winter. This perhaps accounted for the severe broken chilblains that crippled me from December to February every year" (Fleming, 1939, p. 169).

Kipling (1937) stressed the psychological and physical abuse he experienced from "the Woman." Aunty Rosa designated Punch as "'the Black Sheep of the family'" (Kipling, 1900, p. 49). Although Trix was favored by Mrs. Holloway, their relationship presented its own conflicts for her.

Some biographers have suggested that Rudyard's first three years at the Holloways, when he had the support, friendship, and protection of Captain Holloway, were not as dismal as the years after Captain Holloway died. Quite possibly his death and Mrs. Holloway's subsequent bereavement and new burdens increased her resentment toward Rudyard.

Kipling (1937) described "the Woman" as being angry, rejecting, rigid, and sadistic toward him (behavior that she also encouraged from her son Harry, about six years older than Rudyard):

Myself I was regularly beaten. The Woman had an only son of twelve or thirteen as religious as she. I was a real joy to him, for when his mother had finished with me for the day he (we slept in the same room) took me on and roasted the other side. (Kipling, 1937, p. 8)

In "Baa-Baa Black Sheep," Harry frequently tormented Punch:

> "You're a liar-a young liar," said Harry, with great unction, "and you're to have tea down here because you're not fit to speak to us. And you're not to speak to Judy again till Mother gives you leave. You'll corrupt her. You're only fit to associate with the servant. Mother says so." (Kipling, 1900, p. 49)

In his autobiography, Kipling observed: "Yet it made me give attention to the lies I soon found it necessary to tell; and this, I presume, is the foundation of literary effort" (Kipling, 1937, p. 8).

Mrs. Holloway was drawn to Trix, who slept in Mrs. Holloway's room; it was thought she loved Trix as the daughter she never had. Trix commented:

> She ... soon made a pet of me, and did her best to weaken the affection between ... [me and Ruddy]. From the beginning she took the line that I was always in the right and Ruddy invariably in the wrong. (Fleming, 1939, p. 169)

Mrs. Holloway never succeeded in weakening the children's loyalty to each other, however.

Other than the imaginative play the children invented, their daily lives were devoid of pleasure, fun, and intellectual or cultural stimulation. Rudyard's school experiences were also evidently grim. In "Baa-Baa Black Sheep," Punch attended a neighborhood day school with Harry, who gave him a bad reputation. After school, Punch was confined to the home without friends or any significant outside socialization, except for one month a year. Trix observed: "We had 'learnt the meaning of captivity' for nearly six years there" (Fleming, 1939, p. 168).

Both Rudyard and (especially) Trix lacked an outside world. Trix described one lovely, joyful interlude with Jane, the Holloway's maid. When Mrs. Holloway went away for a day, Jane "the ever-friendly" was in charge; "I woke to a fairy world where everybody smiled and nobody scolded, and tea was laid in the greenhouse," Trix recalled (Fleming, 1939, p. 170). Trix formed an alliance with Jane, "the well styled maid-of-all-work" whom Trix "soon loved... only next to Ruddy" (p. 170). Although Jane's relationship to the children was not elaborated on, she appeared to have been a source of support to them, notably Trix.

Captain Holloway

Kipling (1937) in his autobiography refers briefly to the "Captain," the husband of "the Woman," who was protective toward Rudyard, taking him for long walks and telling him stories of the sea and his adventures. When, 3 years later, the Captain died, "I was sorry, for he was the only person in that house as far as I can remember who ever threw me a kind word" (p. 8). Kipling (1900) describes Uncle Harry (the Captain Holloway of "Baa-Baa Black Sheep") as one who:

> ...seldom spoke, but he showed Punch all Rocklington, from the mud banks and the sand of the back-bay to the great harbors where ships lay at anchor.... Punch heard,

too, from his lips the story of the battle of Navarino [during which Uncle Harry had been shot] . . . . "I have got the wadding of a bullet somewhere inside me now." (Kipling, 1900, p. 43)

Kipling described Punch's anticipatory preparation for Captain Holloway's death as well his opportunity to say goodbye. Uncle Harry talked of being tired; some walks ended in a visit to the cemetery, where Uncle Harry would sit on a tombstone for a long time. "'I shall lie there soon,' said he to Black Sheep, one winter evening . . . . 'You needn't tell Aunty Rosa'" (Kipling, 1900, p. 53). Punch was Uncle Harry's special confidante; it is a "secret" between them.

A month later, Uncle Harry, now bedridden, tells his wife, "I've walked my last" (Kipling, 1900, p. 53), and for the next two weeks, "the shadow of his sickness lay upon the house" (p. 54). Then, one night, amid the sobbing from Uncle Harry's room, Punch hears the voice of Uncle Harry singing the song of the Battle of Navarino and responds from his room: "That day at Navarino, Uncle Harry!" shouted Black Sheep, half wild with excitement and fear of he knew not what. A door opened and Aunty Rosa screamed up the staircase:-"Hush! For God's sake hush, you little devil. Uncle Harry is dead!" (Kipling, 1900, p. 55).

Captain Holloway died on September 29, 1874, of liver cancer. Uncle Harry and Punch said goodbye through encoded messages. Kipling loved secrets and codes, which is evident in his fiction. Saying goodbye is another important theme in his work.

Visits to Aunt Georgie

While at the Holloways, Rudyard spent 1 month a year at the Grange, the home of his Aunt Georgie, who was the wife of the artist Sir Edward Burne-Jones. Rudyard's annual visit there was "a paradise which I verily believe saved me" (Kipling, 1937, p. 13). Apparently no one thought of Trix going, and "no one wondered at this" (Flanders, 2001, p. 134). Rudyard always remembered his visits to the Grange. Arriving, he:

> would reach up to the open-work iron bell-pull on the wonderful gate that let me into all felicity. When I had a house of my own, and The Grange was emptied of meaning, I begged for and was given that bell-pull for my entrance, in the hope that other children might also feel happy when they rang it. (Kipling, 1937, pp. 13–14)

Rudyard received "love and affection as much as the greediest, and I was not very greedy, could desire" (Kipling, 1937, p. 14). With Georgie he may have felt a reconnection to his mother. He enjoyed the "smells of paints and turpentine whiffing down from the big studio on the first floor where my Uncle worked" (p. 14), which was probably reminiscent of his father's art school.

Kipling had fun playing and climbing trees with his two cousins, Margaret and Phil, and listening to his aunt reading. He played imaginative games with his uncle, and he and his cousins "could hang over the stairs and listen to the loveliest sound in the world—deep-voiced men laughing together over dinner" (Kipling, 1937, p. 15).

Growing into adulthood, Kipling maintained a special relationship with Aunt Georgie and with his cousins Margaret and Phil; Trix later developed a special relationship with Margaret. Aunt Georgie apparently did not realize how miserable he was at the Holloways:

> Often and often afterwards, the beloved Aunt would ask why I had never told anyone how I was being treated. Children tell little more than animals, for what comes to them they accept as eternally established. Also, badly-treated children have a clear notion of what they are likely to get if they betray the secrets of a prison-house before they are clear of it. (Kipling, 1937, p. 17)

Rudyard and Trix suffered in this foster placement; there was no outside professional supervision. Rudyard makes an astute observation: Children can be fearful of the consequences if they report what happened while they are still "imprisoned."

In a therapy situation, a client told his therapist that he had been in a state-supervised foster home in which he and other boys had been sexually abused by the foster father for 4 years. They were too frightened to tell anyone as long as they remained in that home. Such situations create a complex challenge for social workers supervising foster care—how to assure foster children that they can confide in the social worker and will be safe if they do so.

Adaptation

Rudyard and Trix were devoted to each other. The strength of this relationship also enabled them keep their attachments to their parents alive. Imaginary games and play were vital to them—they created worlds that made their lives tolerable. After reading *Robinson Crusoe,*

> I set up in business alone as a trader with savages... in a mildewy basement room where I stood my solitary confinements. My apparatus was a coconut shell strung on a red cord, a tin trunk, and a piece of packing-case which kept off any other world. Thus fenced about, everything inside the fence was quite real.... I have learned since from children who play much alone that this rule of "beginning again in a pretend game" is not uncommon. The magic, you see, lies in the ring or fence that you take refuge in. (Kipling, 1937, pp. 11-12)

Trix commented: "we had a sort of play that ran on and on for months, in which we played all the parts. I'm afraid there was generally a murder in it; or we ran away to sea and had the most wonderful adventures" (Fleming, 1947, p. 1).

They shared their thoughts with each other through secret knowledge and private codes. Mrs. Holloway was a "Kuch-nay" to them-"a Nothing-at-all, and that secret name was a great comfort to us, and useful, too, when Harry practiced his talent for eavesdropping" (Fleming, 1939, p. 169).

Reading was critical for Rudyard's survival. Punch reflects: "If he were only left alone... [he] could pass, at any hour he chose, into a land of his own, beyond reach of Aunty Rosa and her God, Harry and his tease-ments, and Judy's claims to be played with" (Kipling, 1900, p. 47).

Kipling, initially coerced into reading by Mrs. Holloway, soon discovered the worlds it opened up; it became a means to everything that would make me happy. So I read all that came within my reach. As soon as my pleasure in this was known, deprivation from reading was added to my punishments. I then read by stealth and the more earnestly. (Kipling, 1937, p. 9)

The defense of defiant acting out can "be an indicator of hope and potential for success in the face of adversity" (Dugan, 1989, p. 157). Rudyard, though tormented by Mrs. Holloway, was not cowed by her. His resistance to her control enabled him to remain aloof from her emotionally and to preserve his own emotional integrity. Conversely, excessive compliance with the demands of an abusive or emotionally seductive parent can lead to enmeshment and loss of a sense of autonomy. For example, a client discussed her poor relationship with her mother with her therapist. Because of her defiance, it had been a contentious relationship, one that had resulted in chronic anxiety and feelings of inadequacy. Nevertheless, she was pleased with her own positive family life. She realized that distancing herself from her mother resulted in a better outcome for her than what her compliant sister experienced; the sister remained enmeshed with her mother and had no life of her own.

The Holloways did not have many books, "but Father and Mother as soon as they heard I could read sent me priceless volumes" (Kipling, 1937, p. 9). Rudyard developed keen observational abilities as a means of self-protection. Trix recalls that in his adulthood: "He loved going about and seeing things; he was always observing; he had a camera in his brain" (Fleming, 1947, p. 3).

Eye Problems

Kipling's determination to keep reading led to a serious problem:

> My eyes went wrong, and I could not well see to read.
> For which reason I read the more and in bad lights. My
> work at the terrible little day-school where I had been sent
> suffered in consequence, and my monthly reports showed
> it. (Kipling, 1937, p. 18)

As his eyesight deteriorated, Kipling experienced "some sort of
nervous breakdown ... for I imagined I saw shadows and things
that were not there, and they worried me more than the Woman"
(Kipling, 1937, p. 19). Kipling similarly described Punch's anxiety
as his eyes deteriorated in "Baa-Baa Black Sheep":

> He himself could not account for spilling everything he
> touched. . . . There was a gray haze upon all his world, and it
> narrowed month by month, until at last it left Black Sheep
> almost alone with the flapping curtains that were so like
> ghosts and the nameless terrors of broad daylight that were
> only coats on pegs after all. (Kipling, 1900, p. 65)

When a doctor was consulted for Punch, he declared: "'Good
God, the little chap's nearly blind!'" (Kipling, 1900, p. 69). Kipling
suffered from both weak eyesight and migraine headaches. Rudyard
was unaware that migraine headaches (which were later diagnosed)
can produce visual disturbances. "Although migraine is uncommon
in children, it may have started while [Kipling] was at Southsea,

especially as he was suffering from eyestrain, probably caused by excessive reading in bad light conditions" (Sheehan, 1946). Later, at boarding school, he was the only boy wearing glasses (which were round and thick and strong), and he was often called " 'Gig-lamps' " or " 'Gigger' " (Carrington, 1955, p. 20).

Some biographers have viewed this early crisis as a breakdown with hallucinations. However, the "hallucinations" appear to have been perceptual distortions caused by vision and migraine problems. Kipling suffered from migraine headaches (with some visual distortions) throughout his life, often precipitated by physical or psychological stress.

Epping Forest

Notified of Rudyard's eyesight crisis, his mother journeyed from India, removed the children from the Holloways' home, and rented a cottage in Epping Forest, where they all lived for several months:

> ...for months I ran wild in a little farmhouse on the edge of Epping Forest, where I was not encouraged to refer to my guilty past. Except for my spectacles, which were uncomfortable in those days, I was completely happy with my Mother and the local society. (Kipling, 1937, p. 19)

When Alice initially went to Rudyard's room "to kiss me good-night, I flung an arm to guard off the cuff that I had been trained to expect" (1937, p. 19). He was fearful that Mrs. Holloway had reported his crimes to his mother. But soon he was responding to his mother without fear. Punch comments: "It is astonishing how much petting a big boy of ten can endure when he is quite sure that there is no one to laugh at him" (1900, p. 73).

After several months in Epping Forest, Mrs. Kipling developed shingles. Her sister Georgie came to look after her. Rud and Trix were sent to live in London, with an "ivory-faced lordly-whiskered ex-butler and his patient wife." (Kipling, 1937, p. 18). Mrs. Kipling joined them about a month later.

It was during this London visit that Rudyard developed a sleep disturbance: "for the first time, it happened that the night got into my head. I rose up and wandered about that still house till daybreak, when I slipped out into the little . . . garden and saw the dawn break" (1937, p. 20). He felt that no one would have known about this, except for one incident involving Pluto, his pet toad, from Epping Forest,

> who lived mostly in one of my pockets. It struck me that he might be thirsty, and I stole into my Mother's room and would have given him a drink from a water jug. But it slipped and broke and very much was said. The ex-butler could not understand why I had stayed awake all night. (Kipling, 1937, pp.20–21)

Rudyard and Trix moved to this house without their mother. Symbolically, the "thirsty" Pluto represents Rudyard, a child "thirsty" for nurturing and anxious about his mother's appearances and disappearances. It is unlikely that the only water in the household was in a jug in Mother's room. And somehow the jug slipped, a commotion resulted, and Rudyard received attention and the assurance that Mother was still there.

Kipling (1937) did not "know then that such night-wakings would be laid upon me through my life; or that my fortunate hour would be on the turn of sunrise, with a sou 'west breeze afoot" (p. 21). This is a key event, manifesting his longing for his mother and anxiety about her availability. Separation anxiety would resurface throughout his life, as would Kipling's resilience and adaptability. However, the traumas of loss and abandonment were so deep and so painful that they became embedded in his psyche and his memory. In clinical terms, clients not uncommonly seek help for symptoms of anxiety that have suddenly appeared, stirred up by current circumstances, but which have underlying roots in early trauma.

Validity of Account

Did Kipling exaggerate his abuse at Southsea? Was Mrs. Holloway the cruel and vindictive woman he portrayed? Was his resentment displaced from unacknowledged anger toward his parents for abandoning him? The controversy continues. Some biographers accept the validity of Kipling's narrative. Shengold (1981) described Mrs. Holloway as "a tyrannical, narrow-minded, religiously obsessed woman.... The atmosphere was full of sadism, disguised as religious righteousness" (p. 215). Carrington (1955) and Seymour-Smith (1989) were more skeptical. Seymour-Smith asserted that Mrs. Holloway is a more human figure than portrayed by Kipling. She probably experienced "despair at such savage rejection by a nasty little boy" (p. 27). But if Rudyard was such "a nasty little boy," how can we explain the positive relationship Captain Holloway developed with him?

Ricketts (1999), accepting Rudyard's and Trix's narratives, added that the family situation deteriorated after Captain Holloway's death and that it was these later experiences that "dominate[d] their memories" (p. 18). Mason (1975) emphasized that Kipling's account "is *poetic truth* and represents what he came later to feel had happened" (p. 32, emphasis added). "Whatever may actually have happened, the boy felt that he had been deserted by his parents and that he had been humiliated and ill-treated by a woman he despised and whom he came to hate" (p. 35).

In September 1872 (prior to Captain Holloway's death), Grandmother Hannah and Aunts Louie, Georgie, and Aggie visited Southsea for a week (Ricketts, 1999). Aunt Louie wrote in her diary that the children were " 'very well and happy, improved in every way, & Mrs. Holloway a very nice woman indeed' " (quoted in Ricketts, 1999, p. 19). The aunts and Grandmother Hannah would have viewed the household through their Victorian attitudes about what was acceptable child behavior: ". . . it is almost impossible to look back, with our values now, without feeling that much of what happened then verged on the criminal" (Flanders, 2001, p. 131). No records of observations made by people outside of this family exist. Mrs. Holloway and Harry later moved, fading into the London scene. No one is known to have interviewed them.

Why Alice Kipling placed Trix again with Mrs. Holloway, after another placement elsewhere, is also controversial. Some argue that this decision vindicates Mrs. Holloway: If she were that terrible, Alice would not have replaced Trix with her. Shengold (1981), however, is appalled: "Yet it is a mystery how, even after she knew of Rudyard's suffering and breakdown under [Mrs. Holloway's] care . . . she could have left her daughter Trix—a sensitive and nervous child—or several more years with them" (p. 213). However, did Alice Kipling know what the children had experienced? Mason (1975) suggests that the children may have never complained to her about Mrs. Holloway. "In the story, it is not suggested that Punch told even his mother all that had happened. Indeed, she was clearly puzzled" (Mason, 1975, p. 34). It might have been too painful for the children to discuss: Children "avoid talking of wounds and humiliations and of so deep a shock as desertion" (p. 34).

However, Alice Kipling's behavior as a mother has been questioned. Sending Trix to England at age three seemed extreme and unempathic, even within her social context. Kipling's relationship to her, although close, remained strained; he was closer to Aunt Georgie, his confidante throughout his life. Trix's relationship with Alice also had its strains.

Flanders (2001) asserted that Alice Kipling, living in India, "was pining for her children." As evidence she presents a "poignant verse" Alice wrote. In the last verse, "Little Boy and Girl are gone, / Leaving Mother lonely: / What they shout and run about / Now remembered—only— / He and she, o'er the sea, / Finding other pleasures, / Scarcely miss, Mother's kiss / Rich in childish treasures" (Flanders, 2001, p. 133), the emphasis is on Alice's loss and not the children's feelings of desertion.

There is support for the validity of Kipling's "Ba-Baa Black Sheep" as a narrative of his childhood. Numerous parallels exist between this book, his autobiography, and his life; a consistency and repetition of themes is found. The book has an emotional intensity that rings true: Kipling suffered and wants the reader (and probably his parents) to know this. He probably wanted, as many "survivors" do, to "bear witness" to the horrors he experienced.

Kipling wrote "Baa-Baa Black Sheep" in 1888, when he was 23 and living in India at the home of his friend, Mrs. Hill. She recorded this event in her diary:

> It was pitiful to see Kipling living over the experience, pouring out his soul in the story, as the drab life was worse than he could possibly describe it. His eyesight was permanently impaired, and, as he had heretofore only known love and tenderness, his faith in people was sorely tried. When he was writing this he was a sorry guest, as he was in a towering rage at the recollection of those days. His summing up in the closing words shows the influence on his whole life. (Ricketts, 1999, p. 118)

Ricketts (1999) suggested that Kipling wrote this story at that time because he was experiencing a repetition of past events; he was about to leave India and his parents again, as well as his sister, who was engaged. He was living with Mrs. Hill, another "substitute family" (p. 118).

Kipling referred to his Southsea experience in later life when he wanted to share his experience with his wife, Carrie. When they visited Southsea in 1920, Carrie wrote in her diary: "'Rud takes me to see Lorne Lodge [the Holloways' home] ... where he was so misused and forlorn and desperately unhappy as a child—and talks of it all with horror'" (quoted in Ricketts, 1999, p. 346).

Themes of abandonment, abuse, love, and loyalty can also be found in Kipling's other writings, as can the theme of the hero's skills of adaptation and outwitting his adversaries. In *The Jungle Book,* the hero, Mowgli, is orphaned and becomes the foster child of wolves: "But these wolves were of outstanding decency and dependability with Mother Wolf ready to fight to the death to keep him" (Shengold, 1981, p. 221). By contrast, Shere Khan, the evil Lame Tiger, aspiring to be Mowgli's foster parent, actually had designs on eating him. "Shere Khan stood for Mrs. Holloway, and his sidekick, Tabaqui the jackal, for her son" (Ricketts, 1999). Ricketts pointed out that Kipling seemed to delight in "Mowgli's eventual outwitting and destruction of Shere Khan." (p. 207). In *Kim* (Kipling, 1901), an adolescent boy, also an orphan, cares tenderly and loyally for an elderly Lama, showing extraordinary abilities to cope with dire situations on their journey. He also uses codes, disguises, and trickery, outwitting many.

There is no disagreement that Kipling was in a foster home in Southsea, but the nature of his experience there has been much debated. There are no social case records to read to help assess the quality of this foster home and Rudyard's relationship with the Holloways. Witness accounts of his grandmother and aunts are colored by their values and attitudes about raising children; they also focused on the behavior of Rudyard and Trix, not on the children's feelings about living there. The issues and themes appearing in Rudyard's account also appear in his writings.

Westward Ho!

On January 16, 1878, nine months after leaving the Holloways, Rudyard, 12, entered boarding school: the United Services College at Westward Ho! He found his first term "horrible" (Kipling, 1937, p. 27). His "first year and a half was not pleasant," because of frequent bullying. "Lonely and depressed, he was soon bombarding his mother (who had temporarily remained in England) with letters—sometimes *as many as four a day*. It was, Alice confided to the headmaster, 'the roughness of the lads that he seems to feel most' " (Ricketts, 1999, p. 33). Although we should not minimize his school problems, perhaps more stressful was Kipling's separation from mother.

This new and unique private school in North Devon was attended mostly by army officers' sons, planning military careers, but was not militaristic (Carrington, 1955). The atmosphere, though strict, allowed for a certain flexibility. Cornell Price, its benevolent headmaster and a friend of the Kiplings, was well liked by Rudyard. Price "was a liberal and an aesthete. . . . The school flourished under Price's leadership" (Ricketts, 1999, p. 33).

Rudyard's eyesight remained poor, and he was unable to participate in school sports. The school was located close to the Atlantic Ocean, and Rudyard became a good swimmer, "the one accomplishment that brought me any credit" (Kipling, 1937, p. 29).

Kipling found that "after my strength came suddenly to me about my fourteenth year, there was no more bullying" (Kipling, 1937, p. 29). By then he had two friends with whom he shared a room, and "by a carefully arranged system of mutual aids, I went up the school on co-operative principles" (p. 29). The boys helped each other with their school work, and the academic strengths of one were used to help the deficits of another. They were seen as the "school's intellectuals" and were "at least tolerated" (Amis, 1986, p. 29).

Rudyard conceded that "we fought among ourselves regular an' faithful as man an' wife,' but any debt which we owed elsewhere was faithfully paid by all three of us" (Kipling, 1937, pp. 30–31).

> They took up room on tables that I wanted for writing; they broke into my reveries . . . they stole, pawned or sold my . . . neglected possessions; and—I could not have gone

on a week without them nor they without me. (Kipling, 1937, p. 32)

Rudyard's friends, Dunsterville and Beresford, became characters in his popular book, *Stalky & Company*. Although this book's "high jinks" are a comic exaggeration of Rudyard's life at Westward Ho!, it captures the comradeship of the three boys and their enjoyment of pranks that outwitted both bullies and authorities. Dunsterville and Kipling had a lifelong relationship. Rudyard had the capacity to form significant relationships. His need to be loved and "to belong" were major themes in his life.

Cornell Price taught Rudyard English composition and precis writing and reintroduced the defunct school paper. "When he saw that I was irretrievably committed to the ink-pot, his order [was] that I should edit the school paper and have the run of the Library Study" (Kipling, 1937, p. 40). This was

> ... the first injection into his veins of the printer's ink that he never again worked out of his system. He was delighted with his school magazine, wrote three-quarters of it, sub-edited it, corrected proofs, and took the deepest interest in its production at a little printing shop at Bideford. (Carrington, 1955, p. 27)

Kipling (1937) wrote of "Crom" (that is, Cornell Price) that "many of us loved the Head for what he had done for us, but loved him more than all of them put together; and I think I loved him even more than they did" (p. 41).

At the end of Rudyard's first year at Westward Ho!, he and his father saw each other for the first time since their early separation.

Lockwood took him to the Paris Exhibition. By then, Lockwood had advanced in his career, moving from Bombay to Lahore, where he was principal of the Mayo School of Art and curator of the Lahore Museum (Ricketts, 1999).

Both Lockwood and Rudyard refer to this visit positively but more as a pleasant event than as a momentous occasion of reunion. Lockwood wrote to Crom that he found Rudyard " 'a delightfully amiable and companionable little chap', if somewhat prone to 'vagueness and inaccuracy' " (Ricketts, 1999, p. 35). Kipling (1937) also recalled this visit:

> He allowed me, at twelve years old, the full freedom of that spacious and friendly city, and the run of the Exhibition grounds and buildings. It was an education in itself; and set my life-long love for France. Also, he saw to it that I should learn to read French at least for my own amusement, and gave me Jules Verne to begin with. (p. 28)

Given the long separation, it is surprising that Rudyard was sent off to explore by himself instead of exploring with Lockwood. In his autobiography, Rudyard expressed more affection for Crom than for his father. As an adult, he drew closer to his father. Lockwood even illustrated and advised him on *Kim*.

Several years later, in 1892, the decision was made for Rudyard to leave Westward Ho! to work at a newspaper in India. Kipling wrote that this decision, made by Crom, was unanticipated. He had completed six weeks of the term when "Crom... *told me* that a fortnight after the close of the summer holidays of '82, I *would* go *to* India to work on a paper in Lahore" (Kipling, 1937, p. 41). Kipling added that Lahore was "where my parents lived, and [I] would get one hundred silver rupees a month!" (p. 41).

Educational and financial factors may have led to Kipling's formal schooling ending at 16. Ricketts (1999) questions whether his parents could afford the costs at Cambridge or Oxford. Kipling's eligibility to enter either university was also questionable because of his uneven academic record. Although very bright and excelling in certain courses such as literature, Rudyard "could be vague and inaccurate; and... there were serious doubts about his Latin. A career in journalism, on the other hand, offered distinct possibilities" (Ricketts, 1999, p. 46).

Rudyard's romance with Florence Garrard, which he makes no reference to in his autobiography, likely played a big part in this decision to relocate Rudyard to India. Florence was boarding with Mrs. Holloway; Rudyard met her when he was visiting Trix, who had resumed living there. Rudyard was then 14 and a half and Flo a little older. His character, Maisie, in *The Light That Failed* was modeled on Flo. Carrington (1955) described Florence as

> ... a straight slender girl with a beautiful ivory-pale face and a cloud of dark hair, but badly brought up in continental hotels and very ill-educated. With a shrewd sophisticated manner, she was self-centered and elusive, lacking in sympathy and affection.... Rudyard fell an easy prey. (Carrington, 1955, p. 32)

Rudyard "felt himself to be in love with her for five or six years" (Shengold, 1981, p. 231).

When Rudyard left for India, he and Flo became engaged. "He often mentioned her in his letters to his aunts… but it is still difficult… to judge the depth of his feelings.… It is clear that he was initially strongly involved, and he was again affected when he met her many years later" (p. 231).

Kipling's parents may have become alarmed at his romantic relationship. Lockwood, in a letter to Crom, stated "'I must confess… from what I have seen of Ruddy it is the moral side I dread an outbreak on. I don't think he is the stuff to resist temptation'" (quoted in Ricketts, 1999, p. 47). Planning for Kipling's return to India may have been Lockwood's attempt to thwart Rudyard's romance (Ricketts, 1999). In a later letter to his sister-in-law, Lockwood commented that Rudyard was "'better here [in Lahore] than anywhere else where there are no music-hall ditties to pick up, no young persons to philander about with.… For all that makes Lahore so profoundly dull makes it safe for young people'" (quoted in Ricketts, 1999, p. 56). This effectively put an end to Rudyard's relationship with Flo but not to his feelings for her. He attempted to see her again later, but she emphatically ended the relationship.

Amis (1986) observed that Kipling was 16 and a half when his formal education ended, "to his own keen regret" (p. 31). Kipling's friend Beresford asserted that "Rud left England with very mixed feelings" (Ricketts, 1999, p. 53). Mason (1975) reports that in a letter to an aunt, Kipling expressed his wishes to follow the same path as his cousin Stanley Baldwin: " 'I'd give anything to be in the Sixth at Harrow as he is, with a University Education to follow.' " Mason adds that "for many years [Kipling] would display little spurts of animosity directed at those who did have a University education" (p. 47). On the positive side, however, Rudyard did express enthusiasm about a job in journalism and being with his family.

Adulthood

Return to India

Kipling sailed for India on September 20, 1882, "alone and seasick, in drizzling rain" (Carrington, 1955, p. 33). He wrote:

> So, at sixteen years and nine months, but looking four or five years older, and adorned with real whiskers which the scandalised Mother abolished within one hour of beholding I found myself at Bombay where I was born, moving among sights and smells that made me deliver in the vernacular sentences whose meaning I knew not. Other Indian-born boys have told me how the same thing happened to them. (Kipling, 1937, p. 45)

Kipling goes on to describe his life and work in India. He worked very hard, often under poor conditions, frequently suffering from heat and illness:

> I never worked less than ten hours and seldom more than fifteen per diem; and as our paper came out in the evening did not see the midday sun except on Sundays. I had fever too, regular and persistent, . . . Yet I discovered that a man can work with a temperature of 104, even though next day he has to ask the office who wrote the article. (Kipling, 1937, p. 47)

In spite of difficult working conditions, Kipling was proud of his increasing responsibilities and professional development. He initially "knew nothing" and learned a lot from Stephan Wheeler, the chief editor, who "took me in hand"; however, he adds, "for three years or so I loathed him" (Kipling, 1937, p. 46). As Kipling became more proficient, he was given reporting assignments. He traveled throughout the country. On these travels, "he quizzed and looked and listened, picking up characters for his stories and verses" (Shengold, 1981, p. 232). Writing was important: He felt "the pleasure of writing what my head was filled with" (Kipling, 1937, p. 70).

Kipling lived at home, where his pampered existence contrasted to his difficult work conditions. His own manservant (the son of his father's servant) was very solicitous. He described unbearable physical discomfort during the hot season, which lasted half the year. Illness was rampant: "my world was filled with boys, but a few years older than I, who lived utterly alone, and died from typhoid mostly at the regulation age of twenty-two" (Kipling, 1937, p. 47). Kipling's family went to the cool hills of Simla during the hot spells while Kipling remained in Lahore, working and living at home. He spoke of "the temper frayed by heat to breaking point but for sanity's sake held back from the break; the descending darkness of intolerable dusks; and the less supportable dawns of fierce, stale heat through half the year" (Kipling, 1937, p. 68).

Kipling described his happiness being with his family when they were together in cooler weather:

> But the Mother proved more delightful than all my imaginings or memories. My Father was not only a mine of knowledge and help, but a humorous, tolerant, and expert

fellow-craftsman.... We delighted more in each other's society than in that of strangers; and when my sister came out, a little later, our cup was filled to the brim. Not only were we happy, but we knew it. (Kipling, 1937, p. 46)

The four Kiplings wrote a Christmas annual they named *Quartette,* which received positive public acclaim. In 1885, Rudyard published his book *Plain Tales from the Hills,* a collection of his newspaper stories. The following year, he published *Departmental Ditties,* a collection of poems on Anglo-Indian life. "These things were making for me the beginnings of a name even into Bengal" (Kipling, 1937, p. 74).

Sleeping in the heat was difficult, even on the roof, and so Kipling (1937) would frequently wander the streets at night:

Often the night got into my head as it had done in the boarding-house in the Brompton Road, and I would wander till dawn in all manner of odd places-liquor shops, gambling and opium dens... wayside entertainments such as puppet-shows, native dances.... One would come home, just as the light broke, in some night-hawk of a hired carriage... and if the driver were moved to talk, he told one a great deal. Much of real Indian life goes on in the hot weather nights. (pp. 59–60)

Kipling's anxieties about "the night getting into my head" remained with him, but he made adaptive use of it, wandering through the streets at night, observing the lively scene, and storing up his observations for later use in his writing.

Kipling experienced a turning point in the year " '86 or there-abouts," when it seemed as though "I had come to the edge of all endurance" (Kipling, 1937, p. 71). This occurred during the hot weather, when his family was away. "As I entered my empty house... there was no more in me except the horror of a great darkness, that I must have been fighting for some days. I came through that darkness alive, but how I do not know" (p. 71).

That night Kipling "came across" *All in a Garden Fair* by Walter Besant, a book about a man ambitious to be a writer who ultimately succeeded. This book "was my salvation... and with the reading and re-reading it became to me a revelation, a hope and strength" (Kipling, 1937, p. 71). He also could become successful: "there was no need for me to stay here forever." He would save money and return to London. "I built up in my head... a dream of the future that sustained me" (p. 71).

At his newspaper, Kay Robinson was appointed editor-in-chief. During his "joyous reign," changes were made, including the reduction of space for short articles, most of which Kipling wrote, to "one column and a quarter"; "once more I was forced to 'write short' " (Kipling, 1937, p. 72).

In 1887, Kipling was transferred to the *Pioneer,* "our big sister-paper at Allahabad" (Kipling, 1937, p. 69). Kipling wrote 19 anonymous travel articles about his trip from Lahore to Allahabad for the *Pioneer* called the *Letters of Marque* (Ricketts, 1999).

Omitted from Kipling's autobiography was his good friend Mrs. Edmonia Hill, whom he met shortly after his arrival in Allahabad. Mrs. Hill, 29, was an American married to Alec Hill, a professor of physical science at Muir College from Ulster. Mrs. Hill and Kipling met at a dinner party; the guests were discussing the *Letters of Marque* and their curiosity about the anonymous author. Mrs. Hill wrote:

When we were seated at the table... my partner called my attention to a short dark-haired man of uncertain age, with a heavy mustache and wearing very thick glasses, who sat opposite, saying: "That is Rudyard Kipling, who has just come from Lahore to be on the staff of the Pi. He is writing those charming sketches of the native states... which the Pi is publishing."... Of course I was interested at once, for I had been fascinated by these unusual articles so clearly written.... Mr. Kipling looks about forty, as he is beginning to be bald, but he is in reality just twenty-two. He was animation itself, telling his stories admirably, so that those about him were kept in gales of laughter. He fairly scintillated, but when more sober topics were discussed he was posted along all lines. (Hill, 1936, p. 406)

Mrs. Hill, meeting Kipling for the first time, was drawn to him (perhaps in part because of his celebrity). She described his wit, his storytelling abilities, and the fact that he "fairly scintillated." Whatever anxieties may have been inhabiting his inner self, Kipling's "recruitment" capacities enabled him to come across as outgoing and engaging.

A special friendship developed between Kipling and Mrs. Hill. When she left Allahabad to go to the cool hills near Simla, Rudyard conducted a "voluminous and almost daily correspondence" with her "us[ing] every possible ploy to sustain her interest and attention" (Ricketts, 1999, p. 108), including seeking her editorial help with his writing. "Mrs. Hill was a kinder critic than... Kipling's sharp-tongued mother" (Carrington, 1955, p. 75). The following month, when Rudyard was sent back to Lahore, he continued writing to Mrs. Hill in a "more directly confessional" style.

He wrote about his love affair with a mysterious woman. Carrington (1955) speculated that "the reader begins to suppose her a figment of the young writer's fancy, a projection of Mrs. Hill herself, to whom he must not declare his devotion" (p. 87). Ricketts noted: "The highly artificial manner in which Rud wrote about the affair supports this idea.

The picture presented of himself, powerless in a hopeless entanglement, was also reminiscent of earlier attempts to solicit other correspondents' sympathy" (p. 109).

When Rudyard returned to Allahabad, he no longer had a place to live; Mrs. Hill invited him to live at her home. Rudyard lived with the Hills for his remaining nine months in India. Planning to return to England, Kipling (1937) felt "ripe for change ... [and] had a notion now of where I was heading." With profits from book sales and severance pay from the paper, he was ready to go. "I left India for England by way of the Far East and the United States" (p. 80).

A decisive factor (omitted from his autobiography) in his leaving just then was that the Hills were planning such a trip at the same time. The Hills were important to Kipling; at this point in his life, they eased his separation anxieties. Mrs. Hill had decided to visit her family in Pennsylvania, traveling first through the Far East. Mrs. Hill (1936) wrote:

> Rudyard was planning to go direct to England, when suddenly the idea occurred to him that he would like to see something of the world first, and as he helped us look up routes he begged to be allowed to accompany us. Then Mr. Allen [his editor] asked him to write letters on the trip for the Pi, which would pay his expenses. We agreed to have him join us. (Hill, 1936, p. 413)

There is no confirmation that Rudyard begged to go. He may have, or Mrs. Hill (1936) may have chosen this emphasis. This letter, among several printed in the *Atlantic Monthly,* highlights her importance in his life; she spoke of being "present at the inception of Ruddy's Barrack Room Ballads" (p. 414) and also quoted his "Inscription for my presentation copy" of *Wee Willie Winkie* (p. 413).

In February 1889, Kipling said good-bye to his family in Lahore and left before Trix's wedding. Mrs. Hill wrote: "Here we are, ready to start on our long journey.... Rud has loaded us up with a delightful array of books" (p. 413).

In his travel letters for the *Pioneer,* Kipling described his travels to Asia. He saw a Pagoda in Rangoon, which he would have remembered better "'had I not fallen deeply and irrevocably in love with a Burmese girl at the foot of the first flight of [its] steps'" (quoted in Ricketts, 1999, pp. 121–122). Rudyard's poem "Mandalay" most likely evolved from this memory.

On May 28, the travelers arrived in San Francisco and temporarily parted company. The Hills went to her parents' in Pennsylvania; Kipling, after traveling through the West, joined them in Pennsylvania and met Mrs. Hill's father and her young sister, Caroline. Kipling stayed for 2 months. Professor Hill returned to India early, and Kipling later sailed to Liverpool with Mrs. Hill, her sister Caroline, and their cousin Edgar Taylor (Carrington, 1955).

Return to London

Mrs. Hill's sister Caroline, "a cheerful, plump, young girl," and Rudyard became engaged shortly after their arrival in London (Carrington, 1955, p. 99). "Not much is known about Caroline—and, according to Trix... there was not much to know... Trix's recollections of the women in her brother's life were usually crushing" (Ricketts, 1999, p. 145).

This engagement was short-lived—we know little about this relationship and its ending. Ricketts (1999) asserted that Kipling was interested in Caroline because "she was the sister of the unavailable Mrs Hill" (p. 146). Flanders (2001) described the relationship as "a bit half-hearted," and "an attempt to stay attached" to Mrs. Hill. Comparing the letters Kipling wrote to Caroline with those he wrote to Mrs. Hill, Ricketts finds that "his feelings for Caroline were mostly a *willed fiction*" (p. 146, emphasis added). This behavior mirrors Kipling's engagement to Flo before his first trip to India; "now, returning to England and an equally uncertain future, he got engaged to the equally absent Caroline" (Ricketts, 1999, p. 146).

During this time in London, Kipling by chance came across Flo in the street, "and [he] had realized... that she still retained her power over him" (Carrington, 1955, p. 121). Flo again indicated no interest in seeing him. Several months later, Kipling visited Flo in Paris; this visit appeared to end his involvement with her. This loss led to his first novel, *The Light That Failed,* an account of the relationship between Maisie and Dick Helder, which was based loosely on his relationship with Flo (Ricketts, 1999).

Shortly before they left for India, Mrs. Hill and Caroline helped Kipling decorate his new rooms in his apartment on Villiers Street.

My rooms were small, not over-clean or well-kept, but from my desk I could look out of my window through the fan-light of Gatti's Music-Hall entrance, across the street, almost on to its stage. The Charing Cross trains rumbled through my dreams on one side, the boom of the Strand on the other, while, before my windows, Father Thames under the Shot Tower walked up and down with his traffic. (Kipling, 1937, p. 87)

Initially, Kipling (1937) had little cash and was determined not to borrow money from his relatives. He did, however, dine with and frequently visit them.

My rooms were above … Harris the Sausage King who, for tuppence, gave as much sausage and mash as would carry one from breakfast to dinner when one dined with nice people who did not eat sausage for a living. (Kipling, 1937, p. 88)

Kipling's London visit was a success; he was a known and popular writer before his arrival, and his ongoing work proved very popular. By 1890, he was famous both in London and the United States. Sidney Low, the editor of the *St. James's Gazette,* offered him a job writing short stories for the paper; "the pronouncement gave me confidence" (Kipling, 1937, p. 85).

Kipling met many people, including literary celebrities, and was elected to London's famous Saville Club. "Kipling's conversational powers played as significant a part in his easy conquest of the London literary scene as his existing publications" (Ricketts, 1999, p. 148).

During this time, Kipling wrote "Danny Deever," the beginning of his *Barrack Room Ballads.* These ballads, "Mandalay" and "Gunga Din" among them, all had "the common touch." The British Army's GI Joe, Tommy Atkins, the hero of "Tommy," represented the "ordinary" soldier (Ricketts, 1999, p. 162). Many were put to music. "He had struck the vein that was to become Kiplingesque" (p. 162).

Kipling wanted to share his success with his parents. "What I most needed was that my people should come over and see what had overtaken their son. This they did on a flying visit, and then my 'kick-up' had some worth" (Kipling, 1937, p. 96). Kipling spoke positively about his parents' support and interest. "As always, they seemed to suggest nothing and interfere nowhere. But they were there . . . both so entirely comprehending that except in trivial matters we had hardly any need of words" (p. 97).

During this tumultuous year, Rudyard met an American writer and publisher, Wolcott Balestier, 29, and "developed the deepest friendship of his life" (Shengold, 1981, p. 241). Wolcott worked for an American publishing company, which sent him to London to find British authors who would affiliate with the company. Wolcott, ambitious, diligent, and highly competent, with an appealing personality, was popular with writers; he had a "capacity for making others feel special, allied to the chameleon quality of taking on something of the nature of those he talked to" (Ricketts, 1999, p. 178). As Wolcott and Kipling worked together, their friendship grew: ". . . they referred to each other as 'brother' " (Ricketts, 1999, p. 179). Together they wrote *The Naulahka,* an adventure novel. "No other man ever exercised so dominating an influence over Rudyard Kipling as did Wolcott Balestier during the eighteen months of their intimacy" (Carrington, 1955, p. 137).

Kipling has revealed little of his feelings about Balestier; there is no reference to him in his autobiography. Wolcott "was one of those shadowy figures in Kipling's life about whom little is known, but much has been speculated" (Ricketts, 1999, p. 177); "Kipling liked to keep his friendships in different compartments" (p. 137).

Wolcott's family traveled from their home in Brattleboro, Vermont, to join him in London. Carolyn (Carrie), his sister, became

Wolcott's housekeeper and secretary. Rudyard and Carrie met, and their relationship blossomed. Alice Kipling commented after meeting Carrie: "'That woman is going to marry our Ruddy,' and showed little enthusiasm for the prospect" (Carrington, 1955, p. 141). Lockwood commented that Carrie "'was a good man spoiled .... If I had been in [Rudyard's] place I think I hold have preferred the younger and prettier sister'" (Flanders, 2001, p. 239). "The progress of the love affair, as its two principals would have wished, remained their own secret" (Carrington, 1955, p. 141).

> The only *direct* evidence of [the Balestier-Kipling] friendship is preserved in a fragment of a letter from Wolcott to Kipling [probably written in 1891, when Kipling was on a lengthy voyage]. It was discovered in a bank box in Brattleboro, Vermont, in May 1992: ... "Carrie bears up like the grave child she is. She counts the days; but she is strong.... I want you back most hideously; but not enough to want you till the job's done. Heaven be with you! God bless you! Always and Ever, Your brother, Wolcott." (Ricketts, 1999, p. 180)

Ricketts (1999) added that "the reference to Carrie ... shows that by this time there was already an accepted understanding between her and Kipling" (pp. 180-181).

Wolcott, "probably already sick with the typhoid," went to Dresden, where his illness worsened; he died there on December 6, 1891 (Ricketts, 1999, p. 185). At the time of his death, Kipling was on a voyage and had stopped in India. Shortly after arriving at his parents' home, Carrie cabled him: "'WOLCOTT DEAD. COME

BACK TO ME'" (quoted in Ricketts, p. 185). Racing back to London, he and Carrie were married eight days later, on January 18, 1892.

Life in the United States

Kipling (1937), in his autobiography, without any prelude, mentions his wedding:

In the midst of a London influenza epidemic, "we were married in the church in the pencil-pointed steeple at Langham Place" (p. 116). Carrie Balestier is referred to as "my wife" or as the "Committee of Ways and Means" throughout his autobiography (p. 118). Four adults and two children attended the wedding: Henry James gave the bride away; some invited guests were unable to attend because of illness. Rudyard had arranged a honeymoon voyage around the world and wanted to leave quickly because of the influenza epidemic. Ricketts (1999) asserts that the haste of both the wedding and the honeymoon were related to grief over Wolcott's death.

Kipling's letters at the time of his wedding expressed his joy (Ricketts, 1999).

To his cousin Margaret (Georgie's daughter), he wrote that he was "'idiotically happy'" (p. 186). To Aunt Louie, he said, "'That I am penetrated with the solemnity of things in general is true. That I am riotously happy is yet more true and I pray that... you will bless us, because we have gone through deep waters together'" (Ricketts, 1999, p. 186).

Kipling (1937) wrote that "a few days after... [the wedding] we were on our magic carpet which was to take us round the earth" (p. 116). Arriving in Yokohama, calamity struck. Kipling had deposited most of his money in a Yokohama bank, which suddenly closed and "suspended payment"—his money was gone (p. 118). "I returned with my news to my bride of three months and a child to be born" (p. 118). Apparently, Carrie rose to the occasion, and together they resolved their dilemma. Kipling, wryly referring to Carrie for the first time as the "Committee of Ways and Means," recalls how the "Committee" "advance[d] our understanding of each other" (p. 118).

Kipling (1937) received a refund for the remainder of their unused tickets, and they traveled to Brattleboro, Vermont, where they rented a small "habitable" cottage (p. 119). At the end of the year,

> . . . my first child and daughter was born in three foot of snow on the night of December 29th, 1892. Her Mother's birthday being on the 31st and mine the 30th of the same month, we congratulated her on her sense of the fitness of things, and she throve in her trunk-tray in the sunshine on the little plank verandah. (Kipling, 1937, p. 120)

His daughter, Josephine, is not named in the autobiography. Though keeping his private life private, he adored Josephine and "and was entirely devoted to her" (Carrington, 1955, p. 169). His letters included "the latest besotted bulletin on the progress and accomplishments of 'The Joss'" (Ricketts, 1999, p. 196). Marjorie, Josephine's young cousin, often visited the Kiplings; Rudyard "always had stories for the children, animal stories about camels and whales and the cat that walked in the wet wild woods up the road from Beatty's house" (Carrington, 1955, p. 159). Carrington noted: "Even as a tiny child [Josephine] had a remarkable and endearing personality, with a charm and quickness of mind far in advance of her years" (p.169).

The Kiplings built their own home nearby, and Rudyard was involved with its building and design. Carrie's brother Beatty and his family lived nearby, and Beatty served as a general contractor on the project (Carrington, 1955). The Kiplings called the house *Naulakha* in honor of Wolcott, commemorating Wolcott's collaboration on their book. J. I. M. Stewart noted that this house

> ...had one notable feature, to be reduplicated in essentials wherever the Kiplings subsequently lived. Kipling's study had only one entrance, through a room occupied by his wife. There Carrie would sit at a desk ordering her domestic affairs, and guarding her husband against all possibility of intrusion. (Stewart, quoted in Shengold, 1981, p. 243)

Rudyard was financially successful; he wrote "a note of thanks" in Carrie's diary at the end of 1894 to show "his gratitude for a fortunate year, [and] he noted that he had earned $25,000... a great sum in... those days" (Carrington, 1955, p. 171). Kipling flourished in Vermont: "'The sun and the air and the light are good in this place and have made me healthy as I never was in my life'" (quoted in Carrington, 1955, p. 164). Carrington wrote that "never again was Rudyard so happy, never so sure of himself, as in the honeymoon years at 'Naulakha'" (p. 188).

Kipling was creative and productive during this period, writing verses in *The Seven Seas,* his two *Jungle Books* and *The Day's Work.* He was also writing "M'Andrew's Hymn," "the most elaborate and perhaps the most effective of his dramatic lyrics" (Carrington, 1955, p. 162). Lockwood came to visit. He and Rudyard discussed the latter's work, and Rudyard found his father's interest and ideas helpful.

The Kiplings did not socialize much with the villagers. One neighbor, Mary Cabot, became a close friend. They had prominent friends, including Teddy Roosevelt, then secretary of the navy, with whom they corresponded through the years (Kipling, 1937, p. 133). Arthur Conan Doyle came to visit and taught Kipling to ski, bearing skis as a present for him. But Kipling felt himself to be the object of resentment in Brattleboro:

> I felt the atmosphere was to some extent hostile. The idea seemed to be that I was "making money" out of America— witness the new house and horses—and was not suffi- ciently grateful for my privileges. . . , A meeting of the Committee of Ways and Means came to the conclusion that *Naulakha,* desirable as it was, meant only "a house" and not "*the* house" of our dreams. So we loosed hold and, with another small daughter born in the early spring snows… we took ship for England. (Kipling, 1937, p. 142)

This second "small daughter" Kipling refers to was Elsie, born February 2, 1896.

> Dillingham (2008) expanded Kipling's picture of Brattle- boro's resentment to include both Kiplings: People felt that Carrie, whom they had known as a child, was putting on airs and that Kipling "was lording it over them" (p. 22). [Kipling] skied, rode his bicycle, played golf, entertained important visitors, and wrote for big bucks. He pulled strings to have his own post office nearby so that he would not have to go into Brattleboro for his mail. Carrie made sure that everyone knew that her husband was of extraor-

dinary importance and that not just anyone could see him. Royalty had suddenly established a palace in the Green Mountains of Vermont. (Dillingham, 2008, p. 22)

However, Kipling's comment about hostile villagers is not the whole story. When the Kiplings first came to Brattleboro, they lived near Beatty and his wife, Mai. For two years, the two couples had a warm relationship (Carrington, 1955). Beatty and Mai were well liked:

> They gave memorable parties.... With all the neighbors in, they would dance in the barn till past midnight—ungodly hours for Brattleboro. All the family assembled at Beatty's house for their Thanksgiving dinner and when Conan Doyle came to stay with the Kiplings, Beatty swept him into the party. (Carrington, 1955, p. 159)

Tensions started to build when Kipling employed Beatty as the general contractor for construction of *Naulakha*. His "generous" salary was "doled" out to him, by Carrie, as she saw fit, often in small amounts, "as a means of controlling his extravagance" (Carrington, 1955, p. 159)—Beatty had a history of financial mismanagement, drinking, and debts. After the house was finished, Beatty's work for the Kiplings diminished, especially when Kipling hired another man as a manager and helper.

The Kiplings' relationship with Beatty and Mai markedly deteriorated; financial quarrels developed. Carrie often bailed Beatty out. Finally, "the two families were no longer on speaking terms, and conducted their affairs by exchange of notes" (Carrington, 1955, p. 176). Beatty went into bankruptcy, and "with singular lack of tact," Carrie suggested that Beatty leave the farm and find a job; if he did this, "she would finance him and bring up his daughter, Marjorie" (Carrington, 1955, p. 182). This added fuel to the fire; Mai was especially irate.

On May 6, 1896, while riding his bicycle, Kipling encountered Beatty driving Kipling's wagon; a heated verbal exchange developed, and Beatty threatened to shoot him. Kipling had Beatty arrested. Once this happened, Kipling's "cause was lost; appearing in court, he exposed himself to the full glare of the yellow press" (Carrington, 1955, p. 183). The court hearing became a media circus, both in the United States and internationally; Kipling was subject to "ridicule and humiliation.... The irony of the creator of tough old sweats like Learoyd and Mulvaney calling in the sheriff to protect him against his own brother-in-law was lost on no one" (Ricketts, 1999, pp. 223–224.) All the while, Beatty "had become the town hero" (Dillingham, 2008, p. 19).

Back to England

The Kiplings left for England at the end of August. They said goodbye to their good friend and neighbor, Mary Cabot, who wrote: " '[Carrie] was tearful, but [Rudyard] seemed frozen with misery. He said it was the hardest thing he had ever had to do, that he loved Naulakha' " (Ricketts, 1999, p. 225).

They rented a sunny, spacious house in Torquay, near the sea. Then "a growing depression ... enveloped us both—a gathering blackness of mind ... that each put down to the new, soft climate and, without telling the other, fought against for long weeks" (Kipling, 1937, p. 143). Kipling attributed it to "the Feng-shui—the Spirit of the house" (p. 143). When they confided their feelings to each other, they decided to move elsewhere.

The Kiplings' depression and turmoil about leaving Brattleboro was probably displaced onto this replacement home. Although Carrie had said that *"Naulakha . . .* meant only 'a house' and not *'The* House' of our dreams," it was nevertheless a loss and one not fully mourned.

After leaving Torquay, they "ended almost by instinct at Rotting-dean where the beloved Aunt [Georgie] and Uncle [Ned] had their holiday house" (Kipling, 1937, p. 145). They moved into the Elms, "across the tiny green from them" (Ricketts, 1999). The Kipling's son, John, was born on August 17, 1897.

Rudyard's cousin, Stanley Baldwin, lived close by; the three families often spent time together. Kipling talked of "packing farm-carts filled with mixed babies—Stanley Baldwin's and ours—and dispatching them into the safe clean heart of the motherly Downs for jam-smeared picnics" (Kipling, 1937, p. 147).

The novelist Angela Thirkell, daughter of Kipling's cousin Margaret, often visited, and she "remembered how in the summers of 1897 and 1898 she and her 'bosom friend' Josephine Kipling' . . . would be told early versions of the *Just* So *Stories"* (Ricketts, 1999, p. 239): "'During those long warm summers Cousin Ruddy used to try out the *Just* So *Stories* on a nursery audience. Sometimes Josephine and I would be invited into his study. . . . His telling [was] unforget-table'" (quoted in Carrington, 1955, pp. 220–221). Kipling (1937) recollected that these "were exceedingly good days, and one's work came easily and fully" (p. 147). He started his lifelong habit of joining clubs: "My life made me grossly dependent on Clubs for my spiritual comfort" (p. 154).

"For Kipling, as for most of the rest of the English-speaking world, 1897 was dominated by Queen Victoria's Diamond Jubilee"

(Ricketts, 1999, p. 231). Kipling, in the spirit of the Victorian age, advocated expanding the British Empire and bringing the beneficent influence of British politics and morality to "uncivilized" parts of the world. The white man's responsibility was to bring "'a sane and orderly administration into the dark places of the earth'" (quoted in Ricketts, 1999, p. 231). To honor the Jubilee, Kipling wrote the poem "The Recessional," which "far surpassed his earlier triumphs" (Carrington, 1955, p. 209). Kipling became known as the "unofficial" "'Laureate of the Empire' because of his various 'imperial anthems'" (Dillingham, 2008, p. 24).

In a similar vein, Kipling wrote "The White Man's Burden." Shengold (1981) attributed Kipling's conservatism to his experiences in the "House of Desolation" where he and Trix had suffered:

> not knowing why, or to whom they belonged, or what their place was in the order of things. No wonder Rudyard was to become ... a pillar of the established order. One can see how the Law of the jungle in the *Jungle Books*, assigning a place to everyone ... enforcing "human" decency—represented a wish-fulfillment for Kipling. (Shengold, 1981, p. 221)

Ricketts (1999) emphasized the meaning of England as family to Kipling. "For him 'Mother England' was no empty phrase. He desperately wanted England to act as a caring and protective parent to her imperial children" (p. 303). As his fervor increased, negative public opinion grew; caricatures began appearing in newspapers. "He was in a wholly negativistic sense becoming Kiplingesque, evoking the cartoon image of a bald dwarf with glasses and eyebrows, energetically beating some sort of drum" (Ricketts, 1999, p. 268).

In January 1898, Kipling, Carrie, the children, and Lockwood visited Cape Town in South Africa (Ricketts, 1999). For 10 weeks, Kipling traveled extensively throughout Africa and met Cecil Rhodes and Alfred Milner, the British High Comissioner. All three men felt an enthusiasm for the extension of British imperialism and the prospect of federation between the Empire nations. Rhodes was to become a special friend to Kipling and South Africa a place where the Kipling family spent many winters (Kipling, 1937).

Six weeks after the Kiplings' return, Uncle Ned (Burne-Jones) suddenly died of a heart attack. Kipling wrote: "'He was more to me than any man here'" and that "he felt 'broke-broke-broke, I can't cry'" (Ricketts, 1999, p. 246). There was more tragic news: Trix, upon returning to England with her husband, had become mentally ill: "her mind gave way" (Carrington, 1955, p. 221). "Sometimes she would sit in a kind of catatonic state; sometimes talk endless gibberish" (Ricketts, 1999, pp. 247–248). Although Trix remained under Alice's care, Alice denied that she had a mental illness and refused to seek psychiatric help for her. "'The main point is not to flutter the mother,' Kipling told his Uncle Alfred" (Ricketts, 1999, p. 248). Trix would have periods of remission and relapse over a period of many years until midlife, when she improved and remained well.

Kipling immersed himself in work: He produced the poem "A White Man's Burden," he published *The Day's Work,* and he continued with *Kim.* During the winter of 1899, the Kiplings returned to the United States for six weeks so that Carrie could see her mother and Rudyard could work out a copyright dispute with a publisher. "The crossing was rough and freezing, the children were sick, and Josephine and Elsie developed colds" (Rickets, 1999, p. 248). Matters became progressively worse; Rudyard developed pneumonia and Josephine became critically ill.

Rudyard's pneumonia was severe and difficult to treat, and his survival was in question. The world kept vigil: There were constant bulletins in international newspapers (Ricketts, 1999, p. 249). Carrie, caring for Rudyard, was also keeping a vigil for six-year-old Josephine, bedridden at the home of a family friend.

Tragically, Josephine's condition continued to deteriorate; she did not have her father's "reserve of strength. Always hampered in health by a delicate digestion, she was unable during this time of weakness to retain nourishment" (Carrington, 1955, p. 225). In Carrie's diary: "The entry for 5 March read: 'I saw Josephine 3 times today, morning, afternoon and at 10 pm for the last time. She was conscious for a moment and sent her love to "Daddy and all." The entry for the 6th said simply: 'Josephine left us at 6:30 this morning'" (Ricketts, 1999, p. 250).

Josephine died March 6, 1899, at six years and three months of age. For days, Carrie did not tell Rudyard of Josephine's death because of his frail condition. "Months passed before he recovered from his illness; from the shock of his daughter's death he never recovered; nor did Carrie" (Carrington, 1955, p. 225). Several years later, Rudyard wrote to Mrs. Hill: "'I think that that is the one grief that grows with the years. The others only stay still'" (Ricketts, 1999, p. 277).

More than 40 years later, Trix observed: "'After his almost fatal illness & Josephine's death—he was a sadder & a harder man'" (Ricketts, 1999, p. 251). His cousin Angela Thirkell commented many years later about the distance he started putting between them (Ricketts, 1999).

> I feel that I have never seen him as a real person since that year. There has been the same charm, the same gift

of fascinating speech, the same way of making everyone with whom he talks show their most interesting side, but one was only allowed to see these things from the other side of a barrier. (Ricketts, 1999, p. 259)

In the early summer of 1899, the family returned to their English home, the Elms, which evoked painful memories. Kipling told his mother "that he 'saw [Josephine] when a door opened, when a space was vacant at table, coming out of every green dark corner of the garden—radiant and heartbreaking.' Carrie too was able to share her feelings with Alice" (Ricketts, 1999, p. 258). Kipling deeply loved Josephine; she is the "My Best Beloved" of his *Just So Stories.* In his grief, he sometimes thought he saw her; hallucinations of people who have died is a common occurrence for grieving people. In one study, people reported they were "helped" by "seeing" their loved one (Rees, 1975, p. 70). It can be reassuring for bereaved clients to know that this type of situational hallucination is a normal phenomenon.

The Kiplings' return to England coincided with public fervor regarding South Africa leading up to the Boer War; England declared war on October 11, 1899, and Kipling immediately "threw himself into the British cause" (Ricketts, 1999, p. 260). Kipling felt, as did Conan Doyle, that he must go to South Africa. Kipling and his family sailed for South Africa on January 20, 1900. There he edited a paper for the soldiers, gave recitals, made hospital visits, and was known for "his kindness to the troops" (Ricketts, 1999, p. 263).

Cecil Rhodes, a fervent imperialist, multimillionaire, owner of profitable diamond mines, and past prime minister of Cape Colony, was a major figure at that time. Rhodes built a house near Cape Town, the Woolsack, which Kipling and his family could use whenever they wished. This "became the Kiplings' home-from-home on their annual winter visits to South Africa" (Ricketts, 1999, pp. 263-264).

The Woolsack, within walking distance of Rhodes's home, was "Carrie's ideal house, her 'dear Woolsack' which, every year from 1901 to 1908, she occupied with joy and left with regret" (Carrington, 1955, p. 246). Kipling (1937) spoke joyfully of "this Paradise." When the family arrived, "there was the rush to the garden to see what had happened in our absence; [and] the flying barefoot visit to our neighbors" (p. 180). The family's animal friends, included a "spitting llama.... Our most interesting visitor was a bull-kudu" (p. 181). When the children took walks, "their chaperon ... was a bulldog-Jumbo" (p. 182).

The year 1902 marked the end of the Boer War and was also the year of Rhodes's death. Kipling had frequently visited Rhodes's bedside until his death in March of that year and wrote an elegy for Rhodes's private burial. Kipling also later composed a poem for his memorial shrine. Kipling had worked with Rhodes to set up the Rhodes Scholarships for Oxford and had become one of the scholarship's trustees (Ricketts, 1999, p. 269). Despite Rhodes's death, the Kiplings would continue their stays at the Woolsack until 1908.

Back in England, the Kiplings moved into Batemans, their new home in Sussex.

Kipling lived here until his death. The Kiplings found Batemans's "spirit—her Feng shui—to be good. We went through every room and found no shadow of ancient regrets, stifled miseries, nor any menace" (Kipling, 1937, p. 193). Kipling enjoyed "a settled way of life in Sussex, a home of his own with seclusion and privacy" (Carrington, 1955, p. 287). Kipling was devoted to his children, an aspect of his life that has often been overlooked (Ricketts, 1999, p. 295). He was a "sensitive and loving father to Elsie and John. This is the Kipling one constantly encounters in over 200 letters to them" (Ricketts, 1999, p. 295).

Kipling produced some of his most popular writings during this time. The whimsical *Just So Stories,* published in September 1902, featured Kipling's wry sense of humor, imagination, and playfulness. Each story is addressed to "My Best Beloved," written for Josephine during her lifetime, but references to the Best Beloved continued even after her death. The opening of "How the Whale Got Its Throat" typifies his delightful style:

> In The Sea, once upon a time, O my best Beloved, there was a whale, and he ate fishes. He ate the starfish and the garfish, and the crab and the dab, and the plaice and the dace, and the skate and his mate, and the mackereel and the pickereel, and the really truly twirly-whirly eel. All the fishes he could find in the sea he ate with his mouth-so! Till at last there was only one small fish left in the sea, and he was a small "Stute fish." (Kipling, 1902, p. 1)

Puck of Pooh's Hill was published in 1906 and was part of a series of stories Kipling wrote over five years, which included *Rewards and Fairies,* published in 1910 (Carrington, 1955). This latter book included the poem "If," "probably still the most famous poem in English" (Ricketts, 1999, p. 293). Kipling (1937) commented that the verse "'If,'... escaped from the book, and for a while ran about the world" (pp. 205–206).

These stories had a historical focus, involving interactions between Puck and two children, who would meet with characters from English history. Kipling also wrote some science fiction. *Night Mail* told of an airplane crossing the Atlantic Ocean in 2000; in 1907, he wrote "As Easy as A.B.C," about broadcasting techniques, which he predicted "with uncanny accuracy" (Carrington, 1955, p. 291).

The beginning of the 20th century, as Kipling was losing popularity as a writer in England, "coincided with the publication of some of his greatest work... [such as the] *Just* So *Stories*" (Ricketts, 1999, p. 286). In the meantime, his reputation was growing in Europe, especially in France. He also received honorary degrees and other awards. At Oxford, he walked in the academic procession with Mark Twain, writing to his son John that he and "Twain and a couple of other honourands sneaked out 'like naughty boys' for a smoke 'under a big archway'" (p. 284).

In 1907, Kipling became the first Englishman to be awarded the Nobel Prize in Literature. "It was a very great honour, in all ways unexpected" (Kipling, 1937, p. 216). He was offered a knighthood, on several occasions, which he would decline, usually stating that "he did not want his independence compromised" (Ricketts, 1999, p. 262).

Elsie. As his daughter Elsie grew older, Kipling often discussed his work with her, and occasionally they collaborated (Ricketts, 1999, p. 296). She married Captain George Bambridge on October 22, 1924. The Kiplings liked him but were unhappy about losing Elsie. Kipling wrote to her twice a week. "His love for Elsie and his pride in her were everywhere apparent in the zest of these letters" (Ricketts, 1999, p. 349).

John

Kipling loved John and was supportive of him throughout his young life, which ended when he was killed in World War I at 18. After his death, Kipling's work and writings often commemorated his memory. As a child, John had had poor eyesight, was not a good student, and had progressed slowly. Kipling did not pressure him to achieve, "never saddling him with unrealistic expectations. Indeed, his pleasure at John's small successes, usually at sport, are rather touching" (Ricketts, 1999, p. 301).

John wished to join the navy, but because of his poor eyesight, he was rejected from the navy and later by the army. However, learning that John would be eligible to apply for a commission as an officer in the army, Kipling, using his influence, arranged for him to be commissioned in the Irish Guards (Ricketts, 1999). Ricketts observed that although Kipling was "proud of his son's eagerness to join up, there is nothing to suggest that Kipling put any pressure on the already military-minded John" (p. 314). That said, John may have internalized Kipling's values about patriotism and the military.

Extended Family. Kipling remained involved with his extended family. The years 1906–1910 saw a number of deaths: "Uncle" Crom, as they affectionately called Cornell Price, the headmaster at Westward Ho!, died in 1910, and a few months later, both of Kipling's parents died. Alice died first, of heart failure; Rudyard and Trix were with her. Trix immediately had another breakdown: "Lockwood was almost at the end of his tether, as he tried to find a[n] experienced nurse" (Ricketts, 1999, p. 303). Lockwood blamed her husband, whom Lockwood claimed "'would give a brass monkey depression'" (p. 303). Losing

Alice was very painful for him, and he died shortly afterward from a heart attack.

Politics and World War I

Kipling remained "committed to the development of his other family, the Empire" (Ricketts, 1999, p. 303), and as World War I approached, he gave political and recruiting speeches. All the while, he was continually anxious about John.

On September 27, 1915, the Kiplings learned by telegram that John, wounded in battle, was reported missing. His body was not found, and no details were available. Distraught, Kipling made every effort to learn what had happened. "By early November, Kipling himself seemed to have accepted the fact that John was dead" (Ricketts, 1999, p. 326). Carrie continued to hope. Rudyard and Carrie then concentrated on locating his grave; Rudyard became a member of the War Graves Commission in 1917.

"'I'm as busy as the Devil in a gale of wind at all sorts of jobs that don't seem to matter much,' Kipling told Dunsterville in July 1919. 'Nothing matters much really when one has lost one's only son'" (Ricketts, 1999, p. 341). He was absorbed in writing his two-volume history of the Irish Guards, John's unit, and for all his despair this did mean something. He felt that "'this will be my great work'" (Ricketts, 1999, p. 341).

When the Armistice was declared, Carrie wrote in her diary: "'A world to be remade without a son'" (Ricketts, 1999, p. 340). After the war, Kipling became more bitter and angry and strongly opposed to Germany. He was upset with the rise of Hitler and strongly opposed the Bolshevists. Although not anti-Semitic before the war, he became increasingly so and was highly critical of Einstein, "'a Hebrew'" (Ricketts, 1999, p, 351).

Kipling's Health

John's death left Rudyard physically and emotionally devastated. Rider Haggard, his longtime friend, wrote in March 1917 that "'Kipling looked far from well.... Since [John's death] happened he has changed greatly'" (Dillingham, 2008, p. 79). A year later Haggard saw little improvement. Kipling's health problems increased from 1920 to 1922: He had many gastrointestinal complaints and suffered severe pain. He consulted specialists and tried diets and remedies with no success (Ricketts, 1999). Kipling explained that his "'inside cupboards... [were] disarranged'" (Ricketts, 1999, p. 345). Carrie's diary frequently referred to him in pain or as having a bad night. He had one unsuccessful operation in 1922, followed by a difficult recovery. In 1921, all his teeth were removed. Finally in 1933, in Paris, a definitive diagnosis of "duodenal ulcer" was made, but by then he was too much at risk for surgery (Ricketts, 1999).

Carrie had the major responsibility for caring for Rudyard, which was tiring. Carrie also had health problems; she was diagnosed with diabetes in 1928 (Ricketts, 1999). When the Kiplings took vacation trips, Bath was often included on the itinerary so that Carrie could take the cure.

Social Life

After the war, Rudyard and Carrie thought of some of their friends' and relatives' children as "surrogate children" (Ricketts, 1999, p. 349). Kipling took a special interest in Crom Price's children and contributed to their support. His young friends would remember him as "enthusiastic, sympathetic, and fun" (Ricketts, 1999, p. 358).

Kipling made some new friends and remained deeply involved with his longstanding friends, Dunsterville, Haggard, and H. A. Gwynne, a well-known British journalist, as well as his relatives. He kept in touch with a wide group of friends from different countries and was a frequent guest at gatherings of the royal family. Kipling "wrote several Christmas broadcasts for George V in the early 1930's" (Ricketts, 1999, p. 371). Kipling often spent time at his clubs: "His favourite was the Beefsteak" (p. 361).

Death

On one trip, Kipling became ill in London at Brown's Hotel. He died January 18, 1936, of a "massive haemorrhage" from a perforated duodenum. It was his 44th wedding anniversary. His "death sent almost as many shock waves round the world as his near-fatal illness had done in 1899" (Ricketts, 1999, p. 388). Kipling was cremated at Golders Green. The funeral was held January 23, 1936, at Westminster Abbey. Pallbearers included Stanley Baldwin, the Prime Minister. The recessional was sung, and Kipling was buried in the Poet's Corner, between Charles Dickens and Thomas Hardy.

Conclusion

Rudyard Kipling achieved international fame as a writer and had a stable, happy family life and loyal friends. But as a child inventing his imaginary games in the Holloways' damp basement, would he have predicted this future? Kipling's "abandonment" by his parents and his mistreatment by Mrs. Holloway could have shaped a disastrous adulthood. However, he was resilient, creative, and undeterred by adversity. Storr (1988) has observed that trying circumstances that Kipling and other writers experience foster the development of their "creative imagination . . . [which in turn] can exercise a healing function" (p. 123).

There were many factors contributing to Kipling's capacity to adapt. In the first six years of his life, his basic positive self-regard and confidence developed through the bonds of attachment with his ayah, Meeta, and his parents. Other significant relationships included those with Captain Holloway and Aunt Georgie, his "lifesaver." His relationship with Trix "helped strengthen Kipling's masculinity and also his identity. Toward her he was able to feel and act like the protective parent that both so needed" (Shengold, 1981, p. 247). Reading and imaginative play were restorative, opened up new worlds, and were shared with each other. Kipling's recruitment capacities attracted people to him; relationships were a source of pleasure, not a threat to avoid.

In Kipling's life, however, his early traumatic experiences did not vanish; they went underground, sometimes intruding, as they often did at night. When under stress, problems with his eyes and migraines returned. He referred to having breakdowns, but there is insufficient evidence to evaluate their nature. Kipling wrote about these breakdowns in a letter: "This is the third time it has happened . . .

but this time is the completest … I can do nothing to save myself from breaking up now and again" (Ricketts, 1999, p. 158). As has often been noted, resilience and vulnerability are not an either-or. We find in Kipling's life course the coexistence of both.

CHAPTER 11

Summing Up

One lovely summer afternoon, several years ago, I was walking down a country road in England when I saw an elderly woman walking in the opposite direction. We passed each other and not a word was spoken. She must live in this countryside, I decided. She has probably lived here her whole life. From time to time, her image floats through my mind. What is her story? I will never know—but I would like to. I would guess that her life was "ordinary," with nothing especially spectacular to narrate. But the life she lived could not have been ordinary to her. And if we were to listen to her story, we might see beyond its daily routines and learn about her experiences, her insights, her feelings, and come to know her spirit.

In a book review, Susan Dunn (2013) discussed Jill Lepore's (2013) biography, *Book of Ages: The life and Opinions of Jane Franklin*. Jane Franklin, the sister of Benjamin Franklin, led a quiet life, far from the center of the major current events. Lepore highlighted "the importance of the ordinary," and cited Virginia Woolf on the subject: "'Is not anyone who has lived life, and left a record of that life... worthy of biography—the failures as well as the successes, the humble as well as the illustrious?'"

Biographers have the task of bringing their subjects (whether "significant" or "insignificant") authentically to life for the reader. In a parallel manner, clinicians also must construct authentic portraits of individuals and the process of their collaboration.

Biographies are the stories of lives, whether written by biographers or elicited by clinicians. Parallel activities take place behind the scenes for both, as both are engaged in similar psychological and intellectual processes. Both are emotionally involved in this work, and their subjectivity colors their activities. As noted earlier, Backscheider (1999) asserted that the "presence of the writer [exists] in every biography" (p. 118), sometimes fully acknowledged and openly discussed, sometimes concealed beneath the surface. In choosing a subject or deciding to work with a particular client, the biographer or the clinician is already shaping the biographical or clinical narrative.

The following four major processes that influence both undertakings have been discussed extensively throughout this book. Biographers and clinicians (1) develop relationships with subjects and clients; (2) examine how subjects or clients represent themselves and how they present their stories; (3) collect, evaluate, and interpret evidence; and (4) formulate a biopsychosocial understanding of their life course.

In terms of the life course perspective, biographers are able to present the evolution of subjects over their entire life span. This is a privilege not available to clinicians. The reading of biographical works allows clinicians to follow the developmental progress and the ups and downs of subjects' lives, with their transitions and turning points.

Why read biographies? As noted earlier, Conway (1998) observed that "we *want* to know how the world looks from inside another person's experience, and when that craving is met by a convincing narrative, we find it deeply satisfying."

Biographies are a source of pleasure as well as knowledge and learning to all who love them, whether in their professional or private lives. Reflecting on the processes behind the scenes of their creation can add greater depth of understanding and enjoyment.

References

Acocella, J. (2003, December 8). A fire in the brain: The difficulties of being James Joyce's daughter. *New Yorker,* pp. 128–134.

Akhtar, S. (1995). A third individuation: Immigration, identity and the psychoanalytic process. *Journal of the American Psychoanalytic Association,* 43, 1051–1084.

Allingham, M. (1988). *Dancers in mourning.* New York: Penguin Books.

Amis, K. (1986). *Rudyard Kipling and his world.* London: Thames & Hudson.

Angelou, M. (1997). *I know why the caged bird sings.* New York: Bantam Books.

Applegate, J.S., & Bonovitz, J.M. (1995). *The facilitating partnership: A Winnicottian approach for social workers and other helping professionals.* Northvale, NJ: Jason Aronson.

Backscheider, P.R. (1999). *Reflections on biography.* New York: Oxford University Press.

Barbour, J.D. (1992). *The conscience of the autobiographer: Ethical and religious dimensions of autobiography.* London: Macmillan.

Baker, M. (1978). *Doyle Diary: Last Great Conan Doyle Mystery.* Paddington Press, Ltd. New York & London.

Baron, S.H., & Pietsch, C. (Eds.). *Introspection in biography: The biographer's quest for self-awareness.* Hillsdale, NJ: Analytic Press.

Barstow, D. (2009, April 12). Heir to a sad literary legacy adds a new chapter of grief. *The New York Times*, pp. Al, A16.

Barton, A. (2002, December 19). Byron: The poetry of it all. *New York Review of Books*, 49, 8–10, 14.

Beaucar, K.O. (1999). Grandparent caregivers face hurdles. *NASW News*, 44(10), 12.

Beers, C.W (1925). *A mind that found itself* (Rev. ed.). Garden City, NY: Doubleday, Page. (Original work published 1908).

Belsky, J. (2005). Attachment theory and research in ecological perspective: Insights from the Pennsylvania Infant and Family Development Project and the NICHD Study of Early Child Care. In K.E. Grossmann, K. Grossmann, & E. Waters (Eds.), *Attachment from infancy to adulthood: The major longitudinal studies* (pp. 71–97). New York: Guilford Press.

Beveridge, A. (2006). What became of Arthur Conan Doyle's father? The last years of Charles Altamont Doyle. *Journal of the Royal College of Physicians of Edinburgh*, 36, 264–270.

Bloland, S.E. (1999). Fame: The power and cost of a fantasy. *Atlantic Monthly*, 284, 51–62.

Bios, P. (1962). *On adolescence: A psychoanalytic interpretation*. New York: Free Press.

Blume, S.B. (1992). Compulsive gambling: Addiction without drugs. *Harvard Mental Health Letter*, 8(8),4–5.

Booth, M. (1997). *The doctor, the detective and Arthur Conan Doyle: A biography of Arthur Conan Doyle*. London: Hodder & Stoughton.

Brandell, J.R. (2004). *Psychodynamic social work*. New York: Columbia University Press.

Brockmeier, J. (2001). From the end to the beginning: Retrospective teleology in autobiography. In J. Brockmeier & D. Carbaugh

(Eds.), *Narrative and identity: Studies in autobiography, self and culture* (pp. 247–280). Amsterdam: John Benjamins.

Brockmeier, J., & Carbaugh, D. (2001). Introduction. In J. Brockmeier & D. Carbaugh (Eds.), *Narrative and identity: Studies in autobiography, self and culture* (pp. 1–22). Amsterdam: John Benjamins.

Brockmeier, J., & Harre, R.(2001). Narrative: Problems and promises of an alternative paradigm. In J. Brockmeier & D. Carbaugh (Eds.), *Narrative and identity: Studies in autobiography, self and culture* (pp. 39–58). Amsterdam: John Benjamins.

Brontë, C. (1847). *Jane Eyre.* Retrieved from http://uniteddigitalbooks.com/Books/Jane%20Eyre.pdf

Brontë, C. (1864). *Jane Eyre.* Retrieved from http://books.google.com/books/about/Jane_Eyre.html?id=Lsmgaaaaqaaj

Brontë, C. (1893). *Villette.* Retrieved from books.google.com/books?id=fuwyAQAAMAAJ

Brooks, P. (1984). *Reading for the plot: Design and intention in narrative.* Cambridge, MA: Harvard University Press.

Brown, E.M. (1998). The transmission of trauma through caretaking patterns of behavior in Holocaust families: Re-enactments in a facilitated long-term second-generation group. *Smith College Studies in Social Work, 68,* 267–285.

Bruner, J. (2001). Self-making and world-making. In J. Brockmeier & D. Carbaugh (Eds.), *Narrative and identity: Studies in autobiography, self and culture* (pp. 25–37). Amsterdam: John Benjamins.

Burnette, D. (1999). Custodial grandparents in Latino families: Patterns of service use and predictors of unmet needs. *Social Work, 44,* 22–34.

Campbell, R.J. (1989). *Psychiatric dictionary* (6th ed). New York: Oxford University Press.

Carbaugh, D. (2001). "The people will come to you": Blackfeet narrative as a resource for contemporary living. In J. Brockmeier & D. Carbaugh (Eds.), *Narrative and identity: Studies in autobiography, self and culture* (pp. 39–58). Amsterdam/Philadelphia: John Benjamins.

Caro, R. (1983). *The years of Lyndon Johnson: The path to power.* New York:

Vintage Books.

Carrington, C.E. (1955). *The life of Rudyard Kipling.* Garden City, NY: Doubleday.

Ceconi, B., & Urdang, E. (1994). Sight or insight? Child therapy with a blind clinician. *Clinical Social Work Journal, 22,* 179–192.

Chabon, M. (2005, February 10). Inventing Sherlock Holmes. *New York Review of Books, 52,* 7–18.

Challener, D.D. (1997). *Stories of resilience in childhood.* New York: Garland Publishing.

Clemit, P. (2005). Self-analysis as social critique: The autobiographical writings of Godwin and Rousseau. *Romanticism, 11,* 161–180.

Cohen, M.N. (1996). *Lewis Carroll: A biography.* New York: Vintage Books. Cole, S. A. (2006). Building secure relationships: Attachment in kin and unrelated foster caregiver-infant relationships. *Families in Society, 87,* 497–508.

Coleman, D.J. (1999). Narrative performance mode (NPM) of discourse. In A. J. Solnit, P.B. Neubauer, S. Abrams, & A.S. Dowling (Eds.), *The psychoanalytic study of the child.* (Vol. 54, pp. 233–258). New Haven, CT: Yale University Press.

Conway, J. K. (1998). *When memory speaks: Reflections on autobiography.* New York: Alfred A. Knopf.

Dalsimer, K. (1982). Female adolescent development: A study of The Diary of Anne Frank. In A.J. Solnit, R.S. Eissler, A. Freud, &

P. B. Neubauer (Eds.), *The psychoanalytic study of the child* (Vol. 37, pp. 487–522). New Haven, CT: Yale University Press.

DeLaCour, E. (1996). The interpersonal school and its influence on current relational theories. In J. Berzoff, L. M. Flanagan, & P. Hertz (Eds.), *Inside out and outside in: Psychodynamic clinical theory and practice in contemporary multicultural contexts* (pp. 199–219). Northvale, NJ: Jason Aronson.

Diamond, J. (2002). *Narrative means to sober ends: Treating addiction and its aftermath.* New York: Guilford Press.

Diaz de Chumaceiro, C. (2005). A note on Rudyard Kipling's loss of brother John: "Little Tobrah." *PSYART: A Hyperlink Journal for the Psychological Study of the Arts.* Retrieved from http://www. psyartjournal.com/article/show/ de_chumaceiro-a_note_on_ rudyard_kiplings_loss_of_broth

Diaz de Chumaceiro, C.L. (2009). On Rudyard Kipling's loss of Ayah. *PSYART: A Hyperlink Journal for the Psychological Study of the Arts.* Retrieved from https://psyartjournal.com/article/show/ de_chumaceiro-on_rudyard_kiplings_loss_of_ayah

Diedrich, M. (1999). *Love across color lines: Ottilie Assing and Frederick Douglass.* New York: Hill and Wang.

Dillingham, W.B. (2008). *Being Kipling.* New York: Palgrave Macmillan.

Doka, K.J. (1989). Disenfranchised grief. In K.J. Doka (Ed.), *Disenfranchised grief: Recognizing hidden sorrow* (pp. 3–11). New York: Lexington Books.

Donadio, R. (2005, September 4). Literary letters, lost in cyberspace. *New York Times Book Review,* pp. 14–15.

Douglass, F. (1845). *Narrative of the Life of Frederick Douglass, an American slave.* Retrieved from http://www.gutenberg.org/ files/23/23-h/23-h.htm

Douglass, F. (1855). *My bondage and my freedom.* Retrieved from http://books.google.ca/books/about/My_bondage_and_my freedom.html?id=rakJAAAAIAAJ

Douglass, F. (1882). *Life and times of Frederick Douglass.* Retrieved from *http://* books.google.com/books/about/Life_and_Times_ of_Frederick_Douglass.html?id=fFTcLFXId-wC

Doyle, A.C. (1924). *Memories and adventures.* Boston: Little, Brown.

Dugan, T.F. (1989). Action and acting out: Variables in the development of resiliency in adolescence. In T.F. Dugan & R. Coles (Eds.), *The child in our times: Studies in the development of resiliency* (pp. 157–176). New York: Brunner/Mazel.

Dunn, D. (1908). English epical theory and the heroic poem. *Proceedings of the Royal Philosophical Society of Glasgow, 39,* 121–142. Retrieved from books.google.com/books?id=lJokAQAAIAAJ

Dunn, S. (2013, October 24). The other Franklin. *New York Review of Books, 60,* 26–28.

Du Plessix Gray, F. (2001). Loving and hating Simone Weil. *American Scholar, 70, 5–11.*

Edelson, M. 1993. Telling and enacting stories in psychoanalysis and psychotherapy. In A.J. Solnit, P.B. Neubauer, S. Abrams, & A.S. Dowling (Eds.), *The psychoanalytic study of the child* (Vol. 48, pp. 293–325). New Haven, CT: Yale University Press.

Elms, A.C. (1994). *Uncovering lives: The uneasy alliance of biography and psychology.* New York: Oxford University Press.

Elms, A.C. (2005a). Freud as Leonardo: Why the first psychobiography went wrong. In W.T. Schultz (Ed.), *Handbook of psycho biography* (pp. 210–221). New York: Oxford University Press.

Elms, A.C., & Song, A.V. (2005). Alive and kicking: The problematics of political psychobiography. In W.T. Schultz (Ed.), *Handbook of psychobiography* (pp. 301–310). New York: Oxford University Press.

Fadiman, A. (1997). *The spirit catches you and you fall down: A Hmong child, her American doctors and the collision of two cultures.* New York: Farrar, Straus & Giroux.

Fenton, J. (2003, February 13). Turgenev's banana. *New York Review of Books*, 50, 45–48.

Flanders, J. (2001). *A circle of sisters: Alice Kipling, Georgiana Burne-Jones, Agnes Poynter, and Louisa Baldwin.* New York: W. W. Norton.

Fleming, A.M. (1939, March). Some childhood memories of Rudyard Kipling. *Chambers Journal,* 91, 168–173.

Fleming, A.M. (1947). My brother Rudyard Kipling [Transcript, recorded April 17, 1947; broadcast April 19, 1947). College Station: Cushing Memorial Library and Archives, Texas A&M University.

Frank, A.W. (1995). *The wounded storyteller: Body, illness, and ethics.* Chicago: University of Chicago Press.

Franklin, R. (2004, October 4). God in the details. *New Yorker,* pp. 100–104. Fraser, R. (1988). *The Brontës: Charlotte Brontë and her family.* New York: Fawcett Columbine.

Freeman, M. (2001). From substance to story: Narrative, identity, and the reconstruction of the self. In J. Brockmeier & D. Carbaugh (Eds.), *Narrative and identity: Studies in autobiography, self and culture* (pp. 283–298). Amsterdam: John Benjamins.

Freeman, M., & Brockmeier, J. (2001). Narrative integrity: Autobiographical identity and the meaning of the "good life." In J. Brockmeier & D. Carbaugh (Eds.), *Narrative and identity: Studies in autobiography, self and culture* (pp. 75–99). Amsterdam: John Benjamins.

Freeman, E. M., & Couchonnal, G. (2006). Narrative and culturally based approaches in practice with families. Families in Society, 87, 198-208.

Garner, D. (2011, April 20). Recalling childhood as a Styron. *New York Times,* pp. Cl, C4.

Gaskell, E.C. (1857). *The life of Charlotte Brontë.* New York: D. Appleton. Gaskell, E. C. (1870). *The life of Charlotte Brontë.* Retrieved from books.google.com/books?id=6BUvAAAAYAAJ

Gaskell, E.C. (1896). *The life of Charlotte Brontë.* Retrieved from books.google.com/books?id=lShQQbjOBG4C

Gates, H.L., Jr. (1996). Chronology: Note on the texts. In F. Douglass, *Autobiographies* (pp. 1047-1082). New York: Penguin Press.

Gay, P. (1988). *Freud: A life for our time.* New York: W. W. Norton.

Gediman, H.K., & Lieberman, J.S. (1996). *The many faces of deceit: Omissions, lies, and disguise in psychotherapy.* Northvale NJ: Jason Aronson.

Germain, C. (1991). *Human behavior in the social environment.* New York: Columbia University Press.

Giovacchini, P. (1993). Absolute and not quite absolute dependence. In D. Goldman (Ed.), *In one's bones: The clinical genius of Winnicott* (pp. 241–256). Northvale, NJ: Jason Aronson.

Glendinning, V. (1999). *Jonathan Swift.* London: Pimlico.

Gopnik, A. (2008, December 8). Man of fetters: Dr. Johnson and Mrs. Thrale. *New Yorker,* pp. 90–96.

Gopnik, A. (2010, January 4). Van Gogh's ear: The Christmas eve that changed modern art. *New Yorker,* pp. 48–55.

Grann, D. (2004, November 13). Mysterious circumstances: The strange death of a Sherlock Holmes fanatic. *New Yorker,* pp. 58–73.

Grossman, L. (2006, January 23). The trouble with memoirs. *Time Magazine, 167,* 58–61.

Hamilton, N. (2007). *Biography: A brief history.* Cambridge, MA: Harvard University Press.

Harre, R. (2001). Metaphysics and narrative: Singularities and multiplicities of self. In J. Brockmeier & D. Carbaugh (Eds.), *Narrative and identity: Studies in autobiography, self and culture* (pp. 59–73). Amsterdam: John Benjamins.

Hartmann, H. (1958). *Ego psychology and the problem of adaptation.* New York: International Universities Press.

Herrmann, D. (1998). *Helen Keller: A life.* Chicago: University of Chicago Press.

Hill, E. (1936, April). The young Kipling. *Atlantic Monthly, 157,* 406–415.

Hinchman, L.P., & Hinchman, S.K. (1997). *Memory, identity and community: The idea of narrative in the human sciences.* Albany: State University of New York Press.

Hogan, L. (2001). *The woman who watches over the world: A native memoir.* New York: W. W. Norton.

Hollingsworth, L.D. (1998). Promoting same-race adoption for children of color. *Social Work, 43,* 104–116.

Holmes, R. (1985). *Footsteps: Adventures of a romantic biographer.* New York: Vintage Books. Holmes, R. (2000). *Sidetracks: Explorations of a romantic biographer.* New York: Vintage Books.

Holroyd, M. (1994). *Lytton Strachey: A critical biography.* London: Chatto and Windus.

Holroyd, M. (2002). *Works on paper: The craft of biography and autobiography.* Washington, DC: Counterpoint.

Hutchison, E.D. (2005). The life course perspective: A promising approach for bridging the micro and macro worlds for social workers. *Families in Society, 86,* 143–152.

Ingram, R.E., & Fortier, M. (2001). The nature of adult vulnerability: History and definitions. In R.E. Ingram & J.M. Price (Eds.), *Vulnerability to psychopathology: Risk across the lifespan* (pp. 39–56). New York: Guilford Press.

Ingram, R.E., & Price, J.M. (2001). The role of vulnerability in understanding psychopathology. In R.E. Ingram & J. M. Price (Eds.), *Vulnerability to psychopathology: Risk across the lifespan* (pp. 3–19). New York: Guilford Press.

Isaacson, K. (2005). Divide and multiply: Comparative theory and methodology in multiple case psychobiography. In W.T. Schultz (Ed.), *Handbook of psychobiography* (pp. 104–111). New York: Oxford University Press.

Isaacson, W. (2011, October 17). American icon. *Time Magazine.* Retrieved from http://www.time.comitime/magazine/article/0,9171.2096327,00.html

Jamison, K.R. (1996). *An unquiet mind: A memoir of moods and madness.* New York: Vintage Books.

Jarrett. D. (1999, March 18). The doctor's prescription. *New York Review of Books, 46,* 39–42.

Jones, R. (2008, July 31). Collective memory. *Time Magazine.* Retrieved from *http://* www.time.com/time/magazine/article/0.9171.1828314,00.html

Josselson, R. (1995). Narrative and psychological understanding. *Psychiatry, 580,* 330–343.

Kaplan, H., Sadock, B., & Grebb, J. (1994). *Synopsis of psychiatry: Behavioral sciences/clinical psychiatry.* Baltimore: Williams and Wilkins.

Kaufmann, H., & Wildegans, R. (2008). *Van Goghs Ohr. Paul Gauguin und der Pakt des Schweigens.* Berlin: Osburg. [No English version]

Kegan, R. (1982). *The evolving self.* Cambridge, MA: Harvard University Press. Keillor, G. (2010, December 19). Riverboat rambler. *New York Times Book Review,* pp. 1, 6–7.

Kernberg, O. (1965). Notes on counter-transference. *Journal of American Psychoanalytic Association,* 13, 38–56.

Kinsley, M. (2008, March 17). An old story. *Time Magazine,* 171, 64.

Kipling, R. (1900). Baa-Baa black sheep. In *Wee Willie Winkle and other stories* (pp. 26–75). New York: Books, Inc.

Kipling, R. (1901). *Kim.* New York: Doubleday, Page.

Kipling, R. (1902) *Just so stories for little children.* Toronto: George S. Morang.

Kipling, R. (1937). *Something of myself: For my friends known and unknown.* New York: Doubleday, Doran.

Kohut, H. (1971). *The analysis of the self: A systematic approach to the psychoanalytic treatment of narcissistic personality disorders. The psychoanalytic study of the child* (Monograph no. 4). New York: International Universities Press.

Krupat, A. (1985). *For those who come after: A study of Native American autobiography.* Berkeley: University of California Press.

Lacayo, R. (2011, October 31). The stranger: A new look at van Gogh's life-and death. *Time Magazine,* 178, 66.

Lane, A. (2004, April 19 & 26). Beyond a joke: The perils of loving P. G. Wodehouse. *New Yorker,* pp. 138–149.

Lee, H. (2001, April 12). Tracking the untrackable. *New York Review of Books,* 48, 53–57.

Lee, H. (2005). *Virginia Woolfs nose: Essays on biography.* Princeton, NJ: Princeton University Press.

Lee, M., & Greene, G. J. (1999). A social constructivist framework for integrating cross-cultural issues in teaching clinical social work. *Journal of Social Work Education, 35,* 21–37.

Lepore, J. (2013). *Book of ages: The life and opinions of Jane Franklin.* New York: Alfred A. Knopf.

Levinson, D., & Levinson, J. (1996). *The seasons of a woman's life.* New York: Alfred A. Knopf.

Lichtenberg, J.D. (1985). Psychoanalysis and biography. In S.H. Baron & c. Pietsch (Eds.), *Introspection in biography: The biographer's quest for self-awareness* (pp. 33–68). Hillsdale, NJ: Analytic Press.

Longres, J.E. (1995). Human behavior in the social environment. Itasca, IL: F. E. Peacock Publishers.

Lycett, A. (2007). *The man who created Sherlock Holmes: The life and times of Sir Arthur Conan Doyle.* New York: Free Press.

MacGregor, P. (1994). Grief: The unrecognized parental response to mental illness in a child. *Social Work, 39,* 160–166.

Mack, J. E., & Hickler, H. (1981). *Vivienne: The life and suicide of an adolescent girl.* New York: New American Library.

Mahler, M., Pine, E, & Bergman, A. (1975). *The psychological birth of the human infant.* New York: Basic Books.

Mahoney, M.J. 2003. *Constructive psychotherapy: A practical guide.* New York: Guilford Press.

Malcolm, J. (2003, June 2). Gertrude Stein's war. *New Yorker,* pp. 58–81.

Maluccio, A. N. (1980). Promoting competence through life experiences. In C.B. Germain & A. Gitterman (Eds.), *The life model of social work practice* (pp. 282–302). New York: Columbia University Press.

Maluccio, A.N. (2006). The nature and scope of the problem. In N.B. Webb (Ed.), *Working with traumatized youth in child welfare* (pp. 3–12). New York: Guilford Press.

Mankoff, R. (2007, December 10). Cartoon. *New Yorker Magazine, 38,* 92.

Mason, P. (1975). *Kipling: The glass, the shadow and the fire.* New York: Harper & Row.

McAdams, D.P., Josselson, R., & Lieblich, A. (2001). Turns in the road: Introduction to the volume. In D.P. McAdams, R. Josselson, & A. Lieblich (Eds.), *Turns in the road: Narrative studies of lives in transition* (pp. xv–xxi). Washington, DC: American Psychological Association.

McCarthy. M. (1957). *Memories of a Catholic girlhood.* New York: Harcourt, Brace. McCourt, F. (1996). *Angela's ashes: A memoir of childhood.* London: HarperCollins. McFeely, W. S. (1991). *Frederick Douglass.* New York: Norton.

McGrath, C. (2001, August 19). Boswell's presumptuous task. *The New York Times Book Review,* pp. 12–13.

Mehta, V. (1979). *Daddyji.* Oxford, United Kingdom: Oxford University Press.

Mehta, V. (1984). *The ledge between the streams.* New York: W W. Norton.

Mehta, V. (1987a). *Sound–shadows of the new world.* New York: W. W. Norton.

Mehta, V. (1987b). *Vedi.* New York: W. W. Norton.

Mehta, V. (1988). *Mamaji.* New York: W. W. Norton.

Mehta, V. (2001). *All for love.* New York: Thunder's Mouth Press/ Nation Books.

Mehta, V. (2003). *Dark Harbor: Building house and home on an enchanted island.* New York: Thunder's Mouth Press/Nation Books.

Mehta, V. (2004). *The red letters: My father's enchanted period.* New York: Thunder's Mouth Press/Nation Books.

Mendelsohn, D. (2010, January 25). But enough about me. *New Yorker,* pp. 68–74. Merkin, D. (2009, December 20). The aspirational woman. *New York Times Magazine,* pp. 30–37, 44, 46.

Mercer, S.O., & Perdue, J.D. (1993). Munchausen syndrome by proxy: Social work's role. *Social Work, 38,* 74–81.

Miller, L. (2001). *The Brontë myth.* New York: Alfred A. Knopf.

Mishra, P. (2004, March 25). The first citizen of India. *New York Review of Books, 51,* 11–13.

Mitchell, S. (1988). *Relational concepts in psychoanalysis.* Cambridge, MA: Harvard University Press.

Moffat, W. (2010). *A Great unrecorded history: A new life of E. M. Forster.* New York: Farrar, Straus & Giroux.

Moraitis, G. (2003). The ghost in the biographer's machine. In J. A. Winer & J.W. Anderson (Eds.), *The annual of psychoanalysis: Vol. 31. Psychoanalysis and history* (pp. 97–106). Hillsdale, NJ: Analytic Press.

Mortimer, J.T., Finch, M.D., & Kumka, D. (1982). Persistence and change in development: The multidimensional self-concept. In P.B. Baltes & O.G. Brim, Jr. (Eds.), *Life-span development and behavior* (Vol. 4, pp. 263–308). New York: Academic Press.

Northcut, T.B. (1999). Integrating psychodynamic and cognitive-behavioral theory: A psychodynamic perspective. In T.B. Northcut & N.R. Heller (Eds.), *Enhancing psychodynamic therapy with cognitive-behavioral techniques* (pp. 17–51). Northvale, NJ: Jason Aronson.

Northcut, T.B., & Heller, N.R. (2002). The slippery slope of constructivism. *Smith College Studies in Social Work,* 72, 217–229.

Nuland, S.B. (2003). *Lost in America: A journey with my father.* New York: Alfred A. Knopf.

O'Hagan, A. (2009, October 8). The powers of Doctor Johnson. *New York Review of Books,* 56, 6–8, 10.

Olkin, R. (1999). *What psychotherapists should know about disability.* New York: Guilford Press.

Olney, J. (1998). *Memory and narrative: The weave of life-writing.* Chicago: University of Chicago Press.

Ornstein, E.D., & Ganzer, C. (2005). Relational social work: A model for the future. *Families in Society: The Journal of Contemporary Social Services,* 86, 565–572.

Ozick, C. (2003, June 16). What Helen Keller saw: The making of a writer. *New Yorker,* 79, 188–193.

Pachter, M. (1985). The biographer himself: An introduction. In M. Pachter (Ed.), *Telling lives: The biographer's art* (pp. 2–15). Philadelphia: University of Pennsylvania Press.

Pawel, E. (1988). *The nightmare of reason: A life of Franz Kafka.* London: Collins Harvill.

Peters, M. (1986). *Unquiet soul: A biography of Charlotte Brontë.* New York: Atheneum.

Phillips, A. (2011, November 13). A swell life. *New York Times Book Review,* pp. 8–9.

Poniewozik, J. (2009, November 30). Tuned in. *Time Magazine,* 174, 28.

Rayfield, D. (1997). *Anton Chekhov: A life.* New York: Henry Holt.

Reamer, F.G. (2008). Social workers' management of error: Ethical and risk management issues. *Families in Society: The Journal of Contemporary Human Services,* 89, 61–68.

Rees, W.D. (1975). The bereaved and their hallucinations. In B. Schoenberg, I. Gerber, A. Wiener, A. H. Kutscher, D. Peretz, & A.C. Carr (Eds.), *Bereavement: Its psychosocial aspects* (pp. 66–71). New York: Columbia University Press.

Ricketts, H. (1999). *Rudyard Kipling: A life.* New York: Carroll & Graf.

Rodin, A.E., & Key, J.D. (1984). *Medical casebook of Doctor Arthur Conan Doyle: From practitioner to Sherlock Holmes and beyond.* Malabar, FL: Robert E. Krieger.

Rose, P. (1984). *Parallel lives: Five Victorian marriages.* New York: Vintage Books.

Runyan, W. (1982). *Life histories and psycho biography.* New York: Oxford Univerisity Press.

Runyan, W.M. (2005a). Evolving conceptions of psycho biography and the study of lives: Encounters with psychoanalysis, personality psychology, and historical science. In W.T. Schultz (Ed.), *Handbook of psychobiography* (pp. 19–41). New York: Oxford University Press.

Runyan, W.M. (2005b). How to critically evaluate alternative explanations of life events: The case of Van Gogh's ear. In W.T. Schultz (Ed.), *Handbook of psychobiography* (pp. 96–103). New York: Oxford University Press.

Sadock, B. J. and V.A. Sadock (2003). *Kaplan & Sadoch's Synopsis of psychiatry: Behavioral sciences/Clinical psychiatry,* 9th ed. Philadelphia, Lippincott Williams & Wilkins.

Schlossberg, N.K. (1981). A model for analyzing human adaptation to transition. *Counseling Psychologist, 9,* 2–18.

Scholes, R., Phelan, J., & Kellogg, R. (2006). *The nature of narrative* (40th anniversary ed.). New York: Oxford University Press.

Schultz, W.T. (2001). *De Profundis:* Prison as a turning point in Oscar Wilde's life story. In D. P. McAdams, R. Josselson, & A. Lieblich (Eds.), *Turns in the road: Narrative studies of lives in transition* (pp. 67–89). Washington, DC: American Psychological Association.

Schultz, W.T. (2005a). Diane Arbus's photographic autobiography: Theory and method revisited. In W. Schultz (Ed.), *Handbook of psychobiography* (pp. 112–141). New York: Oxford University Press.

Schultz, W.T. (2005b). How to strike psychological paydirt in biographical data. In W. Schultz (Ed.), *Handbook of psycho biography* (pp. 42–63). New York: Oxford University Press.

Schultz, W. T. (2005c). Introducing psychobiography. In W. Schultz (Ed.), *Handbook of psycho biography* (pp. 3–18). New York: Oxford University Press.

Scott-Stokes, H. (1974). *The life and death of Yukio Mishima.* New York: Farrar, Straus & Giroux.

Seiffge-Krenke, I., & Kirsch, H.S. (2002). The body in adolescent diaries: The case of Karen Horney. In A. J. Solnit, P.B. Neubauer, S. Abrams, & A.S. Dowling (Eds.), *The psychoanalytic study of the child* (Vol. 56, pp. 105–119). New Haven, CT: Yale University Press.

Seymour-Smith, M. (1989). *Rudyard Kipling: A biography.* New York: St. Martin's Press.

Shaffer, M.A., & Barrows, A. (2008). *The Guernsey literary and potato peel pie society.* New York: Dial Press.

Sheehan, G. (1946). Kipling and medicine: Neurological conditions. In *The new readers' guide to the works of Rudyard Kipling.* Retrieved from http://www.kipling.org.uk/rg_med_neurol.htm

Shengold, L. (1981). An attempt at soul murder: Rudyard Kipling's early life and work. In J.T. Coltera (Ed.), *Lives, events, and others players: Directions in psychobiography* (Downstate Psychoanalytic Institute Twenty-Fifth Anniversary Series, Vol. 4, pp. 203–251). New York: Jason Aronson.

Shenk, J.W (2005, July 4). The true Lincoln. *Time Magazine,* 166, 39–43. Shulevitz, J. (2003, April 20). Powers of perception. *The New York Times Book Review,* p. 731.

Silverman, K. (1991). *Edgar A. Poe: Mournful and never-ending remembrance.* New York: HarperCollins.

Spark, M. (1981). *Loitering with intent.* New York: New Directions.

Spence, D.P. (1986). Narrative smoothing and clinical wisdom. In T.R. Sarbin (Ed.), *Narrative psychology: The storied nature of human conduct* (pp. 211–232). Westport, CT: Praeger.

Spengemann, W. C. (1980). *The forms of autobiography: Episodes in the history of a literary genre.* New Haven, CT: Yale University Press.

Spira, M. (2006). [Review of the book *The past in the present: Using reminiscence in health and social care* by F. Gibson] *Clinical Social Work Journal* 34, 125–127.

Stashower, D. (1999). *Teller of tales: The life of Arthur Conan Doyle.* New York: Henry Holt.

Stern, D.N. (1985). *The interpersonal world of the infant: A view from psychoanalysis and developmental psychology.* New York: Basic Books.

Storr, A. (1988). *Solitude: A return to the self.* New York: Free Press.

Stroufe, L.A., Egeland, B., Carlson, E., & Collins, W.A. (2005). Placing early attachment experiences in developmental context: The Minnesota Longitudinal Study. In K.E. Grossmann, K. Grossmann, & E. Waters (Eds.), *Attachment from infancy to adulthood:*

The major longitudinal studies (pp. 48–40). New York: Hamilton Guilford Press.

Styron, A. (2007, December 10). Reading my father: A writer's triumphs and his torments. *New Yorker,* pp. 50–54, 57–58, 60.

Styron, W. (1990). *Darkness visible: A memoir of madness.* New York: Random House.

Sutton, A.L., & Liechty, D. (2004). Clinical practice with groups in end-of-life care. In J. Berzoff & P.R. Silverman (Eds.), *Living with dying: A handbook for end-of-life practitioners* (pp. 508–533). New York: Columbia University Press.

Taylor, K. (2011, January 23). The thorny path to a national black museum. *New York Times,* p. A1.

Thernstrom, M. (2004, April 18). The writing cure: Can understanding narrative make you a better doctor? *The New York Times Magazine,* pp. 42–47.

Tomalin, C. (2002). *Samuel Pepys: The unequalled self.* New York: Alfred A. Knopf.

Tomalin, C. (2007). *Thomas Hardy.* New York: Penguin Press.

Tuchman, B. W. (1979). Biography as a prism of history. In M. Pachter (Ed.), *Telling lives: The biographer's art* (pp. 133–147). Philadelphia: University of Pennsylvania Press.

Ulrich, L.T. (1991). *A midwife's tale: The life of Martha Ballard, based on her diary,* 1785–1812. New York: Vintage Books, A Division of Random House.

Urdang, E. (1991). The discipline of faculty advising. *Journal of Teaching in Social Work,* 5, 117–137.

Urdang, E. (1999). The video lab: Mirroring reflections of self and the other. *Clinical Supervisor,* 18, 143–164.

Urdang, E. (2002). *Human behavior and the social environment: Interweaving the inner and outer worlds.* New York: Haworth Press.

Urdang, E. (2008). *Human behavior and the social environment: Interweaving the inner and outer worlds* (2nd ed.). New York: Routledge.

Urdang, E. (2010). Awareness of self: A critical tool. *Social Work Education: The International Journal, 29,* 523–538.

Vaillant, G.E. (1993). *The wisdom of the ego.* Cambridge, MA: Harvard University Press.

Voneche, J. (2001). Identity and narrative in Piaget's autobiographies. In J. Brockmeier & D. Carbaugh (Eds.), *Narrative and identity: Studies in autobiography, self and culture* (pp. 187–217). Amsterdam: John Benjamins.

Vonnegut, M. (1975). *The Eden express: A personal account of schizophrenia.* New York: Praeger.

Wall, J.F. (1985). A second look at Andrew Carnegie. In SH. Baron & c. Pietsch (Eds.), *Introspection in biography: The biographer's quest for self-awareness* (pp. 209–224). Hillsdale, NJ: Analytic Press.

Wasser, E. (1966). *Casebook on work with the aging: ten cases from the Family Service Association of America project on aging.* New York: Family Service Association of America.

Watzlawick, P., Beavin, J.H., & Jackson, D.D. (1967). *Pragmatics of human communication: A study of interactional patterns, pathologies, and paradoxes.* New York: W.W. Norton.

Wayne, L. (2009, February 3). Buffett cancels event with biographer. *The New York Times,* p. B2.

Weissman, S. M. (1975). Frederick Douglass, portrait of a black militant: A study in the family romance. *The Psychoanalytic Study of the Child, 30,* 725–751.

Wheaton, B., & Gotlib, I.H. (1997). *Stress and adversity over the life course: Trajectories and turning points.* Cambridge, United Kingdom: Cambridge University Press.

Wineapple, B. (2012, March 4). The missing pages. *New York Times Book Review,* p.19.

Wolf, E. S. (1988). *Treating the self: Elements of clinical self psychology.* New York: Guilford Press.

Wolf, E.S. (1994). Selfobject experiences: Development, psychopathology, treatment, therapeutic process, and technique. In S. Kramer & S. Akhtar (Eds.), *Mahler and Kohut: Perspectives on development, psychopathology, and technique* (pp. 67–96). Northvale: Jason Aronson Inc.

Worden, J.W. (1996). *Children and grief: When a parent dies.* New York: Guilford Press.

Wyatt, E. (2006, January 27). Live on "Oprah," a memoirist is kicked out of the book club. *The New York Times,* pp. Al, A13.

Wyatt, F. (1986). The narrative in psychoanalysis: Psychoanalytic notes on storytelling, listening, and interpreting. In T.R. Sarbin (Ed.), *Narrative psychology:*

The storied nature of human conduct (pp. 193–210). Westport, CT: Praeger.

Yagoda, B. (2009). *Memoir: A history.* New York: Riverhead Books.

Young, T.M. (1991). Children. In II. Jackson (Ed.), *Using self psychology in psychotherapy* (pp. 73–90). Northvale, NJ: Jason Aronson.

www.ingramcontent.com/pod-product-compliance
Lightning Source LLC
Chambersburg PA
CBHW070856120626
46546CB00001B/28